IMMORTALITY

THE GROUNDWORK TO THE HISTORY OF WESTERN CONSCIOUSNESS

PART II: IONIAN AND CARTESIAN CONSCIOUSNESS

IMMORTALITY

The Groundwork

to the

History of Western Consciousness

Part Two: Ionian and Cartesian Consciousness

MELAMPUS

Edited by Sigmund Black

Black's Academy Limited

Black's Academy Limited
Kington, England

ISBN 978-0-9926645-3-4 paperback

Contents

List of figures

Preface

This book is the second in a series, *Immortality, the Groundwork to the History of Western Consciousness*. The thesis is that Western cognition divides into three epochs, that I call, primitive materialism, Ionian and Cartesian consciousness, and Kantian consciousness. The first volume examined the history of Western ideation during the first of these epochs, when mankind was bound by a cognitive structure in which he took everything that he experienced to be a vital substance, and hence cognized his soul as a breath or thin air.

At the outset, my aim was to investigate grounds for the belief in personal immortality in response to what I perceive to be a crisis in modern consciousness – the despair occasioned by the rise to cultural dominance of what may be dubbed materialism – a philosophy strong among the academics, being associated with scientific rationalism and Positivism. My views were rooted in the work of Kant, but Kant's *Critique* belongs to the tradition established by Plato; hence, my purpose was in part to trace various arguments, of which the transcendental deduction was prominent, back to Plato.

The problems of immortality and of human identity cannot be discussed in isolation from ethical issues, and the crisis of modernity that we all confront is also a crisis occasioned by an ethical Either/Or – which may loosely be expressed as Either Platonism and its world-denying ethic of puritanism, or materialism and whatever ethic accompanies it – but nihilistic in that it brings spiritual illnesses of its own: the emptiness of hedonism, or the narrowness of egoism; the encounter with despair brought on by the belief in death as annihilation and the impermanence of the self.

There arose too the question of the relationship between Plato and Christianity, which I expected to trace "in a chapter or so". The philosophical justification for the lengthier treatment derives from the way in which the enquiry was subsumed under the question – *what is man?* The subject is philosophical anthropology – the origin not of this or that idea, but of ideation itself. But something personal must also be added to account for the journey, on which I hope the reader will be my companion.

Almost fifty years ago, when I was eleven, the very first book on which I took a systematic set of notes was *The Histories* of Herodotus. I still have those notes. I was fascinated at that time by everything to do with Greece and the Ancient World, and although my life subsequently took me in other directions, I remained devoted to this theme, and studied it when I could. I started to formulate ideas, not original to me, concerning the fusion of matriarchy and patriarchy in ancient cultures, and the evolution of Christianity as a Greek religion. The theological/philosophical concern for the spiritual illnesses of our contemporary age encouraged me to seek the origin of those in our ancient history. As doctors well know, the first step to achieving a cure to an illness, is knowing of its causes, its aetiology. This, then, is the legitimate motive for a work that traces our spiritual condition to its origin. The framework is a history of religion from pre-history to the dawn of the Middle Ages in three parts: (1) the period of primitive materialism, from the Paleolithic to c.600 BCE; (2) from the onset of the Ionian revolution of cognition, the subject of the historical part of this work, to the dawn of the Roman Empire, c.27 BCE; (3) from thence to the inception of Medieval Christianity, c.400 CE.

I little expected to uncover observations on the character of ancient history that if adopted may revolutionize our understanding of it. I observe an omission on the part of historians hitherto, that may be expressed by way of analogy – what would a history of the Renaissance look like without a history of the Reformation? It is not so much that the religious history of Rome specifically was overlooked, but that it had been assumed to be just what the Romans themselves said it was. Since Mommsen, historians have been aware that the annalist tradition represented by Livy may be inflected by much legend and fiction, but the broad idea that Rome was founded as a patriarchy went unchallenged, for example, by Dumézil. But close examination of the evidence calls such an assumption into profound question, for there is every reason to conclude that Rome, just like the Etruscan culture on which it was based, was originally a matriarchy; that, furthermore, the religious reformation, the overthrow of matriarchy, took place at Rome relatively late; as late as c.200 BCE is possible – between the second and third Punic wars.

This was not the only radical thesis of ancient history that the heightened awareness of the evolution of Greek and Roman religion occasioned, and here may be mentioned considerations of the flow of ideas between Greece and India, and the precise nature of events surrounding an episode in the history of the Peloponnesian War, the mutilation of the Hermae.

My primary concerns are philosophical, theological and ethical, but all this is subsumed in the question of philosophical anthropology: *What is Man?* Hence, history. We discover that human history is a case of lurching from one spiritual crisis to another. The crisis of the first millennium BCE was to overcome the practice from within "developed" matriarchy of ritual adult male and child sacrifice. While this was resolved in Ionian consciousness, in the process a new and terrible spiritual illness was constellated: the Either/Or. The resolution of this problem in higher Kantian, subjective consciousness is already amply demonstrated in this volume, but its fuller treatment is found in the third volume.

1

The Ionian revolution of consciousness

While man's consciousness is constrained by primitive materialism, he does not distinguish subjective appearances from objective reality, and his cognition, lacking the concept of infinity is bounded by finitude. Primitive materialism is a form of consciousness akin to **the dream state**. When we dream, objects are perceived, but we do not ask in regular dream consciousness whether those objects belong to us, and are 'internal' to us, or are representations of objects that otherwise exist independently of us.

Waking and dream consciousness. Descartes posed the question, "Can I be sure that I am not dreaming now?" In answer, when we are awake and reflect on our dream experience, we do draw distinctions between waking and dream experience, which we may draw even while dreaming, if dreaming is lucid.[1] In dreams, events are not constrained to follow the 'rules' of consistent waking experience: dream objects exist only for a period, and they may 'disappear'; the 'laws' of causality do not apply; action and reaction, inertia and recoil are possible in dreams, but not mandatory; it is possible to levitate or fly; it is possible for perception to be delocalised.[2]

Dream-objects may be imbued with emotional content in ways that objects of waking experience are not. In a dream, the image of, say, a cat is loaded with emotive significance that the appearance of a cat in waking experience does not have, or if it has, then it is by infusion of emotive content from the psyche into waking experience, and not because the image of the cat itself is charged with emotive content; we call it, perhaps, a 'cat phobia'. The objects of dream-consciousness are 'symbols'. The symbolic aspect of dream objects is the foundation of the **interpretation of dreams**.

Law-like character of waking experience. It may be posited that since man entered the modern period of history, c.1400 CE from the Renaissance onwards, man became increasingly conscious that waking experiences constituted for him an ordered and regular manifold that was radically different from his dream state. This does not imply that men of the ancient and medieval epochs were unable to distinguish dream from waking but posits a qualitative development in modern consciousness of that distinction. Modern consciousness is characterised by a heightened awareness of the law-like character of waking experience.

---

[1] In lucid dreams, the subject, while dreaming, becomes conscious of being in the dream state, and can judge and even 'dismiss' the objects presented as "not-real" only because he is dreaming. In the regular dream state, this question, 'Am I dreaming now?' does not arise.

[2] As Descartes intended by the device of dream scepticism to raise concerns about the nature of experience in general, these observations are not a refutation of his arguments.

Developed memory. Man cannot be conceived without memory at all; we ascribe memory also to animals, but we think that animals do not have as developed a memory as we do. Animals recognise certain images as consistent – a dog will recognise his master or mistress – but if a dog acquires a new owner, what kind of persistent memory will that animal retain of its previous owner, and how long will such a memory last? The memory of animals is tied more to the non-visual senses than ours; they experience and remember smells and sounds more acutely than we do. Our memory is linked to our **eidetic faculty**, our memory of images.[3] We have also **semantic memory**, which is memory of meanings and relations between meanings. The ability to recall a date is an example of semantic memory; if in remembering a date an image is also brought to mind, then there is an association of semantic and eidetic memory. Supposing that one only had eidetic memory and no semantic memory of meanings, then it would be impossible to construct a coherent and consistent representation of waking experience – only the images and perhaps their succession would be remembered; experience would be akin to dream consciousness, though in dream consciousness there is also semantic memory, as the experience of dream symbols is semantic. As knowledge of semantic relations increases, so memory develops. Waking experience is a heightened consciousness of repeated sequences of events that we can recall to mind; these sequences become meaningful for us as **sequences of causes and effects**.

The study of history does show that man over historical time has been in constant evolution from previous states that are different from ours and judged by us to be more 'primitive' and 'less developed'. Once we leave the region of historical time, we enter into archaeological time, and the scientific study of this suggests through archaeology and the fossil record, that man has been evolving from man-like animals for some 500,000 years. The **theory of evolution** posits that this evolution may be extended yet further back, and that man evolved from apes, and all the way back from amphibians, fish, and so on. Accepting the evolutionary theory as a valid scientific, not religious,[4] statement of man's origin, we may posit that it was **working with tools** that raised man's consciousness to a remembrance of cause and

---

[3] The term *eidetic memory* is sometimes used to denote photographic-like memory. I am using the term in the general sense of memory of images, without regard to whether images are formed in this memory, or, if they are, to their intensive aspect, whether vivid or not.

[4] I am very far from accepting that the theory of evolution is a statement from which we should infer religious ideas. Man as spirit, may be a being very different from man as incarnate animal. The theory of evolution is taken for an unquestionable "scientific" truth in our contemporary epoch; not being questioned, it has become a "religious" truth, a form of fundamentalism, the **myth of evolution**. [See Part II, Chapter 6, The body/soul problem, for the Kantian resolution of the problem of freewill and determinism, and Part III, Chapter 15, The wilful overthrow of Kantian consciousness, for the rise of Positivism and the myth of evolution.]

effect, stimulating first the emergence and then the evolution of semantic memory, on which knowledge of cause and effect depends. Tools have meanings. Until the emergence of tool-working, we may imagine that man was, like other animals, a creature primarily of sensation, for whom dream and waking experience were barely distinguishable. Throughout the whole 500,000-year record man-like creatures have always used tools, but as their tools developed in sophistication, so too did their consciousness.

Intensive aspects of consciousness. The consciousness that attends primitive materialism is already a highly developed state of consciousness in which waking consciousness is distinguished from dream consciousness. However, consciousness has an intensive aspect – consciousness may be heightened. We may be more awake and less awake; we may experience more intensely or less intensely. There is also **consciousness of consciousness**; being aware that one is aware. This is not the same as intensity.[5]

The **separation of appearance from reality**. In primitive consciousness man is aware of the distinction between waking and dream experience less intensively than we are, and without that degree of self-conscious awareness that we have when conscious of the world. In this form of consciousness, the waking-world and dream-world are not as separated as they are for us, and the rules of the dream-world are judged to apply in some degree also to the waking-world: the primitive belief in sympathetic magic may be "theoretically" grounded upon the assumption that the subjective associations that belong to the realm of dream-consciousness, also apply to the external world. For in this cognition, one only has to bring about an association in thought, for that to "take effect" in the world. The subsequent elaboration of magical ritual – its correct procedures, incantations and the like – already reflects an awareness of the distinction between the subjective psyche and objective reality, because only those magical associations that are performed in the right way, in the right manner, with the right intonation, etc., have real effects. When rituals are no longer deemed to work mechanically but depend on the reception of the god to whom they are addressed, on sacrifice as propitiation, then the idea of supplication to a divine will emerges, and appearances are further separated from reality, though at this stage, reality is that which the gods will, and not that which exists-for-itself.

It is said that the brain we are born with is the same brain in kind to that of Neolithic man. If it were possible by time travel to go back and bring a new-born baby from 3,000 BCE to our modern world, then that new-born baby would be able

---

[5] Ecstasy may be a state of consciousness in which experience overwhelms self-awareness, so that one enters a heightened state of awareness, with altered self-awareness. In this state one may identify with an archetype, so that consciousness is consciousness of the archetype in a purer form; this may be called possession by a god, or by a daemon.

to learn all that a modern baby learns; it would acquire a modern brain. We infer the immense impact our **upbringing, socialisation and education** has upon consciousness. In the construction we make of waking experience, its causal consistency and solidity with respect to objects, learning is decisive. We are inducted into a way of seeing the world. We place an early emphasis upon **reading and writing**, which develops semantic memory. Induction into **the use of technology** leads us to anticipate the consistency of scientific explanation, to which we are also inducted at school. One of the principal features of this induction is training in **geometric and quantitative reasoning**: we learn about straight-lines, geometric figures, and how to measure distances. It is with these tools that we measure the real world, understand the consistency of distances, and comprehend such things as rays of light. Without mathematical notions it is impossible to conceive of light as radiation, as emanating from a bright source. Then, what is perception?

The causal theory of perception. For us, perception is explained in a causal way: rays of light fall on an object, reflected rays from the surface of that object enter our eyes where they are focused into an image, from whence they are converted to electrical signals which are sent to the visual cortex of the brain, and made into a **mental representation**. Therefore, we distinguish between **real objects existing independently of consciousness** and their mental representations. While this is the starting point for an immense scepticism that gives rise to the **dialectic of realism and idealism**,[6] it starts from a species of consciousness that is modern and distinguishes appearance from reality. This consciousness would be impossible without the use of mathematical and geometric concepts; without these tools of cognition, we would unable to distinguish appearance from reality in the way we do.

Cognition of the Sun and Moon. The immense size of distant objects like the Sun and Moon was only in recent times determined. By 400 BCE an educated Greek knew that the world was a sphere and following Eratosthenes (c.276 – c. 195/194 BCE) he had a good estimate of its circumference that differed by only 15% of our value; but even for us these remain only relatively recent discoveries, and most of the populace were at an earlier state of cognition. When Homer looked up at the sky, he saw a solar and a lunar disk, which man in his day judged to be relatively small. The sun subtends an angle of approximately $0.52°$ to an observer on the Earth; by a striking coincidence, this is almost the same as the angle subtended by the Moon. Yet not only does the size of the moon vary, but it exhibits lunar phases, and this subjectively makes the Moon more important in pre-Ionian consciousness. It was natural to assume these disks are imbued with vital energy; that they are conscious and being conscious are gods or the manifestations of gods. The moon is the source

---

[6] [See Part III, Chapter 14, What Kantian consciousness is.]

of lunar light just as the sun is the source of solar light. The idea that the light of the moon is light reflected from the light of the sun was not known.

Perception in pre-Ionian cognition. Prior to the Ionian revolution man did not explain perception in terms of passive reception of incoming signals from the external object. What then was perception for him, but *seeing?* If he had thought in terms of rays, then it was his eye that sent out the ray to the object – he saw the object, not the object was seen by him. No such theory was ever articulated; because an articulation belongs to a later consciousness. Following the Ionian revolution, in the work of Plato, we do obtain an articulated version of a hybrid theory of perception in terms of rays of light both from the object and from the eye.[7]

The clear separation between external reality and objects of consciousness emerges into Western philosophy with the onset of the Renaissance. It finds expression in the work of Descartes, thereafter in all scientific and philosophical discourse. We see it only in emergent form in Ionian philosophy, not in its systematic detail. I infer that **Ionian consciousness** is a less clear and less distinct form of **Cartesian consciousness**. I now proceed to describe **the historic appearance of Ionian consciousness**.

Thales of Miletus (c.624 – c.546) visited Egypt where he learned geometry. Using similar triangles, he devised a method of determining the distance of ships at sea. He took from the Phoenicians the art of navigating by the stars. Using Babylonian astronomical tables, he is said to have predicted an eclipse of the sun in 585. He seems to have improved on the Egyptian notion of general proof. He proved that a circle is bisected by its diameter. He advanced the theory that in the beginning everything was water, and that earth had been formed by a natural process. He envisaged the world as a flat disc floating in water, and regarded the sun and moon as vapours in a state of incandescence.

Anaximander, also of Miletus, (c.610 – c.546) advanced a theory in which fire, by heating water, increased the volume of mist; the universe took the form of wheels of fire enclosed in tubes of mist circling the earth and sea. He thought that planets and stars are holes in the tubes through which an enclosed fire glows. He thought

---

[7] In the *Republic*, Plato explains how seeing arises from the coalescence of two rays – one emanating from the object, and the other emanating from the mind. [See Part II, Chapter 15, The transcendental deduction.] This theory of Plato, comes after the Ionian revolution has already "taken place"; because it is a hybrid theory, it is a strong indicator that, while there was a distinct revolution in consciousness brought about by Ionian speculation between early C6 and C4, the consequences of that change took the whole history of Western consciousness to be "worked out". We are still working through those changes in contemporary times. *The Causal Theory of Perception*, which is a chapter from H. H. Price's book *Perception*, was published as late as 1932. Though Price writes to criticise the theory, which invites sceptical problems, the late date of this work indicates that the fully-fledged notion that perception takes place as a consequence of the reception of light from an eternal world is a C20 CE philosophy and not a C6 BCE one.

that man evolved from fish, some of which came on land when the land appeared. He stated that the four elements (earth, water, air and fire) are composed of a common indeterminate substance.

Anaximenes, again from Miletus, (c.585 – c.528) advocated that everything was derived from mist, and all things are composed of mist in varying degrees of density. He claimed that rarefied mist is fire, and condensed mist is water or earth.

Existence-for-itself. In Ionian philosophy there emerges the idea that the world exists independently of human consciousness and is made of a separable substance. The world exists-for-itself. Geometrical and mathematical reasoning fostered the emergence of this post-primitive cognition.[8] While a plurality of substances could be considered, the hunt was initiated for the one primal substance out of which all other substances are made. Aristotle describes these ideas in his *Metaphysics*.

> Most of the first philosophers thought that principles in the form of matter were the only principles of all things. ... There must be some nature – either one or more than one – from which the other things come into being, it being preserved. ... Thales, the founder of this kind of philosophy, says that it is water (that is why he declares that the earth rests on water). (Aristotle, *Metaphysics* 983b6 – 11, 17-2.)[9]

The separation between mind (subjective, perceiving consciousness) and matter (objective, external substance) is implicit in Thales's work, and coming at the very watershed between the two great epochs of consciousness we may expect that he had one foot in the past. Hence, we are also told:

> Some say that [soul] is mixed in the whole universe. Perhaps that is why Thales thought that everything is full of gods. (Aristotle, On the Soul, 41 127-8.)

> Some (among them the poet Choerilus) say that he [Thales] was also the first to say that souls are immortal. (Diogenes Laertius, Lives of the Philosophers I 22-28, 33-40.)

The statements "soul is mixed in the whole universe" and "everything is full of gods" **are theoretical statements of primitive materialism**. Thus, Thales not only

---

[8] For example, Polycrates of Samos enlarged and improved the harbour, and commissioned a tunnel to run through the hill of Kastro as an aqueduct; the tunnel was dug from both ends and when the two parts met they were no more than a few feet out. A geometrical construction of how to do this was only provided by Hero of Alexander in the second century CE.

[9] Quoted by Jonathan Barnes in *Early Greek Philosophy*, Penguin, 1987, p.63.

stands at the very gateway between **archaic and post-archaic cognition**,[10] but he articulates a theoretic statement of the primitive materialism that he is effectively abandoning.

Permanence of substance. Thales is said to have drawn the inference, "that souls are immortal". In modern cognition we have tended to a one-sided view of permanence of substance. We ascribe indestructibility to material substance, articulated in our law of the conservation of energy-matter, the primal substance being energy, which we now believe can manifest itself as substance with mass, and as substance without mass.[11] We have not ascribed eternal indestructibility to consciousness. We regard consciousness as a by-product of material processes arising from the material substratum of the brain, and the whole fear of death, and rejection of immortality of our contemporary period, is based on this one-sided calculation: substance is eternal, but consciousness is not. Thales, standing right on the boundary between the two forms of cognition, logically deduces that if the one is eternal, then so too is the other.

These early Ionian philosophers were called by Aristotle in his *Metaphysics* *physilogoi*, "observers of nature", in contrast to earlier *theologoi* or *mythlogoi* who explained phenomena in terms of the gods. Aristotle shows a startlingly clear comprehension of the distinction between the two types of explanation and indicates his strong rejection of the ideas of the *theologoi* in favour of the new awareness initiated by the *physiologoi*, to which the corpus of his entire work is increasingly dedicated.

Hybrid thinking. Aristotle classifies certain philosophers as "hybrids" – those "who do not say everything in a mythical vein."[12] All of these Ionian philosophers exhibit a tendency to hybrid thinking, which persisted throughout the ages.

Alcmaeon of Croton (born c.510) dissected and vivisected animals, discovered the optic nerve and concluded that the brain is the central organ of sensation, thus laying the foundation of the physiology of sensation. According to Theophrastus, "He says that we hear with our ears because there is an empty space inside them

---

[10] It is customary to define the archaic period in Greece as lasting from the close of the Dark Age, c.800 until the second Persian invasion of 480. The Ionian philosophers belong to the archaic period, but they inaugurate the post-archaic consciousness, and their theories are hybrid combinations of elements from both species of cognition.

[11] It is said that the rest mass of the photon of electromagnetic radiation (light, and so forth) is zero, though this is debated. However, the existence in modern theoretical physics of massless particles is not the conceptual point at issue here.

[12] Aristotle, *Metaphysics* 1091b4-10. He cites Pherecydes as an example. It can be argued that Aristotle was himself a hybrid philosopher, for he continued to ascribe real existence to the gods, though he so far separates them from the physical world as to render them uninvolved with human affairs. When is providence not providence? Answer: when teleological thinking appears in the hands of Aristotle.

which echoes: the cavity sounds and the air echoes in return."[13] We should recognise in this statement the earliest emergence of the causal theory of perception (or sensation in this case): a physiological account of how sensation of sound arises through physical transmission from the external world to our bodily presence in that external world.

Empedocles of Acragas (c.490 – c.430) claimed to be a magician, heal-all and weather-worker. He advanced an experiment to demonstrate the corporeality of the air. That air with breath has substance he demonstrated using an instrument called a *clepsydra* (water-sealer). He thought the blood oscillates like a tide. Empedocles believed that the Earth, when younger, had produced a much greater variety of species, but some had died out; this is a precursor of the doctrine of the survival of the fittest.

Empedocles was a hybrid thinker; he mixed a phenomenological account of human existence drawn from Heraclitus that all things were the product of the conflict between Love and Strife (Hate) with the physicist's tendency to make substances out of first principles. But he contributed to the evolution of the Ionian revolution and the foundation of empirical science that went with it. A contemporary scientific rationalist concludes, despite this error, that "Empedocles had not merely shown the corporeal nature of air; he had shown how we can overcome the limitations of our sensuous apprehension and discover, by a process of inference based on observation, truths we cannot directly perceive."[14]

Heraclitus of Ephesus (c.535 – c.475) is notoriously difficult to interpret, but his contribution to the evolution of consciousness is unambiguous. Whatever it means to say that "We step and do not step into the same rivers, we are and we are not,"[15] it asks us to distinguish the substance *water* from object/individual *river*, to investigate the logical relations between the two, and how this relates to human identity, for human conscious, like a river, also flows in time. This goes into the very heart of the substance/matter – soul/spirit distinction and exemplifies a state of differentiated consciousness.

Anaxagoras of Clazomenae (c.510 – c.428), was an Ionian residing at Athens from c.480 to 450, when he was expelled on charges of impiety. He was "the first to put mind in charge of matter… All things were together. Then mind came and arranged them. Hence he was nicknamed 'Mind'."[16] This makes him a hybrid thinker. He believed that there were 'seeds' that act as first principles, infinite in number and variety, which give rise to sensations. In this we might read a precursor of Leibniz's **monadology**. He said that digestion is a sorting out of elements already

[13] Theophrastus, *On the Senses* 25-26. Quoted by Barnes, *Early Greek Philosophy*, *Op. cit.*, p.63.

[14] Benjamin Farrington, *Greek Science*. Pub. Spokesman, 1980; First pub. Penguin, 1944, p.59.

[15] Heraclitus, *Homeric Questions* 24. 3-5. Quoted by Jonathan Barnes in *Early Greek Philosophy*, Penguin, 1987. p.117.

[16] Diogenes Laertius, *Lives of the Philosophers II*, 6-14.

given. According to Aristotle, Anaxagoras repeated the experiment of Empedocles with the *clepsydra*. He demonstrated the limits of perception by transferring black liquid to clear liquid drop by drop: "For if we take two colours, black and white, and then pour from one to the other drop by drop, our sight will not be able to discriminate the gradual changes even though they exist in nature."[17]

Atomism. About **Leucippus** (flourished C5), we know very little, save that he was Ionian. His follower, **Democritus** of Abdera (c.460 – c.370) asserted that the universe was made of **atoms and the void**; the void was infinite in extent and the atoms infinite in number, alike in substance but differing in size, shape, arrangement and position. An atom was physically indivisible and impenetrable. In his 'Nothing is created out of nothing' and 'By necessity were fore-ordained all things that were and are and are to be" he anticipated the doctrine of the **conservation of matter** and the concept of **universal law**.[18]

Mind and matter. Democritus's massive corpus represents the fully emergent altered consciousness for which mind and matter are distinct, and the problem of the existence of either or both, and the relationship between them, is posed as **the metaphysical problem of Western consciousness**.

Philosophy arises. The separation between mind matter is the beginning of **metaphysics**: What is a substance? Is mind a substance? If mind and matter are distinct substances, then how does the one interact with the other? If mind is not a substance, and matter is, then how does mind as phenomenon arise from matter as substance? What is the will? What is purpose?

Epistemology. What is the source of knowledge? Does knowledge come from the senses? Is there a faculty of reason, and can this act as an independent source of knowledge? If we do have reason, what is its relation to sense-experience?

---

[17] Sextus Empiricus, *Against the Mathematicians,* vii 90.

[18] "Democritus thinks that the nature of eternal things consists in small substances, infinite in quantity, and for them he posits a place, distinct from them and infinite in extent. He calls place by the names 'void', 'nothing' and 'infinite'; and each of the substances he calls 'thing', 'solid' and 'being'. He thinks that the substances are so small that they escape our senses, and that they possess all sorts of forms and all sorts of shapes and differences in magnitude. From them, as from elements, he was able to generate compound visible and perceptible bodies. The atoms struggle and are carried about in the void because of their dissimilarities and the other differences mentioned, and as they are carried about they collide and are bound together in a binding that makes them touch and be contiguous with one another but which does not genuinely produce any other single nature whatever from them; for it is utterly silly to think that two or more things could ever become one. ... he thinks that they [substances] hold on to one another and remain together up to the time when some stronger force reaches them from their environment and shakes them and scatters them apart." – A fragment of Aristotle's lost essay on Democritus, quoted by Simplicius, *Commentary on the Heavens* 294.30-295.22 Quoted by Barnes, *Early Greek Philosophy, Op. cit.*, p.247-8.

Logic. We begin the activity of justifying conclusions, deriving one belief from another. How do we know that the inference from *A* to *B* is valid? What does it mean to say that an inference is valid?

Philosophy of mind is that sub-branch of metaphysics where we ask: What is the mind? What are the faculties, powers of the mind? How are mental faculties related to one another? Do these faculties derive from matter?

Philosophical logic and **the theory of meaning**. What are the relations between language, thought and reality? What is meaning? How does meaning arise? What is a concept?

Ethics had already been born. For example, at the appearance of the Zeus-archetype, consciousness rejected human sacrifice and instituted justice. Hence, ethics is the mother and father of philosophy.

Meta-ethics. We see the emergence of questions that are hybrids of metaphysics, epistemology and ethics: What is the origin of our ethical thinking? What is justice? What is good living? What is the relationship of happiness to goodness? How do we justify or prove that ethical living is superior to non-ethical living?

Politics. People live in city states, where there are different economic classes and interest groups. The aristocracy base their power on agriculture, but so too do the citizens who now serve as hoplites in the citizen army, though their land is more marginal. There is a rising merchant class, women have been dispossessed of power, and their wealth in the form of dowries is controlled by men. The constant warfare between the city-states goes with the development of the institution of slavery. Hence arise questions of politics: who qualifies as a citizen, and what are a citizen's rights? What of the position of women in society? Is the institution of slavery justified? What rights, if any, do slaves have? What is the purpose of the state? How does the state arise? What is the best constitution for the state?

All the branches of philosophy arise: Aesthetics, the Philosophy of Religion, the Philosophy of Science and the Philosophy of Mathematics also arise. The History of Ideas encompasses all, and there is also the Philosophy of History.

The **dialectic** is born: different schools of philosophy arise, each with a different collection of answers to the above questions, and each will ask of the other, how do we know which one is the true account?

2

Consciousness, Self, soul, person and ego

Ionian cognition draws a distinction between the external world and internal, psychic phenomena (the mind); the external world appears to operate according to laws independently of the mind.

Consciousness denotes **awareness itself** – the mere "fact" that we are aware. Bare awareness. This conscious awareness is a "primitive" idea of human existence. By this is meant that it cannot be defined; for what is a definition but the reduction of one meaning to another? A reduction implies that there are ultimate constituents of meaning, and if there are, conscious awareness must be one of those.

When we say it is a "fact" that we are aware, we must scare-quote "fact". What is a fact? A fact is, perhaps, a statement or proposition corresponding to a state-of-affairs, as the statement, "The cat is asleep on the chair" points to a cat, a chair, an activity, and relations between these three. The expression "fact" orientates towards the external world, which is the world presented in sensation, but the mind is the ever-present awareness that is the correlative of all experience whatsoever.

Empiricism and phenomenology. Therefore, we may distinguish between two potential sources of knowledge. (a) The facts as they are observed in the world via the senses, which are the source of **empirical knowledge**. (b) Phenomena of which we become aware when we turn our consciousness inward and reflect upon experience as it is presented to oneself, the contents before one's own self-awareness, which is called **phenomenological knowledge**. Empiricism is not to be confused as a concept with that of empirical knowledge. **Empiricism** denies that phenomenological observation is a source of knowledge. When Wittgenstein declares, "The world is all that is the case. The world is the totality of facts,"[1] he announces himself to be an empiricist. **Phenomenology** does not deny that empirical knowledge is a source of knowledge but opposes empiricism by acknowledging phenomenological knowledge as another source. This work is a work of phenomenology; I am opposed to empiricism, as being too narrow; "facts" are not the only source of knowledge. The world is not the totality of facts. Furthermore, empirical and phenomenological knowledge do not exhaust all the possible sources of knowledge; for what is knowledge of history? That history is knowledge, I do allow; but it cannot be either empirical or phenomenological knowledge. Phenomenology studies consciousness, which is the present awareness. Consciousness is not a thing like perhaps an atom might be thought to be, an "object" whose properties are fixed immutably, indestructibly, forever.

---

[1] Ludwig Wittgenstein, *Tractatus Logico-Philosophicus*, trans. D.F. Pears & B.F. McGuinness. Routledge & Kegan Paul, London, 1922. 1 – 1.1.

Qualitative character of consciousness.   Consciousness is attended by qualitative differences that give rise to **the kind of consciousness** that one has.   In the ordinary way of thinking, we recognise this in how we describe another person's character.   We say of people, that they are kind, vain, proud, ambitious, cruel, besotted with self-love, emotionally stupid, intelligent, witty, sarcastic, ironic, happy, outward going, extravert, introvert, intuitive, empathic, loving, aesthetic, generous, avaricious, courageous, cowardly, intellectual, sporting, persevering etc. Each of these terms not only expresses a judgement we make about another person, but also connotes a mode of consciousness of the person itself, how that person's consciousness is like to that person.   What is it like to be that person? – a question addressed by use of imagination and empathy when we pose it of others.

The Subject.   The bare awareness that I have drawn attention to above is the pure awareness belonging to the Self.[2]   It is the subjective consciousness that attends all experience whatsoever.   What are the properties of this subjective Self?

Extension and intension.   Look at a tree or a chair, a material thing; then, as Subject you *perceive* a thing as object.   Contemplate an idea, say the idea of freedom; then, as Subject, you *conceive* of freedom, an object of contemplation, as concept.   The first kind of object is called an **extensional object**, and the second an **intensional one**.   However, they are both objects to consciousness.   Extensional objects, trees and tables, exist in space and time, and it makes sense to ask of them, what is their size, and how long do they last?   They are objects of **perception**. Intensional objects, concepts, meanings, thoughts, are not located in space and time. They are objects of **conception**.   While we are thinking of an idea, that thought has a duration, but the idea itself does not.   We have discovered a "peculiar" property of the mind, its ability to think of intensions, meanings.   But in both extensional and intensional cases, there is a relationship of Subject to object.   What now of the Subject?   Is that an object at all, and if so, is it an object with a spatial size and temporal duration?

The (Kantian) Self.   Kant's answer: "I" as Subject is never presented to itself as object, and never for itself becomes an object, as if consciousness or awareness could double back upon itself and perceive itself or know itself in the same way it

---

[2] Henceforth, the terms *Self* and *Subject* are capitalised whenever they refer directly to the Kantian notion of primal human identity.   This distinguishes them as concepts from other uses of these terms. That the Kantian Self is not the same in conception as the Cartesian soul is the fundamental observation of Kantian consciousness.   The terms *Self* and *Subject* may be regarded as two aspects of the same concept.   In the term *Subject* we think of conscious awareness in relation to the objects of awareness; in the term *Self* we think of it "alone", as if it were a thing-in-itself, though what it is in itself is not known to us, for to know the *Self* would be to make it into an object of its own awareness. The *Self* is transcendent to space and time.   The term *pure apperception* relates to the *Subject* and its experience in general, but abstracts from experience of particular objects, and focuses on its receptivity to experience in general.

perceives a table or entertains a thought. The questions: how large is the "I"? and, how long does the "I" last? are meaningless questions. There is no size or duration to the Self. All subjective experience whatsoever is referred to a single, abiding "I" that is the Self, as to a unity.

The third eye. Visual perception is related through perspective to an apparent point of consciousness that appears to lie behind the eyes at a point located just behind the middle of the forehead that is called the "third eye". It is a **transcendental illusion** to think that the "I", as object, is located at this point in space, so that it does belong to space, and appears to be located at this point, to move with the physical body within external space. On close examination, this is found to be an illusion, for the "I", the **apperceiving Self**, is not so located, but rather it is as if a window had been placed at that point of the third eye, and the "I" was looking through that window into the world of experience. This is the same "I", or "mind", to which we refer all experiences whatsoever. So that if I am looking at a flower, and smell the flower, and think, "That is a fragrant flower," all these cognitions are experienced as belonging to one and the same "I". The Self that sees the flower *appears* to be located at that point of the third eye, but on closer reflection we realise it is not located at all; the smell of the flower is also not located, for a smell is not a spatial object, though it can last a while, and is a temporal object; the thought about the flower is a thought, and thoughts do not exist is space and time; yet it is the same "I" that is involved as self-same Subject in all these cognitions. This is Kant's answer to the question: What is the nature of consciousness?

> The abiding and unchanging 'I' (pure apperception), forms the correlate of all our representations in so far is it is to be at all possible that we should become conscious of them. All consciousness ... belongs to an all-comprehensive pure apperception...[3]

Philosophy presents two alternative answers to this question of the fundamental self-intuition. These alternatives are implicit in Ionian consciousness but appear in explicit formulation relatively late in the history of Western philosophy.

(1) **The Cogito, Cogitans**, and the **soul**. Descartes in the *cogito*, offers, "I think, therefore, I am." He infers the *cogitans*, "I am a thinking thing." Descartes believes, when he reflects on his own awareness, that he experiences himself as simultaneously both subject and object, as subject experiencing itself as object. "But what am I?" he writes: "A thing which thinks. What is a thing which thinks? It is a

---

[3] Immanuel Kant, *Critique of Pure Reason*. Translated by Norman Kemp Smith. Transcendental Deduction A. Deduction of the Pure Concepts of Understanding. Section 3. A. 124, p. 146.

thing which doubts, understands, conceives, affirms, denies, wills, refuses, which also imagines and feels."[4]

By thinking Descartes means awareness, consciousness: "By the word thought I understand all that of which we are conscious as operating in us. And that is why not alone understanding, willing, imagining, but also feeling, are here the same thing as thought."[5] He uses *cogitatio* for thought. His statements are, "I am conscious, therefore I am," and "I am a thing that is aware." He expressly denies the conclusion that a primitive materialist might have provided.

> I am not a collection of members which we call the human body: I am not a subtle air distributed through these members, I am not a wind, a fire, a vapour, a breath, nor anything at all which I can imagine or conceive…[6]

He concludes, "We may thus easily have two clear and distinct notions or ideas, the one of created substance which thinks, the other of corporeal substance."[7] There are two distinct substances, spiritual and material. It is use of the terms "thing" and "thinking substance" that make his conception distinct from Kant. The **soul** designates the Cartesian concept of the self as spiritual substance.

Sum. In the *Critique*, Kant does allow the notion of substance to be attached to the Self, but merely as a manner of speaking, and his version of the cogito may be expressed by the alternative formulation, *Sum*, "I am," or "I am conscious," which entails, so far we know, "I am not a thing" and "I am not a spiritual substance." This denies knowledge of the soul but affirms the Self.

(2) **The bundle theory of the self**. The empiricist alternative to the cogito is provided by Hume.

> For my part, when I enter most intimately into what I call myself, I always stumble on some particular perception or other, of heat or cold, light or shade, love or hatred, pain or pleasure. I can never catch myself at any time without a perception, and never can observe any thing but the perception. When my perceptions are removed for any time, as by sound sleep; so long am I insensible of myself and may truly be said not to exist. And were all my perceptions removed by death, and could I neither think, nor feel, nor see, nor love, nor hate, after the dissolution of my body, I should be entirely annihilated, nor

---

[4] Descartes, *Meditations*: II – Of the Nature of the Human Mind.
[5] Descartes, *Principles of Philosophy*. Principle IX. What thought is.
[6] Descartes, *Meditations*: II – Of the Nature of the Human Mind.
[7] Descartes, *Principles of Philosophy*. Principle LIV.

do I conceive what is farther requisite to make me a perfect
nonentity.[8]

This is called the "bundle theory of the self", and the argument the "theatre of the mind"; by this, Hume opposes Descartes by claiming that there is no self at all, merely individual sensations, and that these bundled together comprise the person. To Hume a **person** is a collection of perceptions and sensations.

Kant wrote after Hume, and in response and reply to him. Thus, Kant agreed with Hume in the critique of Descartes, that Descartes went beyond the phenomenological evidence in concluding that there is non-material, spiritual substance that is the person but opposed Hume for failing to acknowledge the ever-present "I" in all experience, the source of the unity behind the bundle.

The problem of human identity. Contemporary philosophy, materialist in bias, follows the approach of Hume. Under this Humean approach, however, there arises the taxing problem of accounting for human identity. What is a person? If a person is neither an abiding pure Self, nor a Cartesian spiritual substance or soul, then what *thing* is it? The pages, articles, books, volumes, tomes that have been written within the empiricist tradition in response to this problem would be sufficient to form a land bridge over the Atlantic, and yet, it is no great difficulty to see immediately that if Hume is right, then the solution is that the person is No Thing at all, like the answer of Odysseus: "I am Nobody". A constantly changing collection of perceptions cannot be a thing, unless by convention, and it is not existence as a convention that people seek when they ask, *What thing am I?* or *What is the basis of my personal identity?*

Why labour to find a solution to a problem that the "bundle theory of the self" renders impossible? Because this "person" that we are is the "object" of our self-concern and self-love, the "thing" to which we are devoted, and it is therefore surprising and disturbing to discover its very existence is an illusion.

The ego. Hume's theory of the mind as a kind of theatre, as a collection of changing perceptions, is a good description the "object" that we call the ego. By the above, it is an illusion that the ego is a substance, when by ego we denote a real, existing, substantive and abiding "thing", something akin to what we think an atom might be. But that does not mean we cannot ascribe to the ego an existence of another kind. The arrangement of perceptions that forms this bundle is no mere chance collection, but a succession of collections that we may allow to be connected from one moment to the next by association and by causal laws. In a modern analogy, this compares the person to a strip of film as in a movie. Further, Hume believed that time was composed of discrete atoms of time, and hence, at any one moment of time, there was a definite collection of perceptions all associated together with a given person. Then the person's life, or "the person's ego over time", is the

---

[8] David Hume, *A Treatise of Human Nature*, Part IV, Section VI, Of personal identity.

entire "film strip", and any one frame or snapshot of the film strip is "the ego at that moment". Hence, under this conception, the ego exists in a derivative sense. But this is a problematic basis for personhood because (a) a person = ego is not a substantive thing, and has no endurance as a thing over time, and (b) a person = ego does not have freewill, and it is an illusion that this ego brings about any effect in space and time; it is, rather, the product of causes, not the author of them.

The contemporary **fear of death** as annihilation arises from the belief in the material basis of the mind, and parallelly in the Humean conception of person as ego without substantive identity. It immediately follows from this Humean idea, that with the cessation of the film-strip, the person = ego is also annihilated, and that death is annihilation.

The Kantian and Cartesian conceptions of human identity provide grounds for a belief in immortality. In Descartes's case the spiritual substance can conceivably survive its severance from the body, and in Kant's case the Self is a Subject not in space and time. As Kant expressly states:

> Why do we have resort to a doctrine of the soul founded exclusively on pure principles of reason? Beyond all doubt, chiefly in order to secure our thinking self against the danger of materialism. This is achieved by means of the pure concept of our thinking self which we have just given. For by this teaching so completely are we freed from the fear that on the removal of matter all thought, and even the very existence of thinking beings, would be destroyed, that on the contrary it is clearly shown, that if I remove the thinking subject the whole corporeal world must at once vanish; it is nothing save an appearance in the sensibility of our subject and a mode of its representation.[9]

I do not imagine that this statement by Kant will be easily understood, or that it will be sufficient by itself to remove the doubt arising that death is annihilation. Yet, it is my very purpose to deepen the insights provided by Kant. It suffices at this stage of this study of philosophical anthropology, that we have uncovered two alternative concepts of personhood that do not entail the conclusion that death is annihilation. If people do believe that death is annihilation, that is because they explicitly as philosophers, or implicitly as people, accept Hume's account of what it is to be a person.

The empirical self. Kant also calls the ego the "empirical self" and argues that it is an object in much the same way that objects of experience are objects. For, assuming atomism, a table is also an arrangement – not of perceptions, but of atoms, and as such has no abiding substratum, other than the atoms. In the case of the table,

---

[9] Kant, *Critique of Pure Reason*. A. 383.

the issue of annihilation raises no emotional concerns, for a table is not a person, and if it is destroyed, as in the story of the Chippendale chair that was dismembered,[10] then it may be a loss, but not at all equivalent to the loss of a person.

The transcendental Self. For Kant, the "The abiding and unchanging 'I'" is called the transcendental Self, which is a subjective consciousness only, not an object in space and time. Thus, he contrasts Self to ego; he uses the term "Self" expressly to distinguish his conception of human identity from that of Descartes, reserving the term "soul" for the Cartesian concept of soul-thing, object made of spiritual substance.

Ego-illusion. The distinction between ego and Self invites consideration of the illusion of mistaking the ego for the Self. Whether we agree with Hume or with Kant, the ego is not a substantive thing; hence, to believe it is a thing, and to live accordingly, is an illusion. But this illusion seems to be the fundamental and defining character of human life, for if a person goes to bed full of anxieties about what will happen to him or her the next day, whether he or she will be able to earn enough money to put bread on the table, or whether a significant other will continue to treat him or her as significant, what is the "thing" that is the source of the anxiety? It is not the transcendental Self, supposing this notion makes sense, but the empirical self, the ego that is the object of concern. And yet, our analysis shows, it is no substantial thing. This invites us to conduct an enquiry into this concern for our ego, because simply to call it an illusion will progress us not a whit further in ethics, for none of us will give up living because of a mere argument of this kind. If it is an illusion, it may be a necessary illusion, and it may be a harmless one.

Intuitively, there are ethical implications that go with the degree of self-love and self-obsession that we encounter in ourselves and other people. Selfishness is not an illusion, and the selfish person frequently transgresses against other people, and treats them not as persons, but as objects. If we accept also the distinction between ego and Self, we may refer to this as a qualitative degree of **ego-attachment**. In Eastern philosophy, it is customary to refer to ego-attachment, which expresses itself as the notion of **fundamental aggression**.

> There are three categories of suffering or pain in the Buddhist tradition: all-pervading pain, the pain of alternation and the pain of pain. All-pervading pain is the general pain of dissatisfaction, separation and loneliness. ...
>
> All-pervading pain is general frustration resulting from aggression. ... As long as we try to hold on to our existence, we become a bundle of tense muscles protecting ourselves.

---

[10] [An allusion to a story by Roald Dahl in *Kiss Kiss*.]

This fundamental pain takes innumerable forms – the pain of losing a friend, the pain of having to attack an enemy, the pain of making money, the pain of wanting credentials, the pain of washing dishes, the pain of duty, the pain of feeling that someone is watching over your shoulder, the pain of thinking that we haven't been efficient or successful, the pain of relationships of all kinds.[11]

Our attachment to ego correlates with a tendency to project outwards into our social environment behaviours of **ego-defence**, and **ego-priority**. We act as if we were fundamentally in a war with our fellows. People vary in the degree of their ego-attachment; we find that some people are more aggressive than others. If so, then degree and quality of self-love, degree and quality of aggression, degree and quality of ego-attachment are characteristics of consciousness, and part answers to the question: what is consciousness?

Thus, the question – What is consciousness? – invites answers of diverse kinds, answering diverse questions. The question of the transcendental Self as the "The abiding and unchanging 'I'" is an answer to what "fundamentally" consciousness is, but consciousness has qualitative aspects, comes in degrees and appears to have a history.

There is a history of consciousness, which is a history of what it is for an individual to have been conscious at a given historical point of time, and in this sense, we talk of primitive consciousness or archaic Greek consciousness. Concerning the qualitative aspects of consciousness:

(1) Consciousness is attended by levels of awareness, an **intensive degree of consciousness**. This is not a quantifiable scale. There is heightened awareness.

(2) **States of consciousness**. There are also differences between waking consciousness, dream consciousness and sleep consciousness and these are not the same as varying degrees of awareness but are differences in kind. The intensive quality of consciousness may be distinguished from **states of consciousness**, such as in waking, dreaming and sleeping.[12]

(3) Every mode of consciousness is related to a **difference of cognition**, which arises from the collection of concepts through which that consciousness perceives and interprets the world, perceives itself and perceives the relationship between itself and the world.

(4) Consciousness is characterised by a **quality and degree of self-love**, or, if we accept the notion of an ego, by a **quality and degree of ego-attachment**.

[11] Chögyam Trungpa, *The Myth of Freedom*, Ed. John Baker and Marvin Casper. Shambhala, Boulder & London, 1976.
[12] It is possible to be awake while dreaming, for this gives rise to the lucid dream, and it is possible to be intensively aware while in deep sleep, for this is what is called in meditational practice transcendence, the product of concentration, of *samadhi*.

(5) An individual consciousness has a relationship to **fundamental, archetypal patterns of life**. A person in his or her life has a strong tendency to live out an archetype. An archetype presents itself to a person as **an original project** of life and expresses itself as vocation. Most people are not consciously self-aware of living out an archetype.

(6) Consciousness is also characterised by **self-awareness**, which relates to the qualitative aspect of **self-knowledge**. With self-awareness there is an accompanying experience of **degree of self-conscious freedom**. If one is living an archetype, one is not necessarily aware of choosing to live it, but with increasing self-awareness, there is an increasing sense that if one behaves in a certain way, has a certain vocation, follows a fundamental pattern of life, akin to a mythologem, then that is because one freely choses to do so.

These ways in which consciousness can vary are all **qualitative not quantitative differences**. This means that there can be no measurement, as in a mathematical scale, of consciousness and its properties. There is no scale, as in proportionality, to measure the intensive magnitude of consciousness. In 1623 Galileo wrote:

> Philosophy is written in that great book which ever lies before our eyes — I mean the universe — but we cannot understand it if we do not first learn the language and grasp the symbols, in which it is written. This book is written in the mathematical language, and the symbols are triangles, circles and other geometrical figures, without whose help it is impossible to comprehend a single word of it; without which one wanders in vain through a dark labyrinth.[13]

Being an inheritor of the Ionian revolution of consciousness, Galileo can here write of the external world, disregarding wholly the realm of the psyche, consciousness itself. Whether everything in the external world can be quantified and thereby described by mathematics is one question, but it is self-evident that the "subjective" realm of consciousness wholly belies such a description.

---

[13] Galileo, *The Assayer* (1623), translated by Thomas Salusbury (1661), p. 178, quoted in *The Metaphysical Foundations of Modern Science* (2003) by Edwin Arthur Burtt, p. 75.

3

Irony, satire, cynicism and laughter

The **moral argument for the existence of god**. For Homer, who invokes Zeus as the force that ensures oaths are upheld, God and morality are inseparable. But in Ionian cognition, there arises the possibility that the external world, nature, is an unconscious mechanism, whose operations are in accordance with deterministic laws. It follows as a possibility that either (a) there are no gods, or (b) if there are gods, then the gods belong merely to subjective or inter-subjective human nature, or (c) if there are gods, then they are removed from nature, and do not participate in human history. Whatever their differences, these are all **forms of atheism**.

Monotheism. Another possibility arises: to acknowledge that the Graeco-Roman gods are subjective fictions, the products of "lying fables", and hence, do not exist, yet affirm that there is another, higher god, who is a pure form of justice, Zeus = Deus = God, who is wholly good, untainted with any form of earthly evil, the creator of the universe, etc. In Homer, Zeus is sufficiently powerful to overrule all the other gods combined, but he is not omnipotent. Homer does not consider the question: since only a god can be an arbiter of human affairs, it is sufficient that the highest authority be strong enough. The Ionian revolution brought into consciousness the concept of infinity; after that, strong is not strong enough; a tendency to justice is not pure justice, as finite is not infinite. **Omnipotence** is an expression of **the concept of infinity**.

The emergence of the Zeus-archetype constellated latent monotheism. The **Zeus-archetype was forced to ascend** to that of universal, omnipotent and all-benevolent governing power of the cosmos, while the imperfections of the lesser gods must render them not gods at all; or if gods, then infernal ones, opposed to the will of the Almighty. **Ironic detachment** and comment on myth, character, and society were henceforth conceivable and permissible. Permission to poke fun at the gods, to expose hypocrisy, may signify strength in religious consciousness; the contrasting dogmatic, rigid attitude that does not permit of mockery, of laughter, may be a sign of weakness, and impending collapse. Nevertheless, the increasing prevalence of irony, sarcasm and cynicism in Greek culture are expressions of an age that is undergoing religious turmoil. At the onset, we have the scathing attack of **Xenophanes** of Colophon (c.570 – c.475). His comment on Homer and Hesiod has already been exhibited once, but it is so significant, that it is right to quote it again: "Homer and Hesiod attributed to the gods all the things which among men are shameful and blameworthy – theft and adultery and mutual deception."[1] This attacks

---

[1] Quoted by Sextus Empiricus, *Against the Mathematicians* IX 193. Quoted also in Part I, Chapter 18, The Zeus theology of Homer.

the Olympian religion, and hovers in its implications between atheism and advocacy of a new religion, where these dark things – theft, adultery, mutual deception – are expunged from the divine order. Xenophanes is the first expression in Western consciousness of a destructive analysis of the origin of the pagan gods.

> But if cows and horses or lions had hands or could draw with their hands and make the things men can make, then horses would draw the forms of gods like horses, cows like cows, and they would make their bodies similar in shape to those which each had themselves.[2]

This anticipates by more than two millennia the thesis of **Ludwig Feuerbach** (1804 – 1872) that **religion is a projection of the human mind**, where projection is treating something as objective, independent and real, what is subjective.

> In religion, consciousness of the object and self-consciousness coincide. The object of the senses is out of man, the religious object is within him, and therefore as little forsakes him as his self-consciousness or his conscience; it is the intimate, the closest object.[3]

If the experience of God is the experience of self-consciousness, then God is more intimately "known" than external, sensory objects – but this "knowing" is an illusion based on an erroneous projection. In self-consciousness one becomes aware of certain attributes of the self. However, those attributes that are recognised as belonging to self-consciousness are *not* projected. We are unconscious that certain subjective attributes are subjective – it is these that we project.[4] According to Feuerbach, to withdraw a projection is to recognize that an attribute that was formerly unconsciously regarded as an objective attribute, belongs in truth to subjective consciousness. **To withdraw a projection is to advance consciousness**, since the unconscious projection, being withdrawn, is the raising to consciousness of

---

[2] Clement, *Miscellanies V* xiv 109 – 1-3.

[3] This and subsequent quotations are drawn from Feuerbach's *Introduction to The Essence of Christianity*, 1841 – section 2: The essence of religion considered generally. Trans. Marion Evans, London, John Chapman, 1854.

[4] "But when religion – consciousness of God – is designated as the self-consciousness of man, this is not to be understood as affirming that the religious man is directly aware of this identity; for, on the contrary, ignorance of it is fundamental to the peculiar nature of religion. To preclude this misconception, it is better to say, religion is man's earliest and also indirect form of self-knowledge. Hence, religion everywhere precedes philosophy, as in the history of the race, so also in that of the individual. Man first of all sees his nature as if *out of* himself, before he finds it in himself." Feuerbach, *Introduction., Op. cit.*

something that was previously unconscious.[5] It is an advance of self-knowledge. Whatever one conceives as highest in one's own human nature, that is unconsciously attributed to God, and so forms the basis of the God concept.[6]

Feuerbach's argument is a fallacy, because all ideas whatsoever arise in subjective consciousness, and hence by this argument no objective statement about "reality" would be possible. Should we apply these arguments to the conclusions of natural science, and argue that in natural science too we have made the world in the projected image of subjective consciousness? If it is possible to conceptualise an objective reality that is independent of subjective consciousness, then it is also possible to conceptualise God as belonging to that reality. Yet, notwithstanding the limitations of Feuerbach's analysis, his work illuminates the progress of religious consciousness.

Xenophanes represents a stage of religious consciousness in which the **anthropomorphic projection of human nature is withdrawn** from the divine, to be replaced by a new projection, **the projection of love**, of the highest moral order and of justice. Xenophanes is not an atheist, and his speculations on god represent what will, via Aristotle, become prominent features of Greek and Roman religious consciousness. Hippolytus described the opinions of Xenophanes: "The first principle is infinite, changeless and spherical," and Xenophanes "also says that god is eternal and unique and homogeneous in every way and limited and spherical and capable of perception in all his parts."[7] Despite the reference to "limited", we see here the Ionian awareness of infinity, expressed as **the concept of perfection**, a sphere being a perfect geometrical figure.   God, "changeless and spherical", becomes a perfect being separated from imperfect incarnation. In the work of Aristotle, God is placed outside the world as the unmoved mover of the universe, a conscious being endowed with life, yet dwelling only in eternal happiness of self-contemplation.[8] Aristotle believed that the planets were divine intelligences, also involved in self-contemplation, moving in combinations of perfect concentric circles.

---

[5] "Hence the historical progress of religion consists in this: that what by an earlier religion was regarded as objective, is now recognized as subjective; that is, what was formerly contemplated and worshipped as God is now perceived to be something *human*. What was at first religion becomes at a later period idolatry; man is seen to have adored his own nature. ... Every advance in religion is therefore a deeper self-knowledge." Feuerbach, *Introduction, Op. cit.*
[6] "Thou believest in love as a divine attribute because thou thyself lovest; thou believest that God is a wise, benevolent being because thou knowest nothing better in thyself than benevolence and wisdom; and thou believest that God exists, that therefore he is a subject – whatever exists is a subject, whether it be defined as substance, person, essence, or otherwise – because thou thyself existest, art thyself a subject." Feuerbach, *Introduction., Op. cit.*
[7] Hippolytus, *Refutation of All Heresies*, I xiv 2-6. Hippolytus (170 – 235 CE) was a Roman Christian theologian.
[8] Aristotle, *Metaphysics*, 12.1072b, *Nichomachean Ethics*, Book 10, 1178b7-29.

To this work of Xenophanes, we could add remarks of other pre-Socratics: **Heraclitus** of Ephesus (c.535 – c.475), **Hippasus** of Metapontum (fl. C5) and **Anaxagoras** of Clazomenae (c.510 – c.428). In post-Socratic times, this movement is expressed in the religion of Plato, in the irony of Euripides and in the sarcasm, cynicism and laughter of Aristophanes.

Euripides and irony. It is characteristic of the ironic method that the author does not make didactic statements and invites the audience to reflect. Euripides's play *Heracles* (c.416) is an expression of the new ironic attitude. In it, Heracles, son of Zeus, is driven mad by Hera, wife of Zeus, and in his madness murders his wife and children.[9] The irony invites us to recognise the moral and sceptical problems raised by this drama concerning the relation of man to the Olympian gods. Whether the madness of Heracles proceeds from certain hidden recesses of his own nature or not, the cruelty of the Olympian gods appears to be in focus. The all-powerful Zeus stands by, while his jealous wife tortures his son; only the foster father, the man cuckolded by Zeus, is able to act as any kind of break upon the action, and he is a weak force in comparison to the social force of blind, unjust cruelty represented by Lycus, and the tyranny of the gods represented by Hera and those lesser divinities compelled to act on instructions. The sceptical question reaches a climactic expression in the condemnation by Heracles, son of Zeus, of the morality of the gods. Euripides stands in the middle of the whirlwind crisis of faith that swept the ancient world; the revelation that the true identity of the gods, or God, cannot be revealed in the myths as they had them.

> I don't believe gods tolerate unlawful love.
> Those tales of chainings are unworthy; I never did
> And never will accept them; nor that any god
> Is tyrant of another. A god, if truly god,
> Needs nothing. Those are poets' lamentable myths.

---

[9] Amphitryon, who is Heracles's reputed father (the real father being Zeus) is beset with dire apprehensions. Lycus has usurped the throne of Thebes and is proposing to slaughter Heracles's entire family. Megara, Heracles's wife, implores Amphitryon to come up with a solution, but the old man is unable to avert their impending doom. Heracles has gone to Hades to drag up the hell-hound Cerberus, and everyone has given him up for dead. Lycus tells them to prepare for death; the chorus of Theban elders want to prevent the slaughter but are impotent. Megara and Amphitryon pray to Zeus for deliverance. Then Heracles appears. They persuade him, against his instincts, to go into the palace and await Lycus. Lycus arrives and enters the palace where he will meet his death. The goddess Iris and god Madness appear. Iris, on the instructions of Hera, will make Heracles mad. Madness pleads that it does not delight in slaughter, but Iris is adamant, and Heracles is duly sent mad. A Messenger relates the consequences; Heracles has slaughtered his wife and children. Amphitryon was able to bind him to a pillar. Heracles is distraught and wishes to die. Theseus appears. Heracles had rescued Theseus from Hades, and in recompense Theseus does not abandon Heracles, consoles him, and persuades him to endure his suffering and to go with him to Athens.

Henceforth, the expression "lamentable myths" or equivalent will echo through the whole of Greek and Roman history whenever the question of what the true nature of God has been raised. For example, in this opinion of Cicero:

> Thus far have I been rather exposing the dreams of dotards than giving the opinions of philosophers. Not much more absurd than these are the fables of the poets, who owe all their power of doing harm to the sweetness of their language; who have represented the Gods as enraged with anger and inflamed with lust; who have brought before our eyes their wars, battles, combats, wounds; their hatreds, dissensions, discords, births, deaths, complaints, and lamentations; their indulgences in all kinds of intemperance; their adulteries; their chains; their amours with mortals, and mortals begotten by immortals.[10]

In the first of the Tusculan Disputations the myths are called "monstrous inventions of the poets and painters."[11]

Aristophanes and satire. The *Frogs* and *Clouds* by Aristophanes are satirical plays that act as sarcastic responses to one account of the answer the Delphic Oracle gave to Chaerephon, a pupil of Socrates, when he asked it whether anyone was wiser than Socrates: "Sophocles is wise, Euripides is wiser, but of all men Socrates is wisest."[12] *Clouds*,[13] which is a satirical and downright nasty attack on Socrates's reputation, contains plenty of evidence of the transformation of consciousness taking place. Both plays explore the implications of what is called in them the **inferior argument**, the argument that as there is no objective morality, then *everything is permitted*.

In *Clouds*, the state of Athens is such that the "buggers" have it – that is people schooled in the inferior way of argument hold all the power. The caricature who is attacked in this play draws upon the ideas of Anaxagoras but is avowedly a charlatan

---

[10] Cicero, *On the Nature of the Gods*, XVI.

[11] Cicero, *Tusculan Disputations*, I.

[12] Chaerephon, a student of Socrates, is said to have asked the Delphic oracle whether anyone was wiser than Socrates. This is one version of the response.

[13] An elderly member of the Athenian gentry, Strepsiades, enrols himself into the school of Socrates, the Thinkery, to learn how to outwit his creditors, having been plunged into massive debt by his profligate son. We are introduced to some of the quackery of Socrates and his school. In a comic reversal, Strepsiades is rejected from the Thinkery for masturbation, but his son is enrolled in his place. The son adroitly learns the "inferior argument" of might over justice and is taught that he may beat his father and mother, and justify it too; the father laments his folly in going to Socrates. The play forcefully illuminates the background to the charge of impiety on which Socrates was tried, convicted and condemned to death.

and a representative of the kind of Sophist that Plato also made the butt of his arguments in his dialogues.

Socrates	Zeus indeed! There is no Zeus. Don't be so obtuse.
Strepsiades	No Zeus up aloft in the sky!
	Then, you first must explain, who it is sends the rain;
	or I really must think you are wrong.

Explanation in terms of natural phenomena is fashionable, and with that, there is a perceived destruction of values, religion, mystery, respect for the gods, and respect for justice. The idea that "If God does not exist, everything is permitted" is under examination in the debate between superior and inferior logic. Belief in the moral argument for the existence of God has collapsed as a social force.

Frogs[14] is full of witty burlesque. While it was acceptable to show disrespect to Greek gods, Aristophanes' plays expose the underlying problem that the myths do not stand up to critical and "moral" analysis. The overwhelming tendency of Aristophanes is towards scepticism, secularisation, agnosticism, "rationalism" and ultimately atheism.[15] The play is a snapshot of the religious crisis. The Athens of the god-fearing, god-like Aeschylus had overcome the superior mass of Persian armies, not once, but twice.[16] But now Athens in the Peloponnesian war is losing to

---

[14] In the *Frogs* the god Dionysus travels to Hades ostensibly to bring Euripides back from the dead. After bawdy burlesque exchanges between Dionysus and his slave Xanthias, who is more resourceful than the cowardly god, Dionysus consults with his half-brother Heracles about the shortest path to Hades, and is told that hanging, taking poison or jumping off a tower are effective. Croaking frogs provide a seemingly senseless choral interlude, and Dionysus gets into a lot of trouble in Hades by impersonating Heracles, who is unpopular down below for his theft of Cerberus, the Hound of Hell. Dionysus is whipped for telling the truth that he is a god. The dramatic climax of the play is a contest between Aeschylus and Euripides as to which of the two is the better playwright, a contest in which each mocks the other. Dionysus, originally the butt of the all the humour, assumes the role of impresario and orchestrates the cynical laughter at both contestants. Aeschylus wins because his works are literally heavier – they refer to a river, death, crashed chariots and dead charioteers, so weigh more. In the final contest, the two authors must give the best advice on how to save Athens in her hour of need. Aeschylus wins, and his chair in Hades for best poet of the Underworld is given to Sophocles. Aristophanes evidently personally disliked Euripides, who fails to obtain this honour.

[15] Aristophanes is a strange case. His positive value system appears to be one of respect for the old customs, but he is too much at home with the new arguments, modes of explanations and customs to be the consistent advocate Aeschylus reborn. Aristophanes has invented satire, and he effectively mocks stupidity; how, then, can he also be the knight of noble, old-fashioned ideals? His personal attack on another citizen does not evince a respect for persons.

[16] The Persians were first defeated at Marathon, then in the Persian invasion of Xerxes at the naval battle of Salamis (480) and the battle of Platea (479).

the Spartan league. It's not just the influence of Persian money,[17] the rot is everywhere – in the crushing loss of solidarity, in the loss of community, and in the predominance of the power politics of demagogues. The play exposes the rising bias in favour of argument for might over right, the lure of the "inferior argument" and the lure of the life of pleasure. It shows us that Athens is going through a "loss of soul" experience.

The destruction of faith in the pagan gods is the inevitable consequence of the appearance of the concepts, infinite, omnipotent, omniscient, all-good, and perfect. The questions are: Does God exist because there is and must be a moral reality? Must there be a higher order where justice prevails, and the "bad" cannot succeed? Can a society, where faith in God as author of moral reality has collapsed, survive? These are questions for us too. Is Dostoyevsky right? **If God does not exist then everything is permitted**, which is the converse of the moral argument.

> "... he [Ivan Karamazov] solemnly declared during an argument that there was absolutely nothing in the whole world to make men love their fellow-men, that there was no law in nature that man should love mankind, and that if love did exist on earth, it was not because of any natural law but solely because men believed in immortality. He added in parenthesis that all natural law consisted of that belief, and that if you were to destroy the belief in immortality in mankind, not only love but every living force on which the continuation of all life in the world depended, would dry up at once. Moreover, there would be nothing immoral then, everything would be permitted, even cannibalism. But that is not all: he wound up with the assertion that for every individual, like myself, for instance, who does not believe in God or in his own immortality, the moral laws of nature must at once be changed into the exact opposite of the former religious laws, and that self-interest, even if it were to lead to crime, must not only be permitted but even recognized as the necessary, the most rational, and practically the most honourable motive for a man in his position."[18]

This was the moral problem of ancient Athens as it struggled with the implications of the terrible Peloponnesian war that it fought with Sparta and her allies, during which the "buggers", to use the term of Aristophanes, rose to power. A less salacious term, derived from Chinese *Great Treatise*, is the **inferior man**: a man

---

[17] The Spartans gained the upper hand in the war because the Persians funded the construction of their fleet, which was used to sever Athenian corn supplies coming from the Black Sea.

[18] The character Miusov is speaking. Fyodor Dostoyevsky, *The Brothers Karamazov*, trans. David Magarshack, Penguin. 1958, p. 77. Between the ideas of Feuerbach and Dostoyevsky we glimpse somewhat of the religious controversy of the C19, a greater age than our own.

who is so wholly absorbed by himself in this world, that he cannot consider anything worth doing that has no advantage to himself, who believes that "self-interest, even if it were to lead to crime, must not only be permitted but even recognized as the necessary, the most rational, and practically the most honourable motive for a man in his position."[19] The inferior man makes it a principle to treat all persons as objects.

Self-interest. In Euripides we also perceive how the new consciousness affects the dramatic portrayal of character. Just as in perception we may distinguish appearance from reality, the subjective from the objective, the psyche from nature, so in the depiction of character not everything may be really what it seems to be. Deception, insincerity and hypocrisy have entered drama, and these perceptions extend not just to politicians and other members of the citizen body, but to the myths. The heroes come off their pedestals. Heroes that come in for much heavy critique and criticism in Euripides's work are Menelaus and Orestes, which is a stark contrast to their treatment by Homer. Both appear in successive scenes in *Andromache*[20] and are portrayed as villains. One example of the sickening, conscienceless, self-interest on the parts of these characters occurs when Menelaus declares that his promise to spare Andromache's son from death, if she agrees to leave a sanctuary, was a bare-faced lie.

> Menelaus   You men, get hold of her and tie her arms. She won't
>   Like what I have to tell her. I threatened to kill
>   Your son, to induce you to abandon sanctuary

---

[19] From Dostoyevsky's *The Brother's Karamazov*, quoted in full above. The following extract from the Chinese Great Treatise, *Ta Chuan*, Chapter V. 7 is instructive: "The Master said: The inferior man is not ashamed of unkindness and does not shrink from injustice. If no advantage beckons he makes no effort. If he is not intimidated he does not improve himself, but if he is made to behave correctly in small matters he is careful in large ones." The Great Treatise, *Ta Chuan*, Chapter V, 7, *The I Ching*, trans. Richard Wilhelm, Routledge & Kegan Paul, 1951.

[20] Andromache, the former wife of Hector, has been forced into concubinage with Neoptolemus, the son of Achilles. While Neoptolemus is away at Delphi expiating a sin against Apollo, his new and official wife, Hermione, daughter of Menelaus, out of a bevy of negative emotions, plots to murder Andromache. Menelaus enters to back up his daughter. Threatening to murder her son by Neoptolemus, he entices Andromache out of the sanctuary where she has taken refuge. He is prevented from that murder by the timely return of Neoptolemus's grandfather, the hero Peleus, father to Achilles by the goddess Thetis. Menelaus leaves in high dudgeon, abandoning his daughter, who is then overtaken by remorse, self-pity and fear. Orestes arrives, apparently to her rescue, but we learn that he is plotting the murder of Neoptolemus, and hopes to recover Hermione, the rich daughter of the powerful Menelaus, king of the Peloponnese and further his ambitions to succeed him. Not only does Orestes say that he will murder Neoptolemus, but it seems likely that he already has. Neoptolemus is duly reported to be dead by a messenger; he died bravely fighting off his assailants within the shrine of Delphi itself, and Peleus is bereft of son and grandson. The goddess Thetis arrives to bring him some comfort. Andromache has dropped out of view, to be handed on a second time to another man, Helenus.

And freely give yourself into my hands to kill.
That explains *your* position. As regards your son,
My daughter shall decide either to kill him or
Not to kill him, as she pleases.

Does this man fear nothing? Does he not fear the gods? Does he not fear divine retribution? But, of course he does not, for he does not believe in the gods, in retribution. He reckons only on material consequences. Menelaus, a creature of the post-Ionian revolution of consciousness, has worked it out that there are no gods, and divine justice is a fairy tale invention of poets. That is precisely why we must consider the question, what are the supernatural consequences of transgression against moral law? – notwithstanding the appearance that morality has nothing to do with external reality and its mechanical laws.

Orestes   If my comrades-in-arms at Delphi keep their oaths,
              I'll teach Neoptolemus – yes, I, the matricide –
              To beware of marrying a woman who <u>belongs to me</u>.

O brave new world, that has such creatures in it! The words of Ivan Karamazov echo in our ears: "everything is permitted". Menelaus believes it, and so does Orestes.

The collective. A recurring situation that Euripides refers to is the power of the collective thirst for blood. Public opinion has come to be a force against which the individual struggles to find an orientation. No doubt there are brave and yet discrete persons who know, when push-comes-to-shove, that they cannot abandon the principles of justice – they must stand up to the collective lust for blood, but so many of the leaders lack moral fibre and find themselves in situations where things get out of hand. One example is Demophon, the son of Theseus, in *The Children of Heracles*. In this play, the guardian of the orphaned children of Heracles has brought them for refuge to a sanctuary in Athens, fleeing from the relentless pursuit of Eurystheus, who wants them all dead. Eurystheus threatens Athens with war, if the Athenians will not give them up. Demophon resolutely protests that he would rather be dead than hand them over, and he prepares for war. We are impressed. But then, the oracles are consulted.

Demophon   … my preparations are made,
              Athens is armed, victims ready for slaughter stand
              Beside the altars of the appropriate gods; prophets
              Have filled the city with sacrifices. I have assembled
              All the chanters of oracles, and questioned them
              About ancient predictions, whether publicly

Delivered, or in secret, which might indicate
A course of safety for this country; and the experts
Differing in many other points, are all agreed
On this clear pronouncement: they insist that I
Must sacrifice to Persephone, Demeter's Maid,
The virgin daughter of a royal family.
   Now, for myself, I am most anxious, as you see,
To help you; but I will not kill my own daughter,
Nor will I compel any of my citizens
To such an act...

It seems to be an impossible situation. While we are shocked at the way he has caved in, we can hardly expect him to sacrifice his own daughter. In these situations, it is left to the oppressed and obscure to make the decisive step, and Macaria, a daughter of Heracles, offers to die, which resolves the problem of the blood-lust of the masses, and we do not hear of Macaria again.[21]

In *Iphigenia at Aulis* a yet darker instance of the same problem is dramatized. Agamemnon agonises about whether to sacrifice his daughter, his attempts to "save" her are lame, and in the end, he gives way to the pressure to appease the blood-lust of the massed soldiers, and she is sent to be slaughtered at the altar.

Agamemnon   A strange lust rages with demonic power throughout
                The Hellene army, to set sail immediately
                And stop the barbarians from raping Hellene wives.
                If I refuse to obey the oracle, they'll come
                To Argos, and kill me, you, the whole family.
                Menelaus has not made a slave of me, my child;
                I came to Aulis not to serve his purposes;
                I am a slave to Hellas; for her, whether I will or not,
                I am bound to kill you. Against this I have no power.

It is again the girl, Iphigenia, the sacrifice, who achieves dignity and superiority by acceptance of fate.

Mother, I have thought this over; I know now what I must do.
I am resolved to die. Above all things, I want to act nobly

---

[21] Marcaria: "Iolaus, I am myself / Ready to die, and give my blood for sacrifice. /... Even so, I have no hope of a good life; for who / Will choose a wife a girl so destitute, or wish / To beget children from me? Better then to die / Than meet a fate I have not deserved, a fate which might / Better become a girl less notable than I."

> And renounce all cowardly feelings. Mother, look at this with me,
> And you'll see I am right. The power of all Hellas now looks to me;
> All lies in my hand – the sailing of the fleet, the capture of Troy,
> And the future safety of Greek wives from barbarous attacks;
> No more forcible abductions from our happy homes, when once
> Paris has been made to pay the price of death for Helen's rape.
> All this great deliverance I shall win by dying, and my name
> Will be blessed and celebrated as one who set Hellas free.

Euripides reveals his knowledge that the masses lie at an earlier, more primitive stage of consciousness. An Athenian minority have broken away from this mass, and now *know* that sacrifice is wrong, immoral, and offensive to God, and that the gods of Olympus, or the Earth, who demand these rituals are fictions, expressions of the darkness that resides in the human psyche. These dark masses are served, led, incited by religious experts, "chanters of oracles", who represent the theological inertia of the old force. Behind these priests lie vested interests that seek to preserve the rituals and the flow of wealth that arises from their observance.

The priesthood of Greek religion. Greek religion is often said to be a religion without priests. However, it is not true that Greek religion was without vested interests, because the priesthood was supplied by the aristocrats.[22] Many of the cults were hereditary in a family. Each aristocratic family traced its power and prestige to legendary characters associated with given cults. It is a hypothesis that every festival was connected to an aristocratic family. The religion of Athens was deeply conservative. It is not true that the ancient world was one where religious toleration was universally practised, for where vested interests are involved, persecution of religious deviance follows. At Athens, the crime of revealing any part of the Eleusinian Mysteries was punishable by death. Diagoras of Melos was accused of this blasphemy in 415.   Others charged at some time with blasphemy included Anaxagoras, Socrates, Aeschylus, Alcibiades, and a courtesan called Phryne. These are some of the named cases of blasphemy trials. While in each case there may have been political motives, the existence of blasphemy laws indicates that Athens was not a religiously open society.

The conservative element may have become more agitated once society started to come under the influence of the rationalising spirit of Ionia, and real atheism emerged.

---

[22] The Boutadai supplied the priestess of Athena Polias and the priest of Poseidon Erechtheus on the Acropolis. The Eleusinian Mysteries were controlled by the families of the Eumolpidae and the Kerykes. Since the Eleusinian Mysteries became pan-Hellenic under Pesistratos, I suggest they were associated with the Peisistratidae. The Eumolpidae claimed descent from Eumolpus, the son of Poseidon and the legendary first priest of Demeter at Eleusis.

4

The mutilation of the hermae

There are certain social and political events that give expression to a spiritual transformation in religious consciousness. They epitomize the change.

Like the Trojan War, the Peloponnesian War[1] may be taken as **a landmark period dividing two epochs in religious consciousness**. While the foundations of the change were laid continuously throughout the archaic period, as also by the remarkable revolution in cognition in Ionia, this war features prominently as a catalyst that accelerated the religious transformations at work. War is the supreme test of the character of a people, of its cohesion, and of the quality of its constitution. Its mores come under the fiercest of examinations, and the longer the war, the more evenly balanced the two sides are, and the more it becomes a life-and-death struggle hinging on the vicissitudes of single battles, and apparently on the actions of powerful individuals, the greater the test. The Peloponnesian War endured 27 years, during which the population of Athens was halved. The watchword is trauma.[2]

In broad outline, then, the history of **the Athenian constitution** is marked by progressive steps towards the development of a democracy, by which is meant, a situation in which the ultimate legislative power resides in the assembly of enfranchised male citizens, of between 30,000 to 50,000 citizens, about one fifth of the population of Athens taken as a whole.[3] It is hard to imagine what meetings of

---

[1] It is customary to divide the **Peloponnesian War** between Athens and Sparta into three phases: (1) **The Archidamian War** (431 – 421) named after the Spartan king Archidamus II, who routinely invaded Attica. During this phase the Athenians gained the upper hand. The two sides concluded (2) **The Peace of Nicias** (421 – 414). During this period the Athenians launched an invasion of Sicily, attacking Syracuse and its allies (415), that ended in total defeat for them with the loss of their entire force, and brought Sparta back into the war. (3) In the third phase, the **Decelean War** or Ionian War (413 – 404), Sparta with the financial backing of the Persian satraps of Asia, contended with Athens for control of Ionia and the Propontis. By the disastrous defeat at the battle of Aegospotami in 405, the Athenians lost their entire fleet, were cut off from grain supplies coming from the Black Sea, and forced to surrender. The Spartan general Lysander installed an **oligarchy of 'The Thirty Tyrants"** at Athens, but this was overthrown a year later in 403 and a democracy was restored by Thrasybulus. In the subsequent period Athens recovered, and Spartan power eventually declined, while Thebes assumed political dominance within Greece. The independence of the Greek city states, and the constant warfare between them was ended by the victory of Philip of Macedonia over the Greek forces lead by Athens and Thebes at Chaeronea in 338.

[2] The World Wars of the C20 lasted four and five years respectively; but one could call the whole 1914 – 1945 a single period of war, with an extended "peace", equivalent to the Peace of Nicias, separating the two periods of world-wide armed conflagration. By this comparison, we understand the devastation wrought by the Peloponnesian War, and learn something too about the past century.

[3] Emerging from the disruption of the Dark Ages, Greece grew prosperous. The C8 is said to have been a century of population expansion in Greece, resulting in colonisation and changes in the social

and economic structure. The agriculture of Attica could not support the expanding population of Athens, which became a city that relied on manufactures, mining and trade. The wealthier citizens, the aristocrats, owned the more fertile productive lands close to the citadel, and the other citizens were forced to farm more marginal lands. Society became more stratified: (a) the landed aristocracy (*pentacosiomedimni*); (b) other wealthy landed citizens, some called knights (*hippeis*) and other yeomen (*zeugitae*); (c) the merchant and manufacturing class; (d) the poorer citizens; (*thetes*), who worked for wages or had very low farm incomes, and who provided the oarsmen of the navy; (e) resident foreigners, who were probably for the most part merchants, manufacturers and quite prosperous; (f) slaves. Only the wealth owning classes had slaves. There were about as many slaves in Athens as freemen. Around the time of Pericles (c.440) there were about 40,000 male citizens, 10,000 residents, 50,000 male slaves; thus, with the women, who were completely unfranchised, a population of about 200,000 in all. In war, the nobility provided the generals, the knights the cavalry, the yeomen the hoplites, and the *thetes* the bulk of the sailors. Within the landed classes there was a shift of power from the aristocracy to the yeomanry, occasioned by the shift in battle tactics from independent warrior combat out of mobile chariots that we see in the account of the battles before Troy in Homer, to the use of yeoman hoplites in phalanx formation. The superiority of the hoplite armies is reflected in the constant defeat of larger Persian armies by Greek formations. By the time of Homer, the change in military tactics had already taken place. Homer's works were idealisations of the past created for elite audiences. Landed warfare favoured the interests of the landed classes altogether, and naval warfare the lower classes (thetes). The introduction of currency created further social pressure, including the possibility of debt, and hence enslavement through debt.

This dynamic social structure involving economic conflict and general pressure produced a series of political developments in Athens. (1) During the C7 Athens was governed by an aristocracy through the aristocratic council of the Aereopagus. This culminated in the tyranny of Draco (c.621) in which the poorer classes were increasingly oppressed. (2) The resultant pressure led to the reforms of Solon (594). It became illegal to enslave a citizen for debt, all debts were cancelled, mortgages were cancelled, and a new constitution strictly defined property classes, and shifted power to a limited extent from the Aeropagus to the general Assembly. (3) The tyranny of Peisistratus (561 – 527) and of his sons Hipparchus and Hippias may have arisen from an alliance between the aristocratic faction led by Peisistratus with the manufacturers and poorer segments of society. Initially popular, this administration was accompanied by an expanding economy. The aristocracy was divided between three main groupings: the coast party (south-west coast of Attica) headed by the Alcmeonidae; the plains party (Athens and the plains to the north) headed by the Boutadai; the "beyond the hills" party (east coast of Attica) headed by the Peisistratidae, whose estate was at Brauron. (4) The tyranny of Hippias was brought to an end by Spartan military intervention in 510 at the behest of the Alcmeonidae, but democratic reform continued and the reforms of Cleisthenes, himself an Alcmeonidae who had allied himself with the "people" and defeated the conservative party lead by Isocrates, resulted in a reorganisation of the tribes of Attica into new civic units, called demes. This represents both a real and symbolic shift of power to the Assembly away from the aristocratic dominated traditional tribes and phratries, and the constitution further was altered in that direction. The advance of democracy came into conflict with conservative elements: during the reforms of Cleisthenes the Athenian term for a statute was changed from *themos*, signifying a law imposed by the gods, that is the aristocracy, to *nomos*, signifying a law created by the agreement of the people in the Ecclesia. The Alcmeonidae tended to favour collaboration with Persia; the Peisistratidae opposition. However, it was during the political ascendency of Themistocles, a non-aristocratic, popular leader, and Miltiades, an associate of the Peisistratidae, that Athens defeated the first Persian invasion at Marathon.

the assembly were like, with so many potential participants. A quorum of 6,000 of these citizens was required. There are varying estimates as to the capacity of the open-air theatre – the Pnyx – where these meetings were held, from 6,000 to 20,000.

Democracy. Contemporary Western states are said to be democracies, but reflection on how power is distributed within these states shows that the meaning of democracy needs to be clarified. A "direct democracy" is a state where citizens vote on every item of legislation, as in an assembly; a "representational democracy" is one where citizens first elect representatives, who then become the law-makers. In the contemporary world, even a state such as Switzerland, where there is more direct democracy than others, could not be called a "pure democracy". This is because power is not distributed exclusively through such elective procedures, and the distribution of power elsewhere is by other means.

Sources of power and influence: (a) **Birth and inheritance**. By being born into a family with wealth, economic power and "cultural capital".[4] (b) By acquisition of **economic power** – success in business confers political and social influence. (c) By acquisition of power by virtue of position within a **bureaucracy**. Large businesses constitute themselves as bureaucracies, and the state creates many bureaucracies. In a corporation, or by entering the civil service, one may "climb the ladder". Among the most important of the state's organisations is the military. All positions confer political influence and executive power – the authority to press a certain button, or make a certain decision is vested in a position. (d) By acquisition of **prestige**. Certain occupations (film, sport, television presentation etc.) attract a **charisma** that endows the person in that position with influence. Politicians can sometimes be regarded as charismatic star-like people; occasionally, a successful academic, writer, or priest acquires charisma. (e) By acquisition of the **reputation for special knowledge** that is needed by others. Technicians range from plumbers to computer experts and academics. **Academia** forms a bureaucracy, and the combination of a reputation for exclusive technical knowledge combined with positional power – editorship of a journal, head of a faculty, leader of a university – can be powerful. (f) By acquisition of position within a **traditional hierarchy**, such as a family, clan, or racial grouping. (g) By acquisition of position within a **voluntary association**, such as a club.[5] (h) By acquisition of power through a **democratic procedure**. Election as a representative is but one means to power; an individual must acquire power in at least one other sense before acquiring power by election. (i) Power vested in respect for **age** in a traditional society, and power vested in **gender** in a patriarchy. This is historic, it being a moot question whether

---

[4] This term denoting influence through social connections is due to Pierre Bordeaux.

[5] One of the most important of voluntary associations is that of a **political party**. A political party claims to represent the economic or **vested interests of a segment of society**, such as an economic class or racial group, or community. The individual gains power within the association or party, then more power through the backing given by the supporters of that class, group or party.

either of these are sources of power in contemporary society.[6] (j) **Race**. It is a sensitive yet moot question as to whether racial identity is a source of power.[7]

A historical question concerns the power of the **Church**. While historically a certain **spiritual power** might have been felt by people, so that a person perceived to be spiritually elevated above the human average was granted power through the respect shown to him or her, such power has either ceased to exist in contemporary society or has become marginal.[8]

The State requires means by which the various interests of individuals or groupings with power are regulated and harmonised. A state, its constitution, or constitutional practices, amounts to methods whereby a **balance of power** is achieved; a system of "checks and balances". Since there are many powerful individuals and groups within society, society involves conflict, which society, though its constitution and norms, has methods of resolving.

In theory everyone, whatever their position, degree of power or influence enjoys the benefits from living in society; for example, a well-regulated society has low levels of crime, and individuals benefit from this. The individual has a self-interested motive for participating in society, and expresses that participation, by, for instance, paying taxes and obeying the law. This **state of nature theory** concerns not only the question of self-interest, but also whether the individual is morally obligated to join society, supposing he did not find himself already in one.

When people living in a society are aware that the benefits of participating in society outweigh the disadvantages, they experience a satisfaction that expresses itself in social **solidarity**. They feel that their society is "just". Solidarity manifests itself by participation in the norms of civil society – voluntarily paying taxes, voting, abiding by the decisions of plebiscites, obeying policemen, not committing crimes, etc.

---

[6] The idea that older people have acquired **wisdom**, a form of spiritual power, merit respect and political power, does not appear a principle of contemporary society. The elderly are treated as encumbrances by those still of working age. They are anticipated to acquire serious illnesses, including mental or intellectual decay, and are sources of power to those who act as carers, who thereby gain positional or economic power within the caring industry. Regarding the male-female balance, it is a moot question whether we have entered a matriarchy or are progressing towards one. Economic forces dictate that both men and women work, and while women may yet be paid less for work than men, their economic independence liberates them to an extent from the previous norms of patriarchy.

[7] It is likely to be still the case that in Britain, being born white, and with an English name, does advantage the individual and increase his or her opportunities.

[8] The Church is another organisation or "business", and power is acquired within that organisation by acquisition of position in its bureaucracy. A Church, like a political party, represents a community of worshippers. Thus, a person acquires power firstly by position within the Church-organisation, and then through the strength of the community that he represents.

Each person, however, does exaggerate what he or she feels is due to him or her. Furthermore, whatever position one has in society, whether one belongs to a high or low place within it or was born into a family with economic and cultural capital, it is inevitable that one will experience a limitation. In a large society, unlimited power could not be the privilege of any individual. It is also false that "equality of opportunity" exists in any society. Society is and always has been an environment where some are born with more advantages than others. Education is not equally accessible to all, and even if we treat society as one vast competition for power, then that favours those who are better adapted by birth, character or circumstances to the competition.

Corruption. Solidarity and social cohesion break down when society is perceived to be "unjust", and in such circumstances individuals feel that their legitimate ambitions (which are for power) are thwarted by the excessive power and influence of other individuals or groups. When people feel that their society is unjust they also, in their minds first, charge those in power with corruption. They say, in private at least, that society is corrupt. Corruption is the use of power to further the interest of oneself or one's group in ways that are perceived by other individuals or groups as "unfair". This also touches upon the issue of rights and minority rights. A corrupt government may arise through the "tyranny of the majority"; for example, in a society where there is a large racial grouping, that racial grouping may democratically elect a government which systematically engineers the laws and executive power of the state and norms of society to disadvantage minorities. This is one form of corruption, for corruption, like crime to which it is always linked, is a many-headed hydra. The breakdown of social cohesion and the rise of corruption lead invariably to conflict. Where the political system remains to a degree "open" and "healthy" it may express itself in civil ways and thereby bring about redress; in this case the corruption was not endemic to society, and was a temporary phenomenon brought about not through some collective will. But in other cases, where protest is repressed, the civil discord breaks out in civil war, or if the power of the state is too great, in underground opposition and even acts of terror.

Elections. In practice "democracy" refers to the performance in a society of such things as elections at regular periods, in accordance with rules, and established customs, such as plebiscites. In a society such as Britain, democratic procedures are aspects of the constitution, and part of the system of checks-and-balances. The public are good judges of when a government is failing, or in danger of corruption, and the institution of voting quickly restores the norm.[9]

---

[9] Democracy of the British, American, or Western variety, which acts in this way, and is a practical and symbolic process whereby all the people are included in the decision-making process of society, is to be applauded. For example, the two, or multi-party system provides the British people with acceptable alternatives, and the differences of policy between the respective parties are smaller than the parties themselves make out. From the C17 onwards Britain evolved a property-owning

Leadership. The benefits of an excellent democratic system should not preclude discussion as to where "true leadership" lies, or what meanings we may give to "leadership" other than the obvious ones of "having political and institutional power to take certain decisions". According to this latter and popular notion, a man like Napoleon was a leader. But it is a moot question as to whether Napoleon, as an individual, ever did anything that was not the expression of a collective will.[10] I am very far from sharing the opinion of Rousseau in the infallibility of **the general will**. But, then, Rousseau also does not share his own opinion.

> Whether the General Will is Fallible
> It follows from what has gone before that the general will is always right and tends to the public advantage; but it does not follow that the deliberations of the people are always equally correct.[11]

One way of reading the above, is that the first part says, "The general will is infallible", and the second says "The general will is not infallible." A more sophisticated reading might be, "Under certain circumstances the general will is infallible, but in circumstances that may prevail in society, the deliberations of politicians as to the general will may be corrupted by vested interests."

Where the general will fails. Humanity is bound by its cognitive structures, it is restricted by its consciousness, it is constrained by its religious consciousness. In those questions where the solution to a practical problem of politics or ethics lies within the subsisting framework of the cognition or consciousness, then the general will may or may not be infallible, and if it does fail, then that may be due to the corruption of vested interests. But in those questions that lie on the boundary between what is possible to think within a system, and what must be thought by abandoning that system and progressing in consciousness, the general will is at best irrelevant, and more usually a regressive force that prevents progress. This was also the analysis of Euripides, as we have seen in the preceding chapter.

In such cases, the leadership of society always lies with individuals and small groups; but with single persons more than with small groups of persons. In all matters **where consciousness must progress**, true leadership is provided by an individual. Many such individuals were well-known during their lives, and some of them had political influence, but quite a few of them were utterly obscure during

---

"democracy" in which only those who had property were eligible to vote etc. In the C19 this system was rightly overturned through a series of progressive reforms, such as the reform of 1832, and concluding in the inter-war period, when the suffrage was extended to all male citizens and finally to women as well.

[10] Tolstoy, for example, in *War and Peace* was adamant that Napoleon was a mere product of the age he lived in, and in himself, nothing but a small man.

[11] Jean Jacques Rousseau, *The Social Contract*, Book II, Section III.

their lifetimes, and the relevance provided by their leadership emerged after their death. Since the progression of cognition, of consciousness, and of religious consciousness always requires breaking the mould of some previous constraint, every true leader in this sense is a great thinker, a free thinker, a genius.

We see immediately who the leaders of Greece were: Orpheus, Homer, Solon, Thales, Aeschylus, Sophocles, Euripides, Parmenides, Zeno, Pythagoras, Socrates, Democritus, Plato and Aristotle. These are the persons who decisively advanced consciousness, and broke the tyranny held over the collective will by a previous system of cognition that spiritual progress demanded had to be overcome.

Orpheus is least known as an individual and may be a mythical invention. We attribute to him the overthrow of the practice of ritual human, male adult and child sacrifice and the transformation of that religion into the chthonic religion of symbolic festivals. He transformed the archetype of Dionysus. **Homer** instituted the Olympian religion, whose defining aspect is the concept of justice, on which the notion of respect for persons and human rights in Western consciousness and civilization are founded. He instituted the archetype of Zeus and the archetype of the hero. We may attribute to **Solon** the notion of a constitution as securing laws whereby the right balance is achieved between the interests of all classes of society; he turned Athens into a constitutional democracy. **Thales** instituted the Ionian revolution of cognition, making it possible to systematically consider nature objectively as a system that is regulated without reference to human ego and human fantasy. The work of **Aeschylus** and **Sophocles** established the moral foundation of Athens and Western consciousness – absolute respect for justice; suppliants, that is refugees, to be protected even in the face of overwhelming odds; respect for the law, for individuals; mercy to be shown to the defeated; adherence to the rules of humane war; prisoners not to be executed. They advanced the concept of sin as hubris. **Democritus** represents the systematic working out of the idea of nature as objective reality where objects are collections of indestructible particles. He laid the foundation of Western empirical science. The contributions of the other leaders mentioned above will be subject to further discussion.

I wish now to discuss a special sequence of events, marked out from all the events of the Peloponnesian war, whose linking motif is the life and character of Alcibiades and the relationship of Alcibiades to Socrates.

Alcibiades was born on his mother's side into the leading aristocratic family of the Alcmaeonidae. Cleisthenes, one of the reformers of the Athenian constitution, and Pericles, the democratic leader of Athens at the onset of the war, and arguably its greatest ever statesman, were members of this family. Alcibiades was not only fantastically wealthy, extremely well connected, and born to power and influence, but he had enormous beauty and charisma that made him into a star.[12]   Accounts provided by Plato and Plutarch suggest that Alcibiades suffered as a young man from a form of infantile self-infatuation.   They suggest that he was reckless and over-confident, prone to riotous living, and believed he was above reproach.   On their account, his character contributed decisively to his first crisis, which lead to his exile from Athens, and defection to Sparta in 415.[13]

The fate of Alcibiades is an expression of **the failure of Athenian solidarity**. The place of Alcibiades in certain curious events has a pivotal significance.   He became the focal point of every intrigue, in the conflict between various factions.

(1) Plato's work *The Symposium* (composed not earlier than 385) is set in 416. The events are fictional, but the characters are all historical.   In addition to the philosophy of higher love that Plato has Socrates express, the central subject of the work is the relationship between Alcibiades and Socrates.   The context of the events is the run-up to the Sicilian expedition, the policy of Alcibiades.

(2) After **the capture of Melos**, 416/415,[14] the Athenians committed the **atrocity** of executing all male survivors and selling all women and children into slavery.   In this **war-crime**, Athens violated its own mores, as expounded to them by Aeschylus and Sophocles.   When a society betrays its own values, for whatever reason or practical expedient, it becomes moribund.   All moral strength derives from **the consciousness of righteousness**, as it appears to the free conscience within the framework of the religious consciousness of the age.   Euripides in *The Trojan Women* protested.   At a subsequent date, **Alcibiades was scapegoated** for the war-crime.   Plutarch states that "Alcibiades bore a heavy share of the responsibility for the execution of the grown men on the island, since he had given his support in the Assembly to the motion which decreed this."[15]   Plutarch, who is careless with his sources, repeats a charge that may be without foundation.   We may infer is that the

---

[12] He was a very good general.   His brilliant victory over the Spartan navy at Battle of Cyzicus (410) restored Athenian power for a time, and the Spartans sued for peace, which the democracy at Athens rejected.   His defeat at Notium (406), not decisive, was caused by the failure of a subordinate to follow a command, yet it provided the pretext for Alcibiades's dismissal from command, and by that means the Athenian democracy deprived itself not only of Alcibiades but of its other competent commanders, such as Thrasybulus.

[13] The same arrogant character is made to appear in his conduct in Sparta, where according to Plutarch he had an affair with Timaia, the wife of King Agis II, sired an illegitimate son by her, and provoked a plot against his own life.   However, in this instance political forces within Sparta may have been all that was necessary to account for his losing favour.   After losing favour in Sparta, Alcibiades defected to the Persians, before being reinstated by the Athenians.

[14] This occurred during the Peace of Nicias.   The Melians, who were of Dorian extraction, refused the demand of the Athenians that they should join the Delian League, the alliance dominated by Athens. Following a long siege in which the Melians were reduced to an exceptional state of starvation, the city was captured.

[15] Plutarch, *Alcibiades*, 16, 3.

Athenian psyche seized upon Alcibiades as the author of all that was blameworthy in their own conduct.

(3) **The mutilation of the hermae**, 415. Alcibiades was chosen as one of three commanders to lead the Athenian expedition against Sicily. It seems this was the policy of Alcibiades and Alcibiades did attempt to justify the war as pre-emptive. Certain states within Sicily had also appealed to Athens for protection. We judge the expedition to be an act of imperialism that reflects badly on Athenian mores; an offensive war that violated what was even in Greek consciousness the important principle of the **just war**.

Herms were used as boundary markers at important places and were thought to confer protection on those places. Their origin lies in the old matriarchal religion of fertility; they are pillars carrying a head or torso, and nothing else but a large phallus. While preparations were being made for the launch of the expeditionary force, one night, during the festival of Adonis, many of the hermae were mutilated. Their heads were knocked off during a night of riot. There followed a witch-hunt, and public opinion was directed towards Alcibiades; he was indicted in the Assembly by Thessalus for the crime. He pleaded to be allowed to immediately defend himself, but was required to sail for Sicily with the expedition. He was later recalled, and, expecting the worse, he gave his captors the slip, and defected to Sparta.

(4) **Parody of the sacred mysteries**. In addition, as Plutarch explains, "During this period Androcles, the democratic leader, produced a number of slaves and resident aliens, who accused Alcibiades and his friends of having disfigured other secret images and parodied the Mysteries of Eleusis in one of their drunken revels."[16] These acts of impiety were then included in the indictment made by Thessalus, son of Cimon, against Alcibiades.

(5) **Return of Alcibiades** to Athens in 407. The day of his return fell on that day during the festival of Plynteria when the statue of Athena was ritually cleansed. This was interpreted as an ill omen, the bad luck falling on Alcibiades.[17] But the blasphemy charges against him were dropped.

(6) Alcibiades made a **public demonstration of his piety** by organising a military escort for the procession to Eleusis, a ritual that had not been practised during the second part of the war, owing to the Spartan garrison at Decelea.

(7) **Indictment of Socrates.** In 399 Socrates was indicted by Meletus, Anytus and Lycon. The indictment reads:

---

[16] *Ibid.*, 19, 1.

[17] Plutarch tells us, "the Athenians regard that date as the unluckiest in the whole year for business of any kind, and so the goddess, far from welcoming Alcibiades graciously and with goodwill, appeared to be hiding her face and rejecting him." *Ibid.*, 34, 1.

> The following sworn indictment has been brought by Meletus, son of
> Meletus, of Pitthos, against Socrates, son of Sophroniscus, of
> Alopeke. Socrates does wrong in not recognizing the gods which the
> city recognizes, and in introducing other, new divinities. Further, he
> is a wrongdoer in corrupting the young.

One of the accusers, Anytus, had been involved in the democratic overthrow of the
Thirty Tyrants, and had supported the **Amnesty of Eucleides**, under which offences
committed before or during the Rule of the Thirty were granted immunity from
prosecution. He broke with the spirit of that decree by prosecuting Socrates.[18]
Socrates attacked his accusers rather than defended himself; he maintained his trial
was a political and philosophic-religious **act of persecution**, he expected to be
condemned, and took no steps to prevent that condemnation by acts of appeasement
or otherwise. His death may be regarded as an act of self-sacrifice.

   Bias of Plato and Plutarch.   In the spirit of impartial enquiry, I observe
prejudice in the portrayal of Alcibiades by Plato and Plutarch.[19] The account of
events in Thucydides only refer to Alcibiades's reputation for profligate living, when
these are mentioned by his adversaries. The first introduction of Alcibiades by
Thucydides sets the tone in which he describes the political and military acts of
Alcibiades throughout his history.

> The breach between the Lacedaemonians and Athenians having gone
> thus far, the party at Athens, also, who wished to cancel the treaty,
> immediately put themselves in motion. Foremost amongst these was
> Alcibiades, son of Clinias, a man yet young in years for any other
> Hellenic city, but distinguished by the splendour of his ancestry.[20]

Charge of inexperience. But Alcibiades (b. 450) was not so young neither – he was
thirty-four years of age in 416 at the outset of the events described above,
experienced beyond his years with notable political and military successes. One

[18] We have two accounts of Socrates's defence at the trial, one by Plato and the other by Xenophon.
Xenophon was not an eye-witness of the events, being involved as a mercenary at the time of the trial
in the attempt to overthrow the King of Persia, and he based his account on the testimony of
Hermogenes, the son of Hipponicus, who claimed to be at the trial. The two accounts have
differences. Xenophon rationalises Socrates's defence by arguing that he knew he was already
advanced in years, and wished to avoid the pains of old age, but this explanation is superficial
[19] Regarding the bias of Plutarch, his account of Alcibiades's life occurs in the context of his plan to
draw parallels between a Roman and Greek personage who exhibited similar character and moral
failings. He compares Alcibiades to Coriolanus. His aim contaminates his perceptions from the
outset, he draws upon Plato as a source without critical awareness, and he is not concerned with
historical accuracy.
[20] Thucydides, *The Peloponnesian War*, 5.43.

alleged informer in the matter of the hermae and defamation of the Eleusinian mysteries, Andocides, was ten years his junior, being born in 440.[21] Thucydides represents Alcibiades as a serious leader. The **characterisation of Alcibiades** in *The Symposium* presents him as an adolescent of skittish manners.[22] Comparing his pathetic outburst of irresponsible youth with the speech Thucydides attributes to Alcibiades when debating the merits of the Sicilian expedition, we see that Plato has participated in **defamation**. Plato's motive is transparent – the portrayal of Alcibiades **elevates the character of Socrates** and absolves Socrates of culpability for the crimes reputedly attributed to Alcibiades. Plato, who was born between 427 and 423 was between six and eleven years old when the events of the alleged symposium took place. The episode in *The Symposium* is a **fabrication**. In the dialogue, another enemy of Socrates, Aristophanes, is made to appear a fool. A story of how at the battle of Potidaea Socrates saved the life of Alcibiades elevates Socrates at the expense of Alcibiades.[23] Plato joins the enemies of Alcibiades in the practice of **scapegoating** him for the ills of Athens. Referring to Socrates, the fictitious Alcibiades states: "He is the only person in whose presence I experience a sensation of which I might be thought incapable, a sensation of shame; he, and he alone, positively makes me ashamed of myself. The reason is that I am conscious that there is no arguing against the conclusion that one should do as he bids, and yet that, whenever I am away from him, I succumb to the temptations of popularity."[24]

Homosexuality. Was the relationship between Socrates and Alcibiades homosexual? Homosexuality has been condemned for more than two millennia, but we are in a new age that regards a person's sexuality as his or her own affair. A second aspect, of a **relationship between teacher and pupil** is trickier, though here it is the question of sexual relations between academics and their adult students. (The Greeks may have found paedophilia normal, but that is not in question here. The pupils of Socrates are of legal age by our standards.) For the circle to which Socrates belonged, it was "normal" and acceptable behaviour for teacher and pupil to become intimate, but it is not clear that Athenian society as a whole looked upon it that way. We are so used to the commonplace that the Greeks extolled

---

[21] According to Plutarch, Androcles was the chief accuser of Alcibiades. Andocides was later said to have been an informer, but he vigorously denied that charge.

[22] "A moment later they heard the voice of Alcibiades in the courtyard, very tipsy and shouting, wanting to know where Agathon was and demanding to be taken to Agathon. He was helped in by the flute-girl and some of his other companions; he stood in the doorway crowned with a thick wreath of ivy and violets, from which a number of ribands hung about his head, and said:

'Good evening, gentlemen. Will you welcome into your company a man who is already drunk, utterly drunk, or shall we just put a garland on Agathon, which is what we came for, and go away?'" Plato, *Symposium*, 212d – e.

[23] The Potidaean campaign in question is 432/1, making Alcibiades then eighteen years old. The account is suspect; in Sparta, under the Lycurgan reforms, military service began at the age of twenty.

[24] Plato, *Symposium*, 216b.

homosexuality that the possibility of outrage at sexual relations between masters and pupils may have been overlooked. Pederasty may be hinted at in the indictment of Socrates. It is possible that among the accusers of Socrates at his trial, one of them believed Socrates had debauched his son, and another believed that Socrates belongs to a circle of an older man who sought by means of money to debauch his son. But we might say that the young men were of an "age of consent", teacher-pupil relationship or not.[25] I revert to the discussion of religion in relation to these events.

(1) **Ironic reversal of religious values**. Jonathan Miller's play *The Crucible* depicts a ghastly witch-hunt in seventeenth century New England. It is conducted by puritans under the pretext of rooting out the devil in their society. Miller exposes the evil ambition of the perpetrator of the witch-hunt, Thomas Putnam, to persecute and eliminate his political opponents, in the name of hostility to the body. The witch-hunt and persecution that followed the mutilation of the hermae at Athens in 415 was as vicious as the one depicted in Miller's play but done in the service of the religion of fertility – conducted because standing statues with representations of the erect penis had been mutilated. How things run in circles. But this irony is no mere accident. The mutilation of the hermae is **the historical turning point in this reversal of religious values**, marking the boundary between the epoch when the phallus was a symbol of highest religious significance, from the epoch when it was a symbol of all that was un-holy. The greatest significance is that the "sacrilege" occurred.

(2) **Who did it**? Some persons did commit the "outrage". Plato considers that Alcibiades was the author; Plato is at least not at pains to deny it. Plato's portrayal of the character of Alcibiades is so evidently a fabrication, that we could certainly not convict on its basis. The political enemies of Alcibiades seized upon the occasion to cover him in calumny on the eve of this departure for Sicily, and when he was absent, were able to bring a charge against him. Alcibiades knew exactly what to expect on return to Athens, and astutely jumped ship. By the **Count of Monte Cristo principle**,[26] the perpetrators of the sacrilege were the very people who made the accusation.[27]

---

[25] One of the accusers was Anytus, and in Xenophon's account Socrates is stated as saying, "I had a brief association with the son of Anytus, and I found him not lacking in spirit." In Xenophon's account Socrates poured scorn on the occupation of Anytus, who was a tanner. Another of the accusers, Lycon, had a son called Autolycus. In the Symposium by Xenophon, Socrates praises the love of Callias, an older man, for a younger man called Autolycus, whom scholars identify as the son of Lycon. Xenophon's information may not be correct, and the implications are not entirely clear.

[26] After the novel by Alexander Dumas, in which the Abbé Faria explains that the person most likely to benefit from a crime is the one most likely to have committed it.

[27] Andocides figures in the account of Plutarch as an informer. (Plutarch, Alcibiades, 21.) However, Andocides was himself accused of blasphemy in 400, and we have his speech in defence. Citing state corroborated testimony, he refuted the charge of informing against Alcibiades and was acquitted of blasphemy. Based on his speech, it may be possible to determine the perpetrators of the crime.

(3) This sacrilege, which anticipates the **iconoclasm** of the Byzantine period,[28] marks a watershed moment in the history of Western consciousness. Whether it was committed by Alcibiades or his enemies, such **an outrage against the gods of fertility** of the old epoch would have been inconceivable at an earlier date. Supposing it was committed by Alcibiades under the influence of Socrates – then it marks **the rationalist's rejection of sexual impulses as the foundation of religion**.[29]   Alternatively, supposing that the hermae were mutilated under the instructions of the enemies of Alcibiades, with a view to accusing him of sacrilege – then this reflects a transformed consciousness, for it marks **a cynical attitude to religion**. The world has changed, whichever way one looks upon it.

(4) In the Western tradition, the first nameable person historically to reject the body and sexual impulse and grade them as immoral was **Pythagoras**. But it was **Plato** who incorporated this concept into a systematic philosophy. **Plato**, the pupil of Socrates, is the principal originator in the West of the concept of sin as desire of the Flesh. In the matter of the relationship between Alcibiades and Socrates, Plato, no eye-witness himself, is in a state of conflict over the central moral issue. Is sex, specifically homosexual acts within the context of a consenting adult relationship, moral or not? The whole of Greek society was moving in the direction of rejecting the physical. It is summed up in Aristotle's definition of **man as a rational animal**. The Greeks asked the question: what makes man different from the animals? Their answer – reason – became bound up with the distinction they drew between **reason and desire**. Henceforth, only **the life of reason**, as distinct from the life of bodily pleasures, could be moral and spiritual.

(5) Between the generation of Socrates and the generation of Plato we may see a **revolution in sexual mores**. While in *The Symposium* Plato implies that Socrates never had any sexual relations with Alcibiades, that it was Alcibiades that pursued Socrates without obtaining satisfaction, the context as well as other dialogues indicate that sexual relations between men were normal within the group to which Socrates belonged. The symposium is a drinking party of men held at the house of the poet Agathon to celebrate Agathon's winning a prize for his first tragedy at the

---

Though Andocides denies it, it is possible the Hermai were desecrated by gangs of up to 300 men. The ensuing witch-hunt, which was very nasty, targeted the party of Callias, son of Hipponicus. We may speculate that it was the faction opposed to Callias, Alcibiades and their associates who mutilated the Hermai, which was staged to bring Alcibiades and his associates down. The tit-for-tat reaction of Callias is also indicated in the speech of Andocides. Religion entered a new cynical phase.

[28] 726 to 787 CE and 814 to 842 CE – periods of destruction of pagan images.

[29] It is unlikely that Alcibiades committed the crime, but in principle the whole philosophy of Plato represents a rejection of the physical, so it is not inconceivable that this kind of thinking could be present in the circle of Socrates, and that indeed must have been known to the enemies of both men, because the charges stuck. Alcibiades had to run for his life, but was murdered, and Socrates was put on trial and chose to submit to his fate.

festival of Lenaia in 416. All these men are bisexual at least, and Agathon, the central attraction, is, like Alcibiades interested in Socrates, finally joining the couch of Socrates at the end of the party, though Socrates is made to ignore this and is attested to have simply carried on the discussion all night. Elsewhere in the dialogues of Plato the social context in which Socrates is moving is one in which homosexual love is normal. The *Phaedrus* opens with a discussion of the attempt by Lysias to win Phaedrus as a lover. It was a practice normal among the circle of Socrates for an older man to court a younger one for sexual favours. Plato indicates that Phaedrus is reluctant to accept the proposal of Lysias, which is made under the cover of a sophistic argument; Socrates exposes the fallacies in the argument, and it seems that reason has triumphed over sin as desire. Then Socrates hears his divine voice and expounds a **theory of sublimation**. Why does Plato reverse his conclusion of the first part of the dialogue to allow some homosexual practice as morally and spiritually acceptable? Because Socrates, or at least many of his circle, were practising homosexuals, and Plato cannot deny that as a fact, and therefore must rationalise it.

(6) The events illustrate **the state of religious consciousness in the mass**. The Athenian masses are superstitious, irrational and easily manipulated into a collective hysteria. We see the enactment of the mythologem of ritual human sacrifice; Alcibiades plays the part of Dionysus and is pursued by the irrational force of the collective psyche at a more primitive state of development. Symbolically, Plato is right to bring him into the symposium wearing the ivy symbol of the god-who-is-rendered-limb-from-limb and eaten.[30]

(7) A second ironic observation is that every superstitious idea attached to the life of Alcibiades came true. The mutilation of the hermae did presage great disaster for Athens – their expedition to Sicily was an utter failure; they were ultimately defeated. The day that Alcibiades arrived back at Athens was a day of doom for

---

[30] Alcibiades fell into the trap of being made into the scapegoat of this powerful, unanalysed, unconscious force of the collective psyche, and his life exhibits him as the constant victim of that force, which is steered by other demagogues. Whatever his conduct before the mutilation of the Hermai, we may speculate that it had been sufficiently unguarded as to expose him to the charge of impiety. From the moment he is charged with blasphemy, he is playing "catch-up" all his life. We see in his response to the crisis increasing maturity, as well as intelligence and courage. He is finally restored to his homeland and becomes its saviour for a time; his first act is a very public display of piety. But it is not enough, for the force against which he is struggling is too big for any man once it has been unleashed. His successes increased his star-like quality, which served only to make him more vulnerable to fall. Eventually, he sought to withdraw entirely from the situation – by retreating to castles in Thrace. But the relentless enemy of the massed psyche of collective oppression pursued him. The idiots placed in charge of the Athenian navy lost their entire force of two hundred ships – Alcibiades tried to prevent it by warning these commanders of their foolish disposition of the navy – they rebuffed him. With Athens defeated, Spartan power reached everywhere – he was on the run, he made it to the court of Persian satrap Pharnabazus, where he was murdered.

him; whatever he did, he could not shake off the curse of being the target of every superstitious idea prevalent in Athens; he lost his command again, was unable to prevent the final disaster, and was finally murdered while on the run. While we perceive that these superstitious beliefs were self-fulfilling prophecies and were part of the causal mechanism that lead to their fulfilment, there remains a hint of something supernatural or at least symbolic about them. The mutilation of the hermae is a **symbolic statement of a rupture in Athenian religious solidarity**, for sacrilege had been demonstrated to be possible by becoming actual, and such a rupture operates on a plane of historical explanation lying above the causal mechanisms.

(8) The **collective psyche** is left behind at an earlier stage of religious consciousness; being collective, it is unconscious. It re-enacts the drama of the mythologem of Dionysus; it is superstitious, savage and cruel. At Athens, the collective blindness makes it vulnerable, and brings about the defeat of the city. First it is tempted into the hubristic, collective fantasy of invulnerability, and embarks upon a poorly planned attempt at imperialism in the invasion of Sicily. Then, it turns upon the apparent architect of that fantasy, and destroys him, even when that person demonstrates that he alone has the quality as a commander to save them. The collective, under the inspiration of demagogues, rejects the offer of peace from Sparta, and pursues to the bitter end the goal of total victory. It sanctions war-crimes in the pursuit of this chimaera. The collective psyche of the Athens exhibits the character of the failed hero. In the matter of true leadership, the collective does not know what is best to do, because "best" can only mean "what is moral" and the collective is at an earlier stage of moral development. That the **collective is always behind the advanced individual** is most likely a universal **pattern of history**, but the gap between the two can vary. History demonstrates that in any conflict between nations or peoples, one of these collectives may be at a more advanced stage of consciousness than the other. Victory goes to the collective at the more advanced stage. In the conflicts between Rome and Carthage, Rome was more progressed, and therefore was able to overcome Carthage. During the Peloponnesian war the collective mores of the Athenians regressed, their cohesion broke down, and they were unable to resolve their own internal factional politics.

(9) **Theoretical foundation for the aristocratic principle**. It follows that the elevation and progression of consciousness always takes place in an individual, working alone or with a group. Aristocracy is connected to a theory of inheritance of elect status by blood, which reflects the cognition of primitive materialism, where blood is a vital, magical substance, and can be thought of as transmitting spiritual power. Another view that is prevalent in contemporary consciousness is that inheritance is a matter merely of random chance, which appears as an unjust distribution of opportunities at birth. We justify it by **utilitarian arguments**, arguing that the unequal distribution of wealth is a dynamic that through its

economic effects brings about wealth for all. As Western culture is based on the family, we also argue that laws of inheritance are in the best interests of social cohesion. However, under this conception where you are born into the social hierarchy is a matter of random chance, which appears unjust. In the Medieval period, the West adopted the theory of **the Great Chain of Being**, according to which providence elects certain individuals to be born into a higher status, who hence are by birth not only materially but spiritually superior to those below them. The king, who stands at the top of the chain, is closest to God, and derives his power by **divine right**, but the same right filters through the entire chain. Notwithstanding, a monarch or aristocrat must by his deeds fulfil the duties that this election has imposed upon him. Aristocracy is justified not by the election but by the manner the elect dispose of their power. The valid theoretical foundation of aristocracy is that aristocracy must always lead or nurture culture; this alone can justify the privileges that they are born to. Our contemporary consciousness has introduced a spurious, economic justification for aristocracy, and our contemporary aristocracy has become selfish, weak, and inward-looking. An aristocrat in the material sense is anyone who has exceptional wealth, power and prestige. This may be acquired at birth or in life; there is old and new money. The ethical principle is clear: as soon as individual becomes inducted into the aristocracy, he or she is obligated to use his or her wealth, power and prestige for the furtherance of cognition, consciousness and religious consciousness. Since given aristocrats are not always in themselves equipped with that genius that makes this advance possible, they discharge their duty by disposing of their wealth, power and prestige wisely, that is by **patronage**. Historically, the aristocracy has accepted its role as patron, and behind the historical personages who have advanced consciousness we generally see an aristocratic patron. The contemporary era has witnessed a collective retreat of the aristocracy from its duty as patron, and thus we see that individuals working for the advancement of consciousness are left without support. There has never been an epoch in history comparable to our own for the **failure of the aristocracy** to discharge the duty that alone can justify its privileges. We should at once challenge the myth of individualism that has arisen in modern consciousness – namely, that the individual is "self-made", and wins by his own efforts his privileges, which are then inalienable, an idea expressed commonly by "he earned his money, power, position, wealth, and privileges," a statement almost always false as to fact, and used to justify the indifference that an aristocratic feels towards his fellow men. Individualism is a myth, for the individual participates in society, and society grants the rights that give him his privileges. Society makes the laws of inheritance, which society can change or rescind. Society establishes the economic framework whereby an individual can acquire wealth, and society can withdraw that framework and tax that wealth. It is true that no man is an island unto himself, and hence, the duty imposed by wealth, power and privilege must be discharged by the aristocracy.

It may be argued that in our contemporary society the duty of patronage for the advancement of consciousness falls upon the state, and the state sponsors the arts and universities. Even supposing this were true, it would not absolve the aristocracy of their duty to foster culture, to study to be cultured themselves, and to be patrons. It is questionable whether the state has taken over this function, for the state is the expression of the general will, it is elected by it, and hence its sponsorship lies at or close to the level of general consciousness. It sponsors ideas but not transformation of cognition.

(10) **The circle of Socrates** did express the aristocratic principle of society. To the period belong several of the most important leaders of Western consciousness – all connected with Athens, all knowing each other, all known to Socrates. This group included Sophocles, Euripides, Parmenides, Zeno and Plato; Aristotle joined the group later. Among the second rank in this aristocratic group, there are many others: Alcibiades might be one, but also Aristophanes and Agathon among the participants of the symposium, and the great Athenian leaders outside it: Pericles and Thrasybulus. At Athens there were other intellectuals: Protagoras, Gorgias, Anaxagoras, Empedocles, Thucydides and Xenophon.

(11) **Socrates** and **Socratic consciousness**. The distinctive contribution of Socrates is found in the *Apology*, the account rendered by Plato of the trial of Socrates and his speeches at that trial. Socrates defines his vocation in life as the endeavour to understand that oracle of Delphi's pronouncement that he was the wisest of men. He facetiously tells the court how he went from one person to the next trying to find out what they knew and wherein they were wise. Of each one, he reached the same conclusion:

> 'Well I am certainly wiser than this man. It is only too likely that neither of us has any knowledge to boast of; but he thinks that he knows something which he does not know, whereas I am quite conscious of my ignorance.'[31]

This indeed is a divinely appointed revelation. Firstly, the need in **knowledge and belief** to provide a **justification** is brought into Western consciousness for the first time. The theory of knowledge, epistemology, was born. Secondly, the overwhelming conclusion – that **knowledge is impossible**, and that, therefore, we are all fundamentally equal in our beliefs. This is more than scepticism, but the challenge to all to demonstrate sincerely to themselves and to others the superiority of their beliefs and conduct. We call it **Socratic scepticism**. Thirdly, then it follows that the fundamental challenge of human existence may be said to be to achieve faith and to live by faith; thus, **faith is rendered possible**. In our terminology, this is the

---

[31] Plato, *Apology*, 21b.

first statement of the **existentialist philosophy**, which is expressed in the statement of Tertullian – I believe it on the strength of **the absurd**.[32] Fourthly, the ethical foundation of the virtue of intellectual modesty. Not knowing better than another person, one is challenged in at the core of being to justify oneself, **to examine oneself**.

Whether it is possible to transcend this existential state of not knowing – which is the same as not knowing for certain – is the foundational problem of Western philosophy, and other philosophers coming after Socrates, and among these Plato, did claim to know. But the dogmatic position is henceforth always set within the context of sceptical doubt. **Dogmatism** that loses all connection with the possibility of doubt is morally very dangerous and gives rise to persecution, witch-hunts, pogroms and inquisitions.

Doubt and the call for justification ushers in **the dialectic**. Henceforth, there is debate and the interplay of **thesis and antithesis**; for one person to affirm a proposition that another person denies becomes the fundamental truth of the human situation. Combined with the quest for self-knowledge, the dialectical method becomes the **Socratic method**. It promotes tolerance. It is not philosophy or justice when you fail to acknowledge the rationality of anyone who denies your position. Together we may call Socratic doubt and the Socratic method, **Socratic consciousness**.

Socratic consciousness represents a peak in cognitive awareness; it is demanding. People brought into contact with Socratic consciousness experience a resistance. People like to be assured of certain certainties. In terms of the notion of ego-attachment, **to advance consciousness is to retract ego-attachment** and advancement is therefore opposed by ego-attachment. In Socratic consciousness, everyone finds him or herself alone in a sea of experiences, obliged to decide for him or herself what is truth, and confront their own psyche, possibly full of contradictions, as a dark mass of the unknown. For those who embrace this condition, it is uplifting, but for those who fear it, it is terrible. Hence, **ego-resistance**. Individual resistances in combination give rise to a **collective resistance to the advancement of consciousness**, which expresses itself as collective aggression towards those individuals who are perceived to oppose the ego with self-knowledge. The collective will may seek to destroy an advance of consciousness, because in the collective the combination of individual egos becomes a massed regressive force. There is a fundamental aggression on the part of society towards the **intellectual**, who I define here to be an individual to seeks to advance consciousness. We call this aggression, **anti-intellectualism**. All societies are threatened at any time by **atavism** – the reversion to an earlier stage of cognitive

---

[32] A reference to Tertullian, De Carne Christi V, 4. It is elaborated in the theology of Kierkegaard in *Fear and Trembling*.

development – or by **complex forms of atavism**, wherein conscious does not revert, but society lives in bad faith with its own cognition and behaves as if it had not advanced. Of these, the simple atavism is less harmful, for it is like a plant that dies in winter, retracts its energy into the tuber, to be reborn the following spring. But in the complex forms, the plant has not died, but brings forth sickly flowers and poisonous fruit, **the flowers of evil**.[33] One such flower of evil is the indictment of Socrates. Therefore, we may read the trial of Socrates as a collective attempt to force consciousness back into an earlier state, but in bad faith, for the accusers are cynics who do know that their accusation is false according to their own state of cognition, for they too know that the sun is not a god. The trial of Socrates is illustrative of the way the intellectual is threatened with oppression, persecution and death.

From the other dialogues of Plato, we infer that Socrates also introduced the search for meanings; he asked not only – How do you know? – but – What is it that you mean when you claim to know? This sets in motion the search for meaning. He initiated the **theory of meaning**, and the **philosophy of language**. But many other ideas that Plato attributes to Socrates, particularly those regarding metaphysics, were the ideas of Plato.

Death. The attempt to circumvent death is therefore the fundamental error of life. Only ethical existence matters.

> … if I were to claim to be wiser than my neighbour in any respect, it would be in this: that not possessing any real knowledge of what comes after death, I am also conscious that I do not possess it. But I do know that to do wrong and disobey my superior, whether God or man, is wicked and dishonourable; and so I shall never feel more fear of aversion for something which, for all I know, may really be a blessing, than for those evils which I know to be evils.[34]

The only question of importance is what, at this moment in time, does my conscience tell me is the right thing to do? It is not, could this thing be the cause of my death? Doing what is right is more certain than death. "Where a man has once taken up his stand," Socrates tells his accusers, "either because it seems best to him or in obedience to his orders, there I believe he is bound to remain and face the danger, taking no account of death or anything else before dishonour."[35] Socrates tells his accusers that he is neither an idiot nor a coward. He knows full well that he has been

---

[33] [An allusion to the poetry of Baudelaire.]

[34] Plato, *Apology*, 29b.

[35] Plato, *Apology*, 28d.

brought to trial to defend his faith, and he refuses to compromise and bargain for his life. Be it on your head, he says to them.

> I believe that it is far worse to do what he is doing now, trying to put an innocent man to death. For this reason, gentlemen, so far from pleading on my own behalf, as might be supposed, I am really pleading on yours, to save you from misusing the gift of God by condemning me. If you put me to death, you will not easily find anyone to take my place. It is literally true (even if it sounds rather comical) that God has specially appointed me to this city…[36]

But, what of the charges themselves? The material charge is that of innovation in matters of religion. What defence can Socrates offer? For, without doubt, he has innovated in religion; his God is not the same as the gods that his accusers purport to worship, his practices are not the same as those found in the rituals of the Athenian calendar. His mission is to promote change in religious consciousness, an awareness that God and gods are not the same thing. He must be "guilty" as charged.

> Socrates. Do you assert that I believe in no gods at all, and teach others to do the same?
> Meletus. Yes, I say that you disbelieve in gods altogether.
> Socrates. You surprise me, Meletus; what is your object in saying that? Do you suggest that I do not believe that the sun and moon are gods, as is the general belief of all mankind?
> Meletus. He certainly does not, gentlemen of the jury, since he says that the sun is a stone and the moon is a mass of earth.
> Socrates. Do you image that you are prosecuting Anaxagoras, my dear Meletus? Have you so poor an opinion of these gentlemen, and do you assume them to be so illiterate as not to know that the writings of Anaxagoras of Clazomenae are full of theories like these?[37]

Socrates attempts to dance his way out. He does not say that the sun and the moon are not stone and earth; he says, that is the opinion of Anaxagoras, and he has never been heard to say or known to publish such a view. He never refers to any Olympian god as an Olympian. He talks of "god" not of "Hermes" or "Hephaestus" and certainly not of "Hera"; when he mentions Delphi, he talks of the oracle of god, not "Apollo". In their eyes and in their terms, he is an atheist. For us, he is a believer in

---

[36] Plato, *Apology*, 30d – e.
[37] Plato, *Apology,* 26c – d.

God, a theist, but his religion is close to monotheism, not polytheism. He claims direct communion with God.

> I remained at my post like anyone else and faced death, and yet afterwards, when God appointed me, as I supposed and believed, to the duty of leading the philosophic life, examining myself and others...
>
> ... I am subject to a divine or supernatural experience, which Meletus saw fit to travesty in his indictment. It began in my early childhood – a sort of voice which comes to me: and when it comes it always dissuades me from what I am proposing to do, and never urges me on.
>
> The duty I have accepted, as I said, in obedience to God's commands given in oracles and dreams and in every other way that any other divine dispensation has ever impressed a duty upon man.[38]

The members of his circle have been led by his questioning to a related state of consciousness. They have advanced in cognition to the state of scepticism regarding the religious orthodoxy of Athens. They extol reason and virtue founded upon reason above observance of festivals of fertility. So far as the outward display of religious conformity goes, Socrates has been among the most conscientious observers. But the inner attitude is lacking. Socrates himself is too mature to go out of his way to parody the Eleusinian mysteries, or not knock the phallus from a statue, but those are the sort of things that an immature, adolescent, narcissistic sort of person might do who came under his influence in some superficial way. The people who mutilated the statues may very well be among his accusers, or the accusers of Alcibiades, but if so that whole cynical way of looking at things could only arise in the context of Socratic doubt. His accusers are surely in bad faith, for they know that they do not know anything, for they have also heard the seductive voice of Socrates, whispering siren-like from the Rock of Reason.

Socrates is guilty as charged of both religious innovation and inspiring the young with that religious innovation, and his accusers are guilty of bad faith, the cynical use of religion, of persecuting an innocent man, and of judicial murder.

---

[38] Plato, *Apology*, 28e, 31d, 33c.

5

Athanatos

The purpose of this chapter is to analyse further beliefs about death and immortality in archaic Greek consciousness, which remained within the proto-Ionian cognition of developed primitive materialism.

Fundamental principle of cognitive limitation. This enquiry has been delayed to this point in the historical exegesis, because one can only make it from the vantage of post-Ionian consciousness; from within the system of primitive materialism, it is not possible to conduct a self-reflective examination of what death as an event means, and what immortality as a state of consciousness might be. This is an instance of the most fundamental principle of all: *we cannot see outside the confines of our conceptual framework*; cognition frames the questions and delimits the answers. Therefore, in each stage of cognition, there are fundamental problems that cannot be resolved. Within primitive materialism the question – What does it mean to be immortal? – cannot be answered in terms of concepts that do not yet exist. Within the confines of Ionian/Cartesian cognition, the problem of freewill and determinism cannot be solved.

Bounded by finitude. The concept of infinity does not exist in primitive materialism; hence in that system, immortality cannot mean "everlasting". The only idea that can be conceptualised is that of a persistence of *something* into the proximal zone of the future. The extension of that future to a limitless continuity cannot be conceptualised.

Annihilation of consciousness as a concept. Because we exist in post-Ionian consciousness, for us, the notion of death always carries with it the implicit notion and threat of utter annihilation. In Ionian cognition, having separated the external world from the inner realm of psyche, we conceive of the psyche (soul) as incarnated within the body. Therefore, the possibility that the soul is annihilated when the body ceases to function is obvious to us. The concept of annihilation is another outcome of the Ionian revolution.

In primitive materialism, all things are vital substances: consciousness is not conceived as something different from material substance; the concepts "consciousness", "matter" and "substance" have not been formulated, nor distinguished from each other.

Primitive dualism. Death forces the truth of alteration of vital substance: that vital substance, the body, that used to be alive, is no longer alive. Primitive materialism encompasses the idea that life itself is a vital substance, and that at death, this vital substance has departed the body. This vital substance is conceived to be a subtle kind of substance, akin to material substance, but thinner and more refined, so it may be the breath of the living body, or air, or akin to fire, or a substantive double of the body, related to the shadow that the body casts. Separation of body and soul as two vital substances is not merely a possibility but a necessity that follows by inference from the cognition of all things as vital substances. There is no mystery in a state of primitive consciousness regarding what happens to the person after death: a person's soul = shadow = double = life breath simply departs the body and goes somewhere else.

Location of the afterlife. But where does it go? Since the notion of an immaterial "place" has not yet been brought into consciousness, the only answers considered must be what we might call "geographical" – they go somewhere that could in practice be reached by a living person – a geographical location.

(1) Under the ground, to the Underworld, conceived precisely as being directly below the surface of the earth, and a place that can be entered by the living, physically, through certain gateways, not "portals" in our sense, but such things as cracks and fissures in caves or caverns; places leading underground.

(2) Within the tomb prepared for the dead soul, which is like a house, a place of special comfort and dwelling for the soul.

(3) To a location at the boundary of the earth – to the land of the Hyperboreans – or to a distant island – to a magical land, the garden of the Hesperides – or Asphodel – but conceived at the edge of the known world.

Hence, there arises the possibility that different souls = vital substances may depart this world to diverse locations – one soul may go underground, but another may go to the eternally green garden of Asphodel. A variant of the garden-at-the-end-of-the-world idea is the idea of a palace-in-the-sky, up above, for above is better than below – and heaven is first conceived as a place in the sky. Conceptually, the garden and heaven belong to the same stage of cognition.

The Ethical question. There then arises the ethical question: what in life must I do to ensure that I go to heaven/the garden of Asphodel as opposed to merely exist under the ground or within my tomb? A relationship between life and life-after-death emerges. The most primitive answer is the concept that we dub "spiritual materialism" – that the better destiny depends on material – not ethical – actions performed in life, and hence can we can "buy our way into heaven". Ironically, the concept of an indulgence is among the first spiritual ideas mankind has, and spiritual materialism suggests firstly that only the great, mighty, rich and powerful go to the garden/heaven, that is the king and queen, and later the nobles.

During the second millennium BCE, the Greeks remained at a barbarous or semi-barbarous state and continued to worship the Goddess with all her orgiastic rites. They sacrificed men as god-kings or male god-children to the Goddess in fertility-rites. They elevated the sacrificial victim to the status of hero or divine child, son of god, and conceived that their bloody ritual conferred immortality upon the hero.

> In myth, Demeter places the son of the king of Eleusis into the fire on
> the hearth, so that the horrified mother is led to believe that the child
> is being burned, whereas the goddess is actually bestowing
> immortality on the child.[1]

In this extract, Burkert is referring to the myth of the child Demophoon, related in the *Homeric Hymn to Demeter*. This is the mythological basis of the **Mysteries of Eleusis**. In the *Hymn to Demeter* Demophoon survives his ordeal, but in other later accounts he does not. The story indicates ritual child sacrifice by burning. Demophoon was the first-born of the king of Eleusis, Celeus, by his wife Metanira. The ritual indicates a special passport to the afterlife and introduces **the concept of immortality**. To be immortal is a gift granted by the Goddess by burning. Here the self-same ritual of the burning of a child that we find in Phoenicia and Carthage is indicated coupled to the notion of immortality for the victim. The immortality concept may either originate in or be concealed by a later gloss, for the author of the Homeric Hymn does everything possible to conceal the horrible nature of the ritual, and perhaps its author genuinely is ignorant of it. The cult of the hero is linked to the concept of immortality. The adult hero obtains immortality by his self-sacrifice, for by submitting to sacrifice, he sacrifices himself; the child-sacrifice has immortality bestowed upon him.

From our perspective, the notion of conferring immortality is in contradiction with the idea of the survival of the person after death. If in fact the soul is a material, vital substance that separates from the body at death, as in primitive dualism, then the soul is already indestructible, and immortality is inalienable, and cannot be conferred. Naturally, archaic Greeks did not think in such language, which belongs to post-Ionian cognition, but they may have had intimations of such tension from within their system, and this tension may then have stimulated the onset of the Ionian revolution.

The concept of annihilation within primitive materialism. An idea of annihilation did appear within primitive materialism. As early as 2125 in the Egyptian, Theban recension of the Book of the Death, we see failure to be judged worthy of life was punished by immediate annihilation rather than eternal damnation: the soul-body is decapitated and destroyed in pits of fire.[2] Hence, the Egyptians could conceive of a **second death**, when the material, vital soul was also destroyed. But they did not think that annihilation was automatic upon the **first death**, the separation of that vital soul from the body. But this raises the possibility

[1] Walter Burkert, *Greek Religion*. Translated by John Raffan. Basil Blackwell, English translation, 1985, p.288.
[2] [Part I, Chapter 8, Egypt.]

that the Egyptians had anticipated the concept of annihilation of the soul already by c.2000 BCE, which would be a remarkably early in the historical record. I shall discuss this below, after examination of the evidence in the Greek record.

The manifestation of this distinction between the fates of vital souls in the afterlife within archaic Greek consciousness is found in the idea of the different fates of persons at death: the ordinary person becomes a shade in the underworld, but to the extraordinary hero there is the possibility of a special destiny – in the gardens of the Hesperides – or, for the most exceptional, an apotheosis, being raised as a god to Olympus, a fate earned only by Dionysus, Asclepius and Heracles. In these instantiations of the Dionysus-hero archetype we see the transformation of the idea of immortality as something conferred as sacrifice to something earned as hero.

Athanatos – the concept of immortality. The Greek word for "immortal" is *athanatos*, derived from *thanatos* meaning "dying"; the primary meaning of *athanatos* is "not dying", "undying"; its secondary meaning is "eternal", "perpetual". What did the Greeks of the second millennium cognize by *athanatos*?

Bounded by concrete thinking. By the late stage of Hesiod and Homer, Thanatos is a god, not an abstract idea. Abstract thinking such as we know emerges after Hesiod and Homer in the context of the transformation of the Ionian consciousness. Prior to that, what we deem "abstract ideas" first emerge not as abstract but as concrete entities, conceived of as persons.

Thanatos. I suggest that it was in the concrete sense of meeting that the early Greeks first conceived of Death. To die is to meet or encounter Thanatos or be carried off by him. Concerning the death of Sarpedon, Homer has Zeus instruct Apollo in the *Iliad*:

> Then, for his swift conveyance, put him in the hands of Hypnos and
> his twin-brother Thanatos, who will make all speed to set him down in
> the broad and fertile Lycian realm.[3]

Hypnos is Sleep, another god, and the twin of Thanatos. The text does not suggest that Sarpedon is dead (annihilated) in our sense, but merely to be carried to his homeland for burial. A reply to this argument is that Homer intends this description as a poetic device, a personification, perhaps for the purpose of softening the image of loss for the death of Sarpedon. But such a claim is more likely to be a backward projection, for Homer was bounded by concrete thinking. Further, the same pairing of Sleep (Hypnos) and Death (Thanatos) and the same bounded concrete thinking is found in Hesiod.

---

[3] Homer, *Iliad*, Bk 16, 681 – 84.

> Night ... brings Sleep, Brother of Death, and carries him in her arms.
> There [in Tartarus] live the children of dark Night, dread gods, Sleep
> and his brother Death. ... [Sleep] is kind to men and goes peacefully
> over earth and the sea's broad back; the other [Death] has a heart of
> iron; in his breast is pitiless bronze: if he should touch a man, that
> man is his. And even to the gods who are immortal, Death is an
> enemy.[4]

For the archaic Greeks dying is more of an encounter, akin to meeting Hypnos, that
is encountering sleep, akin to a carrying off. Thanatos carries off the dead. In the
later development of Greek religion, the role of Thanatos was usurped by Hermes,
who became the psychopomp, the conductor of souls, which accounts for why
Thanatos did not become a more prominent god, because he was submerged in
Hermes.[5]

I suggest that in Homer and Hesiod Death = Thanatos is a god-like being; death
is not an event in the sense in which we conceive it. For the archaic Greeks, Death =
Thanatos, Ate = Hate ("sin") are god-like personages, vital forces, like spirits that we
might encounter on a dark road or in a bad dream, like the image of the Angel of
Death; we die, when Death, Thanatos comes to collect us. We are *athanatos* – "not
dying" – if Thanatos, the Angel of Death does not collect us.

It is possible that the archaic Greeks had only a limited ability to conceive of
death at all. They probably could not cognize it as annihilation in the sense we do.
The issue for them appears to be not the question whether at death one's soul is
annihilated, but what kind of death one has. Thanatos is the regular death, in battle,
of disease, even of old-age, one is carried off; athantos is not-death, or another kind
of death, or the conferring of immortality by fire, as in the myth of Demophoon; it is
not an encounter with Thanatos. In their primitive cognition, all souls are vital
substances, hence all souls persist, but those that are immortal = athanatos persist in
some special way. The evolution of the very concept of immortality is another
archaeological site. It is easy to slip into the habit of the backward projection of
modern concepts onto previous epochs.

A similar problem arises in the context of Egyptian cognition. As early as c.2000
the Egyptians appear to have a concept of eternal life and of annihilation. This, at
least, is what Wallis Budge indicates.

---

[4] Hesiod, *Theogony* 758 ff. Trans. Doorthea Wender. Penguin. 1973. Minor adaptation.
[5] In the image of the grim reaper or the angel of death prima facie we see a fusion of imagery drawn
from the mythology of Thanatos (Death), Cronos (reaper, fertility god, scythe) and Hermes
(conductor of souls).

But, as according to the cult of Ra, the wicked, the rebels, and the blasphemers of the Sun-god suffered swift and final punishment, so also all those who had sinned against the stern moral Law of Osiris, and who had failed to satisfy its demands, paid the penalty without delay. The Judgement of Ra was held at sunrise, and the wicked were thrown into deep pits filled with fire, and their bodies, souls, shadows and hearts were consumed forthwith. The Judgment of Osiris took place near Abydos, probably at midnight, and a decree of swift annihilation was passed by him on the damned. Their heads were cut off by the headsman of Osiris, who was called Shesmu, and their bodies dismembered and destroyed in pits of fire. There was no eternal punishment for men, for the wicked were annihilated quickly and completely; but inasmuch as Osiris sat in judgement and doomed the wicked to destruction daily, the infliction of punishment never ceased.

The term "annihilation" here would imply that the Egyptians had entered into a state equivalent to Ionian consciousness some 1400 years before the Greeks. The above translation is an unfortunate backward projection of the modern conception of annihilation arising in the context of Ionian and later Cartesian cognition, notwithstanding the great authority of Wallis Budge with respect to Egyptian studies. (1) For the concept of "everlasting" to mean what we mean by it, there must be a corresponding concept of infinity. There is no evidence that such a concept was known to Egyptian mathematics at such an early time. The Egyptians remained in the bronze age until their conquest by Persia (Battle of Pelusium 525 by Cambyses II). (2) Egyptian science is a highly sophisticated and elaborated development of primitive materialism. In this system the afterlife is conceived as a near extension of life, replete with all its life-experiences. They do have a concept of the separation of body and soul, but by soul is meant another substance akin to that of the body – as in primitive dualism. Hence, it is possible to picture in the afterlife the possibility of events like those in life – the possibility of a judgement by a king, and the penalty of judgement as death by decapitation. A concept of a second-death thereby ensues, but it does not follow that the Egyptians have conceived of *everlasting life* in the sense that we, in Ionian consciousness, conceive it. (3) When we refer to the texts, their content does not support the language Wallis Budge uses in his summary. He tells us, "Chapter L enabled the deceased to avoid the block of execution of the god Shesmu," and Chapter CXXXVII is "a series of magical ceremonies that were to be performed for the deceased daily in order to make him to become a 'living soul for ever'."[6] But when we look at these chapters, we see, for example, merely ritual

---

[6] E. A. Wallis Budge, *The Book of the Dead*, The British Museum, 1920, pp 20 -21.

formulas, not so very-well developed, that act as incantations to prevent separation of head from neck in the after-world.

> I have joined up my head and neck in heaven [and] earth. Behold it is Ra who, day by day, stablisheth the knot for him who stood helpless upon his legs on the day of cutting off the hair. The god Suti and the company of the gods have joined together my neck and my back strongly, and they are even as they were in the time that is past; may nothing happen to break them apart!

The Egyptians were highly sophisticated theorists of primitive materialism. Their concept of "everlasting" is not ours; they did not enter a state of Ionian cognition at so early an epoch, but remained, on the contrary, defenders of the theory of primitive materialism and magic-science into the Roman epoch. The concept of immortality is also an archaeological site.

6

The body/soul problem

The purpose of this chapter is to analyse the body/soul problem in the wake of Ionian consciousness. **Ionian consciousness** is a vague form of **Cartesian consciousness**. In Cartesian consciousness, the conception of the soul is clarified as spiritual substance, a notion merely implicit in Ionian consciousness. Cartesian consciousness is a more developed variant of Ionian consciousness. Because the concept of soul as spiritual substance is not articulated at the Ionian stage, it is unstable as cognition, meaning that it is prone to regress to the earlier stage of primitive materialism, where the soul is identified with material substance. The Cartesian concept is not unstable in this sense, because it is internally consistent; but historically, intellectuals in the West remained predominantly at the level of Ionian consciousness until Descartes published *Discourse on the Method* (1637). It is the thesis of this work that Cartesian consciousness is superseded by Kantian consciousness with the publication by Immanuel Kant of *The Critique of Pure Reason* (1781/87). However, the West has resisted the emergence of this higher state of Kantian consciousness in Positivism, an academic philosophy.

Just as we can only analyse primitive materialism from the vantage of Ionian/Cartesian concepts, so the metaphysics of Ionian/Cartesian consciousness can only be analysed from the vantage of Kantian concepts. This is of course problematic in the contemporary context because of the resistance to Kantian consciousness posed by Positivism.[1] Here, the reader is invited to consider a self-contained Kantian analysis of the Ionian body/soul problem.

The external world, reality. Relative to Ionian concepts, and implicit in them, we encounter two interpretations of what is external to us: (1) That which is *perceived* as being external to us, as, for example, the table that I see is also seen as external to my body. (2) That which is *conceived* as being "external" altogether to conscious perception, as in the unseen cause of perception.

On this basis, Kant distinguished between (1*) the realm of experience, of **phenomena**, called **empirical reality**, and (2*) the realm of **objects-in-themselves**, also called **noumena**, belonging to **transcendental reality**. To accept this distinction as valid is to be on the borderline of **Kantian consciousness**. What Kantian consciousness is, is purpose of this entire work to clarify. Since the beginning of the C20 modern philosophy has tried to refute this distinction on the basis that it is meaningless. I shall discuss this attempt in detail subsequently and offer grounds for rejecting it.[2] I believe C20 philosophy to have taken a false path: I

---

[1] [See Part III, Chapter 15, The wilful destruction of Kantian consciousness.]
[2] [See Chapter 15 of this volume, The transcendental deduction, as well as Part III, Chapter 15.]

take it that it is possible to conceive of a thing as existing but never seen, hence acting as the unseen cause of what is seen,[3] and that Kant's conclusion that there is a distinction between empirical and transcendental reality is not only valid, but fundamental to understanding of human existence.

The problem of external reality. If the distinction is accepted, there is the inevitable sceptical problem – since the transcendental realm is thought to be populated by objects-in-themselves that are never experienced, can we be sure that they exist? Is there a realm of reality transcendent to consciousness? Or, if we think that there is such a realm, can we know anything about that realm?

> ... what we directly see and feel is merely 'appearance', which we believe to be a sign of some 'reality' behind. But if the reality is not what appears, have we any means of knowing whether there is any reality at all? And if so, have we any means of finding out what it is like?[4]

This was written by Bertrand Russell and he goes on to state, "Berkeley retains the merit of having shown that the existence of matter is capable of being denied without absurdity, and that if there are any things that exist independently of us they cannot be the immediate objects of our sensations." At the time of writing he explicitly regards the expression "things that exists independently of us" as meaningful; this is identical to Kant's object-in-itself. The chapter from which this is taken is entitled, *Appearance and Reality* – a more explicit announcement of participation in Ionian cognition could not be made.[5] But, in fact, ancient thinkers of Ionian cognition never do consider the sceptical problem of external reality – it is not expressed in such words as those of Russell in ancient philosophy. This further characterises the distinction between Ionian and Cartesian cognition – Cartesian cognition is not only explicit that the soul is a substance of another kind than matter, but by invoking dream scepticism and other arguments relating to the nature of conscious experience

---

[3] In this expression it is possible to substitute for "seen" any term such as "experienced", "sensed", "appears" and "perceived".

[4] Bertrand Russell, *The Problems of Philosophy*, Oxford University Press, 1959, p. 6. First published by Home University Library, 1912.

[5] *Ibid.* Close examination of Russell's work would show that his conception of external reality is confused. This quotation has the merit of demonstrating that no lesser a person than Bertrand Russell himself did at one time accept that the expression "things that exist independently of us" is meaningful. Yet, even at the time of writing the above, he is attempting a construction of reality in terms of phenomena alone. Psychologically, it may be said that Russell arrived at a borderline consciousness of the Kantian distinction between the transcendental and empirical, and then decisively shied away from its consequences. Deconstructing the chapter on *Appearance and Reality* along these lines is possible, but would be the work of many pages.

of phenomena within Cartesian consciousness it is possible to conceive a sceptical position with respect to external reality.[6]

The distinction between phenomena and noumena in Ionian cognition. Let us clarify the position regarding what distinction is made in Ionian cognition between the empirical and transcendental.

Being and nothingness (the void). It was Ionian thought that also brought into consciousness the notion of space and time as a container for things and events. The following idea was attributed to the atomist **Leucippus**.

> Again, he held that being no more exists than non-being, and both are equally causes of the things that come into being. For supposing that the substance of the atoms is solid and full, he said that it was being and that it was carried about in the void, which he called non-being and which he says exists no less than being. [7]

Here non-being = void = the framework of space and time which is occupied by being = the substance of the atoms. Leucippus does not use the term "nothingness" here, but other pre-Socratics do, such as Parmenides and Melissus.[8] In the account of Leucippus there is no indication that he distinguishes the empirical from the transcendental. He not only supposes without sceptical consideration that atoms exist, but he also ascribes existence to the void. Some later Greek philosophers, it seems, did go towards distinguishing between the empirical and the transcendental. For example, **Simplicius**, when discussing the philosophy of **Melissus**, a follower of Parmenides, states:

> And if Melissus entitles his work *On Nature or on What Exists*, it is clear that he thought nature to be what exists and natural objects, i.e. perceptible objects, to be the things that exist. Perhaps that is why Aristotle said that, in declaring what exists to be one, he [Melissus] supposed that there was <u>nothing else apart from perceptible substances</u>. For given that what is perceptible plainly seems to exist, then if what exists is unique there will not exist anything else apart from what is perceptible.[9]

---

[6] These arguments have been misleadingly dubbed, "the argument from illusion" by J. L. Austin. [See Part III, Chapter 14, What Kantian consciousness is.]

[7] Simplicius, *Commentary on the* Physics, 28. 4-15 – quoted in Barnes, *Early Greek Philosophy*, Penguin, 1987. p. 242.

[8] In this way, the non-existence of "nothingness" is inconceivable, and we raise the question, "How is it possible to think of nothing?" which is the subject of Plato's dialogue, *The Theaetetus*.

[9] Simplicius, *Commentary on the Physics*, 28. 4-15, Barnes, *Op. cit.*, p. 146.

In this passage, there is an implicit distinction drawn between empirical and transcendental reality; Melissus and **Parmenides**, whom he follows, are identified with the view that nothing other than what is experienced exists – or **monism**.[10]

(a) The denial the existence of transcendental reality is a doctrine that Kant called **dogmatic idealism**; it may also be called **monism**, because it affirms that only the mind and what is present to the mind exists. (b) The view that affirms dogmatically that there exists a transcendental reality, is called by Kant **transcendental realism**. As this position is dogmatic, it must affirm something definite about that reality, as, for example, it is composed of atoms and the void; that space and time exist independently of consciousness. (c) The view that affirms that there *might* be a transcendental reality, but that we have no knowledge of it as substance, is called by Kant **transcendental idealism**. It is opposed to dogmatic idealism because it does not deny outright that there is no reality transcendent to experience; but it is opposed to (dogmatic) transcendental realism, precisely because it is not dogmatic and refuses to acknowledge that human reason can reach a definite understanding of what objects-in-themselves are. As Kant maintains, a transcendental idealist may be an **empirical realist**, because he affirms the real existence of all phenomena, that is, objects of experience, and maintains that "real" as in "I see a real tree" means that the tree belongs to experience. The position adopted in this work is that of Kantian transcendental idealism. I think it is possible to conceive of a reality that exists independently of myself, but I do not believe I have any substantive knowledge of it. As this work progresses, this position shall be clarified.

The term **realism** is ambiguous. To say one is a realist is to affirm a belief in the real world, but *what is the real world? What is meant by "real"?* The term must be qualified by "transcendental" or some such. If you turn you back on a tree, but think that the tree continues to exist, then you are a transcendental realist. If you think the tree only exists while you look at it, then you are an empirical realist, and have the choice between dogmatic and sceptical (transcendental) idealism.

The body/soul problem in Ionian consciousness. Once we distinguish body from soul, then we have by tradition three possibilities.

---

[10] The reading of Plato is a problem of interpretation. Generally, Plato is contemptuous of the sensible world regarding it as a source of illusion. His allegory of the cave (the *Republic*) implies that sensory data are two steps removed from reality. Yet in one of his last works, *the Timaeus*, he describes without scepticism the creation of the material world out of prima materia by the demi-urge. I suggest that Plato's reaction to sensation is not an expression of scepticism regarding external reality in the C18 CE sense – Plato has not reached the borderline of Kantian consciousness. As he also never formulates a notion of the soul as substance he has also not reached Cartesian consciousness.

1.   **Dualism**. Body and soul are separable.
2.   **Materialism**. Only physical substance exists. Consciousness is either identical to some part of physical substance (for example, the brain) or caused by it.
3.   **Idealism.** (Monism) Only the soul exists. All material objects are merely phenomena arising in or presented to consciousness.

The Cartesian soul. With the advance to Ionian consciousness, the idea that the soul is a material substance can no longer be maintained; the soul is not extended as physical objects are and has no weight – the question, what is the volume of the soul? is absurd.   Descartes introduced the concept of spiritual or thinking substance.[11] If, as in dualism, the soul is thought to exist in time and to be separable form the body, then to say that it is a substance is to say that it exists as a spiritual substance, and not as a material substance. Cartesian dualism is the idea of a persistent thinking substance that is in time, and hence, at death separates from the extended, material substance of the body. Descartes believes he can demonstrate the existence of the soul by introspection.[12]

The Kantian Self. Kant questions the existence of the soul-substance. He draws a distinction between the soul and the Self, attributing the Cartesian notion of substance to the soul-concept, and maintaining of the Self that it is a non-spatial, non-temporal being transcendent to space and time.[13]   But to say that the Self is transcendent does not answer the question as to whether there is also a transcendent material substance. Hence, conceptually there arise distinct forms of this doctrine.

---

[11] I do not find the term "spiritual substance" in Descartes's work, and it is a later gloss. However, as an interpretation it is not in dispute. Descartes introduced the distinction between mind and body as different substances, and he certainly used the term "thinking substance" in direct opposition to "extended substance". For example, *The Principles of Philosophy*, XLVIII.

[12] In the Cogito it is maintained that the Soul becomes aware of itself as an object of its own contemplation. This identifies the Subject (awareness) with the object (soul, spiritual substance) and affirms that Subject can know itself as object in a special act of self-reflective consciousness. Descartes equates "I see myself" with "I see a tree"; that is, "I (subject, awareness) see myself (object, soul)" just as "I (subject) see a tree (object)." *Cogito, ergo sum* = "I am aware, therefore, I am"; that is, "I (subject) am aware, therefore, I am (object)."   *Sum res cogitans* = "I am a thing that thinks"; that is, "I (subject and object) am a thinking substance." Soul = thinking substance persisting in time (not space). The *Cogito*, is the judgement, "I am a Soul".

[13] This is connected to his transcendent idealism, by which he expresses scepticism regarding the nature of transcendent reality of external objects, and affirms that the transcendental Self alone is known, but only ever as Subject and never as object of its own self-awareness. To be aware of the self (self-conscious awareness) is to be aware of Self as Subject, not to be aware of Self as object and substance; it is to be conscious of one's Self as the "abiding" Subject of experience. Hence, Kant replaces both *Cogito, ergo sum,* and *Sum res cogitans*, by *Sum* – "I am" = "I (subject) am transcendent being (not known as object)." [See also Part III, Chapter 14, What Kantian consciousness is.]

The body/soul problem in Kantian consciousness. By the Kantian analysis of the Ionian body/soul problem, there are six distinct possibilities.

1. **Materialism**. (Naturalistic monism,[14] transcendental realism.) There exists only transcendent material substance. Mind and brain (a material substance) are identical.

2. **Epiphenomenalism**. There exists only transcendental material substance: mind is not identical to it, and not a substance, but is a product of this substance.

3. **Cartesian dualism**. There exist two substances, material and spiritual, and there is an interaction between these two substances. Material substance is extended in space and time; spiritual substance has temporal duration but not spatial extension.

4. **Transcendental dualism**. There exist two transcendent realities – the reality of mind which is a substance, but not in the sense of an entity persisting in space and time – and the reality of objects-in-themselves that exist independently of mind/consciousness and are "in time".[15]

5. **Idealistic monism**. Only the mind exists, and it is transcendent to phenomena which are representations arising in the mind. All is one.

6. **Transcendental idealism**. The Self is transcendent to space and time; it is directly acquainted with phenomena of empirical reality. Beyond what is given directly to consciousness, no other dogmatic statement can be affirmed. A transcendental reality of objects-in-themselves might or might not exist.

This classification differs from the previous classification under Ionian cognition by the addition throughout of the term or terms, *transcendental* or *empirical*. Kantian consciousness forces us to be explicit whether the object affirmed (to have being) exists either before consciousness ("in the mind") as a phenomenological/empirical object, or independently of consciousness as a thing-in-itself or transcendent being.

Materialism in contemporary philosophy is not analysed by means of Kantian concepts; hence, the cognizance of materialism as a doctrine in contemporary consciousness is relative to Ionian/Cartesian cognition. Materialism has become a

---

[14] [For the term *naturalistic monism*, see Part I, Chapter 4, The scandal of shadow, p.33.]

[15] In the Christian conception of God as a necessary being and uncreated creator of the cosmos, we have an implicit transcendental dualism. It is only required to conceive of God as a separate spiritual substance, a mind, existing independently of space and time, for this to amount to transcendental dualism. This is implicit in the notion of God the Creator, for God exists first apart from all creation in Eternity, and then by his act of creation brings about a cosmos of space, time and substance. In this classification, transcendental dualism is distinguished from Cartesian dualism in that in Cartesian dualism the mind is a spiritual substance, that is, a persistent identity in time.

cultural norm in Western academic circles; this norm is promoted to the public through the media and by education. Daniel Dennett writes:

> Scientists and philosophers may have achieved a consensus of sorts in favour of materialism.[16]

This is an argument from authority, where the authority is "scientists and philosophers", which is vague. But it is true that in contemporary culture there is considerable momentum in favour of materialism. A lot has been written in its favour, but there are very few arguments, and of these two are prominent: (1) Cartesian dualism is false, therefore materialism is true; (2) **Functionalism**: all the properties of the mind can be explained by a mechanism. Both these arguments feature prominently in Dennett's *Consciousness Explained*.[17]

In these materialist arguments Cartesian dualism is presented as a kind of **straw man** – a straw man in philosophy being a position that no serious philosopher adopts. I am far from considering Cartesian dualism an indefensible position, but the straw man aspect is to present it in such a form as to make it appear to be made of straw, that is, appear to be ludicrous. It is correct to assert that dualism affirms the existence of two substances, material and spiritual, and interaction between them. When considering the interaction, Descartes speculated on the location of a point of contact between body and soul, the pineal gland. Since one side of the interaction, the soul, is not in space, and the other, the pineal gland as a part of the brain is in space, the notion is not promising. It also gives rise to **the ghost in the machine** concept – an idea very close to **the manikin of primitive materialism**, namely that the soul acts as a "driver" operating the body, and to complete the difficulty, Descartes also proposes that the body is a machine, and all other animals are soulless machines. I think in the context of the C17, when the understanding of mechanisms was being formed, such ideas would have been seen to be interesting speculations. However, such speculations on the point of contact between body and soul form no more than a superficial part of Cartesian philosophy, and I believe that if Descartes were alive today, he would retract those that he made. In other words, any critique of the ghost in the machine and the notion of a point of contact between spiritual and material substance is a specious attack on a straw man. It is not a refutation of Descartes to argue: there is no ghost in the machine, therefore materialism is true, nor is it a "proof" of materialism.

Dennett does argue against this straw form of Cartesian dualism, stating that it cannot explain the interaction between mind and body, that it posits a "ghost in the

---

[16] Daniel Dennett, *Consciousness Explained,* Penguin 1993, p.37.
[17] Gilbert Ryle's *The Concept of Mind*, 1949, which Dennett praises, is an earlier version of the same position.

machine", and "wallows in mystery".[18] While he notes the problem of interaction, his argument against it is that it contradicts the principle of the conservation of energy.

> It is this principle of the conservation of energy that accounts for the physical impossibility of "perpetual motion machines," and the same principle is apparently violated by dualism.[19]

In reply, (1) if dualism contradicts the principle of conservation of energy, that does not refute dualism, but invites us to reconsider the principle of conservation, which is not written on tablets of stone handed down by God to his prophet; its validity may be questioned.[20] (2) If mind and body are in any sense distinct, then there is a problem of explaining the interaction between them. But this applies equally to those variants of the materialist philosophy that do not espouse strict identity, such as epiphenomenalism. Thus, supposing the mind to be an epiphenomenon produced by brain states, but not bringing about any alteration in brain states, how then do brain states bring about this one-sided interaction? It is false to characterise this as a problem solely for the Cartesian straw-man. (3) Dennett ignores the solution to the problem advocated by the dualist Leibniz, who argued that there are two world-orders, one material, the other spiritual, that each runs in exact harmony with the other, like two perfect clocks synchronised, and that it was Almighty God who created that harmony when he made the world. This solution is self-consistent; hence, there is no problem of interaction for the Cartesian dualist. However, for epiphenomenalism there is.

Dennett's second argument posits functionalism:

> If you reproduce the entire "functional structure" of the human wine taster's cognitive system (including memory, goals, innate aversions, etc.), you would thereby reproduce all the mental properties as well, including the enjoyment.[21]

This is **the golem** or **myth of Frankenstein**: a man-like machine will be created. This myth is so deeply embedded into contemporary consciousness that I will reserve detailed examination of it. No such golem has yet been made; the above claim is entirely speculative.[22]

---

[18] Dennett, *Op. cit.* p.33. p37.

[19] *Ibid.*, p. 35.

[20] [See also Part III, Chapter 18, Kantian consciousness and the spirit world.]

[21] Dennett, *Op. cit.*, p.31.

[22] [It is the subject of Part II, Chapter 15, The transcendental deduction, and is taken up again in Part III, Chapter 16, Despair and the hope that is despair.]

7

Anatta

Greece, Persia, Babylonia, Egypt and India – the main centres of cultural evolution either of the ancient near east or the regions abutting it – were in constant communication. Though Eastern and Indian consciousness are out of the scope of this work, some reference to the state of Indian philosophy around the time of the Ionian revolution of consciousness is appropriate.

Indian philosophical religion. Some of the principal religious leaders of India at the time include: (1) **Gautama Buddha**, the founder of **Buddhism**. His legendary life is calculated by Edward Thomas[1] as 563 – 483, which makes him belong to the generation of Heraclitus (c.570 – c.475). If so, then he died seven years after the battle of Marathon (490), just before the Persian war (480 – 479) and seven years before the birth of Euripides (490 – c.406). Contemporaries of Buddha may include: (2) **Vardhamana Mahavira**. Heinrich Zimmer tells us that the foundation of **Jainism** is attributed to Mahavira – "a contemporary of Buddha, who died c.526." But Jainas regard Mahavira as just the "last of their long series of Tirthankaras" – a term denoting a saviour.[2] Jainism affirms the existence of an imperishable life-monad. (3) **Maskarin Gosala**. Gosala accepted that idea of reincarnation but specifically denied the existence of freewill and asserted a form of determinism. Gautama Buddha "declared this imposing antagonist's teaching to be the very worst of all contemporary erroneous doctrines."[3] According to Gosala each life-monad, an atom, passes through exactly 84,000 births; at the beginning of this cycle each has but one sense-faculty – that of touch – i.e. weight and pressure, and as it progresses it acquires more faculties. There is no divine grace or human self-salvation. It advocates a form of mechanistic inflexibility as a law of evolution.[4] (4) **Ajita Kesakambali** is said to have been the forerunner of the **Charvaka school** of materialism, empiricism and hedonism. (5) **Pakudha Kaccayana** advocated a form of atomism, stated that there are seven "elements" – Earth, Water, Fire, Air, Joy, Sorrow and Life – that do not interact with one another. The resemblance of this system to that of Empedocles (c.490 – c.430) is remarkable, and in India, Empedocles is known as Pakudha Kaccayana of Greece. However, Empedocles

---

[1] Edward J. Thomas, *The Life of the Buddha As Legend and History*, Routledge & Kegan Paul, 1927. Some scholars date his life about 100 years later, and Thomas quotes the opinion of H.H. Wilson: It is "not impossible, after all, that Sákya Muni is an unreal being, and that all that is related of him is as much a fiction as is that of his preceding migrations." (1856).

[2] Heinrick Zimmer, *Philosophies of India*, Edited Joseph Campbell, Meridian Books Inc. New York, First published August 1956. Part 3. I. 1.

[3] *Ibid.*, Part 3. I. 9.

[4] *Ibid.*, Part 3. I. 9.

belongs to at least two generations after that of the Buddha, accepting the above dates for the Buddha.   (6) **Sanjaya Belatthiputta** expressed agnosticism with respect to death.

According to Surendranath Dasgupta, "All the Indian systems except Buddhism admit the existence of a permanent entity variously called **atman, purusa** or **jiva,**" and disagree as to the details. As Dasgupta mentions the Charvaka school, and there is also the atomism of Pakudha Kaccayana, his proposition here is not precise, but he touches upon a core aspect of Indian thought that makes it so different from Western thought, which is **Indian subjectivism**.   While Western thought, following the Ionian revolution, headed not always linearly, but inextricably in the direction of increasing materialism, so that the identification of reality with the external world is its dominating principle, in Indian philosophy the subjective element is the one that assumes **the character of the real** from the first.   Empiricism, materialism and atomism all appear in Indian philosophy, but the main stream of Indian thought is dominated by the concept of the **soul as a monad** – an elemental, indestructible **atom of consciousness**.[5]

Anatta. In Buddhism we find the doctrine of anatta (Pali) or anatman (Sanskrit), which is sometimes translated as **the doctrine of no-self or no-mind**.

Kantian interpretation.   I suggest that the Buddhist doctrine of anatta is misleadingly expressed by the terms no-self, or no-mind, which give that doctrine the air of self-contradiction, mysticism and nonsense. I advocate that the doctrine should be expressed in Western philosophy using the terminology of Kant: atman (purusa, jiva) refers to the conception of a spiritual substance, one persisting in time, corresponding in Western terminology to the Cartesian soul, and hence anatta (anatman) only means to deny that there is spiritual soul-substance, persisting in time: anatta = there is no soul, in the Cartesian sense of soul. Hence, anatta also asserts the Self as transcendent being, where "transcendent" means not belonging to either space or time. As the ego is also identified by Descartes with the soul, the anatta doctrine also denies the reality or permanence of the ego. The ethical goal of Buddhism is to renounce ego-attachment as an illusion, not only because ego-attachment brings about suffering, but also because the ego has no permanence and it is an illusion to suppose it is a substance.[6] The anatta doctrine is equivalent to the

---

[5] Surendranath Dasgupta, *A History of Indian Philosophy*, Vol. 1, Cambridge University Press, 1922. Chapter IV. According to Dasgupta the Nyaya school say that the soul "is absolutely qualityless and characterless, an indeterminate unconscious entity." The Samkhya school identify the soul with pure consciousness. The Vedanta school say, "It is that fundamental point of unity implied in pure consciousness (*cit*), pure bliss (*ananda*), and pure being (*sit*)."

[6] Buddhism tends to affirm a belief in reincarnation and stresses the importance of ethical living. These do not imply the interpretation that anatta literally means that there is no self whatsoever. Interpreting, atman as the Sansksrit term for the soul in the Cartesian sense, anatta = no-atman translates not to "no mind" but to "no soul".

difference between Kant's *Sum* and Descartes's *Cogito*; to the ascent from Cartesian consciousness to Kantian consciousness.

The meaning of Indian terms – *atman, purusa, jiva* – must be a matter of interpretation; but it is not necessary for us in the West to undertake it in any precise way. We find in our cognition only three concepts of what human identity may be, and these correspond to the three stages of cognition in our evolution: vital substance (manikin) in primitive materialism, soul or spiritual substance in Ionian/Cartesian consciousness, and Self (atemporal being) in Kantian consciousness. It seems likely that the same three concepts exist in Indian cognition. We experience problems arising from confused mixings between the three concepts; we may imagine Indian philosophy experiences like difficulties. For us, the question is whether the impermanence of the soul (anatta) entails impermanence of human identity altogether.

We here run up against the limitations of language and cognition. What does "exist" mean? Usually, to say that something exists is to say that it is an object in space and time, such as a tree. In this sense the Self does not exist, because the Self is not a physical object. Descartes claims that the Self exists as a substance persisting in time, and we denote his idea by the soul, which is also an attempt to make the Self into an object, one comprised of "spiritual substance". One interpretation of anatta is that it is the doctrine that the Self does not exist as soul. Hence, we require another term altogether, so we say, "The Self has being." There is being that is neither a form of persistence as physical object in space and time, or persistence in time alone.

This limitation of language is why terms like "abiding" are sometimes scare-quoted here when used in relation to the Self. When we describe the Self, we are talking of being that is independent of space and time. Sometimes we use the term "Eternity" to describe this state. It seems that there may be two time-orders – one temporal in which objects exist, the other eternal in which we have being. We really need a whole new set of terms and concepts when approaching such a higher-order conception.

What precisely Indian consciousness means by such terms as *atman, purusa* and *jiva* must be a matter for another investigation. What I claim is that Western conceptions contain an analysis of the problem of what the Self is that parallel those of India. Further, the Indian doctrine of anatta is importantly reflected in Western cognition and gives rise to problems that Western philosophy must also resolve, specifically because of the alternative interpretation that we have imposed upon it.

The alternative reading of anatta as utter impermanence. It may be possible to take anatta to be the doctrine that denies the existence of the Self altogether. Then, indeed, it means there is no permanence to the mind whatsoever. This position is occasioned by materialism and empiricism. I have already outlined the view of David Hume that the mind is a kind of theatre wherein perceptions and sensations arise; that these form at any one time a collection, but between successive moments of time, successive collections have no permanence. Hence, there is no "I"; anatta = no self = there is no mind whatsoever. The Self, soul, ego, "I" are all illusions.

The Kantian interpretation is that while soul (Cartesian) and ego are illusions, the Self is not; the Self is a pure, "abiding" Subject, and never an object. The alternative interpretation is that everything to do with human identity is an illusion. I reject the alternative interpretation. It is a pernicious bringing on of despair.

This version of the anatta doctrine is also self-refuting. Is the goal of life, then, to achieve an enlightened state of realisation of the utter non-existence of the Self? Such a goal is self-refuting, because if the Self has no being whatsoever, it cannot reach a state of self-cognition in which it achieves the complete knowledge of its own impermanence, such that I (Self, being) know myself as no-self (no-being). There cannot be self-knowledge if there is no Self.

The contradiction involved in "I, no-being, know myself as no-being" that is entailed by the Humean theatre of the mind, should strongly suggest to us that there is something profoundly wrong with this account of human identity, because the experience of self-identity is truly so fundamental to our human reality. Only by "forgetting the subject" could we be lead to such a self-refuting doctrine. There is no ground in self-awareness to suggest the utter impermanence of the Self; ego-illusion is not the same as the claim that the Self, as an identity, is an illusion. The Self as apperceiving Subject always appears as a single, identical Subject of all experience whatsoever; so, it can only be thought to be an illusion through some form of false cognition.

The Humean analysis of identity in the theatre of the mind is an invitation to profound pessimism. The doctrine of impermanence, anatta = no mind whatsoever, leads to the ethics of **nihilism**, that life is meaningless.[7] If pursued to a "logical" extreme, it gives rise to despair. Yet, philosophers of contemporary consciousness advocate the Humean solution to the problem of "Who am I?" and do so with an air of liberating mankind from folly, as benefactors. For example, Wittgenstein in his *Philosophical Investigations*,[8] and Gilbert Ryle, a pupil and follower of Wittgenstein,

---

[7] This, however, is not the ethics of David Hume, whose ethical thinking is an analysis of people as social animals; implicit within that analysis is the assumption that people are attached to their egos and continue to act ethically as if their egos were substantive entities, albeit that these egos are non-existent illusions. Hume offers a hedonistic basis to human motivation, and his central concept is that of **utility**, with regard to what is useful to the collective, rather than to the individual.

[8] For example, Wittgenstein writes, "410. "I" is not the name of a person, nor "here" of a place, and "this" is not a name." "412... But what can it mean to speak of "turning my attention on to my own consciousness"? This is surely the queerest thing there could be! It was a particular act of gazing that I called doing this. I stared fixedly in front of me – but *not* at any particular point or object. My eyes were wide open, the brows not contracted (as they mostly are when I am interested in a particular

in his *The Concept of Mind*[9] both advocate the doctrine anatta = no mind whatsoever, impermanence.

It seems that contemporary philosophy has set out to threaten humanity with two spiritual illnesses. Firstly, the materialism that it embraces requires everyone to face the possibility of the death of the body as an utter annihilation of their person. Secondly, on even closer examination, following the analysis of Hume, even the ego, the "thing" that we devote all our vital energies to, and make the darling centre of our quest for happiness and power, is an illusion, a no-thing, so that we must in life face the fact of our complete non-being. Contemporary philosophy is also presented as a matter of certainty and proclaims all alternative views as products of bygone ages of bad thinking. Even the consolation of not-knowing, our final hope, is stripped away.

The anatta = no-mind whatsoever interpretation can also appear to arise from within Kantian consciousness. In the following passage **Schopenhauer** accepts the Kantian doctrine that the Self is being outside space and time.

> For permanence has no more to do with the will regarded as the thing-in-itself or with the pure subject of knowing, the eternal eye of the world, than has transitoriness, for permanence and transience are predicates valid only in time, whereas the will and the pure subject of knowing lie outside time.

He calls the Self "the will" and "the pure subject". This is the starting point of Kantian consciousness, but he deems the Self "the thing-in-itself", which makes the

---

object). No such interest preceded in this gazing. My glance was vacant; or again *like* that of someone admitting the illumination of the sky and drinking in the light." Wittgenstein means in this second quotation to mock the Cartesian act of introspection. The tone is sarcastic, and by its tone denies the rationality of the Cartesian position. He completely omits any consideration of the Kantian view. Did he ever read him? The whole of *Philosophical Investigations* may be interpreted as a homily to anatta as the doctrine of no-mind-whatsoever. The quotations are from Ludwig Wittgenstein: *Philosophical Investigations*, translated G.E.M. Anscombe, Basil Blackwell, Oxford, 1953. [See Part III, Chapter 15, The wilful overthrow of Kantian consciousness.]

[9] The *Concept of Mind* is another homily dedicated to the materialist-empiricist anatta – and echoes the *Philosophical Investigations*, making the same elusive points, for example: "'I' is like my own shadow; I can never get away from it, as I can get away from your shadow. There is no mystery about this constancy, but I mention it because it seems to endow 'I' with a mystifying uniqueness and adhesiveness. 'Now' has something of the same besetting feeling." (Gilbert Ryle, *The Concept of Mind*, Penguin, 1963. p. 189.) It is difficult to make any sense of this opaque writing, until one grasp that all that he is hinting at is that there is no 'I' – no such thing to which 'I' refers; that is, a homily to anatta in the sense of no-mind whatsoever. But I wonder what the 'I' he refers to is when he writes, "I mention it because…".

Self into a transcendental object. This goes against the interpretation of Kant, who stops at the sceptical position. Then he reflects on death.

> The inward and merely felt consciousness of what we have just raised to distinct knowledge, prevents, as we have said, the <u>thought of death</u> from <u>poisoning the life of the rational being</u>, in that this consciousness is the basis of that courage which sustains every living thing and enables it to continue to live as if there were no such thing as death, as long as it is focused on life. Yet this consciousness will not prevent the individual from being <u>seized with the fear of death</u>, and trying in every way to escape from it, <u>when it presents itself to him in reality</u>, and specifically to him, even if only in his imagination, and he is compelled to look it straight in the eye. ... when death presents itself to him, he is bound to see it for what it is: the temporal end of the individual temporal phenomenon. ... <u>What we fear in death is the eclipse of the individual</u>, which it <u>frankly claims to be</u>; and since <u>the individual is a specific objectification of the will</u> to life itself, its whole nature struggles against death.[10]

This passage illustrates the transition in Schopenhauer's thought from the life-affirming philosophy of Kant, to self-destructive pessimism.

Life-denial. Schopenhauer is an advocate of the way of renunciation: "the denial of the will to life".[11] He pays a kind of lip-service to the interpretation of anatta as affirming the Self as transcendent being but proceeds to advance a form of the doctrine of anatta in the form of no-mind whatsoever, in the form that the individual does not survive after death. For Schopenhauer the Self has a kind of permanence as will, but the individual does not.

Schopenhauer's statement is profound, because it expresses essentially the **angst of the contemporary consciousness**. He makes in the above the statements: (1) the thought of death poisons life; (2) we are seized with the fear of death as soon as we grasp it as a certain reality; (3) the fear is the fear of the annihilation of the individual; (4) there is no comfort in the doctrine that the Self ("will and pure subject") is transcendent. In these statements, the first three notably, Schopenhauer confirms the conclusion of Dostoyevsky: "... if you were to destroy the belief in immortality in mankind, not only love but every living force on which the

---

[10] Arthur Schopenhauer, *The World as Will and Idea*, Abridged, Edited David Berman, Translated Jill Berman, Everyman, Book IV, 54 – p.184 – 85.

[11] He does discuss the possibility of an affirmation of life, but immediately rejects it. The reader suspects some hidden emotive core of Schopenhauer's psyche at work – a *will to pessimism*.

continuation of all life in the world depended, would dry up at once."[12] Although Schopenhauer allows the Self to abide, he refuses to ascribe immortality to the individual that lives in time; the individual does not survive its death.

I find nothing compelling in Schopenhauer's arguments, which express his bias towards pessimism. (1) The individual that he talks of does not exist in life either, for by his philosophy (and Kant's and mine) this individual is the ego and the existence of the ego is an illusion. The ego is not annihilated in time because it never existed in time. (2) Since life expresses the life of the individual person as opposed to the life of a thing, the individual Self also has transcendental being. The Self is not an impersonal entity, like the quasi-material entity that "the" in his expression "the thing-in-itself" in the first quotation implies. (3) Questions concerning what the individual Self is, or what its relation to other individual Selves might be, may arise. But we do not have to answer these questions, which ask conscious to do more than it can conceivably do within the bounds of its cognition.[13] (4) The possibility that death represents in life the reversion of the individual to the Self as pure being, does not imply that in thus reverting the individual is destroyed. The meaning of life resides in the individual, the spiritual concern of life. (5) The cessation of life as we know it, does not imply that the life-to-come is a diminished version of this life. Since we can and invariably do think in some respects of death as an event in time that involves the end of the individual *in this life*, there is no reason to suppose that the reversion to pure being involves necessarily a diminution of the individual *in eternity*. (6) I write "of death as an event in time", but **death is not an event in time**; events in time include such things as a flower bursting into bloom, or a gun going off; but death does not happen to the ego because the ego does not exist in time; it does not happen to the individual Self, because it is eternal; hence, there is no annihilation. Or at least, if our faith is weak, we may at least hope so. (7) If we must think of death as an event of time, then we must think of it as a great transformation or metamorphosis. Does the caterpillar know what it is like to be a butterfly?

The equivalence of Eastern and Western cognition. We see that contemporaneous to the Ionian revolution, we have attested in India a system of philosophical thinking that has given rise to all the main solutions to the body/soul problem that also appear in Western consciousness. The Buddhist doctrine of anatta connects Buddhism to idealistic monism. Jainism represents a doctrine akin to Cartesian dualism, though the emphasis, as in Indian consciousness generally, is so much upon the soul-monad that the material world is of concern only in so far as it

[12] From Fyodor Dostoyevsky, *The Brothers Karamazov*, quoted in full in Part II, Chapter 3, Irony, satire, cynicism and laughter.]
[13] [See Part III, Chapter 14, What Kantian consciousness is.]

must be overcome. The Charvaka school is equivalent to our materialism.   We
have in Belatthiputta an equivalent of contemporaneous empiricism.

But the biases in East and West are so very different, and this is a point of ethical
significance for we of the West. It seems that Indian consciousness is adapted to
subjective introspection through practice of meditation, and that it conducts these
"experiments" in the context of **asceticism**, the rigorous denial of sense-experience,
of desire, of sexual urges and so on. It is a thesis advanced here that **Western
consciousness is not adapted to ascetic practice**, and that forcing ascetic practice
on Western people causes psychological and ethical problems that all stem from bad
faith. If an individual in full command of his soul, freely commits himself to a life
of asceticism, in the full cognition of what such a life involves, and freely grasping
the dogma as an act of faith, then that is simply a choice. That such a course of
action is recommended to others may be an evil, but primarily if others are forced by
pressure or downright coercion to adopt the same practices in bad faith. Historically,
these ideas of bodily self-denial were imported into Western religion through the
medium of Christianity and express themselves in the concept of sin as desire.
Thenceforth, Western consciousness was infected by bad faith and the split-
consciousness psyche.

Soul-sorrow of the West. In contemporary times there is heightened anxiety in
the context of the overthrow of Cartesian dualism and of Christian puritanism arising
from the victory of materialism and scientific rationalism, generating an acute **fear
of death** at the thought of inevitable annihilation. To counter this angst, some belief
in the Self and its immortality must be reawakened. The contemporary angst must
be overcome.   The materialist philosophy will not bear critical examination.
Furthermore, the essential idea that life is a spiritual phenomenon, which takes form
in Eastern consciousness as the quest for release (*moksha*) from the phenomena of
incarnate existence, and in our Western case, as the quest for ethical and spiritual
life, is the only thing that can provide individuals with a secure framework in which
to achieve happiness. At the bottom of all the soul-sorrow that we in the West are
now experiencing are two thoughts: (1) I fear that at my death I shall be annihilated;
(2) I have nothing to live for other than the pleasures of my ego, and these do not
make me happy.

The Western way. For the West, it is essential to understand that there is a
spiritual path of life that does not require the denial of the body; that what appears in
Eastern consciousness as a mandatory path to "the goal" (call it "**Enlightenment**") is
voluntary in Western consciousness. Those who adopt asceticism voluntarily should
do no more than recommend it by example in their persons to their fellow travellers
in the pilgrimage of life. There has been too much preaching the path of bodily self-
denial and too many attempts to hypocritically force it on others without due
observance in oneself. The use of coercion of all kinds in this respect must come to
an end. I affirm that in so far as both paths can be compared, **the Western way is**

not inferior to the Eastern way. Both paths, Eastern asceticism, Western ethical living, lead in the direction of increased spirituality. For what is the true meaning of asceticism other than simply to renounce an indolent way of living, of taking things as they are, of refusing to awaken and develop culture and consciousness? Hence, whether in the West or East, when one freely and consciously adopts that path that Karl Jung has called **the path of individuation**, one has become an ascetic in the true sense. But this **true asceticism** has nothing to do with giving up bodily pleasures. So far as we can know, the two paths, East and West, are equivalent.

Moksha, mukti, nirvana. A proof of the superiority of the Eastern concept might be attempted from the concept of *moksha* or release. As is well known, Eastern philosophy presents incarnate life as a sorrowful or inferior state of existence. This is an idea with which we in the West are also familiar.

> The weariness, the fever, and the fret
>> Here, where men sit and hear each other groan;
> Where palsy shakes a few, sad, last gray hairs,
>> Where youth grows pale, and spectre-thin, and dies;
>>> Where but to think is to be full of sorrow
>>> And leaden-eyed despairs.[14]

Dukka – **existence is suffering**. Life is perceived as an inferior condition of existence characterised by suffering. The world is a cycle of birth, death and rebirth, subject to *mara* – illusion. The Buddhists express this idea in the doctrine of the four noble truths.

The Four Noble Truths
Dukkha – Existence is suffering.
Samudaya – Suffering has a cause.
Nirodha – Suffering can end.
Magga – The way is the Noble Eightfold Middle Path.

This is elaborated into the **Law of dependent origination**, which traces the cycle of birth, death and rebirth through twelve stages of karmic evolution (cause and effect) extended over three lives – past, present and future.[15]

---

[14] John Keats, *Ode to a Nightingale*.
[15] 1. Ego-illusion (*avidya*), 2. Karma-formations (*samskara*), 3. Consciousness (*vijnana*), 4. Mind and Body (*nama-rupa*), 5. Sense-Organs (*sadayatana*), 6. Contact (*sparsa*), 7. Feeling (*vedana*), 8. Craving (*trsna*), 9. Clinging (*upandana*), 10. Becoming (*bhava*), 11. (Re-)Birth (*jati*), 12. Old-Age, Death (*jara-marana*). From Lama Anagarika Govinda, *Foundations of Tibetan Buddhism,* Rider and Company, London, 1960, p. 246.

(1) We are not obliged in the West to adopt all or any of this. The tradition in the East for formularies of this type is overwhelming, but we may at least re-consider the question in the light of Socratic doubt.

(2) When we examine the Kantian point-of-view regarding the Self, we see that it affirms only that the Self is transcendent being. To this I add in the light of the discussions above, that it is transcendent individual being. This implies that death is a transformation or metamorphosis and we do not have to look in time and space for what that transformation might be. There may be other states of individual consciousness, and why should we not translate to a place more wonderful than this world that we know, and that, after-all, is the hope of Heaven or Paradise. Inevitably, we picture this as a state in time, following the event death, but as we come to grasp that the Self is not in time, then we see too that death is not an event in time, and the transformation does not take place in time. Why should we seek to be definite about this? The hope of happiness in the future life is all that is required for a soundly grounded life.

In the Eastern tradition, this hope has been translated into a more definite picture of reincarnation and of cycles of birth, death and re-birth. The notion of a twofold destiny arises. Either the Self at birth transcends to a higher and different state of consciousness called *nirvana* by Buddhists in a process called release (*moksha* or *mukti*), or the Self is reincarnated in another life. This gives the false impression that reincarnation is a worse state than *nirvana*, and that we ought to do everything to avoid reincarnation.

(3) Yet it is the common foundation of all these systems that release is not achieved through one life-time, and that in fact obtaining release is the work of several lifetimes. Thus, even if we swallow hook-line-and-sinker the entire Buddhist-Hindu philosophy, it does not follow that anytime in the near survey of future lives we will obtain release. These religions all tell stories of the countless reincarnations of their respective saints, who finally obtained release. I suggest that if any reader here is about to enter *nirvana* in this life or at his or her next death, he or she will have strong intimations of it. And, likewise, if one is in the Buddhist sense a "once-returner", one will know it. If you are in any doubt as to your current spiritual state, and likelihood of obtaining release anytime in the cycle of near-future incarnations, then you can surmise that the answer is not in this lifetime. This reduces the apparent superiority of East over West, the superiority of asceticism as opposed to incarnate ethical and spiritual living, to approximately zero. For, why not just get on with living? The whole thing, complete with all its ups and downs, and pleasures, pains, lusts, desires and cravings. Enjoy it, and progress. If you are so certain that the final life, the final stage, is one of renunciation of all bodily desires, the final victory that you hope for under the Bo-tree, then you may look forward to being reincarnated as an Indian with the appropriate subjective framework of

consciousness adapted to yogic practice and extreme asceticism. That will be a boon for you.

(4) And when we look at the formulas, "existence is suffering", "suffering has a cause", and so forth, these propositions in themselves are ambiguous, and only achieve clarity through the various interpretations of the various schools. But, might not these interpretations be wrong, or even subtly misguided? There is an impression that Eastern consciousness enjoys asceticism, and it may for reason of that bias import into the wisdom of the Buddha a dogma not otherwise present. For the contamination of ideas is ever the province of later commentators. Any words that are attributed to the Buddha were written down no earlier than one hundred years after his legendary death.

(5) We may examine this doctrine "existence is suffering" and ask, where does it come from? It certainly cannot come from the contemplation of the beauty of the azure sky, of the magnificence of mountains, of the lush-green verdure of the valleys, or of the sight of dolphins leaping from the blue-green sea. We see no suffering in the mere fact of incarnation in nature. Nor is it suffering, if, as in an earlier age of human life, we exist in a more uneasy relationship with wild animals, and like, in many African countries, cause of death may be "eaten by a lion", for the hunter-gatherer exists in a paradise of nature, and admires the beasts that he kills, and has joy of them.

The cause of human suffering is other human beings, society, and naturally oneself. Oppressive and aggressive society does figure forcefully. We may speculate that at that formative epoch when the Eastern tradition of all-life-is-suffering arose, social conditions were particularly oppressive.

(6) **We must laugh, and we must sing**. The Eastern tradition conveys much practical wisdom about the psychology of self-inflicted pain, how it stems from a bad-attitude, and has repercussions in our dealings with our fellow men. Society is the collective accumulation of individual self-afflictions. So, it is true that society is oppressive because man inflicts suffering upon himself. The psychological dimension of living is overwhelming. But learning from that, and living by it, does not entail asceticism, in the sense of bodily self-denial on account of sin as desire. There is nothing necessarily wrong in desire.[16]

Where there is a good idea, someone has gone there before you. The same conclusion was reached by W.B. Yeats.

> I am content to live it all again
> And yet again, if it be life to pitch
> Into the frog-spawn of a blind man's ditch,
> A blind man battering blind men;

---

[16] [For the phenomenology of desire, see Part III, Chapter 6.]

Or into that most fecund ditch of all,
The folly that man does
Or must suffer, if he woos
A proud woman not kindred of his soul.

I am content to follow to its source
Every event in action or in thought;
Measure the lot; forgive myself the lot!
When such as I cast out remorse
So great a sweetness flows into the breast
We must laugh and we must sing,
We are blest by everything,
Everything we look upon is blest.[17]

What is needed right now is a good blast of **life-affirmation**. The sickly Wittgenstein-led anatta as no-mind-whatsoever, the Schopenhauer-like modern pessimism, nihilism, existential angst, existential fear of death, annihilation and living – all these spiritual illnesses need quickly to come to an end.

---

[17] W.B. Yeats, *A Dialogue of Self and Soul.*

8

The Fall and the doctrine of the mirror

In the matriarchal epoch, there is **sin as transgression of the norms of matriarchal society**, which are crimes committed against maternal blood relatives, the most heinous of which is the murder of one's own mother. The sinful aspect of such crimes is expressed in the existence of **divine matriarchal sanctions** – the criminal is hunted down by **the Furies**.

    Raising of archetypes. Every **departure from an existing norm** raises a new archetype to consciousness. The archetype of Perseus, the dragon-slayer, and the archetype of Zeus, the patriarch and dispenser of justice, were essential to the departure of the hero from the norms of matriarchal society. By classical Greek times the sin of blood-crime against the mother had been subsumed by patriarchal justice; it is a crime, but no longer sinful in its own right. Only by appeal to another moral order, perceived as higher and more masterful, can such a transgression be released from its aspect of matriarchal sin, the one that makes Orestes an utter outcast; Orestes is demonstrated to be acting on the instructions of Zeus the Father, justice, and the Goddess is demoted into the archetype of consort or some other archetype. The mythologem of rape is the forceful demonstration of patriarchal authority. Marriage puts male authority upon a contractual basis and mitigates to an extent its implicit violence over female life.

    People's lives are governed by norms that are embodied in mythologems and acted out in their psyches as archetypes. In primitive consciousness the individual does not get a sharp sense of right and wrong action; this applies even in the context of the Dionysus archetype; the victim and those who sacrifice the victim act out a pre-ordained drama, apparently required by the very nature of things, and though it is murder by our standards, they are not conscious of it. They are conscious of the act of sacrifice as a holy duty, of the frenzy in which they act as divine inspiration.

    Greater **consciousness of sin** emerges from the raising into consciousness of **individual conscience**, a sense of right and wrong. Conscience in the sense of self-righteousness arises when one is conscious of (a) departure in one's own conduct from a norm of society, raising the question – Am I right to depart thus from the customs of my fellows? (b) Awareness that the norms of society are wrong. These are two facets of the same aspect of an individual consciousness breaking away from society. The first question asks what it is permissible to do by way of departure – the origin of the notion of **rights** – rights as permissions to thus depart; the second question asks whether it is one's **duty** to break away from society, which is collectively committed to what is revealed to the individual to be immoral. The rise of complex societies brings diverse situations that prompt the individual to depart from the norms of society. Any departure from a pre-existing norm raises a new norm. Since it is believed that the gods are the moral overlords of life, any departure from a norm represents a religious problem. The religious meaning of sin is departure from the command of the divine order. The raising in consciousness of a new and heightened perception of sin is reflected in the emergence of **sin as hubris**, so this is an appropriate place to examine this conception in the work of Aeschylus (c.525/524 – c.456/455) and Sophocles (c.497/6 – 406/5).

Aeschylus's play, *The Persians*, is set in Susa at the palace of Xerxes a few months after the battle of Salamis, September 480, where Xerxes's massed invasion of Greece was checked.[1] The play looks at the nature of defeat and the terrible loss of life from the point of view of the enemy of Athens and is thereby remarkable for its expression of universal compassion. The blame for the disaster falls entirely on Xerxes. Pride must have a fall, and despite the enormous force Xerxes sent against Greece, the Persians were crushed. The courage and cunning of the Greeks is celebrated, but only to the extent that it is necessary to emphasise the moral failure of Xerxes to understand man's relationship to the cosmos. The invasion is interpreted as a deliberate defiance of the divine order, and the rebellion reaps its inevitable punishment, which the ghost of Darius expresses.

> So now for my whole house a staunchless spring of griefs
> Is opened; and my son, in youthful recklessness,
> Not knowing the gods' ways, has been the cause of all.
> He hoped to stem that holy stream, the Bosporus,
> And bind the Hellespont with fetters like a slave;
> He would wrest Nature, turn sea into land, manacle
> A strait with iron, to make a highway for his troops.
> He in his mortal folly thought to overpower
> Immortal gods, even Poseidon. Was not this
> Some madness that possessed him?
> … Zeus, throned on high,
> Sternly chastises arrogant and boastful men.
> As for my son, since Heaven has warned him to be wise,
> Instruct him with sound reason, and admonish him

---

[1] The Chorus of Persian Elders is expecting news of the campaign led by Xerxes against Greece. They describe the mighty host that was sent against the Greeks. Atossa, mother of Xerxes, enters and relates a series of very bad dreams that she interprets as bad omens. The elders advise her to ritually purify herself. Before she can do so, a messenger enters with news of the destruction of the army of Xerxes, commencing with the battle of Salamis. Xerxes has survived, but the loss of life is unimaginable. They are all dismayed. Atossa proposes to sacrifice to her dead husband, Darius. The Chorus raise the dead spirit of Darius. Darius declaims against the folly of his son in bridging the Hellespont and reiterates the theme of hubris. After his ghost has departed, and Atossa has left the stage, Xerxes enters, stricken with grief; he initiates the period of lamentation for the defeat.

To cease affronting God with proud and rash attempts.[2]

Sin as transgression or as failure of ritual observance are external actions done to others, human or divine. The breach of a promise to a neighbour and the breach of ritual owed to a god provoke alike the other party to revenge. Here sin is not far from the idea of Hate, and it is not surprising that sin in Homer is expressed by Ate, the Goddess of Hate. But in sin as hubris, we have an inner, psychological dimension. It is not so much that an invasion, such as the one Xerxes made, provokes the courage of the enemy, for it might provoke their cowardice or prudent capitulation, it is that one is falling foul of an **inward transgression**. It implies the contrast between spiritual progress and spiritual failure, where hubris stands for the cause and product of failure.

Christianity's equivalent is the **sin of pride**, the greatest sin of all, the sin that Satan (Lucifer) committed in heaven before Man was created, for he rebelled against God, because *he wanted to be God, to be that which he is not*. In the myth, Satan is hardened to obdurate refusal to acknowledge that he is not God, and to obdurate persistence in his futile ambition. Milton expresses this.

> ... Here [in Hell] at least
> We shall be free; th' Almight hath not built
> Here for his envy, will not drive us hence:
> Here we may reign secure, and in my choice
> To reign is worth ambition though in Hell;
> Better to reign in Hell, than serve in Heav'n.[3]

Satan, who speaks in obdurate pride is the author of his own Hell; this illustrates **the psychological analysis of self-begotten suffering** that begins in Greek culture with hubris, and in concurrent Indian culture is reflected in words attributed to the Buddha.

> 1. What we are today comes from our thoughts of yesterday, and our present thoughts build our life of tomorrow: our life is the creation of our mind. If a man speaks or acts with an impure mind, suffering follows him as the wheel of the cart follows the beast that draws the cart.
>
> 2. What we are today comes from our thoughts of yesterday, and our present thoughts build our life of tomorrow: our life is the creation of

---

[2] Darius in Aeschylus, *The Persians*. Darius alludes to Xerxes building a bridge over the Bosporus.
[3] Milton, *Paradise Lost*, I, 258 – 263.

our mind. If a man speaks or acts with a pure mind, joy follows him
as his own shadow.[4]

Xerxes is an insufficient role-model to become the symbolic bearer of the
archetype of sin as hubris. One of the limitations is that his case is too transparent.
He sets in motion vast armies, confident in his arrogant assumption that his vast
numerical superiority will conquer the world for him. This does not invoke the
complex relationship man has with life and fate. Tragedy must engage **the problem
of evil**, the interaction between gods and men, in which the behaviour of the gods
also comes under scrutiny. How, if God exists, if he is benevolent, omnipotent and
omniscient, does he permit evil to exist?[5] The materialist response, that all suffering
arises from chance,[6] mitigated, to an extent, by human endeavour, is not sufficient
for a religious disposition, which seeks rather to understand suffering than to exploit
it as a ground for non-belief in God or super-nature.

The problem of evil arises in Ionian consciousness with the emergence of the
concept of infinity. If the gods are merely "immortals", beings that do not encounter
death, more powerful than men, this leaves unresolved the problem of their moral
stature. Such beings may be thought to walk among men, commune with them, but
it does not follow that their actions are morally good. To counteract this, there must
be a tendency to elevate the gods to a combination of both omnipotence and
benevolence, and to identify the will of god with moral law. This tendency is seen in
the increasing respect shown for the Zeus the Father, who is morphing into
Providence.

---

[4] *The Dhammapada*, Translated by Juan Mascaró, Penguin, London, 1973.

[5] We might express the argument thus, as a refutation of the existence of God. (1) If God exists then
he must be benevolent and omnipotent. (2) A benevolent deity would not tolerate the existence of
suffering (evil). (3) An omnipotent god has the power to alter anything. (4) But the world is a vale of
tears. (5) Therefore, God does not exist.

   Arguments are a form of intensional object (meaningful structure) before consciousness, and their
validity is relative to cognition. The above argument does not prove the non-existence of God but is a
reasoning object present in Ionian/Cartesian consciousness and examined by it. It is found as an
expression of a dialectical conviction of Stoicism, materialism and positivism.

[6] A particularly powerful expression of this problem is *The Plague* by Albert Camus. An Algerian
city has been stricken by plague. It has been sealed off from the outside world, and the inhabitants
fight the plague. Two central characters are Rieux, a doctor, who is also an atheist, and Paneloux,
who is a Jesuit priest. The description of the terrible death of a child and the following exchange
between Rieux and Paneloux is an exceptional statement of the problem, too long to be quoted here.
The death of the child is not only grotesque but arbitrary. Camus's work may be taken as a standard
for the difficulty of reconciling evil in the world to the existence and benevolence of God. But Camus
does recognise the dialectical aspect of the problem; while he makes Paneloux in the dialogue appear
to be the morally weaker force, he represents the two points-of-view, and acknowledges that the
decision between them is existential.

Manichaeism. In the Manichaean defence or "heresy" the omnipotence of God is called into question. God is the opponent of an equal and opposed force of Evil. This arises in the Persian conception of the war between Ahura-Mazda, "the all-wise" and "all-bountiful" and Angro-Mainyus, "the dark intelligence", who is historically the prototype of Satan.[7]

Theological problem of Manichaeism. If the principle of Light (God) is not omnipotent, meaning capable of defeating the Dark principle, then what is the value of the worship of Light? Manichaeism reveals man to be endowed with choice in the war between Light and Dark. Even in Christian theology man, in sinful pride, may choose to align himself with the Dark principle, Satan and Hell, but he does so in despair, for Satan is not God, and cannot be victorious. In the Manichaean version the man who aligns himself with the Dark principle may do so in the hope of victory, because his committal act of support may tip the war in its favour. Furthermore, neither the Light nor the Dark can offer to any individual man, suspended between them, assurance of reward. Fate becomes arbitrary. The good man may be annihilated by the Dark power; he has no assurance of immortality. This may focus the choice of the good as an act of man's will – a free will to live in a world governed by Light, even at the expense of pain and ultimate annihilation. For under this conception it is not only the principle of Light that can cast the bad into Hell, the Dark can also make a hell for the good.

There is a "logical" objection to Manichaeism: the conflict between two principles always implies a third. If Light combats Dark, then they combat over a ground, that amounts to neutral reality, a third principle that is subject to neither power. Once two warriors meeting in a field have thrown their spears, the outcome is down to the laws of nature. Then, we have Three, Light (God), Dark (the Devil) and Nature (the ground on which they fight). Then this reality of three comprises a fourth principle that assumes all three in one. We have Reality comprising Light, Dark and Nature. Is this Reality morally arbitrary (chance like) or providential (directed by spirit)? If the former, the system collapses into a form of materialism, if the latter either the Light or the Dark governs it. Manichaean moral dualism is in danger of collapsing into another position: a form of materialism, or a form of monotheism, as either the supremacy of the Light, or the supremacy of the Dark, which is **pure Satanism**. Perhaps this is what is meant by **the Axiom of Maria**.[8]

One becomes two, two becomes three, and out of the third comes the one as the fourth.

---

[7] [See Part III, Chapter 10, Mazdeism.]

[8] Maria the Jewess, Maria Prophetissima, is a legendary alchemist cited in the works of Zosimos of Panopolois, a gnostic writer who lived c. the end of the C3 or beginning of the C4 CE.

It follows that if there is a God, or moral reality, then a solution that is not Manichaean (dualist) must embrace **evil as part of the godhead**. That means that evil, even the dreadful evil of child mortality, even the ritual of child sacrifice, must be subsumed in the good. Either all evil is an illusion, or it is a consequence of divine benevolence, the working of providence.

> Women of Trachis, you have leave to go.
> You have seen strange things.
> The awful hand of death, new shapes of woe,
> Uncounted sufferings;
> And all that you have seen
> Is God.[9]

The freewill defence. The Christian, Buddhist and Greek answer has tended to perceive the operation of human will in the fate that Man suffers. The Christians call this the freewill defence, the Buddhists have their formulary of dependent origination that traces the fate we suffer in this life to the karmic consequences of our attitude in the previous, and the Greeks have hubris. Implicit in all three variants of the underlying idea is the notion of man's fall from a state of primal grace.

Christianity concludes that we are inherently evil and in a condition of **original sin**. Its theology sometimes traces this state of original sin back historically to Adam,[10] but otherwise interprets the myth of **the Garden of Eden** as an **allegory** for what is every man's primal condition, an ingrained disposition to sin in defiance of God. The imbalance brought about by this idea in the Western psyche has been a persistent theme of this work, which argues that overcoming this concept of original sin is essential to the health of Western society and its attendant shadow problem. In this context we see **materialism as a solution to this problem**, because it rejects altogether all the metaphysics that could be its foundation and teaches us that men evolved from animals. Cruelty originates in animal instincts and is inculcated by social conditions but is not "original" in the religious sense. It is a thesis that the progress of materialism in Western culture, reaching an apogee in contemporary times, owes its force to the dismissal of the concept of original sin on the part of the vanguard of academic Western thinking.[11] So, let us dwell on this.

---

[9] Sophocles, *Women of Trachis*. Concluding speech of Hylas.

[10] The idea that Adam's sin is transmitted by blood to his descendants belongs to primitive materialism. Traces of primitive materialism survive the Ionian revolution. The concept of sin as attachment to the pleasures of the senses arises with the body/soul split and belongs to Ionian consciousness. Hence, the dislike theologians themselves have for trancing guilt by blood to Adam, for it is a confused merging of ideas from two stages of cognition.

[11] It would take a large volume to render it plausible to a sceptic by analysis of cultural material. All beliefs have a motivational aspect, and the materialists (Positivists) disliked the idea of original sin.

(1) Greek consciousness at the late archaic/early classical stage is not yet in the condition of attributing human suffering to original sin caused by desire. In sin as hubris the notion of incarnation as a fallen state is implicit, and achieves expression,[12] but not in sin as desire but in sin as the expression of man's total state of being. It says, this is what he is. In Plato it achieves first explicit expression as the concept of Fallen nature through sin as desire.

(2) **Primal self-examination**. It is a question as to what we directly intuit when we look in upon our own nature and examine ourselves and our actions and the dispositions that are expressed in our thoughts, fantasies and choices. Upon self-examination we find imperfections and some of these we may attribute to desires, but we are not obliged to describe this state as one of original sin or attribute it to desire of the Flesh, or attachment to the senses. I call it, a state of imperfection. In the Socratic tradition, immoral conduct is attributed to **ignorance** rather than will. I think it is both ignorant and wilful, and sometimes wilful ignorance. What I find is that **my total situation as an "incarnate" human being is the perfect expression of the person that I am**, replete with ignorance, imperfection, inappropriate desires, muddy thinking and ego-attachment, and I find that these rebound upon me and contribute to the life that I lead. But I also find other things in myself that are called virtues, such as a desire to learn. Let each person examine him or herself.

(3) In the philosophical myth of the Fall of Man there is a narrative over time. But our state of being is not a condition that has its origin in time. The Fall of Man is a story that postulates a time when we were in an original state of **innocence** – a religious concept of utter importance – but it does not appear to me from any introspective state of mine that I am conscious of ever having been in an original state of purity in the historical sense. (In such matters, each person confronts himself alone; it is a subjective question.) I intuit life as one of increasing development, not of depravity. I do not know how any other person "stands with God", and I avoid absolute judgements. Hence, the myth of the Fall of Man is just one myth. I find it by no means mandatory in explaining my state of existence, which is better expressed as **a state of imperfection**.

(4) Kant attempted to demonstrate that "the human being is evil by nature". He says evil means: "He is conscious of the moral law and yet has admitted the (occasional) deviation from it into his maxim."[13] He is referring to his categorical

---

Materialism and Positivism were constellated in the Western spirt as the first attempt at self-healing from the wound of the shadow problem. [See also Part III, Chapter 15, The wilful overthrow of Kantian consciousness.]

[12] For example, in Heracles's speech in Euripides, *Heracles*. [Quoted in Part II, Chapter 3, Irony, satire, cynicism and laughter, and further discussed in Part III, Chapter 18, Kantian consciousness and the spirit world.]

[13] Immanuel Kant, *Religion within the Bounds of Bare Reason,* Hackett Publishing Company, Inc. Indianapolis/Cambridge, 2009, Translated by Werner S. Pluhar, p. 36.

imperative, which is an expression of the idea of doing to others as we would be done by. But this is not an expression of sin as attachment to the senses, but rather of sin as transgression. A cornerstone of my ethical thinking is that I should aim to treat others as persons and not as things, but even this idea over-simplifies the moral situation. Firstly, contrary to what Kant says, we cannot extract the purpose of life merely from the constraint that we must treat persons as persons, and secondly, in the warp and weft of living, duty ignores the complexities of life's cut and thrust. For example, (a) If I employ a plumber, is he an object or a person, a means or an end-in-himself? (b) If I live with people who treat me as an object, what alterations in my conduct towards them may be entailed? I'm not going to attempt to answer these questions here, but much as I admire Kantian ethics, it is too rigid, and leads one in the question of whether man is evil by nature in the direction of original sin. Kantian ethics is influenced by the Christian ethic with which he is in other respects breaking.[14]

(5) Kant also attempts an empirical proof that man is evil by nature, citing "the never-ceasing cruelty in the vast wastelands of northwestern America," the "long melancholy litany of charges against humanity: of the secret falsity even in the most intimate friendship."[15] He lists many vices as examples, also referring to the behaviour of countries to each other. However, **there can be no empirical proof of the inherent evil of man**; it can only be by direct intuition into my very own psyche that I adjudge myself to be evil. When I personally undertake this, I find imperfection, not evil; if the imperfection I find may be called "an evil", I find it does not appertain to desire as attachment to the senses. I find the senses and attachment to the senses, as attachment to the beauty of the world and to the wonders of nature, holy and pure, and it is in how this attachment relates to other people that it can become contaminated.

(6) I may say that in a sense I directly intuit my spiritual state to be "fallen", and understand for that reason that whatever happens to me in this life may be an expression of that state, but the whole logic that traces this intuition back to a specific cause such as – that I was once in a pure state of existence, and fell from that state through attachment to the senses – is by no means mandatory. My state is a state of ignorance and imperfection, not of immersion in sin as desire. If I wish to call that state of ignorance "fallen", then I may be "fallen", but not in the sense that Augustine meant it, or in the sense that is attributed to the Buddha in the *Agganna-Sutta* – a poetic and philosophical account of the Fall of Man from a Buddhist text.[16] Nor am I obligated to suppose that any words on this topic attributed to the Buddha

---

[14] [The examination of limitations of Kantian ethics is further explored in Part III, Chapter 15, The wilful overthrow of Kantian consciousness.]

[15] Kant, *Religion, Op. cit.,* p. 36.

[16] [The passage from the *Agganna-Sutta* is quoted in Part III, Chapter 1, Either/Or.]

were in fact ever spoken by him, for any such words were written down centuries after the Buddha lived, and who knows what alterations may have taken place in the intervening period? I am not obligated to attribute the concept of sin as inordinate attachment to the senses to any religious hero whatsoever, such as Jesus, Zoroaster or the Buddha, for none of these persons are here to tell us what they thought, did or said. **I am obligated to work it all out for myself.**

The archetype of Oedipus. In the tragedies of Aeschylus and Sophocles the focus is on hubris, which is seen as the **tragic flaw** of the hero. It is in the character of Oedipus in Sophocles's *Oedipus the King* that the archetype of hubris achieves quintessential expression, replete with a profound relation to the problem of evil. Oedipus's history presents the moral problem acutely: (a) he does not know either of his parents at birth and is the victim of their attempt to murder him; (b) he tries to avoid the place where he thinks his mother and father are living; (c) he is the victim of a blood curse originating in the sin of his father Laius; (d) the Delphic oracle drives him to the fit of insanity; (e) he unwittingly kills his father and marries his mother; (f) he rejects violently the crime and inflicts exceptional punishment upon himself. In these episodes, the gods themselves play a role in the mechanism that drives him towards his fate. Oedipus appears as the victim of the gods' caprice; his fate appears arbitrary.

The "solution" of Sophocles is to make Oedipus into an example of hubris. He is (a) irrational, (b) irreligious, (c) arrogant, (d) prone to anger and (e) blind to his own situation. He is also (f) insensitive to the sufferings of his adopted parents, whom he ignores. This hubris places him outside god's grace. He is (g) a serial murderer, since the account he tells of the way he killed his father and his father's attendants does not amount to justified self-defence.

Dual time orders. Dramatically, this produces a profound spectacle, deeply moving and very moral. Nonetheless, it does not answer fully all the religious questions raised by the legend. Furthermore, Oedipus is simultaneous both a good and a bad man. He may have the common fault of humanity – hubris – but he has many virtues as well – a species of honesty is chief among these – and he is seeking God. The position adopted by Sophocles requires further clarification. We need not only the concept of freewill, but also the concept of dual or multiple time. Within normal time, Oedipus is the plaything of the gods and the victim of a blood curse, hence innocent, or not culpable as charged; then, since he is morally guilty of the crime, and not just guilty of hubris, his choice must have been made in eternity, within another species of time. He is born fated to kill his father and marry his mother, because that is what the expression of what he is in his pure Self, transcendent, independent of time and space.

This relates to **the problem of freewill and determinism**, which is the metaphysical problem of Ionian/Cartesian cognition, and cannot be resolved within it. Freewill in the Kantian sense indicates any action not otherwise determined by events in time.

> By freedom … I understand the power of beginning a state spontaneously. Any free act will not, therefore, be itself brought about by another temporal cause that determines it to happen, which is what the law of nature would require.[17]

The idea of freewill has always appeared to be problematic and "impossible" because when one thinks of actions one thinks of an event taking place in time. A typical model of an action is that prior to the act there is a period of deliberation, then, consequent on this "thinking it through", there is an act of will when the person decides to do something; finally, he does it. For example, when I deliberate whether to make a cup of tea or not. After considering the benefits against the effort involved, I decide. Then, I get up and make the tea. It is not difficult to show that this model is not a very good description of how actions are brought about, and the idea of an act of will, as an event, is unsatisfactory. The air of folly arises from the notion of placing an act of will in time.

Kant's resolution to the problem of freewill and determinism. Kant argues that supposing the whole sequence of cause and effect is utterly determined, yet, since the transcendental Self cannot be found in time, it is possessed also of freedom not in time; hence is still morally responsible for the whole sequence because life as a whole is the expression of its freedom. It is as if a Self, prior to being incarnated at birth, chose the whole sequence of his incarnate life, chose his parents, chose the conditions that made him what he is, chose the forces that determined him to commit a crime, if he commits one; the whole sequence. Freedom is not a property of any one event of the temporal sequence; it is a property of the choice of the sequence as a whole.

> Now this acting subject [the transcendental Self] would not, in its intelligible character, stand under any conditions of time; time is only a condition of appearances, not of things in themselves. In this subject no *action* would *begin* or *cease*, and it would not, therefore, have to conform to the law of the determination of all that is alterable in time, namely that everything *which happens* must have its cause in the *appearances* which precede it.[18]

---

[17] Kant, *Critique of Pure Reason*, A533, B561.
[18] Kant, *Critique of Pure Reason*, A540, B508.

The doctrine of the mirror. From this notion of two-time orders, we derive the doctrine of the mirror: life is the mirror of the Self, it is the reflection in time of the transcendental Self in eternity. In "incarnate" life we experience the ego in time as the reflection of the Self. Then we mistake this ego for a substantive entity. This substance is found on examination be an illusion – to be anatta, impermanent. The essence of ego-illusion is to mistake the reflected image of the Self, the ego, for the Self itself and to come to believe that we are actually "in time" as a substantive entity, as a spiritual substance, a soul. Then, on discovering that this ego-soul has no substance and is anatta, impermanent, we experience a despair born of illusion. If we did not mistake the ego for the Self in the first place, we would not experience this despair.[19]

It may be argued that in Greek thought no such idea of two time-orders emerged, but in Plato's *Myth of Er*, we have an allegory that expresses something very close to what we just pictured above.[20] The story goes that Er, having died and witnessed the afterlife, was sent back to life to tell the living what happened after death. Er relates how after a thousand-year cycle of purification, the souls are presented with a choice of lives; how the foolish souls quickly grasp for the seemingly pleasant lives, only to discover that they will be replete with moral evils, while the wise, Odysseus for example, look out for the lives of private citizens or blessed animals, like swans. The point is: first the disembodied souls make their choice, then they live through

[19] Kant, *Critique of Pure Reason* A 541, B 569: "In its empirical character ... this subject, the self as appearance, would have to conform to all the laws of causal determination. To this extent it could be nothing more than a part of the world of sense, and its effects, like all other appearances, must be the inevitable outcome of nature. In proportion as outer appearances are found to influence it, and in proportion as its empirical character, that is, the law of its causality, becomes known through experience, all its actions must admit of explanation in accordance with the laws of nature. In other words, all that is required for their complete and necessary determination must be found in a possible experience.

In its intelligible character ... this same subject must be considered to be free from all influence of sensibility and from all determination through appearances. ... there can be no change in it requiring dynamical determination in time, and therefore no causal dependence on appearances. And consequently, since natural necessity is to be met with only in the sensible world, this active being must in its actions be independent of, and free from all such necessity. No action begins in this active being itself; but we may yet quite correctly say that the active being of itself begins its effects in the sensible world. ... in this way freedom and nature, in the full sense of these terms, can exist together, without any conflict, in the same actions, according as the actions are referred to their intelligible or to their sensible cause."

While Kant's solution is completely satisfactory, so far as regular thinking on this problem goes, I believe that it is not the concepts of freedom and freewill that are incoherent but our understanding of cause and effect, and of determinism. I do not see the law of conservation of energy, which is an expression of this determinism, written on tablets of stone. [See Part III, Chapter 18, Kantian consciousness and the spirit world.]

[20] Plato, *Republic*, Book X, 614 ff.

the inevitable consequences. In this there is implicit the notion of two time-orders, save that, in the allegory, the choice is placed at the beginning of the sequence, and not placed outside the sequence altogether.

In *Oedipus the King*, Oedipus punishes himself as if he were guilty, not of hubris, but of intentional crime of another kind. He does not punish himself as a murderer of a man he did not know, but as the murderer of his father, whom somehow, he did know, and as the lover of his mother, whom somehow he also did know. He knew all along, from the moment that he was mocked as a child for being a bastard, that he was destined to kill his father and marry his mother, and that is why the words of the Oracle drove him mad, and why he did not return to his foster parents, because he knew they were not his true parents, and that he would find his parents elsewhere. Oedipus does not, in this play, treat his own suffering as merely accidental. He acknowledges it as his guilt.

It is as if there are **multiple layers of transcendent personality**. At one layer, Oedipus is sinful man, suffering from hubris, and reaping the inevitable consequence. At another layer, Oedipus is the sage seeking god. Overall, his is a path of ascent, not descent, and he makes that ascent through a wall of pain; he seeks to know himself. He ascends through knowing himself as a sinner, that is, coming to terms with his imperfection, both as a man of hubris, and as a man destined to transgress through murder and incest. He experiences remorse and is saved by it.

9

Remorse and Despair

Remorse is the inward experience of sin. It is only when one touches remorse that one truly comes to know what it is to feel like a fallen being. Remorse is expressed by the thought, *I wish I had not done that.* The reality of the external world is experienced by us subjectively by the thought that our actions have consequences, that these do matter, and once done, an act cannot be undone.

Let us discuss remorse in the context of archetypes. An archetype or complex is a force in the psyche that lives through a mythologem. When an individual lives through a mythologem, the archetype directs choices and acts as the source of fulfilment. An issue is the degree of consciousness that we employ with it, and how we go about it. An archetype, being the expression of the transcendental Self reflected in the mirror of incarnate life, may like life itself be seen as the expression of the freedom of the Self. The mythologems present in a culture represent the range of life-patterns available to people at the time. Archetypes evolve. Over time, new archetypes come into being, existing archetypes split, no archetype, once present in consciousness, wholly fades out of it. The most elementary archetypes of all, so far as we can trace in mythology, are those of the Goddess – matriarch, and Dionysus – sacrificial man-god. Until Dionysus emerged, there may have been no archetype available to men, and the life of men was wholly subsumed in that of women. The **spiritual function of an archetype** is to raise consciousness. He or she who lives an archetype becomes a conscious individual. Even in the archetype of Dionysus man became a conscious individual.

Remorse is a powerful catalyst in the psyche, a dramatic awakening of consciousness, for it brings right to the foreground consciousness of moral pain, the reality of the world as the theatre of actions, where actions cannot be undone, only avoided and if not avoided, repented. Remorse is the most powerful form of pain; and it as far transcends physical pain as a mountain does a valley. We can only know this by living – those who have not experienced both physical and moral pain, cannot compare them. Remorse is qualitatively more painful than physical pain. "Who alone suffers, suffers most i' th' mind."[1] Physical pain once it passes, fades wholly out of consciousness as if it never existed, but remorse lingers in the memory and can torment it.

The archetypes of remorse. Remorse is a term reserved for the strongest form of regret for something done, a word said, an act. I garner the following synonyms of remorse: contrition, regret, repentance, penitence, guilt, bad conscience, compunction, rue, sorrow, shame, self-reproach, self-accusation, self-condemnation,

---

[1] Shakespeare, *King Lear*, III, vi, 105.

pangs of conscience. They all express various aspects of the psychological complex of remorse. The individual is presented with several archetypes when it comes to dealing with remorse.

(1) The **archetype of the sage**, or in Greek mythology, **the archetype of Tiresias**, the blind prophet of Thebes, emerged into Greek consciousness in the time of Hesiod and Homer. He appears in the *Odyssey*, where he is already the wisest man to have ever lived, the guide to the dead, associated with prophecy and the oracle of the dead. This archetype indicates the potential complexity of the situation of avoiding remorse altogether, for the way Tiresias has become a prophet, and hence has stepped outside the cycle of incarnate pain, is indicated to be by **passage through the wall of pain**. His suffering has already transformed him into the seer and man of wisdom, who can avoid the pain of remorse, and foresee the remorse that is the consequence of hubris in others, as in the role he plays in the drama of Oedipus.

(2) In the encounter with remorse, the individual may enact the archetype of self-inflicted punishment; the **archetype of atonement** in Greek mythology is the **archetype of Oedipus**. Through self-blinding, Oedipus becomes the sage. The mythologem involves enactment of the mythologem of hubris, followed by discovery of one's own guilt marked by an expansion of consciousness, followed by remorse, followed by self-inflicted punishment, symbolised by self-blinding, followed by **transcendence through self-knowledge** into the sage. His mythologem is barely distinguishable from that of Teiresias. Both endure the wall of pain, both are blinded, both morph into the sage. The complexity of the mythologem of Oedipus is that it encompasses another mythologem, like a complex molecule containing another molecule, and represents a transformation of archetypes. The **mythologem of hubris** involves: firstly, and above all ignorance. Oedipus is born into **a primal state of ignorance**: he does not know who he is, expressed in the symbol of not knowing who his real parents are. It is ignorance as to his real motives, expressed in not knowing that the man he kills is his father. It is also ignorance as to his passions, expressed in the madness in which he is driven from the Oracle, the passion with which he seeks to escape being taunted with bastardy, his avoiding returning to Corinth and his foster parents, and in the fury with which he commits a serial murder. He has strange luck – luck that is born of his apparent gifts, expressed in the symbol of overcoming **the riddle of the Sphinx**; defeating the monster that is the bane of the Theban people. This elevates him to king, the stimulus to **ego-inflation**, and gives him seeming power over his destiny, to be the author of his own being. In this, we perceive the **illusion of power**, for we understand that the gods are playing with him, and it is not Oedipus who has brought about this wonderful victory, but the gods who have allowed it, so that his hubris can become manifest. The riddle of the Sphinx:

Sphinx	What is the creature that walks on four legs in the morning, two legs at noon and three in the evening?
Oedipus	Man.

This answer of Oedipus is too objective and is the expression of his hubris. Not objectively, "Man", but subjectively, "I, myself, mortal man, man destined to become weak and die." Thus, the third part of the mythologem is the fall, the tragic discovery that the world is not the plaything of my ego, reality defies infantile wishes, I am not the author of my own being, I am guilty, I regret that which I have done, I have sinned against the authority of the cosmos. The enactment of this mythologem is the **archetype of the tragic hero**, the hubris is the **tragic flaw**, and the catastrophe is the **death of the hero**, who is thereby transformed and through his self-realisation and death transfigured into a happier fate in the life to come, **the winning of immortality.**[2]

(3) What if God or the gods, or the moral cosmos, do not exist? What if moral reality is a myth for schoolchildren, and there is nothing but an external world of nature, following its immutable laws of nature? This possibility cannot be excluded from the dialectic. It is what the popularisers of the modern material philosophy tell us; it is the metaphysics of contemporary culture. Hence, **denial of the mythologem of hubris** is a possibility: there are no archetypes, and there is no God or gods. It is the affirmation: I am limited in my individual power only by the limitations imposed on my physical body by nature and my social existence by other people. There is no right, other than that which is created by society, to which I am bound only as a social animal. Under this theory, there is no metaphysics of transgression. Society may punish a criminal, but God does not punish him as transgressor, for there is no God.

(4) The **archetype of Icarus** is the archetype of the failed child prodigy, though it can be acted out by an adult. The child-like person, child or adult, expects to scale Olympian heights, but comes crashing down, unable to realise the promised potential, and leading a mundane or enervated life. It is also the archetype of not amounting to very much in the end. We know the story – the "great man" who while alive is courted by popularity, but as soon as he dies his fame fades into oblivion.

---

[2] This is the fundamental pattern of Shakespearean tragedy, which ends in the death of the hero, but enacts the archetype of Oedipus. In Sophocles, Oedipus continues in life to become the sage, which is his role in *Oedipus at Colonus*. Shakespeare also gave expression to the fully developed archetype in the story of Leontes in *The Winter's Tale*. When Leontes's hubris leads him to falsely accuse his wife, Hermione, his son dies from the shock, and Hermione also appears to die. He goes through the cycle of remorse, self-inflicted punishment, atonement, and redemption. His wife comes back to life, his daughter is found, and he re-enters paradise. This is the Christian variant of the myth.

(5) The **archetype of the persistent sinner**, who is thereby punished. This mythologem has many variants. There is the story of Antinous in the *Odyssey*, the leader of the pack of suitors who persist in the crime of eating up the estate of another man under the pretext of legitimately courting his wife. He is the first to be struck down by Odysseus's arrow – killed in an instant, in the enjoyment of his ill-gotten gains – simply wiped out. This is **the symbol of pointless living**. A life not worth living. The fate of the inveterate sinner is developed in Greek mythology in the **archetype of Sisyphus**, the persistent **trickster**, who attempted to defy death twice, and is punished in eternity by **futility**: the task of rolling a stone up a hill, that always rolls back down again on the brink of success. The **mythologem of eternal damnation** evolves from this.

(7) Mythology treats of the case of an individual who persistently refuses to acknowledge the futility of the challenge to the supremacy of the gods, believing he can make himself the master of his own destiny. This archetype is developed in Greek mythology into **the mythologem of the rebellion of the giants**, the **archetype of Atlas** and the **archetype of Prometheus**; the latter, has a complex mythology that will need to be examined in detail. In Christian mythology it is developed into the **archetype of Lucifer**, the **arch rebel** against the authority of God. This archetype involves the wilful denial of remorse.[3]

The inalienability of remorse. This raises the question as to whether remorse is or is not inalienable. This is another dialectical question. From the material point-of-view, remorse is a biological reaction to a stimulus, and might, in the manner of other biological reactions be "curable" by physical intervention, for example, by taking a drug, or undergoing a course in behavioural therapy. The religious interpretation of remorse indicates that remorse is an inalienable aspect of man's psyche and is a gift of God. Under this conception, if remorse may be cured, the cure is repentance (regretting that the action was ever committed) and atonement (self-inflicted punishment for committing the action).

> Othello   I kissed thee, ere I killed thee: no way but this,
>   Killing myself, to die upon a kiss.[4]

This is **the religious attitude to remorse**, and it affirms the existence of God, the gods or the moral cosmos, invoking the blessing of these powers by self-inflicted humiliation and supplication.

---

[3] Iago in Shakespeare's play *Othello* exemplifies a man dominated by this archetype. Iago: "Demand me nothing; what you know, you know: / From this time forth I never will speak word." *Othello*, V, ii. 16-17.

[4] Shakespeare, *Othello*, V, iii, 375.

From the religious point-of-view, remorse activates the mythologem of **salvation through repentance**, and with the appearance of remorse in *Oedipus the King*, we are getting close to this greatest and most beneficial part of the Christian religion. The pattern is clear: Greek religion is transforming stage by stage into Christianity – for **Christianity is a Greek religion**.[5] This archetype of salvation is called **Christ** or **the archetype of Christ within**.

Remorse emerges in consciousness from the Self, or somewhere close to the Self, a part of it, or it is as if the Self were a part of something else – we might call that the godhead speaking to us, and the faculty through which remorse emerges is conscience – the voice of God in us; it is felt to be inalienable and coming both from within and without.

There is an attempt at a **phenomenology of emotions**, or an introduction to one, in Sartre's *Sketch for a Theory of Emotions*. This work is coloured by an attitude to the emotions that rejects them as a debasement of reason, as delusional and irrational. However, there is a great deal of observation in Sartre's work.

> We can now conceive what an emotion is. It is a transformation of the world. When the paths before us become too difficult, or when we cannot see our way, we can no longer put up with such an exacting and difficult world. All ways are barred and nevertheless we must act. So then we try to change the world; that is, to live it as though the relations between things and their potentialities were not governed by deterministic processes but by magic.[6]

Sartre observes the magical aspect of emotion; anger, for example, seeks to eliminate the source of an offence by the magical power of the emotion itself. Anger leads to curses, and a curse is an invocation of some magical power. Sartre, who belongs to the modern rationalist consciousness, hints that such magic can never be effective, so emotions are irrational.

Magical aspect of remorse. Remorse involves this magical aspect; by it the person expresses the wish magically to transform the past and undo the action that he regrets. But remorse acts as an invocation to a higher, metaphysical, supernatural power; it is a pleading for forgiveness, and by that means, a pleading to alter the world back to the situation that subsisted before the act was committed, not necessarily to make the act as if it never happened, but to restore it spiritually to the

---

[5] The transformations required to bring Christianity into being are found within Greek consciousness. [See Part III, Chapter 13, Plato, Judaism and Christianity.]

[6] Jean-Paul Sartre, *Sketch for a Theory of the Emotions*, Translated by Philip Mairet, Methuen & Co. Ltd., London, 1971, p.63.

state of purity that it had before. Sartre is an atheist; hence he does not believe in the efficacy of remorse, but a religious person does.

The **origin of conscience**. The reader will be aware of scientific or quasi-scientific accounts of conscience that trace its origin to socialisation of the individual. Freud's psychoanalytic theory makes conscience into **the superego**, the **conditioned inner voice of paternal authority** that arises through the repression of the "Oedipus complex". His theory is consistent with materialism, and some form of his theory – with or without the Oedipus complex – is the materialist answer to what conscience is – the internalisation of the rules of society, having no objective existence in the external world, however, subjectively powerful they may be.

When we examine remorse as it appears in consciousness, this appearance says nothing about **the origin of remorse** as such. The experience of an emotion may be compared to that of a sensation. A sensory object, such as the sight of a tree, when it appears in consciousness, we take to be a sign that the tree itself is external to ourselves, for the sight of the tree has the character of appearing to come from nature that exists independently of seeing it. On closer examination, we discover that the tree is only an appearance, and thereby we can consider the question whether reality external to consciousness exists or not.

The emotion of remorse appears to come from a source close to the Self, but not under control of the Self, hence in part appears external to the Self. The part that appears to be external is the judgement of conscience; the pain arising from knowledge and acceptance of this judgement is internal. The objective element is expressed in the fact that remorse is wholly outside our control. All emotions present themselves as arising spontaneously in us, and being to an extent outside our control, but only to an extent. We can learn to manage anger and even love, but there is no detachment from remorse once it has established itself. It can be manged only through repentance. Hence, its external aspect. Modern materialism has concluded that this external source does not exist. Yet, in the dialectic, it remains an open question whether remorse has an external source or not; from the experience of remorse itself, we cannot objectively locate its origin. The problem is dialectical.[7]

Despair. Is it possible to deny the experience of remorse? The individual is touched by remorse, touched strongly, but chooses not to regret.

---

[7] A significant visualisation of remorse in literature is *Crime and Punishment* by Dostoyevsky. The remorse Raskolnikov experiences for his crime of murder is not something that he can bring under control; only after many years is it diminished as is he brought back slowly to the sense of being a part of joyous life; this process is not one of bringing the emotion under control but is the experience of expiation of guilt through penitence. By this, Dostoyevsky implies an interaction with the godhead, and the operation of salvation. In the *Brothers Karamazov*, Ivan Karamazov is a character in remorse, but his ultimate fate is not given. Remorse is the constant theme of Shakespeare.

If remorse disappears quickly, and of its own accord, then it was never truly remorse in the first place. Remorse occurs when a person does something that he or she regrets, and that something cannot be undone, because it is past. The greater the sense of transgression against one's conscience, the greater the remorse. But if the thing that was supposed to have been done, never actually happened, then the remorse disappears immediately, for it was founded on an illusion. When remorse is real, then it is experienced as inalienable, for which the cure, if any, is penitence alone. But, a person may wilfully deny that he or she is in a state of remorse, and thus enter a state of self-deception. It is as if a person lost an arm but refused to accept that the arm was missing.

> A person with limb loss loses part of his or her physical self when they experience an amputation and the change in function and appearance are final. Physically, there is limb loss, stump pain, phantom pain and sensation.   Emotionally there is grieving, depression, anxiety, and poor body image. These challenges are common consequences of limb loss.   These symptoms can be worsened by the presence of phantom limb pain. ... Denial involves a failure to acknowledge the loss, or refusal to accept and adjust to the situation. These responses can increase negative thoughts, negative feelings, physical pain, and seeking needed help.[8]

The above deals with denial of a physical trauma. When remorse, a condition of the psyche, is denied, then the person enters a state of mind called despair. By denial of remorse is meant wilful denial of it, which is done in bad faith and involves an effort of will; hence, it involves processes of rationalisation – the wilful building of excuses, and because the remorse is the underlying reality, these excuses must be constantly worked over and reconstructed. The individual in this condition of pain invests increasingly greater portions of his or her time, energy and willpower into creating the false interpretation.   This is a state of self-deception: the person experiences remorse, but wilfully refuses to accept it. The denial of remorse is not a cure for remorse. Despair is a state worse than remorse itself. It multiplies the pain of remorse; it is self-inflicted pain whose aim is to remove another inalienable pain. It is **pain of pain**.

The conception of self-inflicted pain, whose exemplar is the state of despair, goes to the heart of the freewill defence as an answer to the problem of evil. The issue of natural evils, such as natural disasters, does not lie at the core of the problem of evil, for to blame God for the eruption of a volcano is transparently childish: our human reality is the reality of the inevitability of death. It must come some way. It is in the

---

[8] Anonymous.

human sphere that evil is problematic – the evil that one human commits against another – and it is this evil that we wish to blame upon the godhead. If there is a moral order to the cosmos, then that moral order permits the transgression of one man against another. Such permission is an aspect of the moral reality we encounter. A religious person must accept it. In the case of the self-inflicted pains of the psychological type, of which despair is the core of all, we seem to get an insight into the very nature of the moral problem of freewill. From the phenomenological point-of-view, we experience ourselves as to an extent free – possessed of a power of making things happen not otherwise subject to cause. The freewill that I possess is strongly expressed in the power I have, to assent or dissent from belief. I can **choose to believe**.

Remorse is the judgement in good faith that one has transgressed, combined with the emotive wish that a past action as if by magic had never happened. **Despair is in bad faith, wilfully denying remorse.** The pain in remorse is the pain of knowing that the past cannot be undone. The pain in despair is the pain of knowing that the remorse that is denied cannot be removed by denial.

I have read a contemporary piece of sophistry that there can be no self-deception because it involves contradiction. In self-deception a person both knows and does not know something. For example, the person who denies the loss of a limb knows that the limb has been lost but feels pain in that limb.

If there is a contradiction in self-deception, then it may merely show that the law of non-contradiction does not apply in this case. However, we do not need to go so far, for we understand clearly how self-deception occurs. The judgement that I regret an action I have done forces itself upon the mind, like the missing arm in the mirror, but the mind refuses to pay attention to the judgement, and pushes it away from itself, by an act of will. At the same time, it wilfully brings to awareness another judgement, such as, I am feeling pain in that arm, and forces itself to attend to it. We describe this situation by saying that the person pushes into his or her unconscious the judgement that the limb is missing, and by effort of the will brings to consciousness the judgement that there is pain in that limb. In the case of despair, the wilful aspect of believing excuses for an action that if not maintained by constant effort of the will would collapse as illusions is more evident still. The terms "unconscious" and "conscious" are potentially confusing, for what is unconscious is not wholly eliminated from awareness but is something that presents itself dimly. However, for convenience we say, the judgement, I am in a state of remorse, is unconscious, and the judgement, I am excused from the action that would otherwise make me feel remorse, is conscious. There is no contradiction in self-deception, and self-deception is not merely an accidental feature of human nature but its fundamental expression.

We are always making self-judgements. Whenever we transgress against our conscience there is just such a judgement. Whether we attend to that judgement or not, is the second step. This raises the question: are there people who have no conscience; does the faculty of conscience vary from one individual to another, like IQ? Could we have a "conscience quotient"? Do not children have less developed conscience than adults, and are held to be not morally responsible until they have matured? What of the evolution of conscience? Did the Carthaginians, when they sacrificed their children as first-fruits to Tanith and Baal, do so believing that they were in conscience discharging a religious duty, or against conscience committing sacrilege for the sake of fertile crops or victory in war? To the materialist all these questions are signs that conscience is a social construct; but we are not here concerned with the materialist solution, but with the inward, phenomenological character of conscience. We seek to understand the religious response.

To say that ethics is **absolute** is to say that the same moral rules apply at all times and in all situations. Reaching into the core of ethics, certainly I say that pace Kant, transgression against one's neighbour is morally wrong, and it has never been right to ritually murder another human being for the sake of good crops, or because one believes that the gods have commanded it. On the other hand, our intimate connection with such rules is **relative**. Our individual lives tell us that we were once children, and that our moral understanding was once childish, that the whole history of mankind has been one of evolving consciousness, and hence, there is an evolution in the relationship of conscience to the source of its dictates; an evolution in our relationship to the moral order.

Hence, the punishment inflicted by conscience on the transgressor is relative to the state of cognition of that transgressor. An individual in a state of Neolithic consciousness may commit the sacrilege of ritual murder, maenads may, possessed by the deity, rend limb from limb their victim and consume his flesh raw, and yet suffer no pangs of conscience. Consciousness of guilt in transgression arises relative to the cognition that it is a transgression at a stage in the evolution of cognition. When the archetype of justice arises, then, and only then, becomes it possible to experience the taking of life as a transgression. When Themistocles plunged the knife of ritual sacrifice into the three Persian captives prior to the battle of Salamis (for we take the story to be the narration of real events), did he know that he was committing a sacrilege? Were there those among the witnesses of that horror who were also aware of this as sacrilege, and hence felt themselves to be contaminated by participation in the spectacle? I think we can answer "yes" to both questions – in Euripides's portrayal of Agamemnon in *Iphigenia at Aulis* for example, Agamemnon knows it to be a sin to sacrifice his daughter; yet, he still commits it.

Is **atavism** – reversion to an earlier state of cognition and religious consciousness – an escape from remorse? It can be no escape, for once consciousness has evolved, it does not revert. One cannot to escape the pangs of remorse by wilfully forgetting the very fabric of what one already conceives and knows. I can't will myself in the state of supposing that my actions were committed while possessed by the deity, and hence, are not my actions. This is not a defence against remorse. Nor is it a benefit to be in a more primitive state of cognition, like the cannibal. For that is to be lost in the state of cannibalism.

The phenomenology of remorse and conscience tells us that life is spiritual progress, and that we are always progressing from a lower to a higher state in consciousness. If we adopt the Eastern view of things, and suppose that we pass through countless lives, this leads us to the idea of a spiritual evolution terminating in some future state of release – of emancipation from the cycle of human existence – the attainment of nirvana. We of the West are not obliged to go this far; it is sufficient only that my inward reflection teaches me that this life, the one I am leading here and now, is a path of progressive elevation of consciousness. That is enough to tell me all I need to know. The Eastern myth of reincarnation has the merit of showing us that being at an earlier stage in the evolution of conscience is no boon. Perhaps one is spared the pains of remorse, but only because one belongs to a more elementary stage. It is no way out to have not even begun. The only way out is upwards, though the deliberate exercise of consciousness to attain a heightened awareness of conscience. Thus, there is a "conscience quotient", and some have more evolved conscience than others. For the evolved conscience, transgression leads one to experience remorse in all its fury; the devil experiences the greatest remorse of all, because he has the most heightened conscience of all.

Faustus	Where are you damn'd?
Mephistopheles	In hell.
Faustus	How comes it then that thou art out of hell
Mephistopheles.	Why this is hell, nor am I out of it.
	Think'st thou that I who saw the face of God,
	And tasted the eternal joys of Heaven,
	Am not tormented with ten thousand hells,
	In being depriv'd of everlasting bliss?
	O Faustus! leave these frivolous demands,
	Which strike a terror to my fainting soul.[9]

The more aware you are, the greater the potential for the pangs of conscience. But there are benefits too, for elevated conscience enables one to foretell and forestall consequences. Moral consequences of actions are predictable, as is the remorse that goes with them. Remorse becomes avoidable. "What goes around comes around" is all too true. This is wisdom. We learn too that the best policy of self-interest is to follow the path that avoids remorse. With the raising of consciousness to the experience of conscience, remorse becomes possible. Then, with remorse, self-

[9] Christopher Marlowe, *Doctor Faustus*, I, iii, 71 – 80.

inflicted pain and punishment become possible through denial, and thus, despair is constellated as a possible state of consciousness.

Phenomenology reveals that despair has a metaphysics. The mythologem of hubris as a narrative symbol has elements: 1. Hubris, 2. Ego-inflation, 3. Crisis and discovery, 4. Tragic fall. Remorse occurs from the third stage onwards, which may be followed by death – the fate of the hero in tragedy – or of further development: 5. Reconciliation and redemption, and transformation into the sage, or 6. Denial and despair. What does the whole cycle tell us about despair? During the first two stages, the foundation of the problem is exposed; it is what we call "playing at being god". Ego-inflation is the stage where everything seems to support that illusion, where things go swimmingly well, and one is getting away, even literally, with murder. Then there is the discovery that brings on remorse, which is inalienable. What does remorse tell us? That we are not all powerful, we cannot be god, and that our very being depends on another power, call it God, the godhead, or the very nature of things. Remorse instructs us that we are not a substance. It instructs the individual to seek healing through penitence, that is, by dependence, upon the power whose existence in hubris the individual denied. Whatever it is that I am, I am a dependent thing. I am not the author of my own being, I cannot make myself the author of my own being, I cannot will my soul into existence, I can only acknowledge my dependency upon the cosmos and live in harmony with that dependency. Being a dependent being, I may not transgress against other dependent beings. But it is possible to deny all of this, and then despair.

> In order to want in despair to be oneself, there must be consciousness
> of an infinite self. However, this infinite self is really only the most
> abstract form of the self, the most abstract possibility of the self. And
> it is this self the despairer wants to be, severing the self from any
> relation to the power which has established it, or severing it from the
> conception that there is such a power. By means of this infinite form,
> the self wants in despair to rule over himself, or create himself, make
> his self the self he wants to be, determine what he will have and what
> he will not have in his concrete self.[10]

It is an illusion that the ego is a substance; mistaking the ego for a substance we identify it as a spiritual substance, a soul. Then, in hubris, we assume that the substance of the soul is brought into existence by the soul itself, that through self-consciousness we are the author of our own substance. Our substance thereby is imagined not to depend on anything. But remorse confronts the individual with all

---

[10] Soren Kierkegaard, *The Sickness unto Death*, translated Alastair Hannay, Penguin, London, 1989, p. 99.

these illusions and demonstrates the dependence of the self upon another power. We only exist because we are permitted to exist.

Despair is in bad faith, wilfully denying remorse, wanting, in remorse, to be the author of one's own being, and to have the power to act without moral limitation; despair is wanting, in remorse, to be a self-substantial, self-created being.

10

Prometheus

Prometheus Bound, attributed to Aeschylus, discusses the problem of evil.[1] Whether by Aeschylus or not, it registers profound religious transformations in the archetypes under the pressure of theological debate. The background theology conforms to Hesiod: the Olympians have come to power as the latest in a series of dynasties, a reminder that the Greeks themselves acknowledged an epoch when the Olympians were not the masters in Heaven, and the Titans are an older power. The moral purpose of Zeus is to govern with justice. Zeus holds that the human race is corrupt and must be destroyed to make way for a more perfect race.[2] This hints at the corruption due to the ritual practices of the earlier epoch. Prometheus represents a break on that advance, a force antagonistic to Zeus, preventing the high god from dispensing justice, and a new moral revelation, that mankind must be saved. The play savours some elements of the Manichaean response to the problem of evil, for Zeus, while powerful, is not all powerful. He has not yet become the "Almighty". However, the play dissolves the dualist conflict of justice and rebellion, by resolution in a third force. Zeus is subject to Fate; the supreme power is Necessity.

> Chorus: And whose hand on the helm controls Necessity?
> Prometheus: The three Fates; and the Furies, who forget nothing.
> Chorus: Has Zeus less power than they?
> Prometheus: He cannot fly from Fate.

Zeus is not omniscient. Prometheus has knowledge of Zeus's intended marriage that will bring about another dynastic change, and the downfall of Zeus, unless it is

---

[1] Strength and Violence, who drag in Prometheus, are required, under the management of Hephaestus, to bind Prometheus to a rock. Hephaestus pities Prometheus and does his work reluctantly. Prometheus protests loudly against the cruelty of Zeus, as he does throughout. He relates to the chorus of the daughters of Oceanus that he was able to foresee the victory of the Gods over the Titans and with his mother, Earth, joined Zeus and counselled him. He prophesies that Zeus will fall unless the secret he knows is revealed and proposes to bargain for his freedom. Oceanus counsels him to throw himself upon the mercy of Zeus and offers to intercede on his behalf. Prometheus refuses. Io, the priestess of Argos, enters. She has been driven mad by the lust of Zeus and the punishment of Hera. At her behest and that of the chorus, Prometheus tells not only what has already happened, but what will happen to her: mad wanderings until she is released from her pain and becomes the bride of Zeus. It is her descendant that will liberate Prometheus. The play concludes with the visit of Hermes: Zeus wishes to know what the marriage shall be that will be disastrous for him. Prometheus refuses to give the answer. The further punishment of having his liver devoured by an eagle is pronounced. Prometheus willingly accepts it and is defiant to the end.

[2] An argument we expect would have been developed in the lost sequel, *Prometheus Unbound*.

prevented. The Earth, from which Prometheus also draws his power of prophecy, is another power that is not directly subject to Zeus. It is an older power, from which are begotten the race of Titans and their champions, Typhon and Atlas. In this play, Zeus is akin to a demi-urge, but not a demi-urge, for he has had no part in creation. Zeus is a servant of a higher power, brought to reign by Necessity, and can survive only in so far as he obeys that power.

Punishment, however cruel, is not arbitrary but self-inflicted; it is the sin of pride that is the cause of the position Prometheus finds himself in – the "Kierkegaardian motif" that interprets despair as self-begotten sin of sin. Prometheus, despite his crime, could appeal for mercy, and it is his increasing pride that prevents him from doing so.[3] He is in a state of despair born of defiance. So great is his defiance, that remorse does not appear to enter his thoughts, a measure of his arrogance as he builds a web of illusions to justify his rebellion.[4] He revels in his achievements, and arrogantly claims to have put Zeus on his throne. He will use his knowledge as a weapon to bargain *as an equal* his way out of his prison and punishment.

Prometheus is wracked by pain that he inflicts upon himself by not submitting to Necessity. The theme of the play is *insanity*, and hence the inclusion of the myth of Io in the plot, which is doubly indicated by the fact that Io is the ancestor of Heracles, the hero who will save both Prometheus and Zeus from the consequences of this conflict.[5] Nonetheless, Hermes is right when he states, "It's plain that your insanity is far advanced. / Time has not taught *you* self-control or prudence – yet." The sufferings of Io appear more difficult to comprehend. She appears as the victim of the arbitrary lust of Zeus, and it seems another manifestation of Zeus's tyranny, which is the way Prometheus chooses to interpret it. The Chorus is wiser and gives us the key to the mystery: "That the best rule by far is to marry in your own rank." There is something illicit in Io's love that makes her punishment also self-inflicted. It is the price of ambition.

Strength describes Prometheus as the "rebel". Prometheus is the arch rebel – the defiant god who opposes Zeus – dubbed by Hephaestus as "A god, the enemy of Zeus." According to Prometheus, there has been a series of unlawful dynastic changes in Heaven, that Zeus is the usurper, and that he, Prometheus, stands for the

---

[3] Oceanus tells Prometheus: Then know yourself, / And take upon yourself new ways to suit the time. / … Oh, my unhappy friend, / Throw off your angry mood and seek deliverance / From all your suffering. What I say may seem perhaps / Well worn; but your plight is the inescapable / Reward, Prometheus, of a too proud-speaking tongue. / You will not be humble, will not yield to pain; / You mean to add new sufferings to those you have.

[4] Prometheus: Bow! Pray! As always, fawn upon the powerful hand! / For great Zeus I care less than nothing. Let him do / And govern as he wills, for the short time he has. / Do you think I quake and cower before these upstart gods?

[5] Heracles fights for the gods against the giants in the final rebellion of the earthly powers against Olympian rule, and subsequently liberates Prometheus.

rightful rulers. His thoughts are expressed by the chorus: "Zeus tyrannically rules / And the great powers of the past he now destroys." It is one step only from this to the words of Satan: "Better to rule in Hell than serve in Heaven."[6] Prometheus falls short of a being that could be identified with Satan because he acts alone in defiance of the higher power and not as a leader.[7]

Hubris and pride are clearly marked out as the primordial sins of mankind, and Prometheus is not only the champion of mankind, but also its representative.[8] By giving fire to mankind, Prometheus has given it the ability to stand against the gods and be, in some measure, independent of them. By means of fire mankind has gained the ability to unleash the power of nature. As Prometheus says, with fire "They shall master many crafts." But, just for this reason, it is also correct to say, then, that fire is a gift that mankind *should not possess*, and that to grant it to them is contrary to the will of heaven.

So far as the quarrel goes, then, Zeus is right to act as he does, for according to his conception mankind is a corrupt race that should be eradicated, and he is only the instrument of the punishment of Prometheus, which is self-inflicted. But Zeus can be supplanted because there is yet a higher power and a higher wisdom that he does not know. The destiny of man and god is woven together by Necessity, and if Zeus ignores this then he will also come crashing down. If mankind is the creation of an earlier race of gods, so be it, but once created mankind cannot be arbitrarily destroyed or cast aside to make way for some utopian scheme. This is the rule of love, or sympathy, which Zeus himself does not yet know. He is still young in his power. Prometheus acting out of sympathy, compassion or love, has become the saviour of mankind.[9] But his "love" is infected with his pride. He consults no "bigger picture", and while sympathy is a strong element in his character, pride is even stronger.

Prometheus is a prototype for the dying god, who sacrifices himself out of love for mankind. We see the emergent archetype of Christ. The functions of this second archetype are also carried by the super-hero of Greek religion, Heracles, the *son of god*, who will fight on behalf of the gods, and liberate Prometheus. Then in relation to Heracles, Prometheus becomes *sinful mankind*, released from its torments by the

---

[6] Milton, *Paradise Lost,* I, 263.

[7] Prometheus: My appointed fate I must endure as best I can, / Knowing the power of Necessity is irresistible. / ... And fire has proved / For men a teacher in every art, their grand resource. / That was the sin for which I now pay the full price, / Bared to the winds of heaven, bound and crucified.

[8] Chorus: But I shudder when I see you, Prometheus, / Racked by infinite tortures. / For you have no fear of Zeus, / But pursuing your own purpose / You respect too highly the race of mortals.

[9] Prometheus: Of wretched humans he [Zeus] took no account, resolved / To annihilate them and create another race. / This purpose there was no one to oppose but I: / I dared. I saved the human race from being ground / To dust, from total death.

love of *the son of God*. The play is founded on the opposition of three pairs of archetypes.

Zeus	**Prometheus as Satan/Lucifer**
Protagonist	Antagonist
Justice	Rebel, the Unforgiven, the Crucified

Prometheus as the dying god	**Mankind**
"Son of God"	Chosen of God
The Crucified	That for which the sacrifice is made

Heracles as Saviour	**Prometheus as the Saved**
Son of God	The accursed
The Redeemer	The redeemed

Implicitly, there is a transcendent deity, called Necessity, but as the play rejects arbitrary punishment, it follows that this Necessity must be Love in another guise. Viewed from this higher perspective, mankind must also have a higher purpose, and this is reflected in the myth that the gods can only be saved by the help of a mortal hero, which shall be Heracles. Prometheus does not know everything. This is represented both by the Chorus of the daughters of Oceanus and by Oceanus himself, who may be a representative of the transcendent role. Love is also represented by the compassion of Hephaestus. Love is the transcendent force of the play, the transcendent aspect of the godhead that moves the protagonists even without their knowledge.

The elevation of Heracles into the saviour of the Olympian gods, is an interesting development in Greek consciousness – that the gods themselves should depend upon a mortal saviour. As Zeus came to be elevated to God Almighty, the transcendent deity which he is not here, his salvation became unnecessary; the ultimate power of the cosmos needs no saviour. But the Olympian gods did need a saviour, and having not found one, they were not deleted from religious consciousness, but with the advent of Christianity, relegated to demons. I shall subsequently argue that the gods as archetypes depend for their existence on mankind.[10]

The archetype of Christ. Christ is a complex archetype, and amalgam of the archetypes of Dionysus as the dying god, Prometheus, as the crucified saviour of mankind and Heracles as the ethical superhero. This explains the power of the Christ archetype, because it is a fusion of other already potent archetypes. As Christ acts wholly out of universal Love, he becomes the archetype of the embodiment of Divine Love on earth, the archetypal Son of God, as in the Trinity.

---

[10] [See Part III, Chapter 18, Kantian consciousness and the spirit world.]

11

Orphism

Early influence of Phoenicia. In Phoenician religion, first-born male children were ritually burned alive in propitiation of the Goddess, called Tanith at Carthage. The Greeks had many myths connecting their pre-Greek ancestors with Phoenicia and the near-East, such as the **myth of Cadmus**, the founder of Thebes, who came from Tyre, and the tradition that **the worship of Hera at Argos** was introduced by the first king there, Inarchus, an immigrant from Egypt.[1] His daughter Io, beloved by Zeus, turned into a cow by the jealousy of Hera, is said to have wandered over the whole known world, from Egypt to the Caucasus. The Greeks understood their race to have arisen from the fusion of peoples and that the indigenous peoples, the Pelasgians, were initially lead by immigrants from Egypt and Phoenicia who introduced their religion and founded their principal cities, Argos and Thebes being among these.

    The reformation during the Dark Age of Greece. As the practice of human sacrifice is firmly attested in the religion of the Greeks into the Mycenaean period, and no longer appears in Olympian Greek religion at the time of Homer (c.700), then it follows that a reformation took place.

    Orpheus. The reformation involves the awakening of collective conscience to the sacrilege of human sacrifice, and rejection of it. It is associated by Jane Ellen Harrison with an actual person, Orpheus.[2] **Melampus** is another mythical character who may be connected to a historical person. In his myth he is said to have twice cured the women of Argos of the Dionysiac madness and is said to have become one of three kings there as a result. The myth points also to a reformation of the rites of Artemis. I suggest that the events described are traces of historical events belonging to the Dark Age and projected backwards onto legendary time. Historical events were melded with mythologems of murder and sacrifice that belonged to remoter times, so the myth of Melampus is another "layered text", akin to that of the myth of Heracles.[3]

    The reformation is associated with the rise of patriarchy. We live at the end of a three-thousand-year cycle of patriarchy, so it is scarcely possible for us to imagine a consciousness in which the male-principle is not dominant but absorbed by the female-principle. In the remote times of the Neolithic Near East, we see only one

---

[1] Scholia on Euripides and Sophocles. William Smith, *A New Classical Dictionary of Greek and Roman Biography, Mythology and Geography,* Harper, New York, 1862. Entry on Inarchus.

[2] [See chapter 17, The reformation of the Greek Dark Age.]

[3] In the late epic poem *Dionysiaca* by Nonnus (c.late C4, early C5 CE) both Lycurgus (Sparta) and Perseus (Argos) are enemies of Dionysus and like Pentheus at Thebes battle with him. These could be late survivals of a genuine tradition that explains what the archetype of Perseus overcame. In Nonnus's version Perseus turns Ariadne into stone.

form of religion, the dominant worship of the Mother Goddess. What do the myriads of the Venus figurines attest to but to the power of the female principle in the psyche, and an overwhelming obsession with her magic power of producing life? But as early as 3,000 in Egypt, with the rise of the first dynasty, the male god-king is married in partnership to his sister goddess-queen; even at this early time masculine consciousness has obtained a degree of differentiation from the mother archetype.

We can see in the Dionysus archetype a splitting of the masculine principle from the feminine. Man becomes prominent, not as an independent person with separate rights of self-preservation, but as the sacrificial consort god-king of the Goddess, as Adonis, Osiris, or Attis. Yet, at least, he is important, for the fertility of nature depends on the shedding of his blood. It is the origin of **the archetype of self-sacrifice** for the sake of the community. The next postulated evolution is found in the first form of the Heracles archetype. Originally, Heracles must have been the name of a local incarnation of Dionysus, notably at Argos where he was sacrificed to Hera, but when he began to enact the mythologem of ritual murder of his rival, the predecessor king, either to replace him, or to be driven out of the city as ritually polluted with blood to be hunted down and murdered, by this means man won a further measure of independence. In the archetype of Poseidon, man acquires another more elevated status, as the capable husband of the Goddess. He has secured his personal survival, and perhaps the onerous duty of sacrifice has been pushed onto those least capable of defending themselves, the first-born male children.

After that came the reformation of the Greek matriarchal cult of Dionysus, of ritual male sacrifice, into its chthonic form, arising and running parallel to the Olympian religion of Homer. In this chthonic form the originally bloody rites of Dionysus were mutated into less harmful forms of symbolic sacrifice and sacred rites, and where blood was demanded, the burden fell on animals, or is expressed in symbolic rituals, such as flogging, or the cutting of hair.

The survival of archaic forms of the religion of Dionysus. The evidence indicates that the reformation took place over a protracted period, and even in later times the original religion of Dionysus survived.

The purification of Epimenides. The story of Epimenides of Crete that is related in Plutarch's account of the life of Solon is instructive.

> He made the Athenians more punctilious in their religious worship and more restrained in their rites of mourning; he did this by immediately introducing certain sacrifices into their funeral ceremonies and by abolishing the harsh and barbaric practices in which Athenian women had indulged up to that time. But his greatest service, which he achieved by various rites of atonement and purification and by erecting places of worship, was to sanctify and

consecrate the city and to make the people more amenable to justice and better disposed to live in harmony with one another.[4]

I suggest that the mention of "harsh and barbaric practices" alludes to the continuation of the bloody rites of Dionysus even late into this period, and the passage indicates that the subjugation and subordination of women that we associate with classical Athens was by no means complete at the time of Solon (c.638 – c.558). Epimenides is a semi-mythical figure, but the events described above are consonant with real historical processes and fit the pattern of the subsequent **purification of Delos** under Peisistratus. A clear reference to the continuation of the bloody rites of Dionysus is found in Plutarch's life of the Athenian general Themistocles (c.524 – 459), who commanded the Greek ships at the battles of Artemisium and Salamis in 480 during the Persian War.

> But Themistocles was sacrificing alongside the admiral's trireme. There three prisoners of war were brought to him, of visage most beautiful to behold, conspicuously adorned with raiment and with gold. They were said to be the sons of Sandauce, the King's sister, and Artayctus. When Euphrantides the seer caught sight of them, since at one and that same moment a great and glaring flame shot up from the sacrificial victim and a sneeze gave forth its good omen on the right, he clasped Themistocles by the hand and bade him consecrate the youths, and sacrifice them all to Dionysus Carnivorous, with prayers of supplication; for on this wise would the Hellenes have a saving victory. Themistocles was terrified, feeling that the word of the seer was monstrous and shocking; but the multitude, who, as is wont to be the case in great struggles and severe crises, looked for safety rather from unreasonable than from reasonable measures, invoked the god with one voice, dragged the prisoners to the altar, and compelled the fulfilment of the sacrifice, as the seer commanded. At any rate, this is what Phanias the Lesbian says, and he was a philosopher, and well acquainted with historical literature.[5]

It has been suggested that this account is a slur upon the reputation of Themistocles; but, Plutarch in the passage attempts to clear Themistocles of complicity to an extent, and what we know about the cult of Dionysus, here specifically called *Dionysus Carnivorous*, indicates that the events are historical in the tradition of

---

[4] Plutarch, *Solon*, 12, 5
[5] Plutarch, *Themistocles*, 13, 2-4.

human sacrifice that could and would surface at times of crisis.[6] We also see the role
played here by the collective mass, the entrapment of the leaders by the need to
propitiate the savage and superstitious humour of the collective, so much deplored
by Euripides in his work, and an indicator of the conflict between the collective and
the individual.[7]

Ionian dualism.   The period of moral reformation of the cult of Dionysus
overlaps that of the Ionian revolution in cognition that brings about the separation of
external and internal and makes it possible to conceive of the separation of soul from
body as distinct substances.

The ethical distance between primitive and Ionian cognition.   The idea that
the soul is a different kind of substance from the body not only makes it possible in
cognition to think of diverse ways in which the separation of soul from body at death
can take place, it also brings into consciousness the question of how soul comes to
be incarnate at birth.   In primitive consciousness such questions do not arise; the
problem of the introduction of the soul at birth is not even raised; at death, the soul
goes to its tomb, or somewhere, and can be useful to the living, as an oracle.   The
long-term destination of the soul is not considered; the concept of infinity is not
known; the living are concerned only with life, and how the dead may by useful or
harmful to them.

Orphism.   The idea that the soul has been contaminated by its association with
the body gives rise to **the second reformation of the religion of Dionysus**, the one
that   is   known   as   Orphism.   Ionian   dualism   made   possible   the   idea   of
metempsychosis, **the transmigration of souls**, and the possibility of incarnation in
animals. It is associated with **Pythagoras** (c.570–495).[8] There is sufficient evidence

---

[6] Jane Ellen Harrison remarks that it may have been a slur on the character of Themistocles by
Plutarch's source, philosopher and historian, Phanias of Eresus (active c. 330). I take the events to be
historical. Harison's remark occurs in chapter X of her *Prolegomena.* She also remarks that the story
shows that human sacrifice was conceivable in the C4. Roman history also attests examples of human
sacrifice in parallel circumstances. [The earlier discussion of denial in Chapter 12, No consensus
among the scholars is relevant. See also Chapter 19, Roman religion.]

[7] Further evidence for the long continuance of ecstatic worship at Athens by women is also found in
the following attack by Demosthenes (384 – 322) on his political opponent Aeshcines: "On attaining
manhood you abetted your mother in her initiations and the other rituals, and read aloud from the
cultic writings ... You rubbed the fat-cheeked snakes and swung them above your head, crying *Euoi
saboi* and *hues attes, attes* hues." Demosthenes, *De corona* 260. Demosthenes is the Athenian orator
who was opposed the expansion of Macedonia under Philip and Alexander the Great.   The
expressions quoted by Demosthenes relate to the cult of Dionysus Sabazios. This cult appears to
originate in Asia Minor, and is attested there, but it is also home-spun and universal, belonging to
Athens from time immemorial. Similar events occurred at Rome during the second Carthaginian war.

[8] He was born in Samos, and a pupil of Pherecydes, a Syrian. Legend has it that he studied in Egypt
and on his return, visited the Idaean Cave in Crete accompanied by Epimenides. Then he went to
Babylon. Cicero reports he visited the Persian Magi. According to Apuleius he also visited the
Brahmins. Porphyry reports that Pythagoras visited the Arabians, Hebrews and Chaldaeans. Clement

behind his legend to attest to the existence of Pythagoras as a historical person who travelled widely. The special status of the soul makes it possible to think of it at death as firstly occupying a plane of existence set quite apart from the physical and geographical regions of the living, and then migrating between this region and life. In primitive dualism[9] the soul at death simply departs the body and goes somewhere else, all such processes taking place at the material level. The primitive does not think of himself as incarnate at all; he is a body with his soul, as opposed to a detached soul. But in the Pythagorean picture, the soul departs first to a separate region, and then re-enters another body. This gives rise to the idea that the soul has now migrated between different bodies over countless cycles of birth, death and re-birth and has pre-existed its current incarnation.

Pythagoreanism is the philosophic branch of Orphism. It reforms the Dionysiac cult into a mystical doctrine of the purification of souls, with practices designed to prevent the soul from being reincarnated and thus empower it to achieve release from the cycle of birth and death. These ideas are usually connected in culture with India and suggest that Pythagoras may have learned them there. He would be a **vector of transmission** also of ideas originating in Persia. It is no new thesis of mine that Christianity is in all essence a Greek religion arising in the context of the Pythagorean reformation of Orphism, transforming that religion into a doctrine of asceticism.[10]

Conflation of temporal with eternal time. It may be objected that the idea of transmigration of souls conflates two time-orders of temporal time and eternal time. For, at death, it suggests that the soul reverts first to a non-temporal condition in

---

of Alexander reports that Pythagoras embraced the doctrines of the Indians. There is supporting evidence for his wide travels from Lucian, Pliny, Strabo, Iamblichus and Isocrates. On return he left Samos and went to Crotana in Italy. This was probably because Samos under Persian Darius was no longer governed by Syloran. Aulus Gelinus and Solinus place Pythagoras in Italy at the time of Tarquin the Proud and the rebellion of Brutus. On a visit to Sicily he is reported to have said, "I am a lover of wisdom" and that philosophers seek truth.

[9] [See Part I, Chapter 6 on primitive materialism, where its consistency with primitive dualism is explained.]

[10] Bertrand Russell in *History of Western Philosophy,* (George Allen & Unwin 1946) writes: "They aimed at becoming "pure," partly by ceremonies of purification, partly by avoiding certain kinds of contamination. The most orthodox among them abstained from animal food, except on ritual occasions when they ate it sacramentally. Man, they held, is partly of earth, partly of heaven; by a pure life the heavenly part is increased and the earthly part diminished. In the end a man may become one with Bacchus, and is called "a Bacchus." ... The Orphics were an ascetic sect; wine, to them, was only a symbol, as, later, in the Christian sacrament. The intoxication that they sought was that of "enthusiasm," of union with the god. They believed themselves, in this way, to acquire mystic knowledge not obtainable by ordinary means. This mystical element entered into Greek philosophy with Pythagoras, who was a reformer of Orphism as Orpheus was a reformer of the religion of Dionysus. From Pythagoras Orphic elements entered into the philosophy of Plato, and from Plato into most later philosophy that was in any degree religious."

what we might call eternity, and thence re-enters temporal time. I think we do see this conflation, and we see it most clearly in the most important survival texts of the Pythagorean and Orphic tradition – which are the dialogues of Plato. The problem is a lack of clarity as much as anything else, for transmigration is not incoherent, it simply lacks articulation.

(1) In Cartesian dualism the soul is a spiritual substance that persists in time, thus it is not inconceivable that it reverts to another place in time, and then shortly after re-enters another material body. It is this form of dualism that is implicit in the Orphic religion and the philosophy of Plato.[11]

(2) The idea of a separate time-order of eternity emerges in Western consciousness in the work of Kant, but otherwise in Buddhist literature, some of which may be contemporaneous with Ionian sources. However, the idea of transmigration of souls is also coherent under this hypothesis. It states that the soul, not substance, but pure Self, must re-incarnate itself to fulfil certain karmic patterns initiated in the preceding life. Buddhist-Hindu philosophy indicates that this soul-Self may be "transported" anywhere in the cosmos; theoretically, it could be incarnated in times that would be seen as past in the temporal order from our point in time, or it may be incarnated in other regions. Any region is called a *loka*, which derives from the Sanskrit word for "world" and designates any plane of existence. Buddhist-Hindu philosophy affirms that there are many *loka*. At death, the soul-Self may migrate to any one of these.

(3) Even if one clearly grasps that spiritual substance requires no physical location, the long habit of thinking in terms of physical geography will condition the mind to picture the afterlife of the soul as a journey to and from other physical regions. The term "transported" has been scare-quoted above, because it is a metaphor, transportation being strictly a relation in time. When we think about eternity, we see that normal temporal relations cannot apply, but there may yet be relations in eternity. There is a long tradition that thought about spiritual matters can and must be conducted by means of analogies and allegories; we can only picture the journey of the soul-Self by such devices. Plato does refer to his stories as allegories and myths – for example, the allegory of the chariot in *The Phaedrus*, the allegory of the cave in *The Republic* and the Myth of Er also in *the Republic*. Plato, the most conscious of all these religious writers, is explicit that his descriptions are not to be

---

[11] Modern philosophers sometimes argue, pace Wittgenstein, Ryle and others, that dualism is incoherent. This is done from the vantage of the philosophy of language by assuming an empiricist theory of meaning that renders all metaphysical concepts meaningless, which is circular and "begs the question". Wittgenstein for example advances the theory of meaning that "meaning is use", which is a statement of empiricism. Other objections that are made to Cartesian dualism arise in ways that imply that the author regards the notion of soul-substance as coherent, but false – false for other reasons such as, for example, because the ghost in machine idea contradicts modern physics, or because of the problem of interaction of body and soul.

taken literally but represent to earth-bound and limited understanding states of being that might in reality be quite different from those that he describes.[12]

The metaphysical proximity of primitive and Ionian dualism. In some respects, primitive dualism and Ionian dualism are conceptually close; the latter tends to collapse into the idea of the ghost in the machine that is scarcely distinguishable from the primitive idea of the soul-manikin. In primitive dualism, both body and soul are vital substances, whereas in Ionian dualism, the body is a material substance while the soul is a spiritual substance that acts as the vehicle for consciousness or is identical to the conscious individual. This proximity in metaphysics enables primitive materialism to pull back consciousness into ideas connected to the soul as a material substance, such as water, a breath, air, or blood.

The **backward pull of primitive materialism** is evidenced throughout the history of Western consciousness. To illustrate it, we can take the ideas present in Porphyry's excursus on the cave image in Homer's *Odyssey*; his essay, *On the Cave of the Nymphs*. Porphyry, a pupil of Plotinus, a Neo-Platonist, was an advanced thinker of his day, and his cognition was a product of Ionian dualism; he subscribed to the transmigration of souls. His interpretation of the Homeric image can have very little to do with Homer and is all to do with the state of metaphysics in Romano-Hellenistic cognition. The nymphs of this cave are interpreted by Porphyry to be incarnated souls.

> 4. For we peculiarly call the Naiades, and the powers that preside over waters, Nymphs; and this term also, is commonly applied to all souls descending into generation. For the ancients thought that these souls are incumbent on water which is inspired by divinity, as Numenius says, who adds, that on this account, a prophet asserts, that the Spirit of God moved on the waters. …
>
> 5. It is necessary, therefore, that souls, whether they are corporeal or incorporeal, while they attract to themselves body, and especially such as are about to be bound to blood and moist bodies, should verge to humidity, and be corporalised, in consequence of being drenched in moisture. Hence the souls of the dead are evocated by the effusion of bile and blood; and souls that are lovers of body, by attracting a moist spirit, condense this humid vehicle like a cloud.[13]

---

[12] Empiricists regard such uses of metaphorical language to describe non-temporal relations as meaningless. As their theory of meaning is grounded only in itself, the question whether such allegories have meaning becomes dialectical and a matter of faith and sincerity.

[13] Porphyry, *On the Cave of the Nymphs in the Thirteenth Book of the Odyssey*, Translated by Thomas Taylor, London, John M. Watkins, 1917. Section 4 – 5. W.B. Yeats has a line in his poem, *Coole Park And Ballylee*, (1931) "What's water but the generated soul?"

The conflation of the two different metaphysical ideas is via linking concepts: spiritual substance = ghost in the machine = soul-manikin = material substance of the soul = soul generated by absorption of water. Hence, Porphyry interprets the process of incarnation of a soul as one in which the soul attracts to itself moisture, water, and thus becomes gross mater, and in effect materialises.[14]

The body as tomb. There was the ongoing revulsion from the practices of ritual human sacrifice, whose traces were evident to contemporary Greeks of the C5. Euripides openly acknowledged them. That revulsion increasingly took on a wider aspect – revulsion not just to the shedding of human blood, but to the shedding of all blood, so that animal sacrifice also came emotively to be perceived as revolting and wrong, at least to a significant minority of the population. The appearance in cognition of the idea of the separation of body and soul gave rise to a metaphysical justification for the revulsion. The body came to be judged as the tomb in which the soul was trapped, with the senses as the fetters by which that trapped soul was tied to the corrupt world. Hence, also, we begin to see the formation of the concept of sin as desire.

Greek knowledge of evolution. The Greeks could remember a time when mankind was not civilised but lived as savages. To an extent they knew already the history of man's evolution. In *Prometheus Bound* responsibility for the evolution of man into beings endowed with reason is claimed by Prometheus, who, talking of himself, says, "All human skills and science was Prometheus's gift."

> What I did
> For mortals in their misery, hear now. At first
> Mindless, I gave them mind and reason.
> … In those days they had eyes, but sight was meaningless;
> Heard sounds, but could not listen; all their length of life
> They passed like shapes in dreams, confused and purposeless.
> Of brick-built, sun-warmed houses, or of carpentry,
> They had no notion; lived in holes, like swarms of ants,
> Or deep in sunless caverns; knew no certain way

---

[14] This is a contradiction between the idea of a spiritual substance and an incarnate substance. Only with Descartes does the Ionian dualism become explicitly a dualism of two incompatible substances. Hence, the confusion. The Western psyche ever wishes to return to the primitive state of participation mystique where there was no body/soul split, and hence, no need to fear death as annihilation. Another illustration is the reappearance in Roman cognition of the belief, originally exemplified in Egyptian religion and common to all primitive peoples, that the dead live within the tomb. It is said that this belief is not found in Roman culture before the C1 century BCE but became popular in the Imperial period; Petronius seems to have subscribed. It gave rise to the practice of decorating tombs. See John Ferguson: *The Religions of the Roman Empire*, Thames and Hudson, Great Britain, 1970, p. 134.

To mark off winter, or flowery spring, or fruitful summer;
Their every act was without knowledge till I came.
I taught them to determine when stars rise or set –
A difficult art. Number, the primary science,
Invented for them, and how to set down words in writing –
The all-remembering skill, mother of many arts. ...

He goes on to claim that he gave mankind agriculture, the plough, the horse and chariot, medicine, drugs and the use of herbs, mining, prophecy and the interpretations of dreams, augury, sacrifice and religious ritual. The Greeks knew that they had evolved from previous states, and their way of living was not immutable. As they confronted with horror what it meant to be savage, and rejected savagery, they identified with reason as the distinguishing mark of humanity. The watchwords became temperance, prudence and self-discipline.

Nowadays, we see the theory of evolution as a demonstration of man's material substratum – he is no more than an animal – and evolution has been used as grounds for rejecting the spiritual interpretation of life. The Greeks took a contrary point-of-view and interpreted the ascent of man as imposing upon him yet further religious duties to the gods to live the higher life, which they increasingly interpreted as **a life of reason**. They did not conclude that the ascent of man demonstrates the non-existence of the gods, but rather saw it as reinforcing their decision to abandon savagery in obedience to the Olympians who had supplanted the old gods, the Titans. There arose at this time a feeling that man needed to distinguish himself from animals, reflected in the later definition by Aristotle of **man as a rational animal**. The idea that the life of the senses was irrational, wrong and bestial emerged.

Greek virtue ethics is based on the notion of the authority of reason over passion, with the implicit idea that passions are in themselves of bodily provenance and lead the person astray. This idea lies at the root of Aristotle's virtue ethics of **the doctrine of the mean**, according to which every virtue is analysed as a temperate mean between two extremes, arrived at by balancing one emotion against another. For example, the virtue of bravery is the harmonious compromise between the emotions of fear and confidence; an excess of fear leads to the vice of cowardice; an excess of confidence leads to the vice of rashness. The whole object is **to maximise reason**, for Aristotle argues "The function of man is the exercise of his soul in obedience to reason." The argument Aristotle puts forward is known as **the function argument**.[15]

---

[15] Aristotle writes, "But perhaps the reader thinks that though no one will dispute the statement that happiness is the best thing in the world, yet a still more precise definition of it is needed. This will be best gained, I think, by asking, What is the function of man? For as the goodness and the excellence of a piper or sculptor, or the practiser of any art, and generally of those who have any function of business to do, lies in that function, so man's good would seem to lie in his function, if he has one.

Greek virtue ethics represents the aristocratic end of the religious movement of Orphism. In times when it is principally only the aristocracy that is literate, educated and cultured, we should appreciate that there may be a separation in the ideation of the aristocratic elite and the collective mass. The educated Greek who attended the Academy of Plato or the Lyceum of Aristotle was taught virtue ethics, and the opposition of reason and desire in psychology was an urbane alternative to the emotive aspects of Orphism. The aristocratic elite moved ever in the direction of what Burkert rightly dubs "philosophical religion", but this elite belong essentially to the same transformations of cognition as the general movement of Orphism. Virtue ethics and Orphism belong to one and the same religious milieu. It is to the **emotive symbolism of Orphism** that we now turn.

Transformation of the ritual of bull sacrifice. The mythologem of Dionysus/Zagreus was a focal point. Jane Ellen Harrison states in ritual Zagreus is "a meal shared by all". The ritual victim was a bull, and behind the legend of Pasiphae "lurks some sacred mystical ceremony of ritual wedlock … with a primitive bull-headed divinity." And "of the ritual of the bull-god in Crete we know that it consisted in part of the tearing and eating of a bull, and behind is the dreadful suspicion of human sacrifice." It was the "feast of raw flesh". In the religion of Dionysus, "the sacrificial victim was regarded as an incarnation of the god." And "the mysteries of Liknites at Delphi, like those of Crete, included the sacrifice of a sacred bull, and that the bull at Delphi was called Hoiotes."[16]

Becoming Bacchus. In the Orphic spiritualisation, man can become Bacchus, divine. A *Mystes*, an initiate, becomes divine by "eating raw sacrificial flesh and

---

But can we suppose that, while a carpenter and a cobbler has a function and a business of his own, man has no business and no function assigned to him by nature? Nay, surely as his several members, eye and hand and foot, plainly have each his own function, so we must suppose that man also has some function over and above all these. What then is it? Life evidently he has in common even with the plants, but we want that which is peculiar to him. We must exclude, therefore, the life of mere nutrition and growth. Next to this comes the life of sense; but this too he plainly shares with the horses and cattle and all kinds of animals. There remains then the life whereby he acts – the life of his rational nature. The function of man is the exercise of his soul in obedience to reason." Aristotle, *Nichomachaen Ethics* Book I, some slight adaptation. (1) A good X = an X that performs its function well (for example, a good knife cuts well.) (2) The function of an X = the distinctive property that an X has. (3) Man's distinctive property is his reason. (4) A man will be happy if, and only if, he is good. Therefore, (5) A happy man is one that is rational.

It is an important exercise to demonstrate the fallaciousness of this argument, for the notion that emotions are somehow inherently an evil aspect of our fallen nature is still one that infects our thinking.

[16] The Delphic order of priests were called Hosioi. Plutarch's eighth Greek question and answer: "They call Hosioter the animal sacrificed when a Hosios is designated." A pure unblemished animal was chosen, and when pronounced pure the animal was called Hosios. Hositer means "He who consecrates". The Hosioi are priests; the Hosioter is the victim. Harrison deduces that the five Hosioi at Delphi were priests of Dionysus. Harrison, *Prolegomena, Op. cit.*, p.502.

also holds on high the torches to the Mountain Mother." The bloody rites of Zagreus were transformed into rites of passage from the mundane to the higher spiritual world. The transformed concepts were made to mesh with the Olympian religion. Demosthenes says of Dike (Justice) "whom Orpheus who instituted our most sacred mysteries declares to be seated by the throne of Zeus." From an Orphic hymn we have, "I sing the all-seeing eye of Dike of fair form / who sits upon the holy throne of Zeus."[17]

Contradiction in the symbol of sacrifice. Harrison tells us that "Orphics turned the most barbarous elements of their own faith … into a high sacrament of spiritual purification." We see what an extraordinary project this was. Granted that in the Olympian/chthonic stage the original human sacrifice has been transformed into animal sacrifice, how then can this shedding of blood become an emblem and a gateway to a higher state of purity? The very symbolic act of the ritual shedding of blood must be transformed into a statement of the horror of shedding blood. To the "rational" mind, it is a contradiction. Contradiction or no, we cannot go against the facts, for the history of religion attests that this is what happened. It indicates the progress of religious consciousness was brought about by an overwhelming tide of emotion, and if a contradiction arises in the symbol of sacrifice, that is because emotions do not know of logic.

(1) There is a moral revulsion against the impurity of human existence, the shedding of blood, a rejection of primal facts of incarnate existence, which is based on killing.

(2) There is also an emotive urge to cling to the old forms of chthonic religion, which brought some form of ecstasy from which was derived a huge comfort concerning the afterlife and man's place in the cosmos.[18] This emotion is connected to the overwhelming power of the collective unconscious, which expresses itself through symbols and myths, most of which pay scant regard to the ascetic morality arising from the thought of the contamination of the soul by bodily lusts. To renounce the chthonic rites was to cut oneself off altogether from the vital sources of redemption thought to be found in Nature.

(3) Further, there is the time-honoured practice of sacrifice, and the clinging to the ritual of sacrifice, including its momentous moment of the shedding of sacred blood, as what was demanded by the gods and pleasing to them. A clinging to sacrifice as the method of communion with the gods. To renounce sacrifice altogether was to renounce communion with the gods.

---

[17] Orphic Hymn, LXIL, quoted in Harrison, *Prolegomena, Op. cit.*, p.506.
[18] The overwhelming emotive appeal of the concepts of primitive materialism has been felt throughout all the ages, and accounts for our clinging to the magic stories that we read in childhood – it is the source of that literature that we call **magic realism**. Emotively, *we want the Isle of the Blessed to be still at the edge of the world* – somewhere to which we can reach by physical navigation.

Transformation of the symbol of blood sacrifice. Hence, a system had to arise whereby all these elements were combined into a single totum of belief that appeased all the emotional pressures and ultimately could be made acceptable even to reason. One step was to transform the bull sacrifice into a single, overwhelming statement of participation in fallen, corrupt existence, and at the same time into redemption from it. The doctrine of the fallen state of man affirms that to be alive is to be a sinner. Therefore, in the ritual shedding of blood the mystic could argue: I know that I am a sinner, I acknowledge to myself and the world by participation in this gory rite my sinful state, and through that knowledge and symbolic act, I win salvation for myself by participation in the higher Love, Eros, that is the true author of the cosmos. The shedding of blood can become a symbolic statement of the renunciation of the shedding of blood; it is the symbolic statement of the horror of shedding blood, hence the affirmation that life is horrible because it is sinful and fallen, and in rejecting this state, the Orphic can purify himself, be pure, and gain admittance to heaven. In addition to this process of reason, there remained the lingering yet powerfully potent idea of the magical efficacy of blood. To bathe in blood was to immerse oneself in the vital power of the universe.

Ritual of flagellation. The Orphic cult of Dionysus is attested in a series of **frescoes from Pompei**, painted in the early C1 CE. They record the process of initiation, a process that involves some form of ritual flagellation.[19] Contradictions arise. The flagellation is intensely erotic, with imagery drawn from the original fertility cult of Dionysus, references to coition, sexual union, copulation and sexual ecstasy, but joined to a rite of purification through a humiliating shedding of blood, willingly accepted by the initiate as a submission to the idea that bliss lies through

---

[19] "The lady of the house sits, hieratic, immobile, watching the scene which unfolds. Next stands a neophyte with scarf over her head and hand on hip listening as a young boy reads the prelude to the liturgy under the guidance of a seated matron; there is evidence from elsewhere of a boy reading part of the ritual in Orphic initiation. ... Next we come to the mysteries... the scene immediately to the left ... the more distant unveiling or flagellation ... reminds the worshippers that the road to bliss lies through suffering ... presiding over the whole scene are the figures of Dionysus and Ariadne, and it is they that the worshipper would see first on entering the room. Next a kneeling woman unveils an object – undoubtedly a phallus. Beyond her a great winged figure, perhaps Telete, the very spirit of Mystery-initiation, stands wielding a long rod, and far to her left crouches our initiate, her finery cast off, her hair rumpled, a robe of penitence loosely worn, her back bared for the blows which alike represent the touch of fertility (as in the Lupercalia), the test of endurance, and the ritual death which must precede resurrection. Her head is in the lap of a woman who comforts her; another stands anxiously by. But immediately, blending with this scene, we see the resurrection. The ordeal is over. The initiate has cast off the robe of penitence, and picked up the scarf which lay ready under her arms during the flagellation, the same scarf which swirls over the head of the sea-queen in so many imperial mosaics, and she is clashing cymbals and gyrating in a great dance of Bacchic victory. So finally to a scene of preparation for mystical marriage in re-enactment of that of Ariadne." Ferguson: *Religions, Op. cit.* p. 104.

suffering, in the context of the transformed Orphic religion. The symbolism expresses the emotive union of opposites.

The cult of Dionysus, **the Bacchanalia**, was suppressed in 186 BCE by the Roman Senate. This exemplifies the extreme nature of the "contradiction" involved in the Bacchic rites, for the Bacchanalia is associated in our minds, and in the account of Livy, with extreme sexual licence, intoxication and religious frenzy, yet the Orphic element must always tend in the direction of asceticism.

Another example is **the cult of Sabazios**, which is a Phrygian variant of the Orphic cult of Dionysus/Bacchus. Sabazios contains the root term *dyeus* and is an amalgam of Phrygian Zeus and Dionysus, pointing to its origin in chthonic religion, not Olympian. This cult was imported into the Roman world from C2 BCE onwards.

The idea of the **symbolic immersion in blood** as a rite of purification found explicit expression in **the cult of Cybele**. Though this ritual is not attested until the C2 CE for Rome, it shows the progression of the idea into transformed ritual practice. In the C4 CE the poet Prudentius made a full description of the rite relating how the priest bathes himself in the blood of a newly sacrificed bull.[20] Prudentius, a Roman Christian poet, express his condemnation of the rite, and one must consider whether the rite has been exaggerated out of bias. However, "The evidence of inscriptions reveals a more complex ceremony which might last up to five days."[21] Those who were initiated claimed to have been reborn. The ritual involved a tambourine and a cymbal which seem to have acted as the plate and cup of communion. Christians regarded this as a demonic parody of the Eucharist. In some ceremonies the initiate of the Cybele cult received milk.

---

[20] A gaping wound disgorges its stream of blood,
Still hot, and pours a steaming flood on the lattice
Of the bridge below, flowing copiously.
Then the shower drops through the numerous paths offered
By the thousand cracks, raining a ghastly dew.
The priest in the pit below catches the drops,
Puts his head underneath each one till it is stained,
Till his clothes and all his body are soaked in corruption.
… Then the high priest emerges, a grim spectacle.
He displays his dripping head, his congealed beard,
His sopping ornaments, his clothes inebriated.
He bears all the stains of this polluting rite,
Filthy with the gore of the atoning victim just offered –
And everyone stands to one side, welcomes him, honours him,
Just because he has been buried in a beastly pit
And washed with the wretched blood of a dead ox.
Ferguson: *Religions, Op. cit.*, p. 105.
[21] Ferguson: *Religions, Op. cit.,* p. 105.

The origin of Christian liturgy and **the reformation in Christianity of the rites Dionysus**. It is ironic that Christians should have seen this as a demonic parody of their own rites, when the historical record lies in the other direction. It is Christianity that adopted the rituals and liturgies of Orphism, though with further profound adaptation. In this respect, Christianity represents the outcrop of the Pythagorean wing of the Orphic religion, and as the notion of the body/soul split gained more and more ground in the collective consciousness, so the emotive need to shed blood appeared to drop away. The contradiction involved in a ritual whose aim was penitence and purification but whose mechanism involved the grotesque bathing in bull's blood, could not be ignored. **Christianity further reformed the Pythagorean reformation of Orphism** by transmuting the tendency to actual blood rites into symbolic ones. At the same time, it imported back into the ritual the mythologem of human sacrifice, symbolically transformed from the inflicted murder of the sacrificial victim as Dionysus, the god-king slain and eaten for the benefit of the community, into the self-inflicted self-sacrifice of Christ, crucified by his own permission, to atone for the sins of the world, and thus save all mankind from its fallen state; the actual shedding of human blood in the ritual being transformed into the symbolic participation of his sacrificial body and blood.[22]

The reformation in Christianity of the rites Dionysus into symbolic ones constellates a **dangerous proximity of the two contradictory aspects of Orphic religion**. On the one hand, the claim to ritual purification from the evils of incarnation associated with the desires of the flesh; on the other, the orgiastic tendency of the rites of Dionysus to lead in precisely the opposite direction, to sexual inebriation, to the riot of the flesh. Medieval Christianity is not only founded upon the split-consciousness psyche, but also upon this inner emotional, symbolic, ritual contradiction. Both the religion of Christ and the religion of Satan originate in the Pythagorean-Orphic reformation of the religion of Dionysus; **both Satan and Christ are different manifestations of the same archetype of Dionysus**. This arises from the complex melding of the chthonic and Olympian religion in the wake of the trauma caused by the Ionian revolution of consciousness.

The Roman cult of Mithras is another aspect of the Orphic movement. It is attested in references made by Satitus and Plutarch from the late C1 CE. This cult

---

[22] "Take this, all of you, and eat of it: for this is my body which will be given up for you.... Take this, all of you, and drink from it: for this is the chalice of my blood, the blood of the new and eternal covenant, which will be poured out for you and for many for the forgiveness of sins. Do this in memory of me." *Luke*, 22, 19 – 20; *1 Corinthians* 11, 24-25.

"Be pleased, O God, we pray, to bless, acknowledge, and approve this offering in every respect; make it spiritual and acceptable, so that it may become for us the Body and Blood of your most beloved Son, our Lord Jesus Christ." *Quam oblationem*, from the Roman Rite of Mass. This prayer of the Roman Canon may represent an implicit epiclesis, an invocation to the Holy Spirt to bless the Eucharistic bread and wine. An epiclesis is explicit in most liturgies of the Eastern Church.

has a transparent connection with Persian religion, being based on the Persian cult of Mithra, which is also a development out of the proto-Indo-European god, Mitra, who appears in the Vedas, where he is paired with Varuna,[23] and as Mitra-Varuna is the guardian of treaties and oaths and associated with the dawn and the light of the early-morning sun, a function taken by Iris, Zeus's personal messenger, in Olympian religion.   The Romans themselves attributed Mithraism to Persian Zoroastrian religion.[24]

Chapels dedicated to Mithras were technically called "caves".   The sanctuaries were oblong and had a relief of Mithras and a bull at one end.   Only men were admitted to the sanctuary, and there were seven grades of initiates, each with a separate altar.   The grades were associated with the seven planets; the lowest grades were collectively known as Servitors, the highest grades were known as Participants; the highest grade of all was called the Father.   Initiation seems to have involved symbolic rituals of endurance.   It was also connected to the cult of Cybele, and in some initiations, there was a sacrifice of a bull and baptism in bull's blood.   The central mystery related the journey of the soul – its descent and ascent through planetary spheres leading to judgement by Mithras.   Mithraism was concerned with the battle of light and dark.   There is an Egyptian magical papyrus from c.300 CE that contains a mass of occult ideas connected in some way with Mithraism; it indicates that the cult was concerned with the death and rebirth of the initiate.

The Orphic/Bacchic tablets are inscribed tablets of very thin gold from tombs mostly in Thurii and Hipponiom in Lower Italy but also from Thessaly and Crete containing instructions for the conduct of the dead in the underworld.   They date from C4 BCE.   **The Petelia tablet** contains an "avowal of origin" that acts as a qualification to drink from the Well of Mnemosyne, Remembrance, that will enable a person in the underworld to preserve memory.[25]   The image of Lethe, the river of

---

[23] The deity Varuna in Sanskrit is related to Greek, Uranus, the original god of the sky, who was incorporated in the genealogy of Hesiod as the original ruler of Heaven, supplanted by Cronos.   The common names are indicative of the common origin of the languages, but also illustrate how a religious concept is melded in diverse cultures as the patriarchal and matriarchal elements fight and combine with one another.

[24] Porphyry (c.234 – c.305 CE) in his fascinatingly muddled allegorical reading of a description of a cave in Homer's *Odyssey*, identified "… the Persians, mystically signifying the descent of the soul into the sublunary regions, and its regression from it, initiate the mystic (or him who is admitted to the arcane sacred rites) in a place which they denominate a cavern. For, as Eubulus says, Zoroaster was the first who consecrated in the neighbouring mountains of Persia, a spontaneously produced cave, florid, and having fountains, in honour of Mithra, the maker and father of all things; a cave, according to Zoroaster, bearing a resemblance of the world, which was fabricated by Mithra." Porphyry, *Cave of the Nymphs, Op cit.*, Section 2.

[25] "Thou shalt find on the left of the House of Hades a Well-spring,
And by the side thereof standing a white cypress.
To this Well-spring approach not near.

forgetfulness, appears for the first time in the Myth of Er in Plato's *Republic,* but it was probably already well-established in Orphic circles.

Aversion to the physical. The ritual of aversion arises. To Empedocles is attributed, "to fast from evil was a great and divine thing." There are "wineless" rites in Orphic cult, "the sacrament of their spiritual abstinence." There is no mention of wine in the Orphic confession. Pythagoras did not insist on total abstinence but advised drinking pure water was better. Later, Porphyry in his *Abstinence from Animal Food* advises abstinence for those who desire purity. In **the Compagno tablet** there is an emphasis on ritual atonement of sin as unrighteousness and obtaining a status of purity which shall qualify the believer to obtain memory in the Underworld and have "lordship" there.[26] Orphic rituals are designed to prepare the living for death, the culmination of their rituals was a revelation of 'things to be', "a preparation for the other world".

These ideas are strongly contaminated by what we have called elsewhere spiritual materialism, the idea that one can "buy" one's way into heaven by depositing a certain amount of money, or by performance merely of a ritual. Orphism recognises the state of purity as qualifying the bearer, like a passport, to a better destiny in the afterlife, but the way to obtain purity seems to be through performance of a ritual, by submission to a ritual practice, rather than by any inner transformation, as is suggested to us in our more elevated moments of spiritual enlightenment.

The myth of the Danaids. One image that was particularly popular was the use of the myth of the Danaids to represent lost, errant souls in the afterlife. The fifty Danaids are the daughters of Danaus, king of Argos, forty-nine of whom murdered their husbands, their cousins and the sons of Aegyptus, on the instructions of their father; the fiftieth daughter, Hypermnestra, did not kill her partner, Lynceus, who survived to murder Danaus. According to Orphic symbolism, these forty-nine

---

But thou shalt find another by the Lake of Memory,
Cold water flowing forth, and there are Guardians before it.
Say: "I am a child of Earth and of Starry Heaven;
But my race is of Heaven (alone). This ye know yourselves.
And lo, I am parched with thirst and I perish. Give me quickly
The cold water flowing forth from the Lack of Memory."
And of themselves they will give thee to drink from the holy Well-spring,
And thereafter among the other Heroes thou shalt have lordship…"
Extract from the Petelia tablet.
[26] From the Compagno tablet (b):
"Out of the pure I come, Pure Queen of the pure below,
Eukles and Eubouleus and the other Gods and Daemons.
For I also, I avow me, am of your blessed race.
I have paid the penalty for deeds unrighteous …"

Danaids suffer eternal punishment in the Underworld, Tartarus, by being made to carry water in leaky vessels, sieves. Their task is to wash off their sins, but because the vessels are perforated, they will never succeed; hence, their punishment is eternal, and their afterlives endlessly futile. This reflects how Orphic thinking developed regarding the question of judgement in the afterlife. The image was very popular, and many a Greek pottery was embellished with the scene of the hopeless water-carriers. The pots and vases testify to the preponderance of Orphism.

The Danaid myth is another fabulous illustration of the various layers of Greek religion. (a) There are the transparent references to the matriarchal layer. The Danaids form a college of fifty priestesses and their murder of their "husbands" points directly to ritual human sacrifice in honour not of a king, but of the goddess Da – Danae – Diana – Artemis. A motif present in the myth is that the daughters choose new husbands in footraces, a direct reference to matrilineal succession. There is also present the mythologem of murder. Lynceus kills Danaus and succeeds him by marriage to his daughter Hypermnestra. (b) At the Olympian-chthonic stage the legitimacy of the slaughter of so many men is repudiated, and because the number is so large, it becomes an emblem of monstrous sacrilege. The story is converted into a moralising one, and Hypermnestra becomes an emblem of male regard, a chaste virgin, a creature of independent conscience, refusing the horrible instructions of her wicked father. (c) At the Orphic stage the myth is developed into a symbol of eternal punishment for sin, and the sin of the Danaids is connected to impurity – loss of virginity and murder.[27] The figures are of both sexes and any age. The symbol of the Danaids and their futile water-carrying was developed into an icon of the terrors of the afterlife that await those who do not pay up and quickly get their certificate of Orphic purity.

Trophonios. Jane Ellen Harrison draws our attention to a fascinating passage recorded by Pausanias concerning **the Oracle of Trophonios at Phocis**.[28] This

---

[27] Jane Ellen Harrison discusses a painting by Polygnotus of the descent of Odysseus, which was a fresco at the Lesche of Delphi, and now lost – but described by Pausanias. It showed "above the figure of Penthesilea are women carrying water in broken earthen sherds," and bore the inscription, "of those who have not been initiated." Harrison, *Prologemena, Op. cit.*, chapter 12.

[28] Pausanias's account: "The most famous things in the grove are a temple and image of Trophonius; the image, made by Praxiteles, is after the likeness of Asclepius. There is also a sanctuary of Demeter surnamed Europa, and a Zeus Rain-god in the open.

What happens at the oracle is as follows. When a man has made up his mind to descend to the oracle of Trophonius, he first lodges in a certain building for an appointed number of days, this being sacred to the good Spirit and to good Fortune. While he lodges there, among other regulations for purity he abstains from hot baths, bathing only in the river Hercyna. Meat he has in plenty from the sacrifices, for he who descends sacrifices to Trophonius himself and to the children of Trophonius, to Apollo also and Cronus, to Zeus surnamed King, to Hera Charioteer, and to Demeter whom they surname Europa and say was the nurse of Trophonius.

account of the mysteries of Trophonius is late in the historical record – Pausanias is writing in the C2 CE. He makes it clear that he has himself participated in the rites; hence, his description is one of a ritual current at that time. We cannot say for

---

At each sacrifice a diviner is present, who looks into the entrails of the victim, and after an inspection prophesies to the person descending whether Trophonius will give him a kind and gracious reception. The entrails of the other victims do not declare the mind of Trophonius so much as a ram, which each inquirer sacrifices over a pit on the night he descends, calling upon Agamedes. Even though the previous sacrifices have appeared propitious, no account is taken of them unless the entrails of this ram indicate the same; but if they agree, then the inquirer descends in good hope. The procedure of the descent is this.

First, during the night he is taken to the river Hercyna by two boys of the citizens about thirteen years old, named Hermae, who after taking him there anoint him with oil and wash him. It is these who wash the descender, and do all the other necessary services as his attendant boys. After this he is taken by the priests, not at once to the oracle, but to fountains of water very near to each other.

Here he must drink water called the water of Forgetfulness, that he may forget all that he has been thinking of hitherto, and afterwards he drinks of another water, the water of Memory, which causes him to remember what he sees after his descent. After looking at the image which they say was made by Daedalus (it is not shown by the priests save to such as are going to visit Trophonius), having seen it, worshipped it and prayed, he proceeds to the oracle, dressed in a linen tunic, with ribbons girding it, and wearing the boots of the country.

... Within the enclosure is a chasm in the earth, not natural, but artificially constructed after the most accurate masonry.

The shape of this structure is like that of a bread-oven. ... They have made no way of descent to the bottom, but when a man comes to Trophonius, they bring him a narrow, light ladder. After going down he finds a hole between the floor and the structure. ...

The descender lies with his back on the ground, holding barley-cakes kneaded with honey, thrusts his feet into the hole and himself follows, trying hard to get his knees into the hole. After his knees the rest of his body is at once swiftly drawn in, just as the largest and most rapid river will catch a man in its eddy and carry him under. After this those who have entered the shrine learn the future, not in one and the same way in all cases, but by sight sometimes and at other times by hearing. The return upwards is by the same mouth, the feet darting out first.

They say that no one who has made the descent has been killed, save only one of the bodyguard of Demetrius. ...

After his ascent from Trophonius the inquirer is again taken in hand by the priests, who set him upon a chair called the chair of Memory, which stands not far from the shrine, and they ask of him, when seated there, all he has seen or learned. After gaining this information they then entrust him to his relatives. These lift him, paralyzed with terror and unconscious both of himself and of his surroundings, and carry him to the building where he lodged before with Good Fortune and the Good Spirit. Afterwards, however, he will recover all his faculties, and the power to laugh will return to him.

What I write is not hearsay; I have myself inquired of Trophonius and seen other inquirers. Those who have descended into the shrine of Trophonius are obliged to dedicate a tablet on which is written all that each has heard or seen. ..."

Pausanias. *Pausanias Description of Greece with an English Translation* by W.H.S. Jones, Litt.D., and H.A. Ormerod, M.A., in 4 Volumes. Cambridge, MA, Harvard University Press; London, William Heinemann Ltd. 1918. 9 (Boeotia), 39 ,1 – 14.

certain when the rite in that form was instituted, though its character, I suggest, originates in the C4 BCE, because of its consonance with the Orphic tablets. It is not explicitly an Orphic ritual and represents a conception that is mid-way in the transformation of the religion of Dionysus. Indications of the earlier matriarchal level are present: Zeus as a rain-god, Trophonius as the son of Demeter, the boy attendants are called Hermae, the shape of the chasm-sanctuary is like a bread oven, suggestive of the ovens used by the Carthaginians in their sacrifices; there is a hint of sacrificial death, not just in the myth of Trophonius, but in the fate of a bodyguard serving Demetrius. The rite lies mostly in the chthonic (pre-Orphic) layer. A descent is arranged that induces a state of trance of terror, in which the querent experiences a vision of the future. The whole thing is designed to suggest a journey to the Underworld and back; such experiences belong to the chthonic layer too. Orphic elements are present; we have the waters of forgetfulness and memory, which are Orphic symbols or were adapted by Orphics for their purposes. The writing of a tablet is also Orphic in conception, as we have witnessed in the Orphic gold tablets. There is an emphasis on purity.

The ritual is likely to be a hybrid ceremony of later design, since the rejection of the physical corruption that became an element of Orphism is not dominant. The distinction between this ritual and the Orphic one is, I suggest, that in the Orphic ritual the descent is a decided preparation for death. This ritual, like the one at Eleusis, to be discussed below, endeavours to prepare the querent by a mystic vision of the impermanence of life or the place life has in the cycle of birth, death and rebirth, but the Orphic conception is more definite about the crossing.[29]

The ethical teaching of the Orphics may be inferred from its eschatology, and is almost identical to that of Plato, which reveals his heavy indebtedness to them. The difference between Orphism and Plato is that Plato is careful to divest his philosophy of the cruder forms of spiritual materialism that infect Orphic thinking, thus, for Plato, escaping the terrors of punishment in the afterlife, and the terrors of yet further incarnations can only be achieved through some rigorous ascetic training, so with Plato we move inexorably in the direction of the introduction of eastern-style asceticism into the Western psyche. It is for this reason that Plato can be scathing about the Orphics as peddlers of cheap wares.[30] A spread of responses to the

---

[29] Orphic philosophy bears similarities to Egyptian religious thinking. In Egypt it had already been established for millennia just how to behave during the entry into the underworld, and how to pass the test of Osiris. What distinguishes Orphism from Egyptian religion is that Orphism arises in the context of the body/soul split, is attuned to the doctrine of reincarnation, to the idea of an immaterial soul migrating between life and the afterlife, is connected to the emergent idea of sin as desire and to the quest for purity, links to the notion of the separation of body and soul through ascetic practice, and is attuning itself to asceticism and the rejection of the body.

[30] In the following extract it is Adeimantus, brother of Glaucon, who is speaking, but the sentiments echo those of the educated elite to which Plato belongs. "Mendicant priests and soothsayers go the

religious crisis had been generated out of the need to transform the religion of Dionysus.

(1) **Conservative, chthonic religion**. At one end we have transformations of the chthonic rituals into mystical experiences; in these Bacchus appears as the god incarnated in the rituals. This response is the most conservative of the adaptations. It makes the least possible changes in the rituals and is adapted to primitive materialism. The **mysteries of Eleusis** represent this type.

(2) Orphic religion reacts to the body/soul dichotomy, but it also has several currents, which share a common eschatology, but differ significantly in other respects. In the **philosophic current** represented by Plato, the mystery rites of Dionysus are wholly rejected for their irrationality and for their proximity to the practices of spiritual materialism – the buying and selling of indulgences, the quick and easy passports to a better afterlife. This current is connected to **Pythagoreanism** and develops into Aristotelian virtue ethics.

(3) The other current of Orphism is the more ritually based one that is closely related to **Bacchic practices** but seeks to spiritualise them as well as codify them. It seems likely that this movement, which represents **mainstream Orphism**, is also associated with puritanism or at least incipient puritanism.[31]

The distinctions here between branches of the same movement was also a conclusion of Burkert.

> Within the sphere of *Orphica*, two schools may perhaps be distinguished, and Athenian-Eleusinian school which concentrated on the bestowal of culture allegedly to be found in the Demeter myth and the Eleusinian mysteries, and an Italian, Pythagorean school which

---

round of rich men's doors and persuade them that they have power from the gods, whereby, if any sin has been committed by a man or his ancestors, they can heal it by charms and sacrifices performed to the accompaniment of feasting and pleasure, and if any man wishes to injure an enemy, at a small cost he may harm just and unjust indifferently; for with their incantations and magic formulae they say the can persuade the gods to serve their will. ... And they produce a crowd of books by Musaeus and Orpheus, the descendants of the moon and the Muses, as they say. These are their liturgies, and they persuade not only individuals, but whole cities, that there are modes of redemption and purification from sins for the living and for the departed also, by means of sacrifices and pleasurable amusements which they call mysteries. These redeem us from the evils of the other world; if they are neglected, perils awaits us." Plato, *Republic*, 364b – 365a.

[31] Plato associates this stream with "sacrifices and pleasurable amusements" but this possibly reflects a prejudicial distortion. The words are spoken by a minor character in *The Republic*, and are not necessarily the view of Plato, but a view known to Plato which he presents for consideration. Already by his day mainstream Orphism was infected with the ills of spiritual materialism, which made it an easy target for such opinions; further, the similarity between their rites and those of the more traditional followers of Bacchus created an identity between them, and it is probable that the worshippers too did not always make a distinction.

took a more original path with the doctrine of the transmigration of souls.[32]

I classify he Eleusinian school as belonging to the chthonic religion. The common eschatology held between the two branches of Orphism – the Pythagorean-Platonic on the one hand, and the mainstream-Bacchic on the other – concerns the geography of the underworld, and its nature as a place of punishment and reward. We will examine it detail in the words of Plato, but the evidence that it was held in common by the whole movement is substantial, and that a common imagery and iconography was developed.

Demographics. Can we estimate what proportion of the populace of, say, C4 BCE Athens were involved in each branch of the transformed chthonic religion? I think we can, because the Orphic religion is associated with a change in burial custom. The Bacchic/Orphic gold tablets were recovered because they were attached to burials. Harrison tells us that it is known that "the sect of Pythagoreans had special burial rites, strictly confined to the initiated." Evidence comes from Plutarch in *The Dream of Socrates* in which the disinternment and reburial of a Pythagorean Theban called Lysis is recounted. I have already mentioned the evidence that Burkert records that at Athens thirty percent of burials reverted to inhumation.[33]

The philosophic sect, of whom Plato is a member, represented only a minority view, an elite of aristocrats. We can see this from Plato's account of his own life in his Letters VI and VII.[34] These make his relative isolation in politics clear. Although his influence on men like Dion of Syracuse was significant, he had influence by virtue of his impact on members of an elite rather than by appeal to the "masses". The persecution of Socrates could not have taken place had support for his philosophic religion been widespread among the common people.

The Greeks in the main continued to opt for cremation. The religion at this stage was one in which Olympian and chthonic practices coexisted, and since almost everyone at Athens was initiated into the Elysian mysteries at the time, we can say that non-believers were negligible. Thus, a small minority followed the philosophic religion of Plato, roughly thirty percent were converted to mainstream-Orphism, and seventy percent followed the transformed chthonic rites of Bacchus, now imbued with new symbolism and mystic properties. Destiny was to reverse the situation, so that the philosophic religion of Plato would become predominant, subsuming the Orphic rituals in Christianity; and the Bacchic mysteries of Eleusis and other centres

---

[32] Walter Burkert, *Greek Religion*. Translated by John Raffan. Basil Blackwell, English translation, 1985, p. 300.

[33] [See Part I, Chapter 20, Life after death.]

[34] The authenticity of the letters has been doubted. These letters are written on the occasion of the death of Dion of Syracuse and offer advice to Dion's supporters; they recap the history of Plato's interventions in Sicilian politics. Their authenticity is accepted here.

were to fall away. Plutarch in his essay, *The Obsolescence of Oracles* (C1 CE) was later to observe the dramatic failure of the popularity of the oracles in Greece, with declining numbers of sites, declining observance, and declining numbers of hierophants, and to attribute it spuriously to a decline of the Greek population. He did not see it for what it was, a decline in faith and religious observance. The chthonic religion died. It was Plato who was to win out in the end, at least for a couple of millennia.

The mysteries of Eleusis. Revelation of the secret mysteries of Eleusis was considered a capital offence by the Athenian state. Details of the mysteries were a state secret. Aeschylus was accused of revealing the mysteries on stage, and it is said that the audience nearly stoned him for it. In time, some of the details were leaked, particularly during the Christian epoch, and we have a highly prejudiced narrative by the strained Christian author Hippolytus that recounts what was told to him about them by "a Naasene"; thus, a hearsay account, a second-hand story.[35] His account is very confused, being polemical, mixed up with quotations from the Gospels and muddled with Old Testament theologising involving Adam.

Burkert indicates the impact of the mysteries on the Athenian citizens, who almost all, man, woman and slave participated in them: "the true and universal claim of Eleucis: the mysteries, taking from death its terror, are the guarantee of a better fate in the after-world."[36] – The Homeric *Hymn to Demeter*, Pindar, Sophocles "all leave no doubt about this." He also tells us that the cult could be traced back to the Geometric Age and Mycenaean predecessors. That comes as no surprise. Its origins lay in the matriarchal epoch, when indeed it was no mystery, and the god-king was mated to the goddess-queen, a son was born, and the king or the son was sacrificed. It was transformed into a chthonic ritual during the dark age, and the cult was significantly developed during the tyranny of Peisistratus, when the first hall of initiations, the *telesterion*, was built. This was subsequently pulled down and an even bigger one constructed that could accommodate thousands of worshippers.

---

[35] Hippolytus writes, "And after the Phrygians, the Athenians, while initiating people into the Eleusinian rites, likewise display to those who are being admitted to the highest grade at these mysteries, the mighty, and marvellous, and most perfect secret suitable for one initiated into the highest mystic truths: (I allude to) an ear of corn in silence reaped. But this ear of corn is also (considered) among the Athenians to constitute the perfect enormous illumination (that has descended) from the unportrayable one, just as the Hierophant himself (declares); not, indeed, emasculated like Attis, but made a eunuch by means of hemlock, and despising all carnal generation. (Now) by night in Eleusis, beneath a huge fire, (the Celebrant) enacting the great and secret mysteries, vociferates and cries aloud, saying, "August Brimo has brought forth a consecrated son, Brimus;" that is, a potent (mother has been delivered of) a potent child. But revered, he says, is the generation that is spiritual, heavenly, from above, and potent is he that is so born." Hippolytus *The Refutation of All Heresies* V, 3.

[36] Burkert, *Religion, Op. cit.*, p.289.

Recovering the participation mystique. When man is in the state of primitive cognition, the individual is in a perpetual state of mystic participation in nature, one in which he is not conscious of the distinction between perception and reality. I have already endeavoured to describe this state. Aeschylus had a similar idea.

> … In those days they [men] had eyes, but sight was meaningless;
> Heard sounds, but could not listen; all their length of life
> They passed like shapes in dreams, confused and purposeless.[37]

I suggest that the Eluesian mysteries belong to the third stage of the Dionysian religion, being part of and consequent upon the Orphic movement, but also belonging to that part of the reformed religion that sought unconsciously the conditions of primitive magic, where the pain of the separation of soul from body occasioned by the advent of Ionian dualism could be forgotten. Ionian dualism broke upon Greek consciousness as a muddled doctrine, and its impact was primarily on the most educated sections of society, but inevitably the confused suggestion that the soul was not a substance like water or the breath of air, and that in consequence, death might be annihilation, seeped down to the masses, which included those men who pulled on the oars of the Athenian ships, who benefitted most from imperial wars, had a vested interest in how human sacrifice might help them win them, and whose wives went on the religious processions and attended all the festivals, all of which were chthonic in origin and expression, and most of which were in honour of Dionysus and Demeter.

The Eleusian mysteries represent a device to re-enter the participation mystique of the bygone age – once again to enter the dream world where "life … passed like shapes in dreams". Such a condition is indeed a wonderful thing. It means to re-enter a kind of paradise – a paradise full of ritual murder – where one is liberated from the cares of the world, one becomes like a plant, an indestructible part of nature, whose life is one of natural growth, death and rebirth – like a plant, cut down, sown again and reborn. One gives up being rational, looking at things through the eyes of cold logic and scientific observation, and even great rationalists, like Aristotle, who was an initiate, were not altogether prejudiced against the sublimity and ecstasy of an intoxicating vision. According to Aristotle – the aim was "to suffer or experience (*pathein*) and be brought into the appropriate state of mind."[38] It is also the literal truth. For that is what we are – a part of nature. Therefore, as nature, we are immortal. It is only the obsessive concentration of the perpetuation of the non-existent ego into a permanent, self-begotten substance that makes it hard for us

---

[37] *Prometheus Bound*. It is an early statement of the thesis associated with Levy Bruhl. [See footnote to chapter 6, Primitive materialism.]

[38] This is cited by Burkert and derives from fragment 15 of Aristotle.

to see and experience that. The devices employed in the mysteries were just those well attuned to break down the ego-illusion, make the individual forget that he was a separate "thing" apart from nature, incline him to give up the self-love of that terrible "thing", and just be one with nature. Hence, to participate.[39]

The impact was tremendous. From the *Hymn to Demeter* we have, 'blessed is he who has seen this among earthly men; but he who is unitiated in the sacred rites and who has no portion, never has the same lot once dead down in the murky dark." Pindar and Sophocles confirm, and Isocrates tells us the *mystai* "have more pleasing hopes for the end of life and for all eternity." Euripides wrote in *Hypsipyle*, "One buries children, one gains new children, one dies oneself; and this men take heavily, carrying earth to earth. But it is necessary to harvest life like a fruit-bearing ear of corn, and that the one be, the other not."

Eleusis is the best documented of the backward-looking chthonic versions of the Orphic transformation that set in from the C4 BCE onwards. Other cults include the *Kabeiroi* of Lemnos, who are said to be identified with the Etruscans, and were involved in a cult of Hephaistos, a guild of smiths; and the worship of the gods of Samothrace, which hearkened back to the rites of the pre-Greek Pelasgians. The Great Goddess of Samothrace was Meter, and there was an elaborate mythology. The mysteries were supposed to prevent one being drowned at sea.

These mysteries represent attempts to bring about healing effects on the mind by restoring the person to a more elementary state of participation in nature, where he feels protected by the force of nature – the Goddess – but also experiences a sense of detachment, because as a part of nature, he is indestructible and has nothing to fear

---

[39] We have some idea of the devices used to induce this return to nature. The first sacrifice of a young pig, was preceded by a sea bath taken with the young pig, followed by a purification ceremony. There was the removal of some things called the *kiste* from a basket and placing it back; these were probably "genital symbols", as Burkert says, "something obscene", and possibly a mortar and pestle – instruments for preparing the barley-groats drink – broth seasoned with pennyroyal, a potent and potentially lethal drug that induces a trance. Beyond the entrance there was a grotto – though not a "great marvel of nature" – dedicated to Pluto. During the ceremony in the *Telesterion* the hierophant showed the sacred things. At the centre was the *Anaktoron* – "a rectangular, oblong, stone construction with a door at the end of one of its longer sides" where the throne of the hierophant was placed. He alone could pass through the door. On top of it was a great fire, and earlier mysteries were probably celebrated in the open air around a fire. Terrible things are shown. At the climax, "the hierophant 'appeared from out of the *Anaktoron* in the radiant nights of the mysteries'." Berkert explains this by reference to *Hymn to Demeter*: "In myth, Demeter places the son of the king of Eleusis into the fire on the hearth, so that the horrified mother is led to believe that the child is being burned, whereas the goddess is actually bestowing immortality on the child." A child is then initiated from the hearth. Animals were probably killed and burned. The *mystes* see Kore "who is called up by the hierophant by strokes of a gong"; the hierophant announces a divine birth; 'The Mistress has given birth to a sacred boy, Brimo the Brimos'; the ear of corn is cut in silence. These are all psychological devices, assisted by hallucinogens, to induce an altered state of consciousness; but just because the state has been induced by such means, this does not mean it is not objective and real.

from the future. But such mysteries, no matter how effective in their psychological devices, could not prevent the ongoing scepticism arising from the impact of the Ionian revolution and the revulsion with things of the flesh whose development is also a fact of human evolution. Hence Orphism.

Cloud-cuckoo-land. *The Birds* by Aristophanes was performed in 414, during the disastrous Sicilian expedition, (415 – 413). The mutilation of the Hermae, which occurred in 415, had led to a witch-hunt, a particularly nasty persecution of rationalist thinkers, such as Diagoras of Melos, who was charged with atheism and with divulging the mysteries of Eleusis. It seems he escaped. Alcibiades was also charged.

The Birds lampoons Athenian mores, politics and politicians but most of all Athenian religion. The plot of the play concerns a plan by the comic protagonists, Peisthetaerus and Euelpides, to establish a new religious order that will interpose itself between the people and the gods, and charge duty on sacrifices. This succeeds, and the new religious lords, the birds, then build a city in the clouds, Cloud-cuckoo-land. An army of professional sycophants – represented by a poet, an oracle man, an inspector, and a statute-seller – emerge on the scene with the aim of profiting from the new religion. The older religion of the Titans, previously supplanted by the Olympians, is here referred to under the term Triballians; being "upstairs" from the Olympians, these Triballians look to suffer most from the religious changes. A treaty is agreed – the Olympians and Triballians will pay the duty. Orphism is the main butt of the satire.

Euelphides	[Talking of Tereus, the hoopoe.] I didn't know birds needed servants.
Footbird	Well, he did: having been a man, he'd got used to the idea, I suppose.

The idea of men turning in the afterlife into birds lampoons the Pythagorean doctrine of transmigration of souls. The Orphic cosmogony, which traces everything back to Love, Eros and the primordial world egg is ridiculed.

> Chorus: … We will explain to you the nature of birds, the birth of
> the gods, the genealogy of the rivers, the origin of Erebus and Chaos
> … In the beginning there existed only Chaos, Night, Black Erebus and
> Dreary Tartarus: there was no Earth, no Air, no Sky. It was in the
> boundless womb of Erebus that the first egg was laid by black-winged
> Night; and from this egg, in due season, sprang Eros the deeply-
> desired, Eros the bright, the golden-winged. And it was he, mingling
> in Tartarus with murky Chaos who begot our race and hatched us out
> and led us up to the light.   There was no race of immortal gods till

Eros brought the elements together in love: only then did the Sky, the Ocean and the Earth come into being, and the deathless race of the blessed gods. So you see we are much older than any of the gods.

The idea of Cloud-cuckoo-land anticipates the idea of the heavenly or celestial city – and mocks it in advance. But the play is not an endorsement of the Olympian religion, for that is also exposed as a morally bankrupt illusion, whose gods no longer command thunder and a religion that cannot claim the moral high-ground either: everything comes in for biting satire.

Peisthetaerus	And you can tell the gods they'll no longer be allowed to go rampaging across your territory whenever they want to go down and rape some mortal maiden…
Peisthetaerus	And before he can sacrifice a ram to Zeus, the wren must be appeased with a sturdy uncastrated gnat.
Euelphides	I like the idea of sacrificing a gnat. What price Zeus's thunder now?

The criticism that can be levelled against Aristophanes is that he has no positive solution to propose. But Aristophanes has foreseen the shape of things to come: the establishment of a monopoly on religious ideas by a class of religious specialists, and the institution of theocracy, in this play a nasty one, complete with unpleasant persecution. He represents a healthy comic interlude. It is as if he throws his hands up in the air and exclaims – are we really going to do this? The answer is – yes – we must. Mankind is hotly pursuing yet another illusion. Religion is a serious business, and who more serious than Plato to complete the task that is no less than the construction of Hell?

12

Plato

Plato's thought is vast. He has a claim to having been the most influential person of all time; his philosophical thinking laid the foundations of historical Christian theology.[1] A brief survey of some ideas introduced by Plato will serve to underline his importance: the dialectic; the body/soul divide; the immortality of the soul; proofs of the immortality of the soul; the Fall of Man; the life of reason; the doctrine of reincarnation; the doctrine of recollection; the concept of sublimation; God as absolute morality as the Form of the Good; God as the creator of the cosmos as the demi-urge; the Chain of Being; the Divine Right of Kings; the theory of meaning; the problem and doctrine of universals; number mysticism; the problem of participation; the third man argument.

In contemporary philosophy Plato is an unpopular figure; he is the recipient of projections as the bad or even evil originator of bad ideas. It would be useful to survey the ways in which he can be attacked, and what is prejudicial in them.

(1) Plato's **rationalist theory of knowledge**[2] flies in the face of the positivist, empiricist, realist, scientific bias of our contemporary age. Precisely because his arguments are so challenging, he may be vilified as an enemy of empiricism, and his position may be misrepresented and criticised explicitly or implicitly for making category errors and blunders in the theory of meaning, or some such. Wittgenstein's *Blue and Brown Books* may be taken as an example of this hostility. Under the cover of attacking Augustine's theory of meaning, the work is an assault on Platonism, written from the empiricist point-of-view, assuming an empiricist theory of meaning, and deriving the "nonsense" in Plato's theory of meaning from premises that Plato would never allow. What is prejudicial in this species of attack is that it substitutes one form of dogmatism for another, and denies the dialectic, which Plato never did.[3]

(2) Plato systematised the **Orphic-Pythagorean religion**, its eschatology, its justification in the doctrine of the Fall of Man, its revulsion against bodily desires,

---

[1] The early Christian fathers were Platonists. The *Gospel of John* begins with the words, "In the beginning was the Word, and the Word was with God." St. John wrote in Greek, and his term *logos* is the one we translate as "the Word"; it is the same term that Plato uses for Form; John equates Jesus Christ with "the Word" – that is, with the Form of the Good. The *Timaeus* is the origin of the doctrine of the Trinity.

[2] Rationalism is the epistemology that asserts that man is endowed with higher faculties of reason and intellect that enable him to attain knowledge independently of sense-experience,

[3] In Plato's dialogues whenever empiricism is attacked, a named empiricist is permitted to make a statement of his position, which is then subjected to critique. Wittgenstein does not allow his dialectical opponent to appear in the discussion. His dialectical opponent is a mere ghostly presence.

the psychology of reason versus appetite. He advocated the ego-ideal of perfection as disembodied spirit; the goal of life as the quest for purity; the means to this quest, asceticism. As all these ideas already lay incipient in Greek consciousness, then it is prejudicial to lay at Plato's door all blame for the adverse effects of this philosophy on Western civilisation, which I have here been from the first at pains to acknowledge. However, our revulsion against the worst aspects of this system, our collective desire to escape the philosophy of puritanism, our collective wish to dismantle those aspects of the Christian religion that advocate these things, should not prevent us from seeing that Plato in this respect does not act alone, that he is the manifestation of a collective development of cognition. We should not scapegoat him for our collective moral responsibility. If we are the inheritors of a bad moral system, a system now perceived to be spiritually misaligned, then we all participate in that as a shared, common collective responsibility.

(3) He provided a justification for the rule of an aristocratic elite over the collective majority, he opposed democracy, he defended the institution of slavery, and he defended patriarchy. He is characterised as an enemy of "liberal society", of "democracy" and of "the open society"; he would implement state control over the expression of diverse opinions and censor the arts; he rejects Homer. In Popper's *The Open Society and its Enemies*, Plato is the villain. What is prejudicial in the attack upon Plato in these aspects is that they are taken out of the context of his philosophy as a whole, which if legitimate in any part, add some legitimacy to his political theory, albeit limited. The attacks are taken out of the social context in which Plato lived, the intellectual climate for which he was not alone responsible, the religious climate of Orphism, the social background of class-conflict, and the historical background of destructive war. To criticise Plato is to turn a blind eye to the difficulties of the theory and practice of democracy, or do we forget that democracy failed in the Weimar republic and brought about the dictatorship of fascism in Europe? The criticism of Plato's political theory abstracts from the context of the low level of consciousness in the masses, who were willing, judging by the account in Plutarch's life of Themistocles, to clamour for human sacrifice. The role the masses played in the historical dramas of the C20 should not incline us to think mob-rule is the same as democracy. About slavery, or patriarchy, Plato was not the inventor of these institutions, but they were regarded by his times as fundamental to society – no one criticised them, and it took the West more than two millennia to bring them under scrutiny, and yet they both survive today. For the civilized Greeks, not necessarily aristocrats, living without slaves was to them as living without a fridge or a car is to us – inconceivable if life was to be managed. All persons should be treated as persons, but the Greeks had not elevated their morality to consciousness of that. Plato everywhere exhibits certain compensatory remarks that reveal his compassion and pragmatism and mitigate his dogmatism and preference for "closed society". It is a misconception of his political theory to call it

totalitarian, which is a backwards projection of the ills of modern society. And if, say, the Roman empire was a dictatorship of the military, and hence has some kinship in political form to the totalitarianism of modern societies, then that was not because the soldiers who fought on the frontiers of the Roman empire and elected their generals as emperors, and fought for them too, were intellectual Neo-Platonists.

Getting it just right about Plato is important. It is not just a question of justice to Plato – his greatness will survive any attack – but a question of justice to ourselves. The answer to what is right and wrong about Plato, is the foundation of the answer to what is right and wrong about contemporary cognition, consciousness, religious consciousness, social organisation and politics. I do not suppose that any one reader will agree with every conclusion of mine, but I think it might help if I outlined my position.

(1) **The dialectic.** In the matter of the dialectic Plato was right. It is the foundation of human progress. Our contemporary society is more at fault in this matter than ever Plato or Greek society was, for we have eliminated certain forms of opinion altogether from intellectual life and classified them as false, superstitious and meaningless. Our academic culture is not committed to the dialectic.

(2) **The Open Society**. In so far as Plato became a dogmatic thinker and advocated any form of persecution upon the ground that he knew what was true, right and valid, and his dialectical opponents did not, he was wrong. We should defend open society and free debate. Plato, both historically and in his epistemological construction of ideas, began from Socratic doubt; but because he thought he solved irrefutably the problems thereby raised, he tended to transform into a dogmatic thinker. Simultaneously Plato is an advocate for the dialectic and an open society, and an advocate for his dogmatic form of Orphism, and a closed society. That this is a contradiction in him, should not prevent us from perceiving that it may be a contradiction also in us.

(3) **Elitism**. In so far as Plato was an advocate of aristocratic government we must allow that the system of government we have evolved in Western "democracies" is superior; it would be a blunder to revert to a more elitist form of government. Whether we wish also to say that Plato was wrong about his own society is almost an irrelevant question for us; we could not wish to institute his political theory in our own.

(4) **The aristocratic principle**. In all matters the progression of consciousness, consciousness advances first through the efforts of individuals who are willing to conflict and "do battle" with the bulk of mankind, still wedded to an earlier stage of cognition. Hence, we have a theoretical basis to the aristocratic principle, which is no mere theory in respect of history. Plato's political theory did inform and inspire the aristocracy of the West for a two thousand-year cycle, and aristocrats and monarchs everywhere understood that it was their duty as well as privilege to nurture culture. There could have been no Renaissance had not

aristocratic patrons undertaken to promote it. There is no Ficino without Cosimo de Medici, no Petrarch without Francesco da Carrara, no Leonardo without Lorenzo de Medici and Ludovico Sforza, no Michelangelo without Piero de Medici and Pope Julius II, no Galileo without Cardinal Alessandro Orsini, no Shakespeare without Henry Carey. All these patrons were inspired by that vision of the elevated character of aristocracy that Plato first formulated. Plato by this means became a great benefactor of mankind. In practical management of royal prerogative, while Plato's theory was the foundation of the theory of the divine right of kings, a theory to which we no longer subscribe, he benefitted mankind by inculcating into the European monarchy the highest sense of responsibility. We should not be blinded by all the wars they conducted, and the occasional, even frequent, appearance of tyrannical behaviour among them from acknowledging that monarchs of Europe, even perhaps Emperor Frederick II, felt obliged to govern in a manner that befitted their station as regent for God, and plenipotentiary of justice.

(5) **The Either/Or**. In so far as Plato placed the religion of Orphism upon a systematic and rational foundation, and thereby laid the ground of theological, medieval Christianity the matter of his contribution is as complex as Christianity itself. He did contribute to the development of what I have called the split-consciousness psyche, and the emergence of the shadow problem of the Christian epoch. He provided philosophical justification for the developing hostility to the body, to the passions, desires, appetites, emotions and to sex; he provided philosophical justification to the practice of asceticism; he defended a form of puritanism. The value of all these ideas is a matter for the dialectic. I have already expressed my view that separating what is good in Plato from what is bad does provide us with means whereby to reject all these puritanical conclusions, and thereby transmute all the practises associated with them into free choices as opposed to mandatory conditions of spiritual life. This is by far the biggest problem when dealing with Plato. The most dangerous contribution Plato made to Western civilization was the inculcation of an either/or attitude to spirituality – either puritanism, or hedonism. There is a middle way.

(5) **Rationalism** and **opposition to empiricism**. It must be possible in an open society to deny empiricism. The debate between rationalism and empiricism is dialectical, and so perhaps in the final analysis it comes down to a choice between them – I might say, "I believe it on the strength of the absurd" – which means, in all sincerity, that is the way things look to me. **Universals**. Plato introduces in the theory of meaning, in our knowledge of meanings, the issue that is known as the "problem of universals". The term "problem" is confusing – it is only a problem for empiricists – for the rationalists it is the cornerstone of their theory. Plato's theory of meaning is his most important contribution to Western cognition. It poses a challenge to empiricists and provides a ground over which that debate can be fought. It is still a choice, but there is a ground to choose as well.

(6) **The transcendental deduction**. Plato deduced from this theory of meaning metaphysical consequences, such as the doctrine of recollection, the pre-existence of the soul, the existence of the soul, the possibility of its existence after death, and so forth. Valid or not, his deductions expose a principle of utmost importance: *We understand human identity by understanding what human faculties are.* There arises *the transcendental deduction* from the theory of knowledge to the nature of the human soul. Identifying just what is and what is not valid in this deduction is of utmost importance, and the introduction of the argument itself is an important contribution to the dialectic.

(7) **Moral objectivity**. Plato insisted that ethics must be based on the objectivity of ethical decisions – that there is a **moral reality** that is the source of the dictates of our conscience, and acts as the judge and source of sanctions. Whether morality is objective or subjective is another matter of dialectical debate, and like all great questions comes down to sincere self-examination. For myself, I agree that subjectivism cannot provide an answer to the hard ethical-problems of conflict as an individual against the tyranny of naked power. Like Dostoyevsky I agree that "if god does not exist, then everything is permitted" – the permissions include the most abject cowardice in the face of any evil, including the fear of death.

(8) **Philosophical religion**. Since the intuition of a moral reality amounts to an intuition of the godhead and supplies in the moral argument for the existence of the godhead grounds for believing in that godhead, the objectivity of morals is the ground of philosophical religion. Moral reality is precisely that which we encounter in life as super-nature. I do not speak of the supernatural, of ghosts, or gremlins, or of angels and demons; on this matter I prefer to be silent, though the relation between super-nature and the supernatural needs to be investigated.[4] However, in so far as Plato provided philosophical grounds for the belief in super-nature, I consider his contribution to be important and wholly good.

(9) **Censorship**. Plato's dogma that poetry and the arts should be censored for the benefit of imposing moral discipline is wrong. It is as foolish as puritanism, which, since the validity of puritanism is a dialectical issue, makes censorship also a dialectical issue. It may be observed that Plato was through the allegories he constructed, one of the greatest poets ever to have lived.

(10) **Immortality** stands for the fundamental condition of human existence without which it is inconceivable to imagine human life as other than a state of permanent despair. Immortality stands in direct opposition to the concept of the utter impermanence of human identity. I agree with Dostoyevsky that without the belief in immortality it is not possible to make sense of human morality. Therefore, in providing both emotive appeals and intellectual arguments for the notion of immortality, Plato was a great benefactor of mankind.

---

[4] [See Part III, Chapter 18 - Kantian consciousness and the spirit world.]

13

East and West, the Immortality of the Soul

The East. Plato adopted and systematised the beliefs of Orphism. The proximity of Orphism to Eastern ideas cannot be overlooked. The similarity between the metaphysics of the afterlife in Persian and Greek religion is transparent.[1]

The origin of Orphism. Since Orphism contains elements resembling Persian and Indian thinking that we *assume* pre-date the adoption of those ideas in Greek consciousness, the natural assumption is that the Greeks imported them from those places. Pythagoras, an important reformer of the chthonic religion of Dionysus, great in influence upon development of Orphism, represents the ideal vector for bringing Persian and Indian ideas into Greece.

The journey to the East. Greek thinkers started travelling. Their first port of call was usually Egypt, but they did not stop there. Those who travelled include Solon (c.638 – c.558) who visited Egypt, and according to legend, stopped off in Lydia during the reign of Croesus. Plato attributes the introduction of the legend of Atlantis to Solon, who is said to have imported it from Egypt. Solon also visited Cyprus, a cultural meeting point. The fabulist, Aesop (c.620 – 564), whose moral stories are so modern in cognition, was also said to have worked at Sardis in Lydia. Herodotus (c.484 – c.425) was by his own self-report the most famous of travellers, and his inquiries often concerned religion. Ionia lies on the boundary between the Greek and Persian spheres of influence and changed hands many times during their wars; we may reasonably expect it to be a melting pot for ideas. Anaximander published the first map of the world, Pherecydes came from Samos, Melissus was a naval commander of Samos. Epimenides, according to Diogenes Laertius, met Pythagoras in Crete, where they went to the Cave of Ida. Plato also visited Egypt; later, he travelled to Syracuse. The habit of inquisitive travel, whose purpose is to find out knowledge, possibly arcane knowledge, became popular. Pyrrho of Elis (c.360 – c.270), credited with the foundation of scepticism, travelled to India with Alexander the Great's army and studied with the magi and the gymnosophists.[2] According to Arrian of Nicomedia (c.86/89 – c.146/160 CE), Alexander also encountered these Indian ascetics.[3] The meeting and events may be legendary, but if

---

[1] [For the Persian religion, see Part III, Chapter 10, Mazdeism.]

[2] A term used by the Greeks to denote "naked philosophers"; we use the term "yogis".

[3] Arrian writes, "In Taxila, once, he [Alexander] met some members of the Indian sect of Wise Men whose practice it is to go naked, and he so much admired their powers of endurance that the fancy took him to have one of them in his personal train. The oldest man among them, whose name was Dandamis (the others were his pupils), refused either to join Alexander himself or to permit any of his pupils to do so. ... On the other hand, another of these Indian teachers, a man named Calanus, did yield to Alexander's persuasion; this man, according to Megasthenes' account, was declared by his

not historical, the account demonstrates that the Graeco-Romans of the early C2 CE were familiar with the ascetic practices of the East, and not only respected them, but applauded them. The highways between East and West had long been opened by trade and war, and there was constant commerce of philosophers and ideas between the major centres of thought.

It is normal to assume that the philosophical ideas of Pythagoras were imported from the East. Examination of the dates suggests that the commerce of ideas may have gone in the other direction. Solon had already been travelling in the century before the dawn of the Ionian revolution that commences with Thales (624 – 520), whose life predates and overlaps the legendary life of the Buddha (563 – 483); Pythagoras was a contemporary of the Buddha. Indian texts are notoriously difficult to date – the invention of historical time and the philosophical notion of real time is a Western one. The principal texts of Buddhist literature are contemporaneous with the Hellenistic period, and not the classical period and follow the impact of Alexander's invasion. The high mark of Indian sculpture, works from Gandhara, are from the Indo-Greek kingdom of Bactria (c.250 BCE – 10 CE). Not until this period did Indian art begin to make representations of their deities; the first are found in the coinage of Greco-Bactrian king Agathocles (ruled 190-180). To this kingdom belong the first anthropomorphic depictions of the Buddha; until this period the Buddha was represented through symbols – an empty throne, the tree of Enlightenment, the footprints of the Buddha, and the wheel. We are so used to seeing the beautiful Gandhara representations of the Buddha as the epitome of Indian art and expression Indian religious consciousness that it may come as a shock to realise that they are the product of the fusion of Greek-Hellenistic with Indian culture. We are likewise used to thinking that iconic representations of Hindu

---

fellow teachers to be a slave to fleshly lusts, an accusation due, no doubt, to the fact that he chose to renounce the bliss of their own asceticism and to serve another master instead of god.

... I have mentioned this because no history of Alexander would be complete without the story of Calanus. In India Calanus had never been ill, but when he was living in Persia all strength ultimately left his body. In spite of his enfeebled state he refused to submit to an invalid regimen, and told Alexander that he was content to die as he was, which would be preferable to enduring the misery of being forced to alter his way of life. Alexander, at some length, tried to talk him out of his obstinacy, but to no purpose. Then, convinced that if he were any further opposed he would find one means or another of making away with himself, he yielded to his request, and gave instructions for the building of a funeral pyre under the supervision of Ptolemy son of Lagus, of the Personal Guard.

... At last he [Calanus] mounted the pyre and with due ceremony laid himself down. All the troops were watching. Alexander could not but feel that there was a sort of indelicacy in witnessing such a spectacle – the man, after all, had been his friend; everyone else, however, felt nothing but astonishment to see Calanus give not the smallest sign of shrinking from the flames.

We read in Nearchus' account of this incident that at the moment the fire was kindled there was, by Alexander's orders, an impressive salute: the bugles sounded, the troops with one accord roared out their battle-cry, and the elephants joined in with their shrill war-trumpettings." Arrian of Nicomedia, *Anabasis*, trans. Aubrey de Sélincourt, Bk. VII, 1.5 – 3.6.

religion, notably sculptures of Shiva, are ancient; we may be unaware that Hinduism arose not earlier than 500 BCE, that it was a reaction to Buddhism, that the Hindu synthesis is the period 500 – 200 BCE, and that classical Hinduism covers the period c.200 BCE – 1100 CE.

Contrary to appearances that suggest that Western religious ideas were imported from Persia and India, it is equally likely that the religion of the East was the product of the impact of the Ionian revolution upon Persian and Indian consciousness. The initial response of the West to the shock was the development of Orphism, now seen as more internal to Greek evolution than an import from the East; this shock took form in the systematic philosophy of Platonism. Despite this initial reaction of the West, which drove it in the direction of an Eastern-style asceticism, the predominant response of the West was to develop the materialism and atomism of Democritus and the concept of real time. In the East the shock stimulated the predominant bias of Indian consciousness towards subjective introspection, towards phenomenology and the belief in the unreality of time, the emergence of idealism.

The tracing of **the layers in Indian religion** is of utmost importance not just to the history of ideas, but to the living quest for the truth about human existence. That these layers can be constructed is possible, for it is likely that Chinese literature will contain sufficient data to produce a history and map of the exchange between the Greece, Persia, India and China. When this is achieved, Indian consciousness may be discovered to have evolved in response to the shock of the Ionian revolution rather than have been its progenitor.

Buddhist philosophy is idealist – grounded upon the notion that all is mind. The first historically attested expression of this philosophy is not in the East, but in the West in the work of **Parmenides** of Elea; the school he founded is known as the Eleatic school, whose chief proponents, in addition to Parmenides, are Melissus and Zeno. In *The Way of Truth*, Parmenides expresses the doctrine of the unreality of time.

> For nothing either is or will be other than what is.

> … being, it is ungenerated and indestructible, whole, of one kind and unwavering, and complete. Nor was it, nor will it be, since now it is, all together, one, continuous.[4]

Parmenides was born in either 540 or c.515,[5] which makes him just a little older than the legendary Buddha; however, those explicit expressions of idealist philosophy that we encounter in Buddhist literature belong to a later period.

---

[4] These verses of Parmenides were ecorded by Simplicius in his *Commentary on the Physics* 144.25-146.27. The translation comes from Jonathan Barnes in *Early Greek Philosophy*, Penguin, 1987. p.134.

> Verily, I declare unto you, that within this very body, mortal though it
> be, and only a fathom high, but conscious and endowed with mind, is
> the world, and the waxing thereof, and the waning thereof, and the
> way that leads to the passing away thereof.[6]

This beautifully clear statement of the idealist doctrine comes from the *Anguttara-Nikaya*, one of the discourses said to have taken place between the Buddha and his disciples. It is a document belonging to the Theravadan Pali Cannon of Buddhist Scriptures, committed to writing during the Fourth Buddhist Council in Sri Lanka in 29 BCE. The Scriptures are said to have been transmitted orally from the time of the Third Buddhist Council of 247 BCE[7] held in Asokarama in Pataliputra, under the auspices of Emperor Ashoka. But the purpose of the Third Buddhist Council was to purge Buddhism of heretical movements, which raises the possibility that idealism was introduced as a doctrine at this council, and by backwards projection attributed to Gautama Buddha. Thus, **idealism in India** is first attested in the written record in 29 BCE, attributed in oral tradition to 247 BCE, and may never have been part of the ideation of the Buddha. I do believe that idealism is the core of Buddhist metaphysics, but I can entertain as a possibility that the Indians took idealism from the West, and not the West from the East. One natural conclusion is that there was a two-way traffic. Idealism is re-expressed Western philosophy again, with startling clarity, in the work of Immanuel Kant,[8] whose words below could be taken as a paraphrase of the *Anguttara-Nikaya* were it possible to suppose Kant knew of it.

> … it is clearly shown, that if I remove the thinking subject the whole
> corporeal world must at once vanish; it is nothing save an appearance
> in the sensibility of our subject and a mode of its representations.[9]

> The abiding and unchanged 'I' (pure apperception), forms the
> correlate of all our representations in so far as it is to be at all possible
> that we should become conscious of them. All consciousness as truly

---

[5] In *Parmenides*, Plato a youthful Socrates meets Parmenides. Socrates was born c. 470. If Socrates was twenty at the time of the meeting, and Parmenides was born in 515, then Parmenides would be 65 years old at the time of the meeting. It is likely that the entire meeting is a fiction. Diogenes Laertius places the birth of Parmenides c. 540.

[6] *Anguttara-Nikaya II, Samyutta-Nikaya I,* quoted by Lama Anagorika Govinda, *Foundations of Tibetan Buddhism*, Rider and Company, London, 1960, p. 66.

[7] For example, see Edward J. Thomas, *The Life of the Buddha As Legend and History*, Routledge & Kegan Paul, 1927, p. xviii.

[8] Dogmatic idealism finds first expression in the work of Berkeley. [See Part III, Chapter 14, What Kantian consciousness is.]

[9] Kant, *Critique,* A383.

belongs to an all-comprehensive pure apperception, as all sensible intuition, as representation does to a pure inner intuition, namely to time.[10]

Kant clarifies this idealism by designating it **transcendental idealism**.

> By transcendental idealism I mean the doctrine that appearances are to be regarded as being, one and all, representations only, not things in themselves, and that time and space are therefore only sensible forms of our intuition, not determinations given as existing by themselves, nor conditions of objects viewed as things in themselves.[11]

It is the habit of contemporary consciousness to assume the reality of time – that there was a time and an existence that "came before" consciousness – that birth is the incarnation of consciousness into a body, rather than the coming into consciousness of representations in space and time. We have grown up with this habit. However, let us consider what the alternative – the unreality of time, idealism – implies about the body/soul problem.

The relationship of body to soul under idealism. To be a transcendental idealist means that one accepts that everything of which one is aware is a mental representation – for example, every perception is accompanied by consciousness, by awareness. The transcendental idealist also claims that one cannot have any direct knowledge of transcendental reality that exists wholly independently of our consciousness – though we may speculate about such a reality, we cannot form any definite knowledge of it. The transcendental idealist draws attention to the cognition, were I not aware of *this*, it would not exist (for me). Therefore, all mental representations are "before" the mind, or we sometimes say "in" the mind; but here "before" and "in" are metaphors that draw upon spatial relations to express a relation that is non-spatial.

Though everything we experience is a mental representation before the mind, we distinguish between kinds of experiences (mental representations) of which we are directly aware. There are representations in us that belong to both space and time, and others that belong only to time. Those belonging to space and time are perceived by us to be outside our bodies, located at a distance from a "focal point" of consciousness; they are called **physical objects**. The other kind of representation are those not located in space but located as experiences in time only. For example, sounds, smells and thoughts last for a period, but they do not have spatial extension. These we designate **mental objects**, which taken collectively make up the empirical

---

[10] Kant, *Critique,* A124.
[11] Kant, *Critique*, B155 – 158.

ego.   On this ground we distinguish the physical from the mental, and then, mistaking the empirical ego to be a substance, and calling this the soul, we mistakenly come to believe that the soul is located inside the body.   But this is **transcendental illusion**.

For physical objects are in the fullest sense also mental objects, and the empirical ego is not the true self, but rather the refection, as if in a mirror, of the transcendental Self.   Physical objects are mental representations presented to consciousness of things located in both space and time.   Mental objects are mental representations presented to consciousness of things in time, but not in space.

Kantian doctrine of body and soul.   From this point-of-view, it is a fundamental misconception (transcendental illusion) that the mind is "inside" the body, located in the brain.   The Kantian reply is to reverse the image – it is not the soul that is in the body, but the body that is "in" the soul, now designated by Self to distinguish it from the mistaken notion of spiritual substance.   Here "in" is a metaphor, and it is more accurate to say that the body is one of those collections of representations of which the mind becomes aware.   Being only a representation of the mind, the body cannot be the *thing* (substance) in which the mind takes its seat of origin.   To regard it as such is to view the body not as an empirical object, but as a transcendental object-in-itself, of which, following Kant, we have no direct knowledge (acquaintance).[12]

The origin of the transcendental illusion.   The habit of thinking of the soul as a substance is an inevitable consequence of being alive, of being conscious, for to be alive is to be conscious.   We are aware of the past as it fades out of the present and we anticipate the future.   We conceive of real time as an extended kind of "thing" and correlate our experiences and what we learn about history with it; we make dates and calendars.   Hence, we cannot help thinking of the soul as a substance, a thing enduring in time.   The idealist conception punctures this idea as an illusion, but it is mesmeric and compulsive.

Nothing comes of nothing.   That soul = substance (*atman, jiva*) is an idea born of transcendental illusion.   Then, we conclude that, on account of our birth, which is an event in real time, our soul was created.   Likewise, subsequent to our death, an anticipated event also in time, this soul-substance shall be annihilated.   And yet, we don't take the same view of physical substance, which we suppose to endure

---

[12] "How the 'I' that thinks can be distinct from the 'I' that intuits itself (for I can represent still other modes of intuition as at least possible) and yet, as being the same subject, can be identical with the latter; and how, therefore, I can say: "I, as intelligence and thinking subject, know myself as an object that is thought, in so far as I am given to myself as something other or beyond that I which is given to myself in intuition, and yet know myself, like other phenomena, only as I appear to myself, not as I am to the understanding" – these are questions that raise no greater nor less difficulty than how I can be an object to myself at all, and, more particularly, an object of intuition and of inner perceptions." Kant, *Critique*, A.107, p.136.

immutably over all time.   This treatment of the body/soul problem, even in the context of Cartesian consciousness, is one-sided.   Melissus (born c.500), made a prose summary of the arguments of Parmenides.

> If it is nothing, what could be said about it as though it were something?   If it is something, either it came into being, or it has always existed.   But if it came into being, it did so either from the existent or from the non-existent.   But it is not possible for anything to come into being either from the non-existent (not even something else which is nothing, let alone something actually existent) or from the existent (for in that case it would have existed all along and would not have come into being).   What exists, therefore, has not come into being.   Therefore it has always existed.   Nor will what exists be destroyed.   For what exists can change neither into the non-existent (the natural scientists agree on this) nor into the existent (for in that case it would still remain and not be destroyed).   Therefore it always has existed and will exist.
>
> Since what comes into existence has a beginning, what does not come into existence has not got a beginning.   But what exists has not come into being.   Therefore it has not got a beginning.   Again, what is destroyed has an end, and if something is indestructible, has not got an end.   But what has neither beginning nor end is in fact infinite.   Therefore what exists is infinite.

This is the doctrine: *Nothing comes of nothing. (Ex nihilo nihil fit.) It is not possible to create out of nothing.*   As much as anything a statement like this one forces us to break our heads against our conceptual limitations.   The thought of creation *ex-nihilo* strains imagination.   In physical science we do apply this Parmenidean principle and call it **the conservation of energy and matter**.   In the atomic theory of Democritus[13], we apply this to the theoretical atoms that are the ultimate constituents of reality.   These, we say, have existed immutably for all time, and undergo neither creation nor destruction.[14]

"Proof" of the immortality of the soul.   But when it comes to consciousness, we do not apply this principle.   We say, consciousness arises in the body at birth, or sometime thereafter, and consciousness will be annihilated with the body at death.   Thus, we say consciousness is created *ex nihilo* and is destroyed *in nihilum*.   To say

---

[13] Democritus is said to have been the pupil of Leucippus, and Leucippus the pupil of Melissus.

[14] I am here laying aside the difficulties of modern physics, which complicate our notion of what an atom is, but do not alter the philosophy of the problem.   We are not here taking of that atom that the physicists have split, but of the theoretical atom of Democritus that cannot be altered.   In modern physics these might be called "quanta" or "string" or some such.

that consciousness is a "thing" is transcendental illusion – at least, I think so – the error committed in Cartesian dualism, which says consciousness is a thinking thing, a spiritual substance – *Sum res cogitans*. But if consciousness is no "thing" then it still is. We may say the Self has Being, to capture this notion of being that is not the existence of substance. Being is neither created nor destroyed, at least, we cannot conceive of it as such; creation, destruction are terms that apply in time, while Being is not in time.

Whichever way one conceives of consciousness, either as a soul-substance existing, or as a Self with Being, it is neither created nor destroyed. If it is a substance in time, then – *non potest ex nihilo nihil fit* – it is not possible to make nothing out of nothing – and the soul is immortal. If it is not a substance and stands as Self outside space and time altogether, then it is not subject to the laws of generation in time and is immortal.[15] Hence, the soul is immortal.

The functional or harmony theory of the soul. Quoting from Aristotle: "This is the thesis that the soul is a kind of harmony. This assumes that the harmony in question is a mixture and composition of opposites and that the body is composed from opposites. However, the harmony itself is a kind of ratio or composition of the ingredients in the mixture, and the soul cannot be either of these."[16]

In this passage, Aristotle dismisses the idea almost as soon as he considers it, so hopeless does it appear to him as an explanation of the soul. To understand it in our terms, replace the term "composition of opposites" by "arrangement of atoms", to obtain the theory: "the soul is an arrangement of atoms" or "the soul is the harmony produced by an arrangement of atoms". The first is consistent with our materialism (mind-brain identity theory), and the second could be an expression of epiphenomenalism, the harmony being suggestive of a musical tune produced once the arrangement is made. Aristotle dismisses the view in one line: "the soul cannot be either of these". Why not? He goes on to clarify.

> Nor can the production of movement be a feature of a harmony, and yet it is to the soul that all theories assign this above all, so to speak.

> Of what parts, then, and in what ways are we to suppose the intellect to be a composition, and of what the perceptive and desiderative faculties?[17]

If, for "intellect" we here substitute "mind", "consciousness" or "awareness", then we see immediately that to create an arrangement can in no wise be said to constitute

---

[15] The meaning of "immortal" in these two expressions is not identical. In the first it means "of infinite duration in time", in the second it means "not subject to events in time".

[16] Aristotle, *De Anima*, 407 b.

[17] Aristotle, *De Anima*, 408 a.

consciousness (mind-brain identity) and to say it gives rise to consciousness (epiphenomenalism) is to say that consciousness is created *ex nihilo* when the arrangement is constituted and falls foul of Parmenides's principle. Aristotle simply dismisses it. In the above extracts other faculties of the mind constitutive of consciousness are mentioned: will, perception and desire. In contemporary philosophy, the harmony or ratio theory presents itself as functionalism.

> If you reproduce the entire "functional structure" of the human wine taster's cognitive system (including memory, goals, innate aversions, etc.), you would thereby reproduce all the mental properties as well, including the enjoyment.[18]

This states that an arrangement of material particles called a "functional structure" either constitutes or produces mental properties, that is, consciousness. This contemporary theory of Daniel Dennett and many others is hailed by them as a new discovery – but was very well known to the Greeks; it was discussed and "refuted" above by Aristotle, who dismisses it for what it is – transparently false.

Yet to consider this claim further, what is an arrangement? It is a collection of atoms. Since these atoms have always existed, then it follows that the collection of atoms, just those atoms that make me conscious right now, has always existed. But this collection has not always been conscious, it is only now in their arrangement in my body that they are conscious. Hence, by bringing together that self-same collection of atoms, here and now in close physical proximity we have an arrangement. Prior to the making of the arrangement, the collection was not conscious, upon making the arrangement, the collection is conscious. If it is the arrangement alone that makes the collection conscious, consciousness is created *ex nihilo* in the arrangement.

I am willing to concede that it is a dialectical matter and put it down to questions of faith and sincerity. If in good faith Dennett affirms that it makes sense to him, and he in good faith believes it, then I am willing to accept that. In good faith it looks like nonsense to me.[19]

The annihilation of the soul. I have described despair as *in bad faith, wilfully denying remorse, wanting, in remorse, to be the author of one's own being, and to have the power to act without moral limitation; despair is wanting, in remorse, to be a self-substantial, self-created being*. The state of despair makes us aware that our soul is dependent for its being upon another power and cannot exist save by the "grace" of that other power. Hence, in despair we can conceive of the annihilation of the soul as the just punishment for crime sufficiently proportionate to justify a

---

[18] Daniel Dennett, *Consciousness Explained,* Penguin 1993, p.31.

[19] [The problem is reconsidered in Part III, Chapter 17, The "paradox of incarnate existence".]

benevolent power from withholding its consent to one's being. This opposes the above "proof" of immortality, for it demonstrates that we are only immortal if the gods, or godhead deem us worthy of immortality. Immortality (being) may be inalienable, but we can never count on it. Then it follows that in morality there can be both a creation *ex nihilo* and an annihilation *in nihilum*. The "fallacy" of the "proof" given above is that it treats of existence as if existence were in no wise connected to morality. The argument here affirms that only if we are moral are we immortal, though it does not state what it is to be moral. In religious terminology being depends on grace.

The possibility of a complete and utter annihilation of the soul as the result of heinous crime may have been considered by Greek philosophers.

> ... but in reality the only punishment of those who have lived ill is infamy and obscurity and utter annihilation, which hurries them off to the dark river of oblivion, and plunges them into the abyss of a fathomless sea, involving them in uselessness and idleness, ignorance and obscurity.[20]

When we conceive of matter, particularly of the ultimate constituents of matter, such as atoms, we think of them as unchanging. We apply to them the principle that *out of nothing, nothing can be created*, and conceive of them has never altering, never created nor destroyed, subject to the law of conservation of energy-matter. But when we come to consciousness, which is always present to us as phenomenon only, then we experience consciousness as subject to qualitative differences, and differences of intensive magnitude. We may be more conscious or less. We can think of consciousness as either "increasing" or "decreasing", and hence we may imagine a decrease to a state bordering on oblivion. But only bordering, for a decrease is not a decrease from some intensive magnitude to no magnitude whatsoever.

If the soul is in time and is subject to alteration qualitatively and in intensive magnitude, this creates the possibility of a diminution of being that is akin to, though not the same as, annihilation. Considering the latter, point, it would be foolish to suppose that how one conducted oneself in life did not affect one's state of being.

---

[20] Plutarch, *Morals*, George Bell & Sons, London, 1898. Whether "Live Unknown" be a wise precept, vi – vii. Note the translation, "utter annihilation" is immediately contradicted in the extract by the phrase "involving them in uselessness and idleness, ignorance and obscurity," which implies continuous existence and a form of damnation. Whether the contradiction belongs to an unguarded translation, or to the confusion of Plutarch is a matter of scholarship.

14

The Construction of Hell

Plato and the underworld. *The Phaedo* presents an overview. Plato tells us that the Earth comprises a series of concentric hollow spheres. It is vast, and the known part, the Mediterranean and Black Sea basin, is just a fragment – it is a "hollow place into which water and mist and air have collected."[1] The Earth is beautiful beyond description, and there are regions above and below the one we inhabit. Those above have temperate climates far superior to ours and people live longer in them. In these places, "They also have sanctuaries and temples which are truly inhabited by gods, and oracles and prophecies and visions and all other kinds of communication with the gods occur there face to face." **The underworld** has four streams: two of these appear to girdle the region and flow in opposite directions; the other two seem to be at opposite ends. It is a very deep chasm into which all rivers flow; this chasm is called "Tartarus" by poets. For Plato, Tartarus is the lowest part of this region, the deepest hell. The outermost river is Oceanus and bounds the whole region. The second river, concentric lying inside Oceanus, is Acheron. It "passes underground and arrives at the Acherusian Lake" which is the gathering and departure point for the "souls of the dead". Between these two rivers, "halfway" the third river, Pyriphlegethon, "has its rise, and near its source issues into a great place burning with sheets of fire, where it forms a boiling lake of muddy water greater than our sea." It follows a circular course in which it "winds round inside the earth [and] it comes at last to the margin of the Acherusian Lake" without joining it, and thereafter plunges back into Tartarus. Directly opposite this river there is "a wild and dreadful place all leaden grey." (The Greek word is *cyanus*.) This also does not mingle with the other rivers but falls into Tartarus on the opposite side to Pyriphlegethon. It is called Cocytus and on entry to the region forms the lake Styx.

    Spiritual meaning of these places. At death, the soul separates from the body. It is conducted by its guardian spirit to an assembly point, the Acherusian Lake where the soul is judged. There are four kinds of judgement. (1) Those who have lead neutral lives are sent to Lake Acheron where those "undergoing purification are both absolved by punishment from any sins that they have committed and rewarded for their good deeds." (2) The "incurable" are "hurled by their appropriate destiny into Tartarus, from whence they emerge no more." (3) All those "guilty of sins, though great, [that] are curable" are initially sent to Tartarus. Those guilty of manslaughter are carried by the Cocytus back up to the margin of the Acherusian Lake; those guilty of offending against their parents are carried by the Pyriphlegethon in like manner. This occurs on a yearly cycle. At this margin they

---

[1] Plato, *Phaedo*. 600 – 624.

entreat those whom they have wronged for forgiveness, and if they receive it are cast out of the fire into the Acherusian Lake. (4) Those judged to be holy are "redeemed" and dwell on the Earth's surface; or the best of these, those that are really pure, "reach habitations even more beautiful".

Heaven, Hell and Purgatory. All the elements of orthodox Christian teaching on the afterlife are present. (1) Heaven is the abode of the pure souls and corresponds to the higher regions of the Earth. (2) Hell is that region of absolute and eternal no-return, equivalent to damnation, and is either Tartarus itself, or the lowest region of Tartarus. (3) Purgatory comes in various forms in this myth. There are three regions: (a) The Acherusian Lake for the lesser sinners, where a mild form of purification takes place, and the souls are released back to the Earth – either to our region or one of the others – higher or lower. (b) The two other rivers, which are for the two most difficult kinds of sin that can be remitted, correspond to the fires of purgatory.

Comparison with Homer. The elaborate myth of the geography of Tartarus, its relation to the various spiritual states is not found in Homer. In Homer, the underworld is called the "House of Hades". It is crossed by traversing to the boundaries of Ocean. The dead are ghosts or shades; they are concerned with their former lives to which they are emotionally attached. The prototype of judgement is present: there is a judge, Minos, and punishments are meted out to the worst criminals – Tityos, Tantalus and Sisyphus. There is no conception of purification.

The Myth of Er is found in the *Republic*.[2] Er, the son of Armenius, is said to have fallen in battle. His body did not rot and on the twelfth day, just before being cremated, he awoke and had a tale to tell. He had "journeyed along with a great company" to "a certain ghostly place", where he witnessed souls undergoing judgement; the just went by a road to the right to heaven, the unjust went by the road to the left "downward" to Tartarus. Judgement and rewards are meted out on a tenfold principle – hence, the cycle is one-thousand years – each bad deed is enacted upon the miscreant ten-times and so on. The fate of very bad sinners, for example, a tyrant called Ardiaeus the Great, is ambiguous; their souls are seen to be struggling to break out of their torments, but "the mouth would not receive them" and they are thrust back by "fierce men, like coals of fire to look upon". On the return journey back to life, the souls look upon the spindle of necessity, a column of light, like a chain, on which the eight circles of the heavens revolve. Each whorl is surmounted by a siren and "The whole spindle is turned on the knees of Necessity". The operation of all is "a single harmony". Around the spindle are seated the three Fates, "daughters of Necessity, Lachesis and Clotho and Atropos", who are "clothed in white". These help to turn the spindle. The returning souls go to Lachesis ("what has been"). Lots are cast for "your angel". Each soul choses its next life in the order

[2] Plato, *Republic*, Book X, 10.614 – 10.621.

of the lots. As "virtue has no master, and as a man honours or despises her, so will he have more of her or less. The responsibility is on him that chooseth. There is none on God." Each chooses a life, but most souls do this rather hastily and are tempted by apparent goods, and hence many choose very bad lives that also involve great moral wrongs. Those who sojourned in heaven tend to choose bad lives; and vice-versa. Lachesis is in this "the prophet" and she also states, "Even for him that comes last, if he chooses with understanding, and takes heed in his life, there is laid up a life that is not evil, with which he may be content". Then the choices of several souls are described, including those of characters famous from legend or myth, ending with Odysseus, who searches carefully and chooses the life of a private citizen. Once chosen, they are lead to the spindle of Atropos, "so that the threads might be made unalterable". Finally, the souls drink from Lethe, the river of forgetfulness and they are then carried to their birth. Er was exempted, so he remembered the events.

Judgement in the afterlife. The central theme of Tartarus is that of judgement – and in this vision, all is subsumed in purgation. The purpose of incarnate life, which goes through possibly many one-thousand-year cycles, is to test and purge the soul of all vice, and perfect it in virtue. We see only those souls who are undergoing the test, and even the fate of the greatest tyrant is not certain to be beyond **redemption**. However, two other states are implied: firstly, the state of absolute **damnation**, a state of no-return from Tartarus, of permanent punishment; and secondly, the state of absolute release – permanent residence in **Heaven**, and release from necessity and further incarnation.

This is all-but a description of the Christian conception of afterlife. It differs in that Plato's cycle of purgation is linked to the belief in reincarnation, so that life is not a one-off test, as it is in Christianity.[3] The idea of redemption is also implicit merely. The symbol of Tartarus is approximating to the Christian concept of Hell and Purgatory – even in significant detail, with the fiery looking men acting the parts of devils, who punish and control the evil souls.

Plato's caveat. "Of course, no reasonable man ought to insist that the facts are exactly as I have described them." This cleverly indicates that the reader does not have to take this all literally, but as an allegorical description of something that cannot otherwise be described. I call it a **transcendental illusion** to give a physical location to a phenomenon that could not have a physical location. Since Plato concludes with his caveat, he distances himself from one aspect of this illusion. But he remains a source in the Western tradition of this illusion. (a) Despite the caveat, he creates a physical location for the region of the afterlife. (b) He treats the soul as a quasi-physical substance. (3) He treats immortality as if it were an infinity of time

---

[3] The Christian father, Origen (c.184 – c.253 CE) advanced a theology which advocated reincarnation, but this was later pronounced a heresy.

without beginning or end, treating the soul as a "real" thing with substance, a thing that endures in time.

We find it difficult to think of the afterlife as anything but a continuation in time of this life and we seek to locate the altered state after death in a physical place, even if imaginary. By his approach, Plato has made belief in the concept of the afterlife vulnerable to the discovery that the Earth is not a collection of concentric spheres, or the discovery that it is not possible to dig underground and locate Tartarus. Scepticism is thereby induced. This is obvious to us, but it was not obvious to Plato or his audience. Plato's conception of the soul, like the Cartesian spiritual substance, is in danger of reverting to the primitive conception of soul as material substance. Cartesian dualism hovers precariously close to the idea of a manikin, a ghost-in-the-machine. If in conception spiritual substance collapses into material substance, then any belief in the soul may quickly collapse into out-and-out belief in its impermanence.

Can humanity "get by" without a notion of judgement in the afterlife?

This question is the subject of Plato's dialogue the *Gorgias.* The participants, in addition to Socrates, are Gorgias, Polus, Callicles and Chaerephon. The last figures in the dialogue only as a polite acquaintance of all three men, introducing each to the other. The discussion commences with an investigation into the art of public speaking, and Gorgias, a reputed teacher of rhetoric, undertakes to defend the thesis that it is a skill that can be taught. Socrates turns him inside out, and his place is taken by Polus, an aggressive young man. The underlying theme of the discussion emerges – the issue of whether it is worse to inflict injustice (or rather pain) than to suffer it. Polus is driven into contradiction, whereupon the unpleasant and even more aggressive Callicles, takes over, to pronounce **the doctrine that might is right**, and threaten Socrates with trial and death. Contrary to what Russell says about Socrates being "quite bland and urbane toward the people who would not listen to him,"[4] in this dialogue at least Socrates trades insults with his opponents, gives as good as he gets, makes fools of them even in their own eyes, and in his final pronouncement of a day of judgement for Callicles brings the dialogue back to the question of judgement in the afterlife as well as here on earth. The dialogue is a fiction of Plato; the historical Socrates might have refrained from parrying mental blows with three such stupid and unpleasant people. Of the three, it is Gorgias who is much the nicest, and Plato's device serves to bring into stark contrast the fundamental issue of the existence of moral reality, which is uncovered by the three stages of the argument – Gorgias, representing an urbane, soft shell of the problem, only wishes to help the people achieve their political ends by being more persuasive,

---

[4] Bertrand Russell, *Why I am not a Christian,* lecture given to the National Secular Society, Battersea Town Hall, 1927, from, Bertrand Russell, *Why I Am Not a Christian and Other Essays*, ed. Paul Edwards, 1957.

and hides under the pretence that he teaches only the means to an end, and what people do with the skills they acquire is a matter for their conscience not his. Polus represents a confused younger man under the influence of corrupt older men, and the principle he advocates is really the philosophy of cowardice. Callicles is a thoroughly aggressive man who would easily become a tyrant if circumstances would allow it; he is full of the puffed-up certainty that *there is no judgement* other than social judgement, which is only a convention. There is the background context of war and civil strife; two important examples are presented.

The example of Archelaus [5]

Polus: "Why of course he's unjust! The sovereignty he now holds doesn't belong to him at all, given the fact that his mother was a slave of Alcetas, Perdiccas's brother. ... he's committed the most heinous crimes. First he sends for this man, his very own master and uncle, on the pretext of restoring to him the sovereignty that Perdiccas had taken from him. He entertains him, gets him drunk, both him and his son Alexander, his own cousin and a boy about his own age. He then throws them into a wagon, drives it away at night, and slaughters and disposes of them both. And although he's committed these crimes, he remains unaware of how "miserable" he's become and feels no remorse either. He refused to become "happy" by justly bringing up his brother and conferring the sovereignty upon him, the legitimate son of Perdiccas, a boy of about seven to whom the sovereignty was by rights due to come. Instead, not long afterward, he throws him into a well and drowns him, telling the boy's mother Cleopatra that he fell into the well chasing a goose and lost his life. For this reason now, because he's committed the most terrible of crimes of any in Macedonia, he's the most "miserable" of all Macedonians instead of the happiest, and no doubt there are some in Athens, beginning with yourself, who'd prefer being any other Macedonian at all to being Archelaus."[6]

Polus mocks the view that Socrates has been advancing that to commit a crime is to be "miserable" and "unhappy" and advances the thesis that it is possible to commit a crime (serial murder) for personal gain (winning power) without feeling remorse, without suffering inward negative states, and without material consequences.

---

[5] Archelaus I, King of Macedon (413 – 399) is credited with administrative, military and economic reforms, transforming Macedon into a stronger power. He did, however, murder his uncle, Alcetas II and cousin Alexander.

[6] Plato, *Gorgias*, 471a – 471d.

The example of Pericles, Themistocles, Cimon and Miltiades

Socrates: "I do know clearly and you do, too, that at first Pericles had a good reputation, and when the Athenians were "worse", they never voted to convict him in any shameful disposition. But after he had turned them into "admirable and good" people, near the end of his life, they voted to convict Pericles of embezzlement and came close to condemning him to death, because they thought he was a wicked man, obviously. ... Let's go back to Cimon. Tell me: didn't the people he was serving ostracize him so that they wouldn't hear his voice for ten years? And didn't they do the very same thing to Themistocles, punishing him with exile besides? And didn't they vote to throw Miltiades, of Marathon fame, into the pit, and if it hadn't been for the prytanis [the president of the Council] he would have been thrown in?[7]

Socrates mocks the so-called power of oratory: these most famous speakers were not able to save their own skins by means of it; but he also sharply draws out the dangers of mob-rule and the fickleness of democracy in that all four of Athens greatest leaders and military geniuses were subject to the violent changes of democratic opinion.

The example of Archelaus goes to the very heart of the problem. Firstly, we should note that the issue is not about the historical person Archelaus as such, even though he did commit the several murders described here, he serves as an example. People do commit murder and other heinous crimes for self-advantage – to win power. Polus implies that he would be willing to murder his uncle, half-brother and nephew for the sake of power, so long as he could be assured of getting away with it, which must include being assured that he would suffer no remorse either.

Socrates	Doing what's unjust is actually the greatest of evils.
Polus	Really? Is *that the* greatest? Isn't suffering what's unjust a greater one?[8]

What if all deterrents are removed? What if a person is presented with an opportunity to commit what is socially deemed to be a crime, in the confidence that in the normal course of events, the crime will go unpunished? Our everyday experience is full of examples of people willing to take related risks, people willing

---

[7] Plato, *Gorgias*, 515e – 516e.
[8] Plato, *Gorgias*, 469c.

to make any use of other people for their own gains, under the assumption that their actions cannot be detected.

To commit a crime according to Socrates is bad and makes one unhappy and miserable. The terms "bad" and "unhappy" do not mean for Socrates any subjective state; they do not mean "contrary to the laws of the land" or "feeling miserable" but signify an objective state of the person's soul, a spiritual, metaphysical state of being. Both Polus and Callicles do not recognise any such state; for them, the only states that exist are those that are either physical states or states of mind that arise directly from physical states. To believe that "bad" is a metaphysical or spiritual condition is already to raise the possibility of a retribution for wilfully entering such a state, for committing a crime. It's clear that both Polus and Callicles have no belief in God or the gods as the guardians of justice, but that would not prevent them from sitting in the jury at the trial of Socrates and pronouncing "guilty" on a charge of atheism and blasphemy.

So, the question is whether we can get by without the idea of super-nature in this matter? Is it possible to substitute man-made conventions and states for the objective conceptions that Socrates adheres to? For Socrates, to say that someone or some action is bad, is to make an objective judgement; it posits that the cosmos is conscious and moral, and that it too makes or reflects that judgement. To be bad is a state of being, not an inter-subjective statement of breach of social rules, or a subjective feeling akin to having an upset stomach.

Subjective reasons for resisting temptation are not in question. Most people like and love their relatives and would not be prepared to consider harming them for the sake of power. But this is no answer. It does not make you a good man that you refuse a temptation that is not a temptation for you. You must resist something that you do want to know what "being good" means for you. What would we be prepared to suffer for the good? And if we answer, "a lot", can we get by without the idea of super-nature to explain why?

Contemporary philosophers separate the two issues – the issue of explaining from whence moral judgements arise, from the issue of what those moral judgements are – thus, meta-ethics or second-order ethics is distinct from ethic or first-order ethics. To the former belong statements like "all ethical judgements are objective" and to the latter statements like "we ought to live a life of pleasure". On this basis the philosophers argue that one cannot deduce a first-order statement from a second-order one. Perhaps that is true. But let me record what I see in relation to this question.

(1) It makes difference to **the psychology of crime** if one believes that one's criminal actions are objectively bad. This entails that any remorse attaching to the committing of the crime is inalienable, and remorse is the instant self-inflicted punishment for an action, that being objectively bad, places one in a bad relation to God or the godhead, on whose benevolence remorse and despair teach that one

depends for being. Not offending one's own conscience is the best policy of "self-interest", granted that conscience is inalienable. But this is not to provide a form of spiritual materialism for "being good", because anyone contemplating a crime is likely to take the view that the crime itself has no metaphysical consequences, and that includes the psychological aspects.

(2) **We rationalise our actions**. Where the criminal conceives of the action as bad and yet commits it, he or she will rationalise that action to justify it or explain it away. If a person wills to commit a murder, then that person is most likely to wilfully believe that the judgement, "this is murder", has no objective content. Both ignorance and freewill combine and we are wilfully ignorant. Then we choose in bad faith to believe that there is no objective moral order. Our actions are expressions of the cosmos that we wish to live in. If there is a moral reality and actions are objectively good or bad, and if the dictates of conscious say to us, "such and such is wrong", and we reason that away by denying the objectivity of that judgement, then we place ourselves in a state of wilful illusion. We choose not to recognise reality for what it is. Not only is the crime objectively bad, but we compound that corruption by a corruption of our understanding. The state of bad faith adopted in crime is a state of self-deception.

(3) **The witnesses to crime**. There is always at least one witness to every crime that is committed. This witness is the criminal him or herself. Every crime is remembered. But in addition, our psyche does not function in this respect as if it were "one"; for our conscience is subjectively perceived to be a separate part of the psyche, and there may be a "separation of consciousness" as between the judgement of the criminal, "I have profited by my crime," and the judgement of conscience, "but by doing a bad thing." We can talk of a separation of the ego and Self. If the ego says, "I've done well, now I have what I want, and am powerful," but conscience says, "You have been brutal and disregarded the feelings of others, used persons as objects, transgressed against them and your own better self, and have acted badly," then there are two judgements not one. People do believe that the voice of their conscience is in such matters the voice of God or the godhead speaking to them. It behoves everyone out of "self-interest" to consider carefully what the dictates of his or her conscience or inner voices really are. I call it a sign of immaturity to believe that everything is permitted, but it is a further sign of immaturity to suppose believing "everything is permitted" is even the same as believing "everything is permitted to me."

(4) The step from belief in the idea of judgement to the belief in **the idea of retribution** or consequences stemming from an action is a small one. Thus, if you conceive of an action as bad "before God" in any sense of God, then it is inevitable, as a psychological law, that you will conclude that "God" wills the opposite to your will, and that you have placed yourself in conflict with God and the moral order. Hence, you expect retribution. This arises naturally, and I should say, validly, from

the experience that the judgement of your conscience conflicts with the judgment of your ego. Such conflict results in remorse, and if remorse is denied, then in despair. The punishment for crime is meted out in such psychological states, and it is advisable on a policy of self-interest to avoid going against the dictates of one's own conscience.

(5) **Retribution applies to all**. What you ascribe to your own actions, you will have no compunction in ascribing to the actions of others. If an act that you judge to be bad is committed by another person, and you contemplate that act, you will invariably conclude that the other person will receive a retribution or consequence of his or her action, and that this will be meted out by God in accordance with the moral order of things as they really are.

(6) From this arises **the concept of the afterlife as a place of retribution**. It is a moot point whether there is an afterlife at all; that is, in the sense provided in the descriptions and allegories of Plato or by Christian authors. That the afterlife is a location, that it occurs in time, are all debatable issues. We literally do not know. It is right and proper to have faith in our "immortality" but equally right and proper to reserve a little uncertainty about what that immortality amounts to. Does the caterpillar know what it is to be a butterfly? Notwithstanding, the term "immortality" stands for that which we wish in life to preserve, and "afterlife" stands for the idea of the consequences of our lives extending beyond the visible part of them. In a recent, popular film, a character announces, *What we do in life, echoes in eternity*, and to believe that is a surely the most natural impulse we have. And by this statement we affirm that we are immortal and that there is an afterlife, though we do not know exactly what these are. Then, we also affirm that our actions in life have moral implications in eternity and conceive of reward and punishment in the afterlife.

(7) **Self-examination**. It is appropriate to be more concerned with the state of one's soul, than with the state of the soul of other persons. In the *Chinese Book of Changes* we read:

> ... in fear and trembling
> The superior man sets his life in order
> And examines himself.[9]

The superior man or woman fears the punishments, that is consequences, meted out to him or her by the moral order of things, and is not so concerned with those meted

[9] From the image to hexagram 51, Chen, The Arousing (Shock, Thunder). *I Ching*, trans. Richard Wilhelm, rendered into English by Cary F. Baynes, Foreword by C.G. Jung, Routledge & Kegan Paul, London, 1951, p. 198. Richard Wilhelm glosses as follows: "The superior man is always filled with reverence at the manifestation of God; he sets his life in order and searches his heart, lest it harbour any secret opposition to the will of God. Thus reverence is the foundation of true culture."

out to others. Hence, it is an error to inquire too precisely into the punishments in the afterlife provided for those who in our judgement have transgressed the moral law. We "give it to God"!

(8) Certainly, we observe that many religious thinkers have in history been ready to imagine **the terrors and torments of the damned in Hell**, into which they readily cast others. But it is not necessary that we agree with them. We may yet "give it to God". It is too easy to pay ourselves the wages of **sanctimonious self-righteousness**. But it is not correct to argue, because there are sanctimoniously self-righteous, cruel people in the world who inflict in their sermons countless tortures on those that have offended them, that there is no objective meaning to judgement, the afterlife and retribution.

(9) Plato in his descriptions of Hell is discretely silent on **the issue of eternal damnation**. Though he is setting out on the path of imagining torments in the afterlife, he predominantly pictures the scene as one of redemption through cycles of lives. The objective truth of reincarnation is not to be surveyed here, but as a symbol of the afterlife it is not committed in principle to the image of cruelty that we encounter in medieval Christianity. In dropping the notion of reincarnation altogether, the Christian fathers further fashioned the Hell that they inherited from Plato into a place of absolutes, and pictured life accordingly. Either you are eternally saved, or you are eternally punished; and in a later addition, you may be saved after enduring a period in purgatory.[10] Therefore, in life, you earn a place in Heaven or in Hell, or in Heaven by remission of sins in Purgatory. We are not obliged to adopt this schema. But it does not follow, because this schema is both too absolute and too knowing about the afterlife, that there is no meaning to judgement, the afterlife and retribution.

(10) Having then examined the phenomenology of judgement, we discover that those pains that a transgressor suffers when he or she suffers remorse are self-inflicted pains. We do not need to step outside the confines of life to understand that **judgement is immediate, painful and self-begotten**. The following are states of self-inflicted retribution: guilt, remorse, despair, the desire for death, penitence, the desire for purification through punishment. I have no doubt that many of these states are associated with morbid and unnatural psychological states, so that **self-harm** is a real mental illness having nothing to do with genuine remorse and there are **morbid states** brought about by the cruelty of others, for example, the abuse by parents of their children, physically, sexually and emotionally. That such morbid states exist does not prove that in every case guilt and remorse are merely subjective

---

[10] "The man who has cultivated that remote land [Gen 3:17] and who has gotten his bread by his very great labour is able to suffer this labour to the end of this life. After this life, however, it is not necessary that he suffer. But the man who perhaps has not cultivated the land and has allowed it to be overrun with brambles has in this life the curse of his land on all his works, and after this life he will have either purgatorial fire or eternal punishment." Augustine, *Against the Manichaeans*. 2:20:30.

psychological states and should be removed by any other means than the fulfilling the objective desire for penance.

(11) **The inner states of others**. What Polus says to Socrates is essentially: "Archelaus got away with murder (literally), prospered and never suffered any psychological consequences. He was happy in life." Even if that be so, we should more pity a man who has no conscience. It is not a human state of being. But we do not know the truth of Polus's description of the "happiness" of Archelaus, and nor does Polus. The inner state of any other person is usually hidden from us. We do not know for certain whether Archelaus transgressed moral law, though it certainly appears such; we do not know the inner condition of his soul. The ideation of Polus is the fantasy-laden thinking of an immature person. Anyone contemplating committing a serious crime, would do well, if he or she can still think clearly enough, to consider the profound literature written on this problem: *Crime and Punishment* by Dostoyevsky, the character of Bulstrode in George Eliot's *Middlemarch*, *Confessions of a Justified Sinner* by James Hogg, and all the work of Shakespeare, where we look inside the man, when the mask comes off.

> O, my offence is rank, it smells to heaven,
> It hath the primal eldest curse upon't,
> A brother's murder![11]

(12) The great symbol of the Christian religion is **redemption**, and it is for this reason that Christianity has always had a huge message for those who commit crime. In crime we bring ourselves closer to God, for it is in encountering remorse that we find our dependency in forgiveness upon the benign force of the universe; and in the Christian symbol of the salvation in Christ, through atonement by the shedding of His blood, man has for two millennia found a solace in his despair worth more than all the precious jewels of the manifest Earth combined.

> See, see where Christ's blood streams in the firmament!
> One drop would save my soul, half a drop. Ah, my Christ! –
> Rend not my heart for naming of my Christ![12]

Therefore, though Christianity has in the hands of some been a symbol of unflinching and cruel justice rather than mercy, it is not necessary to agree.

This concludes my defence of Socrates. Two things should be added about Plato's *Gorgias*, and Plato's conception of Hell. Firstly, in his endeavour to clarify what sin is, Plato continues in this dialogue, as everywhere else in the dogmatic part

---

[11] Speech of Claudius in William Shakespeare, *Hamlet*, III, iii. 36-38.

[12] Christopher Marlowe, *Dr. Faustus*, xix, 147-9.

of his philosophy, to lay the foundation of the conception of sin as desire. He wishes
to give a rendering of what it is to corrupt the soul. Confined by the limitations of
his cognition and the emerging Greek consensus, he ramifies the theory that sin
arises from bodily incarnation and is a defeat of reason by desire.

> Perhaps in reality we're dead. Once I even heard one of the wise men say
> that we are now dead and that our bodies are our tombs.[13]

> As long as the soul is corrupt, in that it's foolish, undisciplined, unjust and
> impious, it should be kept away from its appetites and not be permitted to do
> anything other than what will make it better.[14]

> I say that if the self-controlled soul is a good one, then a soul that's been
> affected the opposite way is a bad one.[15]

> Death, I think, is actually nothing but the separation of two things from each
> other, the soul and the body.[16]

This identifies sin with desire.

Secondly, when dealing with brutes like Polus and Callicles, Plato was
"tempted" to use threats. If brutes do not understand justice, tell them that their
crimes will be punished in the afterlife. Tell them frankly what they can expect.
Socrates includes in the *Gorgias* another explicit version of the judgement in the
afterlife, when souls are stripped "naked" and carry none of the appendages of
incarnate existence, no titles, powers, monies, friends and so forth, and must stand to
judgement as they really are, naked. If any man has even the remotest touch of a
belief that his soul might survive in any sense whatsoever his death, then this
warning is effective. Unfortunately, it is written for brutes, perhaps should not be
attempted, and takes us in the direction of the medieval conception of Hell with all
its infernal fires. Brutes like Polus and Callicles are not amenable to any form of
argument, or intimidation. They pose a constant threat for people who wish to live
in civil society.

---

[13] Plato, *Gorgias*, 493a.

[14] *Ibid.*, 505b.

[15] *Ibid.*,507a.

[16] *Ibid.*,524b.

15

The Transcendental Deduction

Empiricism. Empiricism is the doctrine that all our knowledge derives from the senses. It is a popular misconception to immediately equate empiricism with the method of natural science. **Natural science** aims to arrive at general laws that are grounded in systematic observation of nature by means of the senses. However, it is debatable how natural science goes about this – there is no single theory of scientific method that gains everyone's assent – and in the process of arriving at Laws of Nature the natural scientist (a) uses language in general – words and sentences, and the meanings and propositions they stand for; (b) may import general principles that cannot be gathered from direct observation, and (c) almost always uses mathematical reasoning, the source of whose truth is in question. Hence, it is wrong to equate empiricism with the method of natural science. One statement of empiricism is found in Hume's *Enquiries*:

> … all our ideas or more feeble perceptions are copies of our impressions or more lively ones.[1]

Empiricism is not just a statement about the origin of knowledge; since knowledge subsumes knowledge of meanings, it is primarily a **theory of meaning**. In the above statement meanings ("ideas") are derived ("copied") from our senses ("impressions").

(1) **Impressions and ideas**. How do we distinguish ideas from impressions? An empiricist *might* wish to say that impressions come from the external world, and ideas arise subjectively in our minds, but he must avoid this for to do so would be circular; if we are empiricists we must derive our knowledge of the external world from our senses, so we cannot assume knowledge of the external world from the outset. Hume's way of dealing with this is to first introduce an internal criterion whereby we may distinguish ideas from impressions.[2] He says that ideas are feeble and impressions "more lively perceptions"; he uses the strength of the experience to

---

[1] David Hume, Enquiry Concerning Human Understanding, II, 13 – Of the origin of ideas.

[2] "Here therefore we may divide all the perceptions of the mind into two classes or species, which are distinguished by their different degrees of force and vivacity. The less forcible and lively are commonly denominated *Thoughts* or *Ideas*. The other species … let us … call them *Impressions*; employing that word in a sense somewhat different from usual. By the term *impression*, then, I mean all our more lively perceptions, when we hear, or see, or feel, or love, or hate, or desire, or will. And impressions are distinguished from ideas, which are the less lively perceptions, of which we are conscious, when we reflect on any of those sensations or movements above mentioned." *Ibid.*, II, 12 – Of the origin of ideas.

distinguish them. Clearly it may be doubted whether this internal criterion will suffice. We have lively sensations that we do not judge to be the products of the senses, such as **dream sensations and hallucinations**; it is even possible to produce such experiences by effort of the will in concentration exercises, or by the more indolent method of the use of drugs. The inability to distinguish ideas from impressions consistently by this internal criterion is among the first applications Descartes makes of his use of the Method of Doubt.[3]

(2) A second problem for Hume is that his theory does not deal with **emotions**. From what impressions are emotions copied? To meet this objection Hume introduces **inner sense** as well as external sense, and it is with inner sense that we experience emotions. Hence, for emotions too, we have the first impression of an emotion, say raging anger, and then subsequently the idea of an emotion, the thought, perhaps, of that state of anger some years later. But we hold emotions are part of our subjective mental world, and in that case the distinction between impression and idea becomes inconsistent.

(3) When Hume writes, "all our ideas or more feeble perceptions are copies of our impressions or more lively ones" he uses the word "copies". His empiricism is the **copy theory of meaning**.   But ideas, thoughts, meanings, propositions, conceptions, notions are simply not copies, that is, faint copies, of sense-impressions. Wittgenstein, in his *Blue and Brown Books* commences ostensibly to attack the theory of meaning of Augustine that in turn is derived from Plato, but he is equally scathing about the theory of meaning advanced by Hume.

> If I give someone the order "fetch me a red flower from that meadow", how is he to know what sort of flower to bring, as I have only given him a *word*?

---

[3] "At the same time I must remember that I am a man, and that consequently I am in the habit of sleeping, and in my dreams representing to myself the same things or sometimes even less probably things, than do those who are insane in their waking moments. How often has it happened to me that in the night I dreamt that I found myself in this particular place, that I was dressed and seated near the fire, whilst in reality I was lying undressed in bed? At this moment it does indeed seem to me that it is with eyes awake that I am looking at this paper; that this head which I move is not asleep, that it is deliberately and of set purpose that I extend my hand and perceive it; what happens in sleep does not appear so clear nor so distinct as does all this. But in thinking over this I remind myself that on many occasions I have in sleep been deceived by similar illusions, and in dwelling carefully on this reflection I see so manifestly that there are no certain indications by which we may clearly distinguish wakefulness from sleep that I am lost in astonishment. And my astonishment is such that it is almost capable of persuading me that I now dream." Descartes, *Meditation I*, from *The Philosophical Works of Descartes*, Translated, Elizabeth S. Haldane and G.R.T. Rose, Cambridge University Press, 1911, p.146. Descartes considers the criterion that Hume advances, and rejects it; Descartes was writing in 1647, and Hume, who was certainly aware of the work of Descartes, in 1748.

> Now the answer one might suggest first is that he went to look for a red flower <u>carrying a red image in his mind</u>, and comparing it with the flowers to see which of them had the colour of the image. ...[4]

According to Hume's theory, when we exchange words in conversation, these elicit ideas in each other, which are copies of impressions. Hume's theory entails that as ideas are copies of impressions then a conversation would be more effectively carried on if one were able to produce impressions from which they are copied. Why not, then, conduct a more meaningful conversation by carrying around in a knapsack examples of the things you wish to talk about?[5]

Hume's theory is a form of the ostensive theory of meaning, that words acquire their meaning primarily through **ostensive definition** – so that I may teach the meaning of the word "book" by pointing to a book and saying "book". Wittgenstein in his *Blue and Brown Books* and in his *Philosophical Investigations* mocks this idea and makes difficulties for it.[6]

---

[4] Ludwig Wittgenstein, *The Blue and Brown Books,* Basil Blackwell, Oxford, 1972, p. 3.

[5] This idea was lampooned by Jonathan Swift in his description of the Academy of Laputa in *Gulliver's Travels*. "We next went to the school of languages, where three professors sat in consultation upon improving that of their own country. ... The other project was a scheme for entirely abolishing all words whatsoever... An expedient was therefore offered, that since words are only names for *things*, it would be more convenient for all men to carry about them such *things* as were necessary to express the particular business they are to discourse on. And this invention would certainly have taken place, to the great ease as well as health of the subject, if the women in conjunction with the vulgar and illiterate had not threatened to raise a rebellion, unless they might be allowed the liberty to speak with their tongues, after the manner of their forefathers; such constant irreconcilable enemies to science are the common people. However, many of the most learned and wise adhere to the new scheme of expressing themselves by *things*, which hath only this inconvenience attending it, that if a man's business be very great, and of various kinds, he must be obliged in proportion to carry a greater bundle of *things* upon his back, unless he can afford one or two strong servants to attend him. I have often beheld two of those sages almost sinking under the weight of their packs, like pedlars among us..." Jonathan Swift, *Gulliver's Travels*, Voyage to Laputa, Chapter 5.

[6] Since Wittgenstein is an empiricist, what is his alternative? He advocates the theory that **meaning is use.** This is the view that we know the meaning of words and sentences when we respond in a behaviourally recognised way to those words and sentences. Wittgenstein's theory of meaning eliminates cognition, consciousness and mental states altogether. That is in a way rather clever, but is it believable? Does anyone really believe that their conscious state has nothing whatsoever to do with their understanding? Wittgenstein's theory is pure anatta in the form of utter impermanence of the soul. Under it, all conscious states are irrelevant to communication, and cognition with regard to it is an illusion. If we reverse this theory we see that the existence of the soul, or rather Being is essentially connected to cognition. To be, is to understand. Wittgenstein's theory of meaning also shows that the definition of empiricism advanced by Hume must be modified for empiricism to survive, because the copy theory of meaning is untenable.

(4) **Associationism**. A fourth objection to Hume's theory is that in sentences words are connected, and in thoughts and propositions ideas are brought together. What is a thought or proposition, and how are ideas in thoughts connected? Hume's answer is the mechanical association of ideas. Ideas are associated when they are in some way proximate to each other.[7] According to Hume: (a) All thinking is the result of association of one idea with another; (b) All association is built upon one relation only, that of resemblance, which is another application of the copy theory of meaning; (c) When ideas that resemble one another are repeatedly associated in time, we form the notion of one idea being the cause of the other; (d) This all occurs mechanically – there is an unconscious, mechanical faculty of the mind whose function is to produce these associations; this faculty is called *custom* by Hume; (e) Hume later posits, anticipating the theory of evolution, that this mechanical faculty has arisen in man because it enables him to survive. The unconscious mechanical faculty of the mind has been produced by unconscious mechanical forces of nature.

This account clears up the relationship of Wittgenstein to Hume. From Wittgenstein's point of view, any reference to ideas smacks too much of the mind, and he deletes the" unnecessary notion" of ideas from the theory. If man is a machine operating unconsciously in adaptation to the forces of nature, there is no need to posit any association of ideas; association alone, or association of behavioural patterns, is all that is required. Wittgenstein deletes from the theory of Hume the remaining implicit appeal to cognition that is a residual trace of the opposing ideology.[8]

---

[7] "'Tis plain, that in the course of our thinking, and in the constant revolution of our ideas, our imagination runs easily from one idea to any other that resembles it, and that this quality alone is to the fancy a sufficient bond and association. 'Tis likewise evident, that as the sense, in changing their objects, are necessitated to change them regularly, and take them as they lie contiguous to each other, the imagination must by long custom acquire the same method of thinking, and run along the parts of space and time in conceiving its objects. As to the connexion, that is made by the relation of cause and effect, we shall have occasion afterwards to examine it to the bottom, and therefore shall not at present insist upon it. 'Tis sufficient to observe, that there is no relation, which produces a stronger connexion in the fancy, and makes one idea more readily recall another, than the relation of cause and effect betwixt their objects." David Hume, *A Treatise of Human Nature*, ed. L.A. Selby-Bigge. Part I, Section IV, Of the connexion or association of ideas. "... Now as we call every thing CUSTOM, which proceeds from a past repetition without any new reasoning or conclusion, we may establish it as a certain truth, that all the belief, which follows upon any present impression, is deriv'd solely from that origin. When we are accustom'd to see two impressions conjoin'd together, the appearance or idea of the one immediately carries us to the idea of the other." *Ibid.* Part III, Section VIII, Of the causes of belief.

[8] If one comes to see things the way Wittgenstein does, then there is no arguing one's way out of it – this doctrine of anatta = utter impermanence is a labyrinthine philosophy, inducing a stupefying miasma, from which there's little hope of escape. Or, perhaps, this is the escape – the thread of Ariadne to lead one out of the labyrinth – one just sees it all for the utter nonsense it really is.

Rationalism. The opposed theory, which is called rationalist, says that meanings cannot be copied or derived from the senses, that there is something in knowledge more than what is given to the senses. It is customary to designate the opposed, rationalist, theory of meaning as the "innateness" hypothesis – the claim that some ideas, at least, are innate. This notion is attributed to Descartes, who did introduce the term, albeit in passing.[9]

The **innateness hypothesis** asserts that human nature (or human understanding) supplies the concepts that enable us to understand our world.[10] It is possible that at first glance the idea of innate concepts may appear paradoxical and confusing. Concepts are used in understanding to make sense of the world, so how can they arise other than in the world? By this line of thinking, concepts must be abstracted in some way from our sensory knowledge; they cannot arise independently, supplied by the mind. I suspect that some such argument must lie behind the appeal of empiricism.

What the world is. The error in this line of reasoning is that it mistakes what the world is. It is natural for us to assume that the world exists independently of us, and certainly that is what we *see*. But it is also forgotten that what we see is in all respects a mental representation, and hence, the world as we see it belongs to the mind and is "before" or "in" the mind because we must be conscious of it, if it is experienced at all. Were we not conscious, we would not have any experience of the world. Of course, that does not preclude the possibility that there is a reality existing independently of all consciousness whatsoever, but this is not the world that we see, nor ever do we have direct knowledge of it.

Hence, the rationalist alternative to empiricism is not only coherent, but makes sense of the world as we know it. To understand the world is to perceive it as a network of relationships; we experience things in the world as things in time, subject to a certain duration, extended to a certain extent, and similar and dissimilar to other things. There is nothing incoherent in the thought that all these aspects of the world are supplied by the understanding and arise not in the data as such that we may suppose reaches us from a reality that is transcendent to our consciousness. The

---

[9] "Among my ideas, some seem to be innate, some to be caused from the outside, and others to have been invented by me. As I see it, my understanding of what a thing is, what truth is, and what thought is, derives purely from my own nature, which means that it is innate·; my hearing a noise or seeing the sun or feeling the fire comes from things outside me; and sirens, hippogriffs and the like are my own invention. But perhaps really all my ideas are caused from the outside, or all are innate, or all are made up; for I still have not clearly perceived their true origin." Descartes, *Meditations*, *Op. cit.*, Meditation III.

[10] It is interesting that in the footnote to the section in which Hume introduces his copy theory of meaning, Hume acknowledges that the opposed theory is called the innateness hypothesis, but he attaches meanings to "innate" that could not belong to Descartes, and thus affects to be completely unaware of Descartes's views, or to consider them unworthy of his attention. See, Hume, *Enquiry*, *Op. cit.*, II, 17 – Of the origin of ideas.

world as we know it, is not transcendent but is before consciousness and understood by it. Hence, that world may be the synthesis of something that arrives to the mind from a transcendent source, and concepts originating in the mind; for **the world is not transcendent**.

Custom or **instinct**. To explain this understanding, Hume posits an **unconscious faculty of the mind**, which he calls custom, and which we would probably call instinct, whose function is to copy incoming impressions and fashion them into ideas, and thereafter mechanically associate ideas that resemble one another and are contiguous in space and time. If this is essential to an explanation of empiricism, then it is no incoherence in the rationalist thesis to make the same explanation and posit an unconscious faculty of mind that supplies concepts of the understanding.

Rationalism of Descartes superseded by Kant. In this account I have already stepped from the picture presented by Descartes to the solution of the problem found in Kant's *Critique of Pure Reason*. The traditionally rationalist account of human understanding is that it is supplied with concepts that are implanted at birth by God. There is nothing incoherent about this theory either, for if God, a necessary being that is both benevolent and omnipotent, wanted to make creatures that could understand the world, then God would supply those creatures directly with the concepts they need. The origin of the human mind and its understanding are not directly known to us. We know that we understand the world, though we cannot know what the means are that enable us to understand it, or that it is a mechanism. Something passes out of our direct apperception and becomes transcendent. Hume arrives at the notion that this "transcendent something" is a machine and represents instinct in us; the rationalist takes it to be something more.

Imagination. Kant calls this transcendent faculty of the human mind "imagination". He means by this something far more than simply the ability to think up a metaphor.

> Thus the order and regularity in the appearances, which we entitle *nature* we ourselves introduce. We could never find them in appearances, had not we ourselves, or the nature of our mind, originally set them there.[11]

Kant supposes that sensory information arrives at the mind in the form of appearances, but these are immediately synthesized by the Imagination into perceptions though their admixture with concepts. In fact, we experience perceptions not appearances, for in Kant's terminology, a perception is an interpreted appearance; further, without concepts there would be no appearances either.

---

[11]Kant, *Critique*, A.123.

What is first given to us is appearance. When combined with consciousness, it is called perception. (Save through its relation to a consciousness that is at least possible, appearance could never be nothing to us; and since it has in itself no objective reality, but exists only in being known, it would be nothing at all.) Now, since every appearance contains a manifold, and since different perceptions therefore occur in the mind separately and singly, a combination of them, such as they cannot have in sense itself, is demanded. <u>There must therefore exist in us an active faculty for the synthesis of the manifold. To this faculty I give the title, imagination.</u>[12]

Kant's theory of understanding bears some close resemblances to **Plato's theory of perception**.

For Plato the mechanism of sight involves three kinds of 'fire' or light. (1) Daylight, diffused by the sun; (2) a visual current, the same in kind as daylight, which is contained in the eye and is directed from it towards the object seen; (3) 'fire' or light which streams off the body seen, joins with the visual ray, and produces effects which result in colour vision.[13]

"Because the stream and the daylight are similar, the whole so formed is homogeneous, and the motions caused by the stream coming into contact with an object or an object coming into contact with the stream penetrate right through the body and produce in the soul the sensation which we call slight."

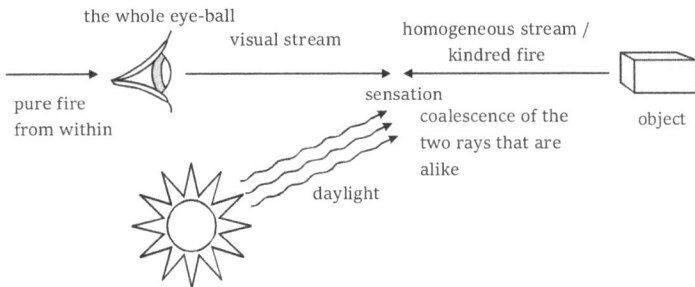

Figure 1. Plato's theory of perception.

---

[12] Kant, *Critique*, A.120.

[13] Summary of Plato's theory made by Desmond Lee, in his translation of the *Timaeus*. My diagram of Plato's theory draws upon terms used by Plato in that dialogue. *Plato, Timaeus and Critias*, trans. by Desmond Lee, Penguin, 13, p.62. This summary is followed by a quotation from the *Timaeus*.

To obtain the theory of Kant, we must modify this diagram. Plato's reference to the eye is spurious, for everything occurs in the mind.

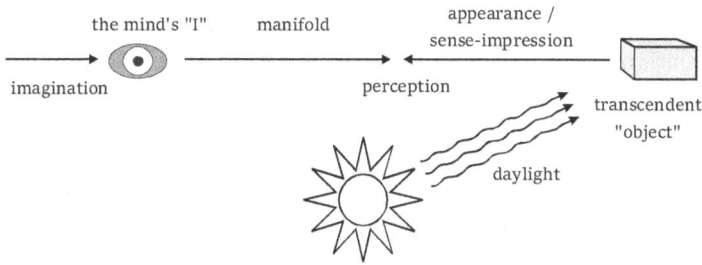

Figure 2. Kant's theory of perception.

Plato was writing at a time when the physics of light was barely understood in terms of rays of light and reflection. I propose that his theory, which seems very confused at first glance, is an excellent account of the **phenomenology of perception**. If we reflect on our sensory experience we are aware that it arises from the synthesis – Plato uses the term "coalescence" – of a part that comes from the external object (appearance), and a part that comes from the mind (concept).

Light taken subjectively. Another pertinent remark is that the light that we "see", the light of which we are conscious, is not the "light" that is described in textbooks of physics. It is a "subjective" phenomenon produced by the mind.[14]

Universals. The world as we know it, which is the world that we see, is populated with objects. In philosophy these objects have been called **individuals**. But these individual objects are also perceived to have properties. For example, in the judgement that a *tree is green*, green is a property of an individual tree. In a manner of speaking, we perceive and "see" not only individual objects but also their properties. According to the Kantian theory described above, this presents no difficulty, for the objects that we see are a synthesis of concepts with appearances brought about by imagination in the mind, and together concepts and appearances form perceptions. (Concept + appearance = perception.) Hence, both individuals and their properties are "real", and this doctrine has been called "Platonism", for it was Plato who first advanced it. The properties have been called *Universals*, and **Platonism** is the belief in the existence of universals. The opposed point-of-view is **nominalism**. We may study nominalism in the following statement of Hobbes.

---

[14] It is also possible in meditation, through emptying the mind of all thought whatsoever, to experience this as pure light, to "see" so to speak, nothing but pure light. This exercise demonstrates the nature of light, and for those who achieve this state provides assurance of the transcendent nature of the mind. [See Part III, Chapter 4, Vision, identity and immortality.]

> Of Names, some are Proper, and singular to one onely thing; as Peter, John, This man, this Tree: and some are Common to many things; as Man, Horse, Tree; every of which though by one Name, is nevertheless the name of divers particular things; in respect of all which together, it is called an Universall; there being nothing in the world Universal but Names; for the things named, are every one of them Individuall and Singular.
>
> One Universall name is imposed on many things, for their similitude in some quality, or other accident: And whereas a Proper Name bringeth to mind one thing onely; Universals recall any one of those many.

In this passage Hobbes denies the existence of universals, claiming that the only things that exist are individual. Hobbes appears to contradict himself when he writes of "similitude in some quality". A similar contradiction may be found in Hume. Having introduced his empirical theory of knowledge: "… all our ideas or more feeble perceptions are copies of our impressions or more lively ones," he throws down the challenge: "Those who would assert that this position is not universally true nor without exception, have only one, and that an easy method of refuting it; by producing that idea, which, in their opinion, is not derived from this source."[15]   The reply to his challenge is: *the entire philosophy of Plato*; that is to say, every universal, infinity, every mathematical and logical concept, every scientific concept, and every idea whatsoever. However, since Hume's thesis is precisely to deny these answers, one can hardly level that charge against him in the context. It is what he himself immediately goes on to acknowledge that constitutes his most severe problem of self-consistency.

> Suppose … a person to have enjoyed his sight for thirty years, and to have become perfectly acquainted with colours of all kinds, except one particular shade of blue, for instance, which it never has been his fortune to meet with. Let all the different shades of that colour, except that single one, be placed before him, descending gradually from the deepest to the lightest; it is plain, that he will perceive a blank, where that shade is wanting, and will be sensible, that there is a greater distance in that place between the contiguous colours than in any other. … this instance is so singular, that it is scarcely worth our observing, and does not merit, that for it alone we should alter our general maxim.

---

[15] Hume, *Enquiries*, Section II. (Of the Origin of Ideas), 15.

The missing shade of blue. This admission is bizarre, for it refutes in a single instance the copy theory of meaning. The concept "blue" is not a copy of any particular shade of blue. If the concept blue is a copy of an impression, then it must be possible to say exactly what impression it is a copy of. But there is not, nor cannot be, any such impression, for the concept blue covers precisely an entire range of particulars, and even particulars that one has never had an impression of, as in the missing shade. Having once grasped what blue *means*, one can identify a shade of blue that one has never encountered before, *as blue*. The way the colour wheel is divided has conventional, that is "man-made" features to it, and it is common to observe that in diverse cultures there are different colour terms, or that in Eskimo culture there are many more words to describe different shades of white. All that is irrelevant; the mind really does identify differences in colours and can classify experiences accordingly. These are universals. It is not unintelligible to suggest that the world that we actually see and experience is constructed out of our understanding of it, and this understanding involves a meeting between a concept originating in the mind, and some prima material originating in the object – not the object that we perceive, but the transcendental object that is unseen cause of what we perceive.

In case the notion of a universal remains difficult for the reader, there is a good introduction by Bertrand Russell.

> The way the problem arose for Plato was more or less as follows. Let us consider, say, such a notion as justice. If we ask ourselves what justice is, it is natural to proceed by considering this, that, and the other just act, with a view to discovering what they have in common. They must all, in some sense, partake of a common nature, which will be found in whatever is just and in nothing else. This common nature, in virtue of which they are all just, will be justice itself, the pure essence the admixture of which with facts of ordinary life produces the multiplicity of just acts. Similarly with any other word which may be applicable to common facts, such as "whiteness" for example. The word will be applicable to a number of particular things because they all participate in a common nature or essence. This pure essence is what Plato calls an 'idea' or 'form'. (It must not be supposed that 'ideas', in his sense, exist in minds, though they may be apprehended by minds.) The 'idea' justice is not 'identical' with anything that is just: it is something other than particular things, which particular things partake of. Not being particular, it cannot itself exist in the

world of sense. Moreover, it is not fleeting or changeable like the things of sense: it is eternally itself, immutable and indestructible.[16]

This also has the merit of relating the general problem of universals to the way in which they arose for Plato. We would say that Plato started at the wrong end regarding universals and set out initially to investigate the most abstract of common terms, such as justice, beauty and goodness, and passed over the **sensible universals**, such as colours and similar sounds, that form the first layer of our intelligible world and comprise the basis of our **understanding**. Russell also has a useful further gloss on the problem. In the following passage he is discussing the attempt of Berkeley and Hume to deny the existence of abstract properties.

> But a difficulty emerges as soon as we ask ourselves how we know that a thing is white or a triangle. If we wish to avoid the universals whiteness and triangularity, we shall choose some particular patch or a triangle if it has the right sort of resemblance to a universal. Since there are many white things, the resemblance must hold between many pairs of particular white things; and this is the characteristic of a universal. It will be useless to say that there is a different resemblance for each pair, for then we shall have to say that these resemblances resemble each other, and thus at last we shall be forced to admit a resemblance as a universal. The relation of resemblance, therefore, must be a true universal. And having been forced to admit this universal, we find that it is no longer worth while to invent difficult and implausible theories to avoid the admission of such universals as whiteness and triangularity.

This makes us aware that the fundamental universals of all are **resemblances**, or as Wordsworth more poetically expressed it – "the accuracy with which similitude in dissimilitude, and dissimilitude in similitude are perceived."[17] [18]

---

[16] Bertrand Russell: *The Problems of Philosophy*, Oxford University Press, 1912, Chapter 9: The World of Universals.

[17] William Wordsworth, *Preface to Lyrical Ballads*, 1801. Wordsworth is thinking of the character of poetic inspiration.

[18] With such arguments being advanced by Russell in 1912, one wonders how it was possible that he himself did not advance to the position taken up by Kant, and how the C20 could turn its back on universals and adopt nominalism. Regarding the first of these questions, it would not be difficult to demonstrate that Russell did not understand Kant's theory, nor did he take the trouble to investigate it further. In the *Problems of Universals*, Russell is at the least a transcendental, Cartesian dualist, if not holding to the belief in a plurality of distinct types of being. But he does not investigate the relations that might exist between those various categories of being, and such an investigation would run contrary to the deeper motives of his thinking, which is to rationalise science. The desire to cleave to

In the *Theaetetus* Plato explicitly argues against the empiricist doctrine that "perception is knowledge", which he ascribes to the sophist Protagoras, who stated "man is the measure of all things." Plato advances the doctrine that the meanings of common-terms, which he equates with forms, are apprehended only by thought; knowledge of meanings cannot be abstracted directly from particular sense-experience.

Synonyms of "universal" include: property, accident, quality, and form. Notwithstanding this plethora of terminology, I also recommend that one thinks of universals as structures. When, for instance, I look at a blue object, I see not only the object, but its structural similarity to other blue objects; this structure is as much a part of my experience of the world as the individual object is.

The Realm of Forms. There is more than one way to treat of the real existence of universals. Plato's approach is to separate the universals into a realm of Forms; that requires one to postulate a special faculty of the mind for apprehending this realm (existence *ante re*); then there arises the question of how the forms participate in the material world – **the problem of participation**. Plato raises this question in the *Parmenides*. However, one does not have to go this far. The universals need not exist separately from the individuals – this is Aristotle's alternative approach – and they need not be thought of as entities at all (existence *in re*). Kant's theory corresponds to existence *in re*, but he still postulates the existence of a transcendental faculty of Imagination to provide the concepts that makes this existence *in re* possible.[19]

The transcendental deduction in the *Theaetetus*. It is this question of how we know universals that leads us to the transcendental deduction. If the mind can know abstract structures (forms, properties, universals), then the mind is not a material entity. *There are faculties of the mind that could not possibly be reproduced in a mechanism.* Plato in the *Theaetetus* makes this step when he argues that the power of the mind to make judgements about different species of sense-object, that is, to compare and contrast them, indicates that the mind itself is independent of the sense-organs.

---

science is the core of his emotive being, the source of his "irrational part". By accepting the existence of universals, he has strictly rejected empiricism, and yet he ever remains sympathetic to empiricism. His work is an attempt to construct a real world of physical entities out of sense-impressions, and to analyse language accordingly. All this as a foundation to rational science, and as a means of avoiding religion.

[19] It is commonplace in contemporary philosophy to distinguish a universal – that which can be instantiated – from an abstract entity – that which has neither spatial nor temporal location and is "causally inert". A "realist" is said to be someone who believes in universals; a "Platonist" someone who believes in abstract entities. The term "realism" here could be confusing; for the belief in a real world of physical entities is also called "realism". The distinction is distracting, because universals are abstract entities, and the "problem of universals" remains, regardless of whether one believes in them *ante re* or *in re*. For, if we know them, then the question is how do we know them?

Socrates	Now take sound and colour. Have you not, to begin with, this thought which includes both at once – that the both exist?
Theaetetus	I have.
Socrates	... Then through what organ do you think all this about them both? What is common to them both cannot be apprehended either through hearing or through sight. Besides, here is further evidence for my point. Suppose it were possible to inquire whether sound and colour were both brackish or not, no doubt you could tell me what faculty you would use – obviously not sight or hearing, but some other.[20]

This is a powerful argument for the transcendence of the mind. Of what impression is the judgement (idea, thought) that "there is music coming from that black box" a copy? Is it a copy of the sound-impression, or a copy of the colour-impression? It cannot be either, nor can it be both. Hence, we are led to the conclusion that it is the mind that supplies the manifold (unity) that makes understanding possible, and *how* the mind does this is a mystery for us, equivalent to the mystery of the synthesis of conscious awareness itself.

Inference to the immortality of the soul. From the existence of universals, Plato believes he has established that the mind (soul) is non-material, and he steps from there to the immortality of the soul.

Men's souls are immortal. Souls pass through death and are reborn, but they are never really annihilated.

The soul, since it is immortal, has been born many times, and has seen all things both here and in the other world. It has already learnt everything that is. So we should not be surprised if we discover that the soul can recall the knowledge of virtue or any other matter that it formerly possessed. Nature forms one whole, and the soul has already learned everything, so when a man has recalled a single part of knowledge – that is, what we commonly call learnt it – there is no reason why he should not go on to discover everything else, especially if he is courageous and does not tire in his researches; for discovery and learning are in fact both forms of recollection.[21]

---

[20] Plato, *Theaetetus*, 151E, from F. M. Cornford, *Plato's Theory of Knowledge*, Routledge & Kegan Paul, London and Henley, 1979 p. 185. (First published 1960.)
[21] Plato, *The Meno*, 81c.

On the one hand, we have knowledge through the senses of particulars, and on the other, we have knowledge of universals. Since we cannot abstract knowledge of universals from knowledge of particulars, how is it possible that we know universals? He answers this with his doctrine of recollection: we pre-existed our birth, and existing as disembodied souls, we were able to know the universals directly as cognition of a realm of Forms. (**Doctrine of Forms**.) Subsequently, we experienced a Fall into incarnate existence through contamination with desire and were born. (**Doctrine of the Fall**.) But our ability to understand the world resides in our remembrance of the Forms that we recollect. (**Doctrine of Recollection**.) This is Plato's argument for the existence of the soul, and for the real distinction between mind and body. This lays the ground for his belief in the immortality of the soul.

Since Forms also bear resemblances and differences between each other, it is a simple step to argue that there are **Forms of Forms**. From there we obtain the idea that all forms are assembled under one single master Form, the Form of the Good. Whence, we obtain the doctrine of **the Form of the Good**, or **the Doctrine of the Logos**. (The term "logos" being the Greek term for "form".)

To contemporary consciousness, these arguments are obviously flawed and fail to explain those things they set out to explain. Their force, as it appeared to Plato, and to generations that followed him, lay in their emotive connections, for by this means Plato was able to connect the logical part of his philosophy with the religious and emotive part. These arguments supplied a rational groundwork to Orphism, but the conviction-energy that explains why they were subsequently adopted came from the already overwhelming tide in favour of Orphism. Orphism came first, then Plato systematised and rationalised it. He made Orphism appear logically unassailable, and chief in the means he employed for this purpose were the doctrines of Forms, recollection, Fall, and the Logos.

Yet, the false steps in these arguments should not blind us to what is genuine in them. It is this argument from the transcendence of understanding and imagination to the transcendence of the mind that I call the transcendental deduction. I maintain that a transcendental deduction does follow from the doctrine of universals. This doctrine identifies the mind as possessed of understanding, reflected in its knowledge of meanings that are on the face of it not abstracted from sensations. Universals, being abstract and therefore, not in space and time, cannot be known by a causal process in space and time. Hence, the faculty of understanding cannot be replicated in a machine.

The transcendental deduction
There are faculties of the mind that could not possibly be reproduced
in mechanism (an arrangement of material atoms).

The reverse transcendental deduction

All the faculties of the mind can be reproduced in a mechanism.

In contemporary philosophy it is this reverse transcendental deduction that is very much in focus. The critique of this contemporary project I shall reserve for a subsequent chapter.[22]   In this context I shall pursue the refinement of the transcendental deduction in the work of Immanuel Kant.[23]

---

[22] [Part III, Chapter 16, Despair and the hope that is despair.]

[23] **The philosophy of mathematics**. In the *Meno*, Plato illustrates his doctrine of recollection in an episode in which Socrates "teaches" a slave boy the meaning of the irrationality of the square root of two. (A number is *irrational* if it cannot be written as a fraction.) His demonstration, which proceeds by question and answer, is intended to illustrate the process by which the boy is brought to *remember* mathematical knowledge that he must have known prior to his incarnation at birth. The episode strikes at the heart of the modern debate as to whether mathematics is discovered or created as an invention of man. Contemporary philosophy has rejected the notion of a mathematical reality, opting for the view of Protagoras that "man is the measure of all things". This is the debate between **Platonism** and **Formalism** in the philosophy of mathematics.

   Formalism. For a definition of formalism, we might turn to one provided by Haskall Curry. "According to formalism the central concept in mathematics is that of a formal system. Such a system is defined by a set of conventions ... we start with a list of elementary propositions, called axioms, which are true by definition, and then give rules of procedure by means of which further elementary theorems are derived. The proof of an elementary proposition then consists simply in showing that it satisfies the recursive definition of elementary theorem."[1] A statement such as this will immediately induce a mental cramp in a non-specialist, and it is an illustration of how difficult this crucial frontier of philosophical debate has become for the bulk of humanity, a situation that could not have obtained in any previous epoch. To explain it for the layman then – formalism is the doctrine in the philosophy of mathematics that says that everything that can be done by man by way of mathematical argument can be reproduced by a machine, a digital computer. That necessarily affirms a nominalist position regarding universals, and assumes the reverse transcendental deduction, specifically, that it is possible in principle to reproduce mathematical reasoning in a mechanism.

   Prima facie, there is nothing at all about mathematics that suggests that it is a formal system at all. (1) There are **the entities of mathematics**, which are in the first-place numbers and rules between numbers called in mathematics functions and relations. If one accepts that there are universals at all (Platonism, realism), then it is immediately transparent that numbers, functions and relations are universals, and Plato must be right about those. In fact, in the philosophy of mathematics there is a current vogue for the view that all mathematics can be written in terms of a special language called set theory. This language appears to have only one primitive concept, that of membership of a collection called a *set* or *class*. It is surprising, but the number of structures that this single relationship can give birth to are countless upon countless; infinities upon infinites of collections can be made, and the complexities of the relationship between those collections is a dark pit into which only the minds of brilliant and obsessed mathematicians can penetrate. And yet, there never was a more avowedly Platonist theory than set theory. Its very objects, collections, sets, classes, its very primitive relationship, that of membership, are so avowedly universal and abstract that one wonders how on earth formalism can be so popular. One is aware of the attempts to circumvent this plain truth, some of which are very sophisticated indeed, such as that of Quine, but examination of these

Kant and the transcendental deduction. To examine how Immanuel Kant refined the arguments of Plato and further honed the transcendental deduction, it is best to understand Kant's arguments in the light of the model of human reality that he advances and which I have already explained – namely, that the mind constructs reality as a synthesis of concepts that originate with the mind with something coming from "outside the mind" – we think of these latter as the sense-impressions (appearances) of objects that exist independently of the mind. The existence of such objects-in-themselves is not known, and the wisdom of Kant is to conclude that we do not need to know them. It is very helpful in this exposition to bear in mind that the human reality that you and I know and see is for Kant (as it is for myself) nothing other than a mental representation and does not exist independently of the consciousness that apprehends it.[24]

---

would take us too far astray, and I shall not trouble the reader with arguments that may appear tedious to him or her.

But let us continue to survey the subject as lightly as we may. Then we see that deployed in mathematics are very special concepts, and special among these is **the concept of infinity**. Infinity if it is grasped at all by the mind is the best candidate there is for a universal and abstract concept. The formalist response is to treat infinity by means of the symbols used to denote it, and then to regard manipulation of those symbols as part of a formal system. That this entails a contradiction of sorts may be conveniently overlooked – for any formal system is finite, and yet we say that all our understanding of the infinite may be comprised by manipulations in a finite system. Furthermore, from the time of Aristotle onwards, it has been customary to distinguish between two types of infinite collection – the potential and the actual infinite – but how such a distinction could be made in a formal system is a mystery that no formalist has even considered addressing, let alone solving.

Thereupon we see also that mathematical reasoning involves inferences that are not easily rendered into the language of formal systems. Chief among these is a principle known **as the principle of induction**. Of course, in this context, I can only point the reader in the general direction of where the objections to formalism lie, rather than delve into the particulars that would make this into a work of a very different kind.

In the recent history of the debate, I know of two attempts to oppose the current overwhelming prejudice. These are (a) the attempt by Mr. J. R. Lucas to advance a species of the transcendental deduction by arguing that that a theorem in logic known as Gödel's theorem demonstrates that human logic transcends anything that can be deployed on a machine. (b) An attempt by the theoretical physicist Roger Penrose to advance a similar idea, in his book *The Emperor's New Mind*. [2] I am under the impression that both attempts met with massive opposition from the collective body of contemporary philosophy. It seems likely that J.R. Lucas was subjected to some unpleasantness, and Dr. Penrose's book was opposed by a consensus who undertook to refute it. [3]

References: [1] Haskell B Curry, *Remarks on the definition and nature of mathematics*. Original publication in Dialectica, 8, 1954, 228 – 33. Reprinted in Paul Benacerraf and Hilary Putnam, Hilary, Eds., *Philosophy of Mathematics*, Selected readings. Second edition. Cambridge University Press, Cambridge, 1987, p.203. [2] Roger Penrose, *The Emperor's New Mind*, Vintage. Oxford University Press, 1989. [3] Behavioural and Brain Sciences. 13 (1990), issue 4.

[24] Concerning a sceptical problem of **solipsism** that is said to arise in Kant's philosophy: if I now equate my consciousness that apprehends the real world with myself it is barely possible to "infer" from this solipsism, the doctrine that I alone exist. However, this is not a necessary consequence of

Kant hones the transcendental deduction in two directions: (a) by a further clarification in the theory of knowledge advancing the concept known as the *synthetic a priori*, and (b) by a direct consideration of what it is to be conscious. It is to the latter that he grants the name "transcendental deduction", but I think it best to see the whole of the *Critique of Pure Reason* as a single whole whose original is the transcendental deduction of Plato. He calls it a "critique" because he wishes to distinguish his arguments from the earlier attempt by Descartes to achieve a related synthesis of Plato's work. Kant is essentially writing, like Descartes, in the tradition of Plato. Of these two arguments it is the second that I consider to be the more profound.

Concerning the first argument, the term *synthetic a priori* can best be understood by grasping fundamental idea that lies behind Kant's explanation of the synthesis by which human reality/the world as we know it is fashioned.

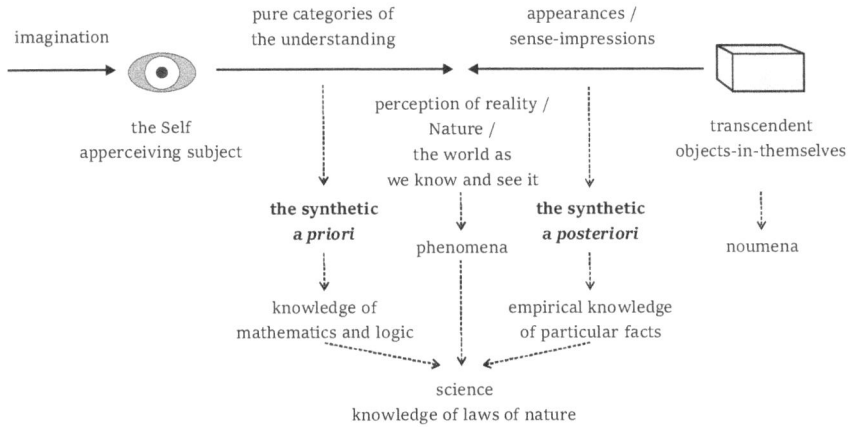

Figure 3. The synthetic a priori *and* a posteriori.

The transcendental faculty of imagination supplies the structure of experience in the form of certain pure categories of the understanding. It is these that supply the ground of mathematics and logic; hence, Kant provides a justification of mathematics and logic by deducing their principles from the categories; it is because the mind plays a role in the construction of reality that these principles are true and

this Kantian approach, for not only is the Kantian approach consistent with the existence of other minds, it is by no means certain that the "I" that apprehends reality has not within it some structure that makes it akin to mind in general. For example, while it most certainly is a unity, within that unity it has a tendency to manifest itself as distinct "persons", most especially in the "I" that is the agent of those actions that I call voluntary – actions of my freewill, and that "I" that is the critical observer of those actions, which I call "my conscience" but which contains an element of communication from that "other" that is often called God, the gods or the godhead.

justified.   The term **synthetic a priori** is used to describe the character of mathematics and logic. Since particular experiences have the sense of coming from a source outside the Self, from transcendent reality populated by objects-in-themselves (noumena), these form the basis of empirical knowledge, and are characterised as *synthetic a posteriori*.[25]

---

[25] **The synthetic a priori**. Accepting that the world that we see and understand is in part a construct of the mind, then it follows immediately that it is the mind itself that supplies the structure to experience, and that there must therefore be knowledge that originates from that structure. The Kantian model is that the mind inserts individual experiences whose information may originate from "outside" the mind into a structure that includes space and time, and mathematics and logic are valid descriptions of that structure. So, mathematics and logic derive their truth from the structure that the mind supplies and not from the incoming data. Such a theory is self-evidently meaningful.

Kant's slant on this issue is to focus not on *meanings* but on *judgements*. Meanings force one in the direction of universals, that to understand a meaning is to grasp a universal. Judgements are assemblages of meanings (concepts). It seems that a fundamental assembly of meaning in judgement involves the joining of two concepts together which is expressed by a sentence. A sentence is a physical object but is taken to refer to a mental object called a **proposition**. Sentences express propositions, that is, make judgements.

Subject and predicate. Take, for example, the sentence, "This leaf is green", then in grammar we say that "This leaf" is the subject of the sentence, and "is green" is the predicate, or "is green" is predicated of "this leaf". So much for grammar. Then in the judgement, which is a mental structure, "this leaf" refers to an object – the leaf I am looking at for instance – and "is green" is a property of the object. So, the sentence, "this tree is green" expresses the proposition, that is, makes the judgement, that the object leaf has the property of being green.

If follows that we may examine the relationship between the concepts involved in a proposition. On this ground, propositions may be classified as either analytic or synthetic. An analytic proposition/judgement is one in which the meaning of the predicate is "contained" in the meaning of the subject. A standard example is "A bachelor is a married man". This is an analytic judgement because a bachelor just is a married man. Analytic judgements are definitions or based on them. The function of analytic judgements is to fix the language by defining relationships between words. It is said that in the English language there are no two true synonyms, and this is probably true, and yet the classification of synonyms and antonyms is the business of analytic judgements.

The bulk of propositions made are not analytic, and the sentence, "This leaf is green" expresses a proposition that is synthetic. That simply means that by consideration of the meaning of "leaf" I will in no wise come to see that "leaf" means something that is green. We say, the concept "leaf" does not "contain" the concept "green". If "This leaf is green" is true, then it is something about the world that makes it true. We tend to say that the proposition expresses a true judgment as to fact. I go up to a leaf, look at it, and say, "This leaf is green".

The second issue concerns the origin of the information that renders a judgement true or false. The proposition, "This leaf is green", if true, derives its truth from observation. I go up to a leaf, look it, and then say, "This leaf is green". The judgment derives its truth from a particular experience of a leaf. The experience is an event in my conscious life, has coordinates in objective space and time, and so forth. We call such statements *a posteriori*. Judgements that cannot be so tied to particular experiences, or to any collection of particular experiences, are called *a priori*.

Now it seems that all analytical statements, for example, "a perfect box is cuboid", are not related to particular experiences, so we readily agree that all analytic propositions are also *a priori*. This seems to involve no special philosophical consequence. But then, Kant turns his attention to mathematical statements and argues that these must also be both synthetic and *a priori*.

The first argument he advances is that mathematical knowledge could not be analytical, (definitional) knowledge as it conveys real information about the world, and hence is synthetic. "We might, indeed, suppose that the proposition 7 + 5 = 12 is a merely analytic proposition, and follows by the principle of contradiction from the concept of the sum of 7 and 5. But if we look more closely we find that the concept of the sum of 7 and 5 contains nothing save the union of the two numbers into one, and in this no thought is being taken as to what that single number may be which combines both. The concept 12 is by no means already thought in merely thinking this union of 7 and 5; and I may analyse my concept of such a possible sum as long as I please, still I shall never find the 12 in it. We have to go outside these concepts, and call in the aid of the intuition ... Arithmetical propositions are therefore always synthetic. This is still more evident if we take larger numbers. For it is then obvious that, however we might turn and twist our concepts, we could never, by the mere analysis of them, and without the aid of intuition, discover what the number is that is the sum." Kant, *Critique*, B.15.

Does the meaning of "the sum of seven and five" contain by way of definition the meaning of "twelve"? If you answer "yes", then for you "7 + 5 = 12" is analytic, and if you answer "no" then it is synthetic. I answer "no", and I agree with Kant. The second issue is whether "7 + 5 = 12" is *a posteriori* or *a priori*. "But though all our knowledge begins with experience, it does not follow that it all arises out of experience. For it may well be that even our empirical knowledge is made up of what we receive through impressions and of what our own faculty of knowledge (sensible impressions serving merely as the occasion) supplies from itself. If our faculty of knowledge makes any such addition, it may be that we are not in a position to distinguish it from the raw material, until with long practice of attention we have become skilled in separating it. ... It has to be noted that mathematical propositions, strictly so called, are always judgements *a priori*, not empirical; because they carry with them necessity, which cannot be derived from experience." Kant, *Critique*, B.1. (Almost the opening statement of the second edition of the *Critique*.)

Kant's argument is that mathematical knowledge could not be a hypothesis of science, because no hypothesis of science can ever have the degree of certainty which mathematical knowledge has. I also agree with Kant. Hence, I agree with Kant that mathematical judgements, such as "7 + 5 = 12" are synthetic *a priori*.

Philosophers disagree about the status of "7 + 5 = 12". Some say that mathematical knowledge is empirical, which in Kant's terms makes "7 + 5 = 12" synthetic *a posteriori*; some say that it is conventional, which makes it definitional knowledge or analytic *a priori*, and Quine advances a sophisticated theory in which it is both (but certainly not synthetic *a priori*). So, this is a matter of debate, and belongs to the dialectic. What I think could be said about this, is that given that the issue is dialectical the current complete absence of advocates of the Kantian point-of-view expresses some oddity about our contemporary philosophy. It is as if the debate had been proscribed.

But if mathematical and logical knowledge is synthetic *a priori* then there must be an explanation for that, and Kant explains it by arguing that it is knowledge of the structure of experience imposed by the transcendent faculty of imagination. This makes sense. But I prefer here to reverse the direction of the exposition, and rather than infer the existence of this structure from the synthetic *a priori*, explain the synthetic *a priori* from the structure of experience.

That experience is structured by the mind must be allowed to be a dialectical issue; and yet, so far as I am concerned it is as manifest to me as anything I can claim to know. I only have to close my eyes to become aware that *the world that I see and know* depends on my perceiving it, and the only space and time that I know of, is the one in which those perceptual objects are located. These belong

The transcendental deduction from the synthesis of the manifold. The second argument that Kant brings forward in defence of the transcendental deduction, is the one that he himself calls the transcendental deduction.[26]

Suppose that I am counting: 1, 2, 3, 4, … . As I progress from one number to the next in succession I retain within one and the same consciousness, memory of the preceding numbers I have already counted. Counting is an act of synthesis of the mind in which separate items are brought together in a single number. If this process were not referred to a single awareness, then there could be no understanding of number.

Hume claims in the *Treatise* that time is composed of discrete atoms, indivisible units of time. Suppose this were the case, and I were to count through successive atoms of time.

Figure 4. Counting "atoms of time".

Hume tells us that there is no unity of consciousness, only successive perceptions. But in that case, there would no retention of the act of thinking number 1, once I had had passed to the number 2, and so forth. When I reach the number 2 in the count, I would have no consciousness that I had passed from 1 to 2, and that there were two moments of time, and so on. I might perhaps argue that when I have reached counting 2, then I have a memory trace present at that same moment of the previous instant when I counted 1. But then I must bring this memory trace and the present instant in which I attend to the number 2 into a single unitary manifold of conscious awareness.[27] Whichever way one looks upon the matter, consciousness must be

---

to my mental representation and as for the world independent of that representation, I have no knowledge, and, for aught I know, it may not exist.

[26] From the *Critique*: "If we were not conscious that what we think is the same as what we thought a moment before, all reproduction in the series of representations would be useless. For it would in its present state be a new representation which would not in any way belong to the act whereby it was to be gradually generated. The manifold of the representation would never, therefore, form a whole, since it would lack that unity which only consciousness can impart to it. If, in counting, I forget that the units, which now hover before me, have been added to one another in succession, I should never know that a total is being produced through this successive addition of unit to unit, and so would remain ignorant of the number. For the concept of the number is nothing but the consciousness of this unity of synthesis." Kant, *Critique*, A 103.

[27] A second rendering of the same argument from the *Critique*: "For experience as such necessarily presupposes the reproducibility of appearances. When I seek to draw a line in thought, or to think of the time from one noon to another, or even to represent to myself some particular number, obviously the various manifold representations that are involved must be apprehended by me in thought one

treated as synthesising the unity of which we are aware and counting numbers would have no meaning at all for us, were it not for that unity.

> There can be in us no modes of knowledge, no connection or unity of one mode of knowledge with another, without that unity of consciousness which precedes all data of intuitions, and by relation to which representation of objects is alone possible. This pure original unchangeable consciousness I shall name *transcendental apperception.* That it deserves this name is clear from the fact that even the purest objective unity, namely, that of the *a priori* concepts (space and time), is only possible through relation of the intuitions to such unity of consciousness. The numerical unity of this apperception is thus the *a priori* ground of all concepts, just as the manifoldness of space and time is the *a priori* ground of the intuitions of sensibility.[28]

Nowhere does Kant state in plain words that the mind, through its transcendental faculty of imagination, synthesises time and space, so that experience becomes possible for consciousness. The formulas "the manifoldness of space and time", "representations in space and time", "space and time are represented *a priori* not merely as *forms* of sensible intuition, but as themselves *intuitions* which contain a manifold"[29] occur repeatedly throughout the *Critique* and in connection with "the reproductive synthesis of the imagination" which "is to be counted among the transcendental acts of the mind" and entitled "the transcendental faculty of imagination."[30] So, we can say that according to this theory, **the mind synthesises subjective space and time**, and experiences are "dropped" into space and time, and rendered coherent.

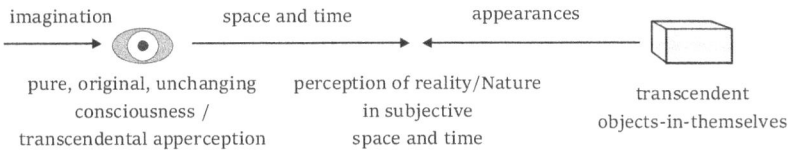

Figure 5. Synthesis of subjective space and time.

after the other. But if I were always to drop out of thought the preceding representations (the first parts of the line, the antecedent parts of the time period, or the units in the order represented), and did not reproduce them while advancing to those that follow, a complete representation would never be obtained: none of the above-mentioned thoughts, not even the purest and most elementary representations of space and time, could arise." Kant, *Critique*, A 101.

[28] Kant, *Critique*, A 107.

[29] Kant, *Critique*, B 160.

[30] Kant, *Critique*, A 101.

Subjective and objective space and time. Philosophers are agreed that human consciousness comprises or contains a mental representation of phenomena. This mental representation is within subjective space and time, which may be studied through introspection and provides the data for phenomenology. Objective (real) space and time is a **theoretical construct**, and it could even be argued that as such it is incoherent.[31] Assuming it is coherent, we presume the mind does not synthesise it. It is subjective time that is the product of the synthesis of Imagination. The structure of objective time is a construct of theoretical physics in combination with philosophy; it is usual to regard objective space and time as composed of points.[32] That is the idea we have in mind when we give a particle coordinates in space and time. We treat time as a fourth dimension and believe that it makes sense to talk of a particle located in three dimensions and time. How, then, does subjective space and time differ from objective space and time?

Subjective experience of space. Space is given not as a collection of points but as an extended manifold presented before consciousness. So, it is not subjectively presented as it is in objective space where it is conceptualised as a collection of points. Likewise, subjective time is presented as extended. We call this feature of subjective time the continuous present, and it is to this continuous present that Kant in his argument about counting draws our attention. In other words, when we reflect inwardly on our intimate experience of time, what we find is something like this: that consciousness is associated with a continuous present in which a motion or direction of time is experienced, so that events in time are constantly sensed as falling out of the present, fading into the past, and other events in time are coming before consciousness in the continuous present – we say that they are coming into being.

We may believe that there is no objective space and time whatsoever, or we may believe that there is an objective space and time; whichever way, it is subjective space and time that is before consciousness and "known" primarily and intimately. We see that subjective and objective space and time have very little in common. Subjective time is a representation in a continuous present of what may be imagined to be a portion of objective time, but it is a portion that overlaps with the past and future and contains what may be conceived as an infinite collection of moments in objective time. Another way of putting this is that subjective time is experienced, objective time is never experienced, but is a conception. Kant calls the experience of subjective time, **intuition**. Therefore, how can subjective time be abstracted from

---

[31] [Zeno's arguments are discussed in a footnote to Part III, Chapter 14, What Kantian consciousness is.]

[32] A point is a theoretical part of space-time that has no magnitude, and yet, space-time is composed of an infinity of them. The infinity in question can be shown in set theory to be *non-denumerable*, meaning not isomorphic (one-to-one) to the infinity of counting numbers. Hume holds the view that objective space-time is composed of atoms, which are very small parts of space-time with magnitude.

objective time? Alternatively, how can subjective time be a mechanical product of objective time? Hence, we have the transcendental deduction.

The transcendental deduction of subjective time
The synthesis of subjective space and time by transcendental imagination could not possibly be reproduced in a mechanical arrangement of material atoms in objective space and time.

Whichever way one looks at it, "pure, original, unchanging consciousness", the "transcendental apperception" that is "I", the Self, (a) stands outside (subjective) space and time, that is transcendent to subjective space and time, and (b) is not known or experienced as a part or product of objective space and time, which is a mere conception. It is barely possible to conceive of the subjective Self with its subjective space and time as the "product" of processes taking place between "things-in-themselves" occupying objective space and time, but any detail as to the mechanism by which this is produced has so-far proven beyond human ingenuity to bring forth. It is a complete and utter mystery. Consciousness is not to be explained by mechanisms posited in objective (real) space-time.

We can conclude that the conception of objective space and time, and the whole of theoretical physics that describes processes in objective space and time, are inadequate as concepts to account for the generation of subjective consciousness, with its attendant subjective time. Since the goal in this work is never to establish a new dogma, and hence a new ground of persecution, then merely, "It is required that you do awake your faith."[33] We have grounds in faith for supposing that pure consciousness (Self) is a being outside space and time, and is not affected by perceived alterations in space and time; and hence, it is not subject to death, which is an event conceived as belonging to objective space and time.

---

[33] [An allusion to the last scene of Shakespeare's *Winter's Tale*.]

16

The decline of paganism

Cicero's *The Nature of the Gods*, composed between 45 and 44 BCE, is a snapshot of Roman thought on the eve of the demise of the Republic. In it, three Roman aristocrats debate the "nature of the gods, the noblest of studies for the human mind to grasp,"[1] the conversation being recorded by Cicero, who remains a silent fourth voice. In the dialogue, the Epicurean position is defended by Gaius Velleius, the Stoic position is defended by Quintus Lucilius Balbus, and a third position that might be called "Roman pietist" is defended by Gaius Cotta. Cotta dominates the debate: he is allowed not only to critique without reply the positions adopted by Velleius and Balbus, but he concludes unopposed the dialogue. The fourth position, agnosticism, is that of the sceptical observer of the debate, Cicero.

The work discusses two questions: (a) do the traditional gods of the Graeco-Roman pantheon exist, and, if so, what is their nature? (b) Is there a creator of the universe, and if so what is that creator's nature?

Breakdown of faith. The modern reader of this work is struck by the extreme state of scepticism, agnosticism and disenchantment expressed which borders at times on modern cynicism.[2] The defences provided of the "old gods" are unsatisfactory intellectually, and even more hopeless emotionally. Cicero's essay is a record of a decided breakdown in faith and anticipates the collapse of paganism that was to follow in the ensuing centuries. The book represents the vacuum, which the new creed of Christianity filled.

Monotheism. Materialism is presented as an option attractive to Roman intellectuals and members of its elite governing class, but we also see the rise of monotheism. Thus, God not gods. The acceptance of the monotheism of Christianity in the C4 CE was wholly prepared by a powerful tidal movement in its favour that had been developing over the intervening centuries.

United around virtue ethics. There are other pertinent observations. The debate gets quite heated at times, but a core of urbane politeness enables all four gentlemen to get along quite nicely. This is rooted in a consensus that whatever position is adopted intellectually about God or the gods, they are unified in their adherence to virtue ethics, the life of reason as opposed to desire. At one point the Epicurean, Velleius, comes under some attack from Cotta with respect to the

---

[1] Cicero, *The Nature of the Gods*, Bk. I, 1.

[2] It is necessary to append "modern" here, because there was an "ancient" cynicism that is not identical to it. This ancient cynicism may be studied in the anthology of Robert Dobbin. Ancient cynics acted the part of "ego-shrinks" and came close to the world-denying attitude of the Indian yogis (gymnosophists). Their principal ethical idea was that of detachment. The most renown of these cynics was Diogenes of Sinope, a contemporary of Alexander the Great.

preference among Epicureans for the pleasures of eating, but in the background is the
ideal of temperance. By the time of Cicero, the debate about the nature of the old
gods had already become academic; the consensus had already moved in the
direction of monotheism, and God Almighty shall be Father of Virtue, the God of
Reason. There is no hint in this work of that passion called "enthusiasm" that leads
to religious persecution. This consensus goes far to accounting for the religious
toleration that has often been regarded as a happy feature of Roman culture.

Predominance of materialism. Since **Platonism** was to become the core of
Christian theology, it is surprising that it is absent in Cicero's work. Cicero was
himself a devotee of the **Academy of Athens**, but he does not speak directly in the
discussion, which he pretends only to record. As shall be shown, **Neo-Platonism**
and **Stoicism** became the two opposed main alternatives in Roman cognition, but
here Platonism is has not acquired separate expression.[3] This shows that the Roman
intellectual culture at the time of writing was dominated by what we would call
materialism.   The two alternatives to the Roman piety of Cotta presented, the
Stoicism of Balbus and the Epicureanism of Velleius, are at this stage both confused
expressions of naturalistic monism (materialism) into which superfluous
justifications of the existence of the old gods are introduced.

The absence of a party representing **Aristotle** and his **school of Peripatetics** is
apparent only, for the consensus between the four speakers could be described as the
common ground represented by Aristotle, and the works of Aristotle are often cited
in the discussion. Although Neo-Platonism will revive belief in an intellectual world
of Forms, and the Logos as the Form of the Good, there is an Aristotelian consensus
operating in this Roman dialogue that the senses are the source of knowledge – thus,
a bias towards empiricism.

Rejection of superstition. Although in defence of Stoicism Balbus attempts a
defence of the religious practices of divination, astrology and the interpretation of
dreams, etc., another consensus is forming that superstition is bad and should be
separated from what is true in religion. This also reflects the emergent bias towards
materialism and empiricism.

Decay of intellectual vigour is illustrated by the dialogue. Cicero is urbane,
highly cultured and well-informed, but the **absence of passion** in the work is
indicative of a loss of intellectualism. With the possible exception of Cotta, and only

---

[3] Somewhat earlier than this dialogue, the founder of the "so-called Fifth Academy", Antiochus of
Ascalon (c.125 – c.68 BCE) had already taken steps to revive the Platonism of Plato and had sought
rapprochement with the Stoics. By the time of this dialogue, the Academy of Plato, in pursuance of
the Socratic Method, had evolved into a position of scepticism. If to every question, there is a
dialectical yes and a dialectical no, then can anything be known? This stage of Platonism, historically
belonging to the philosophers Carneades and Philo of Larissa, both of whom Cicero admired, had not
yet evolved back into a statement of the faith that Plato himself found in his middle and later
dialogues.

to a degree, the postures adopted by the three principal speakers should not be mistaken for faith, and in the detachment of the narrator, Cicero, we find expression of the dominant tone of Roman society. The participants enjoy debate but they are not going to treat the outcome as a "life and death" matter. While faith may lead to enthusiasm, and enthusiasm to persecution, the energy supplied by it adds intellectual substance. It may be useful to contrast Cicero with Augustine, who is by far the "bigger" thinker.

There is a **lack of rigour** in the argument. While picking over details may be a sign of decadence, the need to "get things right" and meet objections with replies is fundamental to progress in the dialectic. The positive positions outlined by Velleius and Balbus are too obviously flawed to be taken seriously even by them, and Cotta easily subjects both to critique. At that point, a reply by either or both could develop the debate forcefully, but no reply is permitted. It's all over. Thus, we see intellectual decay. It is not dialectic, but a series of harangues.

Cynical abuse of religious ideology. The main outcome is the expression of agnosticism bordering on cynicism, and in this the principal character, Cotta, leads. The hollowness of his position is revealed by what he says of himself.

> 'In this investigation of the nature of the gods, the primary issue is whether they exist or not. You say that it is difficult to deny it. I agree, if the question is posed in public, but it is quite easy in this type of conversation conducted between friends. So though I am a *pontifex* myself, and though I believe that our ritual and state-observances should be most religiously maintained, I should certainly like to be persuaded of the fundamental issue that gods exist, not merely as an expression of opinion but as a statement of truth; for many troubling considerations occur to me which sometimes lead me to think that they do not exist at all.'[4]

As a pontifex, Cotta holds one of the highest priesthoods in the State religion of Rome, but he is privately willing to admit that he is not sure that the gods to whom he officiates at sacrifice exist. He is prepared to discuss this in private, but he is not prepared to risk a disturbance in the polity by making such speculations public. It is one rule for the elites and another for the masses. They are not "democrats" to be sure, but this borders upon a cynical abuse of religious ideology, and indeed, the possibility that the gods are inventions of man for political purposes is raised by Cotta himself.

---

[4] Cicero, *The Nature of the Gods*, Trans. P.G. Walsh, Oxford University Press, 1998, Bk. I, p.61.

'To begin with, was anyone ever so blind in his survey of realities as
not to see that these human shapes have been ascribed to the gods for
one or two possible reasons? Either some strategy of philosophers
sought to divert more easily the minds of the unsophisticated from
debased living towards observance of the gods; or superstition
ensured that statues were furnished for men to worship in the belief
that they were addressing the gods themselves.'[5]

Cotta's position borders on **hypocrisy**, and the feeling that he above all, as pontifex,
should have a firm belief in the gods is brought up by the other participants. Balbus
tells him:

'If, Cotta, you were to heed my advice, you would argue the same
case. You would reflect upon your position as leading citizen and as
priest; ... to argue against the existence of gods, whether from
sincerity or for the sake of argument, is a debased and impious
practice."[6]

Epicureanism. Velleius represents the answer of Epicurus on the nature of the
gods. Lucretius, another Epicurean, wrote *The Nature of the Universe* (c.60 BCE).
In the work of Lucretius, as in the account presented by Velleius, there is a form of
dualism. Concerning matter, the Epicureans build on the theories of Democritus,
postulating that matter is composed of atoms and the void. Souls are said to be
similarly composed, but of spiritual substance. Lucretius may be sincere in
proposing the dualist scheme, but the obvious philosophical comment is that spiritual
matter (not spiritual substance) is incoherent as a notion and redundant as an
explanatory principle, and hence the Epicurean system reduces to materialism. In
Cicero's dialogue Velleius offers this Epicurean justification for the existence of the
gods, but Cotta's reply seems correct: "So undoubtedly closer to the truth is the
claim made in the fifth book of his Nature of the Gods by Posidonius, whose
friendship we all share: that Epicurus does not believe in any gods and that the
statements which he made affirming the immortal gods were made to avert popular
odium."[7] He says this because the arguments are so weak. The first proposed is
"that gods exist because nature herself has imprinted the conception of them in the
minds of all... Epicurus terms this prolepsis."[8] This is not entirely ridiculous but is
portrayed in the dialogue as a superficial evasion introduced by Epicurus and

[5] *Ibid.*, Bk. I, p. 77.
[6] *Ibid.*, Bk. II, p. 162
[7] *Ibid.*, Bk. I, p. 123
[8] *Ibid.*, I, p. 43.

redundant in his philosophy as a whole. Epicurus is described as maintaining that the gods are indifferent to human affairs, thus taking away the motivation to worship them. Hence, Epicurus has no answer, and analysis of his statements leads towards atheism. Another consensus is building in Roman society – that if the gods exist, they lead a life of contemplation or perfect self-containment of their own pleasures in their own separate sphere and have no concern for human affairs. This denies the whole point of religion. The pagan gods are being abstracted into nothings.

Stoicism fairs no better than Epicureanism. It postulates that the world is a machine and identifies the universe with God. "Now we observe that some parts of the universe possess sensation and reason..."[9] and that "... the universe must be God, and its entire energy must lie in that element which is divine."[10] This is a statement followed by an exaggerated panegyric on the perfections of the universe, that again cries out for the challenge – what of natural and human evil? – "The universe alone has no deficiencies."[11] It is all too strained: "the universe is alive, and endowed with consciousness, intelligence, and reason; and the logical conclusion from this is that the universe is God."[12] A catalogue of natural phenomena all of which are worshipped poetically in an exaggerated mood of enthusiasm – Sun, Moon, the whole lot – leads emotively to the praise of Providence, and we again cry out – what of the problem of evil?

There are rationalising arguments such as the proof of the existence of god from the design of the world, and even the ontological argument,[13] which is attributed to Chrysippus, but both cry out for refutation, and it is Cotta, the pontifex, who delivers the blows of natural and human evil in the subsequent reply, which will echo through this history of ideas as far as Hume's *Dialogues Concerning Natural Religion* and beyond.

> 'Either God wishes to remove evils and cannot, or he can do so and is unwilling, or he has neither the will nor the power, or he has both the will and the power. If he has the will but not the power, he is a weakling, and this is not characteristic of God.'[14]

But to these rationalising arguments are adjoined confused arguments from revelation – apparitions such as when "Castor and Pollux appeared fighting on

---

[9] *Ibid.*, II. p. 29.

[10] *Ibid.*, II. p. 30.

[11] *Ibid.*, II. p. 37.

[12] *Ibid.*, II. p. 47.

[13] The ontological argument for the existence of God, is the argument that the concept of God as a perfect being implies His necessary existence.

[14] *Ibid.*, III. p. 133

horseback in our battle-line"[15] and "prophecies and premonitions of future events. These constitute nothing less than a declaration that the future is being revealed, portended and predicted to men."[16] Balbus endorses the Sibylline prophecies and the work of augers and soothsayers.[17] That makes, Stoicism into a perverse alliance of rationalising tendencies with crass superstition.

Allegorical interpretation. When one is embarrassed by one's own gods, one interprets them allegorically or naturalistically. "By Saturn they seek to represent that power which maintains the cyclic course of times and seasons."[18] Regarding Demeter/Persephone – "they regard her as the seed of the harvest."[19] Disgust can't help but show through: "But though we reject these stories with contempt, we shall be able to identify and grasp the nature of the divinity pervading each and every natural habitat, as Ceres on earth, as Neptune on the seas, and as other deities in other areas."[20] Such naturalistic identifications reveal that the Stoics have no idea from whence these gods came. We know their origin lies in the matriarchal layer of human consciousness, in the religion of Dionysus before it was reformed. When Euripides wrote, he had more than a vague inkling of the origin of religious myth, and he wrote frankly about it, but in this work of Cicero that origin has been forgotten, and the debating partners are at a loss to account for the stories.

The dialogue expresses a loss of faith, stemming from the perceived immorality and irrationality of the ancient myths and the gods and heroes they celebrate. So much for "these outstanding gifts of the gods to mankind,"[21] so much for the perfection of our bodily parts and "universal abundance,"[22] and who cares about "the frequent epiphanies of the gods"?[23]

Cotta rightly exposes the hollowness of both the Epicurean and Stoic solutions, but his own defence of religion amounts to an **intellectual rationalisation of anti-intellectualism**. His view is that Roman religion was handed down to *we Romans* by our forebears, and we should observe its forms unswervingly, without asking questions.

> 'The religion of the Roman people in general has two separate aspects, its ritual and the auspices, to which a third element is added when, as a result of portents and prodigies, the interpreters of the

[15] *Ibid.*, II. p. 6.
[16] *Ibid.*, II. p. 7.
[17] *Ibid.*, II. p. 120.
[18] *Ibid.*, II. p. 64.
[19] *Ibid.*, II. p. 66.
[20] *Ibid.*, II. p. 71.
[21] *Ibid.*, II. p. 140.
[22] *Ibid.*, II. p. 157.
[23] *Ibid.*, II. p. 166.

> Sibyl or the diviners offer prophetic advice. I have never regarded
> any of these constituents of our religion with contempt; I have come
> to the firm view that Romulus by his auspices, and Numa by
> establishing our ritual, laid the foundations of our Roman state.
> Certainly Rome could never have achieved such greatness without the
> supreme benevolence of the immortal gods.'

This anti-intellectual position of "Roman religion is best" is a mask for bad faith; it amounts to an **identification of Roman religion with patriotism** and assumes that the gods exist to make Rome great, which is a variant of the myth of the chosen people, and a rationalisation of Roman violence. Cotta's view amounts to, "We, Roman patricians, we don't know why, but we do know best."

Scapegoating. The rest of Cotta's diatribe is an attempt to put the blame for any intellectual difficulties in religion on the shoulders of the Greeks and draw a distinction between Roman and Greek religion by divesting all Roman religion of mythologem, myth and archetype and narrowing it into the performance of rituals for the good of the state. The distinction between Roman and Greek religion is appropriate. Whereas Greek religion developed out of ritual into myth by expanding its abundant store of mythologems and archetypes, Roman religion contracted myth into ritual by divesting myth of narrative. But given that the conversation is taking place on the eve of the destruction of the Roman Republic, the onset of the decay and perversion of the notion of Roman *virtus*, the position Cotta adopts may be viewed by us with extreme irony.

Roman bargaining religion. The limited scope of Roman religion by the time of Cicero[24] can be gauged from the following remark.

> Behind all this ceremonial lies the fundamental fact that Roman
> religion was a bargaining religion. Roman commanders in the field
> vowed public thanksgivings and shrines provided that victory was
> granted them. The characteristic formula in ceremonial prayer is: 'If
> you deities duly lend your aid, we in return will reward you.'[25]

Cotta's conception of religion is based on the idea that the gods and all that is benevolent in the universe exists for the sake of a small group of persons. Romans saw their relationship with the gods to be one of contract – on their part, the payment

---

[24] This qualifying remark is needed. In the history of Roman religion may be traced all those layers that we find in Greek religion, and it seems the Romans led the civilised world by their overthrow of Carthage, which still adhered to the practice of child-sacrifice. However, Roman religion mutated into a state religion; a monopoly of the Patrician caste over that state religion is being reflected here. This priestly monopoly is embodied by Cotta, and, to a lesser extent, by Cicero.

[25] P. G. Walsh, Introduction to Cicero's *The Nature of the Gods*, Oxford University Press, 1998, xxv.

of dues of sacrifice and fulfilment of obligations undertaken in oaths, which imposed on the part of the gods an obligation to grant them victory as due compensation. Consultation with the gods took the form of a forensic science and is almost indistinguishable from a modern conception of science – namely, that nature or the gods can be controlled and manipulated provided the technology is rightly applied.[26]

Hence, **the myth of Rome's destiny** is built up out of a will to preservation and domination; Virgil's *Aeneid* caters to the demand for it, wherein the gods convey to Aeneid his mission in a visionary dream while Aeneas in flight has stopped at Crete.

> It was night and sleep held in its grasp all living things upon the earth. There as I lay, the holy images of the gods, the Phrygian Penates[27] whom I had rescued from the thick of the flames of the burning city of Troy, seemed to be standing bathed in clear light before my eyes, where the full moon streamed in through the unshuttered windows. At last they spoke to me and comforted my sorrow with these words:

[26] To this Hegel's summary of the nature of Roman religion could be added. He tells us in his lectures on the Roman World that the "highest characteristic" of the Romans was expressed in Religion, though it is the religion of constraint. Greek and Roman religions are not at all the same, as is popularly supposed. The Greek divinities "were more or less introduced among the Romans" but that does not entail that they are identical. The Roman spirit "remained satisfied with a dull, stupid subjectivity"; which is reflected for their preference for doing things in secret, in the preference for concealment. They did not develop the religious thrill of awe. All relations are made into bonds and cemented by sacra – including oaths, the *confarreation*, [traditional and strict form of marriage.] the auguries and auspices. "The knowledge of these sacra is utterly uninteresting and wearisome, affording fresh material for learned research as to whether they are of Etruscan, Sabine, or other origin." The patricians identified themselves with these sacra and became "sacredotal families" – the "sacred gentes – the possessors and conservators of Roman religion: the plebeians then become the godless element." The Pontifex Maximus presided over all the "sacra" "and gave them such a rigidity and fixity as enabled the patricians to maintain their religious power so long." Roman Religion is characterised by projections onto their deities of "certain voluntary aims": "The Roman religion is therefore the entirely prosaic one of narrow aspirations, expediency, and profit. The divinities peculiar to them are entirely prosaic; they are conditions [of mind or body], sensations, or useful arts..." For example, *Pax, Tranquillitas, Vacuna* (Repose), *Angeronia* (Sorrow and Grief). Jupiter as "Jupiter Capitolinus" "represents the generic essence of the Roman Empire, which is also personified in the divinities "Roma" and "Fortuna Publica"." Romans introduced the practice of making vows to their deities. They did not worship disinterestedly. Mention of the Greek gods is "lifeless and exotic in their hands". Virgil, for example, has "a frigid Understanding". "The gods are used in these poems as machinery, and in a merely superficial way". [Georg Wilhelm Friedrich Hegel, *The Philosophy of History*, trans. J. Sibree, Dover, New York, 1956, p.298. pp 290 - 292]

When Hegel writes about history, and his whole work is a philosophy of the spirit in history, his observations are at best loosely grounded in historical data, sources and scholarship; his assessment of most cultures is vague. His lecture on Roman religion is no exception but contains some insight into the spirit of Roman religion.

[27] [See footnote in Part II, Chapter 19, Roman religion.]

'Apollo here speaks the prophecy he will give you if you sail back to Ortygia.[28] By his own will he has sent us here and we stand at your door. We followed you and your arms when Troy was burned to ashes. With you to lead us we have sailed across unmeasured tracts of swelling seas, and in time to come we shall raise your sons to the stars and give dominion to your city. Your task is to build great walls to guard this great inheritance. You must never flag in the long toil of exile, and you must leave this place. Delian Apollo did not send you to these shores. Crete is not where he commanded you to settle. There is a place – Greeks call it Hesperia – an ancient land, strong in arms and in the richness of her soil. The Oenotrians lived there, but the descendants of that race are now said to have taken the name of king Italus and call themselves Italians. This is our true home.[29]

In the times of Cicero, there were two opposed cultural tendencies in patrician Roman society – one part, represented by Virgil and Ovid, wished to integrate their mythology into that of the Greeks, and sought to mythologise the foundation of their sacerdotal families down to the times of Aeneas and the fall of Troy; the other, represented by Cotta, sought to separate their Roman religion from the "corruption" of Greek religion, and trace back their traditions perhaps only as far back as Romulus and Numa.

Roman destiny. Both parties were agreed on the core notion of idealising Roman destiny to rule the world.

But (I must believe) it was already written in the book of fate that this great city of ours should arise, and the first steps be taken to the founding of the mightiest empire the world has known – next to God's. The Vestal Virgin was raped and gave birth to twin boys.[30]

Such a narrow conception of divine providence must break up once the debasement of patrician culture sets in. This culture was already at an advanced stage of decay by the time of Cicero.

… traditional attitudes, idealized as characteristic of the early and middle Republics, were by Cicero's day being increasingly called into question. Ritual practices began to fall into disuse. The office of

[28] Ortygia is a name of Delos, the mythological birthplace of Apollo.
[29] Virgil, *Aeneid*, Trans. David West, Penguin, 1990. III. 147-167.
[30] Livy, *The Early History of Rome*, trans. Aubrey de Sélincourt, Penguin, 1960, 1.3. The Vestal Virgin is Rhea Silvia, and the twins are Romulus and Remus.

> *flamen Dialis* remained unfilled between 87 and 11 BC. Balbus in his
> treatise laments the abandonment of taking the auspices before
> battle.[31]

Under the Roman empire the patrician ideal would suffer a continuous erosion. Patrician families continued to dominate civil life, but their political influence was constantly diluted.[32]

It is this moribund religion that Cotta represents by his bad faith in practising rituals to which he can attach no mythological, that is, religious content, but serve merely as an expression of Roman bullying of supernatural powers. Cotta then goes on, by repeating the findings of "secret and abstruse books", to subject mythology in general to a withering attack of reason. The work Cotta refers to is the *Antiquities* by Marcus Terentius Varro (116 – 27 BCE), which was a theological work, now lost, in the tradition that Cotta represents, rejecting Greek mythology as superstition and advocating a purer Roman religion in which the legendary king Numa is extolled. Varro exposed the irrationality of Greek religion. Cotta, citing Varro, mentions six different deities identified as Hercules.

> The most ancient was the son of Jupiter – the Jupiter who is likewise
> "the most ancient", for in old Greek works we find that there are
> several Jupiters as well. From this ancient Jupiter, then, and Lysithoe
> is sprung the Hercules who, we are told, struggled with Apollo to
> seize the tripod. There is a second Hercules who is said to be
> Egyptian, the son of the Nile; they say that he composed the Phrygian

---

[31] P. G. Walsh, Introduction to Cicero's *The Nature of the Gods*, Oxford University Press, 1998, xxv. The Flamen Dialis was the high priest of Jupiter, and subject to many ritual prohibitions.

[32] Three dates may be singled out as significant landmarks in this lengthy process, which is studied in the work of Gibbon. (1) The Edict of Caracalla (212 CE) extended Roman citizenship to all free men in the Roman Empire; and the rights of Roman women to all free women in the Roman Empire. This was done to raise taxes to pay for the military dictatorship but is a symbolic as well as practical statement of the end of the exclusivity in the concept that Rome is a single family of patrician families – the legend that the patrician families (*gentes*) derived descent from the one hundred fathers (*patres*) that Romulus appointed as senators. (2) The Edict of Galienus (259 CE). During the crisis of the C3 CE, the Roman empire nearly collapsed under the onslaught of barbarian inroads of the Franks, the Suevi (the Alemanni), the Goths and the Persians. At one point an invasion of the Alemanni penetrated Italy. The Roman senate organised an effective resistance, the Allemanni retreated and were eventually defeated by an army of emperor Gallienus. Gibbon describes how Gallienus was alarmed at the actions of the senate and issued an edict prohibiting "the senators from exercising any military employment" [Gibbon, *Decline and Fall*, Vol 1. X], and how the senators thereafter descended into luxuriousness. (3) Foundation of Constantinople (330 CE). This represents the practical and symbolic shift of power from Rome to the Eastern Empire.

The protracted decline of the military, civil and religious monopoly of the patrician *gentes* is surely one of the long-term causes of the collapse of paganism and the rise of Christianity.

writings. A third Hercules hails from the Digiti of Mt. Ida, to whom the folk of Cos sacrifice. There is a fourth who is the son of Jupiter and Asteria, the sister of Latona; he is worshipped especially by the people of Tyre, and people say that Carthago is his daughter. There is a fifth in India, who bears the name Belus; a sixth is the one we know, whom Alcmena bore by Jupiter – Jupiter mark three, that is, for as I shall presently explain, we are told of several Jupiters as well.

It is an error on Cotta's part to suppose that this cynical attack on pagan mythology can be conducted in such a manner as to leave the "pure" Roman religion of patriarchal violence unscathed.[33] In Cicero's rendering of the debate, Balbus, the Stoic defender of allegorical interpretations protests Cotta's withering reduction of Greek myth to utter nonsense. "So you regard them as fairy-stories, do you?" – a charge whose truth was to haunt Roman conscience henceforth. We see, however, that Cotta is not merely in full retreat from myth on the ground that they are lying fables, but he is unconsciously revolted by their true origin in what we can interpret as ritual human sacrifice instituted in the matriarchal religion.

Wither the crisis of faith leads. Let us examine where the crisis of faith and scepticism arising in the dying embers of the Roman Republic led. A good example is Arnobius of Sicca (d. c.330 CE), who was a Christian apologist of Berber origin living during the reign of Emperor Diocletian (284 – 305 CE). His *Against the Pagans* is a defence of Christianity at the time of the persecution of Christianity by Diocletian. It is a longish work in seven books. In the first two books Arnobius defends a heterodox variant of Christianity that betrays only scant knowledge of the Gospels; the bulk of the work comprises demonstrations of the absurdities of pagan religion. Here is an example of his writing from the seventh book, attacking the pagan ritual of sacrifice.

Do the gods of heaven live on these sacrifices, and must materials be supplied to maintain the union of their parts? And what man is there so ignorant of what a god is, certainly, as to think that they are maintained by any kind of nourishment, and that it is the food given to

---

[33] The passage, however, provides valuable corroborative evidence of all the themes that we have been exploring. Cotta's geography is vague: the India he refers to is Babylonia, where Belus is the title of Ba'al, Lord, god-king and sacrificial consort of the Goddess, or Queen of Heaven, Anat, Anath, Astarte, Inanna, Tanit, Juno or Caelestis. The same Ba'al to whom the little male boys were burned alive in Carthage, identified at Tyre as Melqart, whom the Greeks called Tyrian Heracles; we are not surprised to learn that the goddess Carthago is his legendary daughter. The Romans identified Juno = Hera as the goddess who took special delight in Carthage, which in turn identifies Heracles as Ba'al Hamon at Carthage, and throughout in his original manifestation as a sacrificial fertility god of the Semitic peoples.

them which causes them to live and endure throughout their endless immortality? … But if a god, as is said, has no body, and cannot be touched at all, how is it possible that that which has no body should be nourished by things pertaining to the body, - that what is mortal should support what is immortal, and assist and give vitality to that which it cannot touch?[34]

This extract represents the collapse of pagan belief in the light of Ionian cognition. Arnobius has advanced to a clear and distinct understanding that if the gods are immortal, immaterial and perfect beings, then they cannot require feeding by sacrifice. The concept of sacrifice as feeding the gods or as a symbolic gesture, and the interpretation of myths as allegories are not sufficiently compelling to a reason thus constituted to make the continuance of the practice seem justified. Hence, paganism has become moribund.

The bulk of Arnobius's book deals with many of the other aspects of the same problem. What we are hearing throughout all of this is the ridicule of gods whose reputed actions place them in the arena of human passions – the criticism of Xenophanes multiplied a thousand times over. "Homer and Hesiod attributed to the gods all the things which among men are shameful and blameworthy – theft and adultery and mutual deception." To this is added a critique of anthropomorphism and idolatry; and the critique of Varro is expressly included as demonstrating the absurdity of the multiplicity of the gods and heroes, the several Hercules problem and other problems of similar ilk are liberally drawn upon. Paganism has rotted from within and died.

But that does not endow the work of Arnobius with intellectual vigour – it has the lethargy of a system that has already been well honed – the criticisms of paganism had been in circulation for almost a millennium. Arnobius knows next to nothing about Christianity as a revealed religion. His arguments for Christianity are shallow in comparison to his arguments against paganism. His work amounts to: "Paganism is false, therefore, Christianity is true." His theology is a mishmash.[35]

---

[34] Arnobius, *Adversus Gentes*, Ed. Rev. Alexander Roberts and James Donaldson, T & T Clark, Edinburgh, 1871. II. 36 Arnobius, Adversus Gentes, Ed. Rev. Alexander Roberts and James Donaldson, T & T Clark, Edinburgh, 1871. VII, 3.

[35] While orthodox Christian theology is based on Platonism, it dropped the theory of reincarnation advocated by Origen in favour of the conception of life as a one-off trial. Pre-existence was also dropped, and we arrived at the notion that human beings are brought into existence at birth, subjected to suffering in life as a test of their ability to resist temptation, tried on that basis at death, and sent to Heaven, Hell or Purgatory accordingly. The Day of Judgement makes an awkward companion to this schema and is "resolved" in the idea of a resurrection of the body, when the saved are brought back to life and enjoy Earthly paradise once again. In Arnobius's work an alternative schema is tried out. He writes, "The divine Plato, many of whose thoughts are worthy of God, and not such as the vulgar hold, in that discussion and treatise entitled the *Timaeus*, says that the gods and the world are

This mishmash will be eventually sorted and resolved by a much greater intellect than Arnobious – by Augustine. But we cannot call Augustine an exponent of the dialectic. He is a man in faith arriving at the solution to a problem, but unconscious of how his conclusions are bounded by a much-reduced framework of cognition.

---

corruptible by nature, and in no wise beyond the reach of death, but that their being is ever maintained by the will of God, [their] king and prince: for that that [even] which has been duly clasped and bound together by the surest bands is preserved [only] by God's goodness; and that by no other than by him who bound [their elements] together can they both be dissolved if necessary, and have the command given which preserves their being. If this is the case, then, and it is not fitting to think or believe otherwise, why do you wonder that we speak of the soul as neutral in its character, when Plato says that it is so even with the deities, but that their life is kept up by God's grace, without break or end." [Arnobius, *Op. Cit.* II. 36]

The schema that is confusedly presented in Arnobius's work goes along these lines: the soul is neither mortal nor immortal at birth and may become immortal through faith in Christ. This is a development of the idea, seen in Plutarch's brand of Neo-Platonism, that the evil soul could be punished in the afterlife by utter oblivion, now supplemented by the correlative idea of the reward of immortality for the good. The passage above reflects: (1) the common starting point that Christian theology arises from reflection on "divine" Plato. (2) An impulse to negate the potential for life-affirmation in that theology, by denying the possibility of repeated trials through further incarnation. (3) The impulse to make life into a one-off trial, whose consequences are not just the alternatives of damnation and heaven, but alternatives of utter annihilation and immortality. (4) Hostility to the body and lust, not shown in the above quotation, but demonstrable from the text, and hence an interpretation of that one-off trail in terms of the challenge to resist bodily temptations. (5) The above extract contextually allows existence to the (pagan) gods but denies them immortality. (6) Immortality, then, as the end to be won through devout life. (7) All of this projected onto the archetype of Christ, which we must call an archetype, for the historical personage of Jesus of Nazareth has little to do with it. (8) An impassioned tone that excludes impartial discussion – an "I'm right, your wrong" attitude that is strained out of all proportion to the "objective" inquiry – what is life about? What may I expect at death? (10) Humanity is heading in the direction of persecution – whosoever comes out on top in this overly impassioned debate will send any opponent to the fire, both in this life and the next. It is a disease of the spirit. (10) An admixture in Arnobius's text of some ideas belonging to Manichaeism, in that it is possible that the creation of man is the work of the devil rather than god.

17

The Roman anomaly

We have in Roman religion the same problem as Greek religion – there is no consensus among the scholars. Reaction to Frazer's *Golden Bough* again lies at the core of the problem. Frazer's work advertises itself as an interpretation of Roman religion; it opens by describing the cult of *Diana Nemorensis*, Diana of the Wood, whose centre was the lake and grove of **Aricia**. Aricia was the centre of the cult of Diana common to all the Latin peoples, of which Rome was in its earliest days one member.[1] This is what Frazer tells us happened at the grove at Arica.

> In this sacred grove there grew a certain tree found which at any time of the day, and probably far into the night, a grim figure might be seen to prowl. In his hand he carried a drawn sword, and he kept peering warily about him as if at every instant he expected to be set upon by an enemy. He was a priest and a murderer; and the man for whom he looked was sooner or later to murder him and hold the priesthood in his stead. Such was the rule of the sanctuary. A candidate for the priesthood could only succeed to office by slaying the priest, but having slain him, he retained office till he was himself slain by a stronger or craftier.[2]

This cult does require explanation. Frazer tells us, it survived into the times of the Roman empire, and we have it on the authority of Suetonius that Caligula "caused the *rex Nemorensis,* who had held his priesthood for many years, to be supplanted by a stronger adversary."[3] We have already learned the essential ingredients of Frazer's answer to the mystery of why this took place – that the king of the wood was the personification of the spirit of nature that must be married to nature – as Goddess – and die for the sake of nature's fertility. This king of the wood assumed the name of Virbius, just as every man chosen as the consort of Cybele, was called Attis. He might also be called Zeus, or Adonis, or Heracles, or Dionysus.[4]

---

[1] When Rome became dominant among the Latin peoples, when it had defeated and raised to the ground its founding city of Alba Julia, the cult of Diana was established on the Aventine, one of the seven "sacred" hills of Rome.

[2] Frazer, *The Golden Bough*, Chapter 1. The King of the Wood.

[3] Suetonius, *Life of Caligula*, section 35.

[4] Frazer writes, "He may have personated in flesh and blood the great Italian god of the sky, Jupiter, who had kindly come down from heaven in the lightning flash to dwell among men in the mistletoe – the thunder besom – the Golden Bough – growing on the sacred oak in the dells of Nemi. If that was so, we need not wonder that the priest guarded with drawn sword the mystic bough which contained

Collective amnesia. Evidence for the existence of such a stage of ideation that is attested throughout all the pages of Frazer's work, as in others, has also been amply supplied here. I have called the cognition that frames such rites *primitive materialism*. Its existence is related to the question – did or did not ancient peoples practice animal and human sacrifice? And if so, why? The presence of animal sacrifice is utterly incontestable; the presence of human sacrifice is also utterly incontestable. But it has been frequently ignored. We may call this collective amnesia. If animal sacrifice "makes sense", then so too does human sacrifice. The one rite implies the other.

Why sacrifice to the gods? Because in some sense the sacrifice is pleasing to the gods, that it feeds the gods, and that the gods demand it. Because, the fertility of nature somehow depends on the blood spilled. Because, the primordial aggression in man, subject to such-and-such an occasion, breaks out in divine possession, and a victim is selected and literally rendered limb-from-limb in an ecstatic outpouring of blood that manifests the presence of the god or goddess. The gods impel it. Then, if all this be so, how much more pleasing, efficacious and compelling is the shedding of human blood to animal blood?

It demands a moral revolution to distinguish human from animal sacrifice – a moral revolution in which the dignity of human life comes to the fore, in which human beings acquire, or at least begin to acquire, rights. That such a revolution took place in ancient Greece sometime in the Dark Age, between 1200 and 800 has been already shown. It remains to ask, when did this revolution take place in ancient Rome?

Denial. We have already encountered among scholars of Greek religion the phenomenon of denial – that human sacrifice never did take place among the ancient Greeks – that the attestations are few and accidental, and human sacrifice was the practice of another peoples, the Phoenicians perhaps, but was never an institution among the Greeks. That is false as to fact. The Greeks did practice it.

The same impulse to denial – a turning away, an averting of the eyes – may be found in the interpretation of Roman religion. That Romans did practice human sacrifice is attested from reliable historical sources, but it is still possible to turn away from this practice and perceive it as non-essential to Rome.

We expect to see in Georges Dumézil's *Archaic Roman Religion* a thorough discussion of Frazer's position, if only to reject it. We do not. "I confine myself here to these considerations," is the polite starting point. "They suffice to suggest, not the inaccuracy, but rather the incompleteness of the idea held by Frazer of the Latin kingship, in the line of *Wald- und Feldkulte*, that the essential element of its

---

the god's life and his own. The goddess whom he served and married was herself, if I am right, none other than the Queen of Heaven, the true wife of the sky-god." Frazer, *The Golden Bough*, LXVIII.

office was magical control of the fecundity of nature."[5]   What we find here is some lip-service respect for Frazer, followed by cursory rejection of the whole thesis. Dumézil turns away, only to return when he must, in his cursory discussion of the cult of Diana, where he tells us that "In spite of Frazer's fine studies, nothing allows us to believe that this rex had ever been a real king."[6]   It is an averting of the eyes. Whither, then, do his eyes turn? Towards the Indo-Europeans, and ancestors of the Italic peoples, of which the Romans are one.

The Indo-European heritage. Dumézil traces the structural similarity between some part of archaic Roman religion and the religion of the Indo-Europeans, who migrated into Europe as elsewhere from the fifth millennium onwards, being established then in Europe as the Danubian and Starcevo cultures, being established in the Caucasus as the Iranians by c.2250, migrating into Greece and Italy between 2000 and 1600, and invading Mesopotamia and the Indus valley as the Mitanni and Aryans respectively c.1600. The common origin of the Indo-European languages attests to the migrations, and the conclusion that there was a migration is supported by the evidence of archaeology, and by the evidence of mythology. In this aspect the scholarship of Dumézil is important. He demonstrates the common core between the religious structures of the Vedas, the Iranians (Zend), the Celts, the Scandinavians, together with the Romans and Latins.

The Archaic Triad. This common core finds expression in Roman religion in what Dumézil refers to as *The Archaic Triad* of Jupiter, Mars and Quirinus. In addition to these three male gods, there is one important female deity – Dawn – who in Rome is worshiped as Mater Mutata, the deified name for the "break of the day". He regards the triad as an Indo-European structure and calls it the "ideology of the three functions", which are (a) Jupiter, kingship, leadership, justice; (b) Mars, war; (c) Quirinus, agriculture. According to him the three major deities comprised the original archaic religion, and to each corresponded a dedicated priest called a *flamen*. These priests of Jupiter, Mars and Quirinus are served by the *major flamens*, but there were twelve other *flamens* serving lesser deities.

To see how this triad might act in a practical situation, consider war between two Latin peoples, say between Rome and Alba Longa, the legendary mother city of Rome. In the first place, religious duty requires that the war be a just war. Alba

---

[5] Georges Dumézil, *Archaic Roman Religion*, trans. Philip Krapp, John Hopkins Press, London, 1966, p. 17.

[6] Dumézil, *Archaic Roman Religion, Op. cit.*, p. 408. The reference is to *Wald- und Feldkulte* by Wilhelm Mannhardt, 1904. While acknowledging at Aricia, "Excavations have brought to light a number of votive offerings whose meaning is plain: images of the male and female organs, statuettes of nursing mothers or of women clothed but with the fronts of their bodies exposed," which all point to the context of fertility, Dumézil tells us that Virbius " is a complete mystery". All Dumézil offers is an ex-Cathedra dismissal of the whole theory of Frazer. The idea that Frazer calls the *rex Nemorensis* a "king" is an overlooking of all the subtleties that Frazer attaches to this idea.

Longa must have given just cause for Rome to declare war upon it, and this must amount to more than mere cattle-rustling. This issue of legality falls under the auspices of Jupiter. The college of *fetiales* must be consulted. This is an advisory body of priests whose duty is to see that the war be just in principle, and that the declaration of war be conducted in the right manner. For example, war cannot be declared before reparations have been demanded and refused, and corresponding bodies of *fetiales* from the antagonistic cities have conferred. Hence, a declaration of war does not involve Mars – it involves Jupiter and may involve Quirinus. Only once war is declared is Mars involved; the symbol of Mars is the lance, and hostilities are initiated by throwing a lance onto enemy soil, as we see illustrated in many episodes from Virgil's *Aeneid*. The reason why a declaration of war may involve Quirinus, the god of the third function, the agricultural aspect, is, as Dumézil speculates, that the Romans did away with the Vedic distinction between warrior and agrarian castes quite early, and men were alternately citizens and soldiers as the occasion demanded. At the earliest stage, the Romans conceived of themselves as primarily a peaceful people, and hence placed the Temple of Mars (War) outside the city wall, with the gates of the temple shut during peacetime, indicative of the normal condition. He quotes from a commentary by Servius on the *Aeneid*, "Quirinus is the Mars who presides over peace [*qui praeest paci*] and is worshiped inside the city, for the Mars of war [*belli Mars*] has his temple outside the city."[7] Quirinus only became associated with a warlike function through his later assimilation to Romulus, and in the fact that Romans were alternately agrarians and soldiers.

This account of the role of the three functions in the declaration of war illustrates the difficulties that Dumézil's thesis encounters in his attempt to make it a comprehensive account of archaic Roman religion. It ignores the possible presence of any other element and tends to flatten the development of Roman religion by focusing only on what he considers to be its primordial core.

There are problems as to detail and problems as to essence. Let us examine first some of the details. Here, one issue that arises is the assimilation of the function of Mars (war) to that of Quirinus (agriculture) and conversely of Quirinus to Mars. In other words, while Mars and Quirinus may be in theory distinct, in practice they tend to coalesce. To maintain the purity of the separation, Dumézil is obliged to oppose the theory of an agrarian Mars or of a martial Quirinus.[8]

---

[7] Dumézil, *Archaic Roman Religion, Op. cit.*, p. 262.

[8] It is always comforting to find support of another expert; thus, Wissowa who "forcefully defended the warlike Mars against W. Roscher, J.H. Usener, and especially A. von Domazsewski." Dumézil affirms that Mars has essentially to do with war, but his one example to support this – the temple vowed by Decimus Junius Brutus Callaicus and dedicated in 138 BCE, is late in the historical record and ambiguous as evidence. He then opposes the argument attributed to H.J. Rose's that "the ritual of the October Horse, two peasant ceremonies described by Cato, and the words of the *carmen* of the

Focusing on the problem of an agrarian Mars, Mars is associated with a horse sacrifice that is most brutal as to details. This sacrifice was carried out annually on October 15. After a series of two horse chariot races were conducted on the Campus Martius, the right-hand horse of the winning team was immolated by a spear, the head and tail were cut off, and a fight was staged for the right to display the head. The tail, or more precisely the penis, covered with blood, was carried along the Via Sacra to the Regia, the residence of the high-priest, the *Pontifex Maximus* of Rome, and the blood was sprinkled on the Roman hearth, which I take to indicate the sacred fire maintained in the Temple of Vesta adjacent to the Regia. How is it possible to deny a connection between this ritual and fertility? Dumézil's response is "the king is the beneficiary". What does that mean? For another example of this fudging, his response to the second rustic ritual described by Cato, Dumézil writes, "Mars must be interpreted here as what he is always and everywhere: the actual or virtual fighter, the sentinel ready to keep the enemy at a distance or defeat him."[9] From whence the "must"? And finally, he concludes, "To sum up, from whatever side one views the problem, whether at Rome, or at Iguvium, or in Etruria, a strict checking of the arguments leaves Mars in his traditional role as warrior god and god of the warriors."[10] This counter-argument is not convincing for it is nothing but assertion of his thesis.

Dumézil has demonstrated an important structural connection between Roman and Indo-European religion but has exaggerated its significance to the exclusion of other elements. Further, while one would expect this structural element to be archaic, deriving as it does from the beliefs of the original Indo-European (Italic) immigrants to the Italy peninsula, his claim to have demonstrated this as such is suspect. The reason why this is important is because the establishment of a second triad, the Capitoline Triad of Jupiter, Juno and Minerva, is attributed by legend to the last Etruscan king of Rome, Tarquinius Superbus, and it is a cornerstone of Dumézil's interpretation of Roman religion that this Capitoline Triad is not the original archaic form of the Roman pantheon. We shall find reason to question this conclusion.

The problem of sources. But first, let us consider the most fundamental problem of all in the interpretation not just of Roman religion, but of Roman history, and this is the problem of sources.

Writing was introduced to Italy via the Greek colony of Cumae during the seventh century. If written records were kept during the period of the Roman kings, then they did not survive. One exception is the discovery of a broken stone pillar

---

Arvales" illustrate the counter-thesis of an agrarian Mars. – Dumézil, *Archaic Roman Religion, Op. cit.*, pp. 205, 215.

[9] Dumézil, *Archaic Roman Religion, Op. cit.*, p.236.

[10] Dumézil, *Archaic Roman Religion, Op. cit.*, p.245.

under the Lapis Niger in the Roman Forum bearing an inscription in archaic Latin that may contain the word for a king and a dedication to an unknown deity. In c.390 Rome was sacked and subsequently burnt by the Galls; according to tradition various cult objects and records survived, but this event created difficulties for subsequent Roman historians. Virtually everything we know about early Roman history comes from the work of later Roman historians and annalists. However, even this work has not come to us directly. Many of these works have been lost, and their contents may only be partially reconstructed from surviving fragments or references in the works of other later writers. The standards of these historians do not match the standards of modern historiography. Their work is heavily influenced by bias.

Roman historians only started working on Roman history during the last quarter of the third century BCE.[11] There followed several "annalists". An "annalist" is someone who embroiders historical events as opposed to someone we regard as a historian, who exercises judgment over his use of sources. These annalists added material for which they had doubtful sources and allowed myth-making to predominate in their accounts. As the years progressed the work of successive annalists grew longer, indicative of the accretion into the original account of extraneous material.[12] The *Annales Maximi* published c.131 BC by Publius Mucius Scaevola is a work of another kind and is regarded as the most reliable Latin source for ancient Roman history. There are references to Rome in Greek works dating from the fifth century. These in turn are referenced by Dionysius of Halicarnassus.[13]

---

[11] Fabius Pictor (c.225) and Lucius Cincius Alimentus (c.210) wrote histories of early Rome – both wrote in Greek, and their work has been lost. The poets Gnaeus Naevius (c.270 – c.201) and Quintus Ennius (c.239 – c.169) created literary works based on traditions; they wrote in archaic Latin, some fragments of which have survived. Cato the Elder (234 – 149) was the first Roman to write history in Latin and his *Origines*, now lost, contained an account of the early history of Rome and Latium, the early Republic and the First Punic War.

[12] The first analysts were Lucius Cassius Hemina (c.150), and Lucius Calpurnius Piso Frugi, known as Censorinus, (born c.180). Another annalist was Gnaeus Gellius (fl. c.125) who wrote twenty books covering the period 500 – 300. The works of Valeris Antias (fl. c.100) and Gaius Licinius Macer (died 66) are regarded as mainly fiction and their historiography is at a very low level. None of these sources survive.

The annalists of the first century BCE, the Roman Livy (Titus Livius Patavinus, 64 or 59 BCE – 12 or 17 CE) and the Greek, Dionysius of Halicarnassus (c. 60 BCE – after 7 BCE), are credited with adding no more fiction, but they also did not apply rigorous standards of criticism to their material. Not all of these materials survive, but it is at this point that we arrive at continuous narrative as to Rome's origins.

[13] Greek writers mentioned include Hellanicus of Mytilene (490 – c.405) Theopompus (c.380 – c.315), Aristotle (384 – 322), Callias of Syracuse (c. 300 BCE), Theophrastus (c.371 – c.287 BCE), Hieronymus of Cardia (354 – 250 BCE), Timaeus of Tauromenium (c.345 – c.250). All these works only survive in fragments. The Chronicles of Cumae may have referred to Rome and Latium. The emperor Claudius (10 BCE – 54 CE) is known to have used Etruscan sources for his work on Etruscan history. Claudius's work, now lost, was used subsequently by Tacitus (c.56 – c.120 CE) as a

Roman history prior to the empire is divided into approximately the following epochs. (1) The Latin period of the Alban kings, from the legendary foundation of Alba Longa by the son of Aeneas, Ascanius, in 1151 down to the last Alban king, Amulius, who was supplanted by his nephew, Romulus. (2) To Romulus is attributed the foundation of Rome, traditionally dated as 753. There followed the period of the Roman monarchy, whose successive monarchs were Romulus (753 – 716), Numa Pompilius (715 – 673), Tullus Hostilius (673 – 642), Ancus Marcius (642 – 616), L. Tarquinius Priscus (616 – 579), Servius Tullius (578 – 535) and lastly L. Tarquinius Superbus (535 – 509). (3) Roman Republic from 509 to 264 – conquest of Italy and the conflict of the patrician and plebeian orders. (4) Roman Republic during the struggle with Carthage, First (264 – 241) and Second (218 – 202) Punic Wars. (5) Roman Republic during its establishment of dominance of the Mediterranean – from the conclusion of the second Punic War to the election of Tiberius Gracchus in 133. This period includes four wars with Macedonia, the Roman-Seleucid War and the Third Punic War leading to the destruction of Carthage in 145. (6) Roman Republic during the period of social upheavals and civil wars; at the same time the Roman dominance extended to the acquisition of Asia, Syria and Gaul. Includes the Social War (91 – 86), the civil wars of Marius and Sulla (88 – 83), the Servile Wars, the Mithridatic Wars, the First Triumvirate (59), the death of Julius Caesar (44), and the Second Triumvirate (43 – 33) up to the establishment of the Roman empire under Augustus in 27.[14]

In relation to the sources Roman history only becomes reliable from the fourth of these epochs onwards – from the onset of the struggle with Cartage in 264. While much is known about the political and military history of Rome during this period, knowledge of its religion is scantier and open to interpretation. The subdivision of

---

source. The work of the Greek historian Diodorus Siculus, active in the first century BC, probably used Fabius Pictor as a source. The histories of Polybius (c.200 – c.118 BC) a Greek, covered the period of 264 – 146 BCE in detail.

[14] For early Roman history the most reliable sources are: (1) *Consular Fasti*. Official lists of the chief Roman magistrates, which were compiled into single publications by Mucius Scaevola, Pontifex Maximus in 130 in the record known as the *Annales Maximi*, and later by Atticus, a friend of Cicero, into a book called the liber Annulis. (2) Foreign Treaties. Texts of foreign treaties between Rome and other powers survived to the first century BC – for example, the treaty with Gabii, and the *Foedus Cassianum* (a treaty with the Latins, 485) and the treaty with Carthage (509). (3) Tabula Pontificum. The work of Scaevola, the *Annales* Maximi, also contained records of the religious calendar that had originally been written on a whitened board (tabula pontificum) and stored in the Regia. (4) The Code of the Twelve Tables was made around 450. (5) Census records. The figures quoted by Roman writers for the various censuses are creditable. (6) *Acta populi*. Enactments of the popular assembles were subsequently engraved on bronze tablets and stored in the temple of Saturn. (7) Senatorial records. Records of senatorial meetings were from 449 onwards stored first in the temple of Ceres and then in the temple of Saturn. (8) Oral tradition. Individual Roman aristocratic families preserved legends about their family history and these were passed down orally and sung in ballads at feasts.

the first three epochs may be accepted in rough outline, but until Tarquinius Superbus we do not reach a definite historical character, and all the kings prior to him may be regarded as mixtures of legend and some historical content, with the legendary character increasing the further back one proceeds. The date of the foundation of the Roman Republic is doubtful. Concerning the periods of monarchy, it is unlikely that Romulus ever existed as a historical person, and the foundation myth that relates Alba Longa to the dynasty of Aeneas is extremely doubtful as history.

I here address again the questions – what is the relationship between myth, legend and history?[15] How is myth formed? There are, I believe, doubtful responses to these questions: (a) That myth is founded upon ritual. This view is attributed to Frazer, though I do not find it in his work. (b) That myth concerns events projected into "primordial time". This distinguishes myth from legend, which are events projected into historical time. (c) That myth is not the work of literary genius or conscious design, and springs up spontaneously in the collective. (d) That myth relates to permanent underlying structures of the collective human psyche, which are called archetypes.

Each of these viewpoints expresses insight and truth, but it is the claim made of universality that makes them suspect. To deal in reverse with these.

(1) **Evolution of archetypes**. Jung identifies certain primordial images in the human psyche, which he calls archetypes, and because they influence human actions, they are also complexes. His archetypology is developed out of his interpretation of dreams and clinical practice. Though his subjects are contemporary Westerners, he assumes by backward projection that his archetypology is evidence of primordial structures of the human psyche.[16] Accepting that archetypes exist, examination of history indicates that they evolve. There is also a distinction between male and female archetypes. The primal male archetype is that of Dionysius, which is an archetype defined in relation to the fundamental female archetype of the Goddess Earth Mother. The relation of Jung's modern archetypes to the historical evolution of archetypes is a matter of open investigation.

(2) **The work of individuals**. The dynamic between what is conscious and what is unconscious in myth formation is another open question, but literary and other genius, in other words, individuals, have played a significant part in it. Examples

---

[15] [See Part I, Chapter 16, Prologue to the study of myth.]

[16] Although his philosophy-theology-psychology is best placed upon a phenomenological/idealist basis, in a genuflexion towards contemporary materialism and empiricism he frequently asserts a genetic basis for these archetypes, and claims that they are transmitted through genetic inheritance, a mechanism, which upon examination is too insubstantial to bear the weight placed upon it. A genetic basis is possible and to be expected, because in Kantian consciousness there is no contradiction between freewill and determinism. However, the Ionian/Cartesian context makes it appear that it is genetics that causes psychic phenomena, whereas the higher perspective is to see them as correlated.

include Hesiod and Homer for Greek religion, and all the annalists and poets of the Roman tradition, particularly Virgil, and to a lesser extent Ovid. At one extreme, we have the conscious manipulation of myth – cases of impostors and charlatans.[17] Conscious inventions of genius can and do play a part in this process. Another aspect is that of divine inspiration. Poets do claim to be impelled towards creative genius through possession by their Muse; it is in the most highly conscious individuals that the powers of collective and unconscious forces are most profoundly expressed.

(3) **Dynamic of myth formation**. The view that myths must be expressed as occurring in primordial time is false. The greatest example of this is the life of Jesus of Nazareth, for clearly there are mythic elements in his story. To say that something is myth, is not immediately thereby to deny that it is false as history and did not occur in historic time.[18]

---

[17] An example is Alexander of Abonoteichus (c.105 – c.170 CE) who makes an interesting case study. He invented an incarnate god called Glycon and was very influential for a period. Lucian regarded him as a contemptible fraud. An example of a state religion that, if not actually constructed by the state, was decidedly fostered and developed by it, is the cult of Serapis that was instigated by Ptolemy I Lagos (Soter) as a syncretic amalgamation of Egyptian and Greek features and was very popular throughout the Hellenistic and Roman period. Soter had a vision in the night of a new form of worship and decided to bring a statue of Pluto from a temple of Jupiter in Sinope to act as the centre of a new cult. A theology combining Egyptian and Greek forms was constructed. An Egyptian priest Manetho and a Greek priest Timotheus conferred upon the attributes of the new god and gave him his name, Serapis, with a temple at Serapeum. The sculptor Bryaxis, of the school of Scopas, made a cult image in the middle of the C4 BCE. The language of liturgy was Greek. Serapis was presented as a healer who performed miracles. The Athenian philosopher Demetrius of Phalerum was said to have been cured of blindness by him, and he wrote paeans in his honour. By the second century CE there were forty-two temples (Serapeums) in Egypt. Worship of Serapis spread abroad. His cult was maintained also on Delos, which was the centre of the slave trade. It also spread to Rome: in 38 CE Caligula built a temple to Isis, who shared worship with Serapis, in the Campus Martius. In its service we are told that science "became the handmaid of religion and was applied to the production of miracles in the Serapeums and other temples of Egypt". [1] Some of these are described by Hero of Alexandria. They are mostly based on ingenious applications of the mechanisms of the siphon and the expansive power of heated air. For example, a device to counterfeit the turning of water into wine was invented; a mechanism using expanding air was invented to propel the statue of a deity forward and salute the worshipper. There is an account by the poet Claudian of the use of a magnet to simulate the love between statues of Mars and Venus. Myth becomes popular because it responds to emotional needs, mostly unconscious, of the worshippers.
Reference: [1] Benjamin Farrington, *Greek Science*, Spokesman, 1980 (First pub. Penguin, 1944) p. 199.
[18] That does not mean that none of the events described of him did not occur. But they are not initially located in primordial time; the whole point of the myth is that God became incarnate in Man at a specific historical moment. Certain events that we may believe as occurring in a species of primordial time were constructed over this basis – such as the myth that Jesus, as Christ, is the Son of God, the Word, and is the demi-urge through which all of creation was brought into existence. For a religious person, a believer, to have faith is to merge myth with reality – to believe that, as a matter of

(4) **Myth and ritual**. Ritual concerns religious observance – actions performed in the worship of deity. The picture presented of early man in Frazer is of a creature bound by his cognitive limitations and existing only on the threshold of consciousness, subject to unconscious and/or collective forces. Hence, ritual is spontaneous. But in general ritual is not necessarily spontaneous in this sense, and runs parallel to ceremonial, which may also develop very early in the historical record. Beliefs about gods and their narratives, that is, beliefs in myths, may or may not issue in ritual or ceremonial. To believe that the gods really did destroy the world and mankind in a universal flood is not necessary to institute a ritual regarding that flood. Myth can precede ritual, or ritual precede myth, or their connection may be loose.

In conclusion, (a) there are no certain lines of demarcation between myth, legend and history, and (b) the interactions between the three are dynamic and complex.[19] With these principles in mind, then, let us examine the formation of Roman myth.

The Roman anomaly. A first observation, on which there appears to be universal agreement, is that Roman religion is peculiar in the absence of events depicted as occurring in primordial time; it appears to have **no mythology whatsoever**. Dumézil remarks that "This kind of almost completely demythologized religion, surviving only in rites whose mythological and even theological justifications have been forgotten, is seldom found in other parts of the Indo-European world."[20] He affirms that "Like all the other Indo-European peoples, the Romans at first loaded their gods with myths and based their cultic scenarios on the behaviour of the adventures of the gods. Then they forgot all that."[21] Assuming that Dumézil is right, and that the Romans did have a mythology, then their **collective amnesia** as to what it was needs to be explained. It is a very intriguing problem. "At what stage," writes Dumézil, "did Rome lose its mythology? One can only guess. Personally I would not put the beginning of this process very far back. In any case, it was certainly hastened and completed by the invasion of Greek mythology, which was much richer and much more prestigious."[22]

---

history, such-and-such really did happen. That might extend to primordial time – A Greek might believe that Cronos really did beget Zeus, that Hermes really was born of Maia. Such believers fuse primordial with historic time. However, the view that myths must be depicted in primordial time, and similarly are fashioned only in the prehistoric stages of human cultural evolution is false.

[19] Because a historical narrative involves depiction of miraculous events, that does not thereby make it into false history and mere legend, for to assume such is to take a philosophical stance that *miracles never happen*. Of course, establishing the truth of a miracle borders on the impossible, but to say that miracles never happen is likewise an *a priori* position that is not an induction from evidence. The presence of miraculous events in a narrative does not automatically make the narrative false as to history.

[20] Dumézil, *Archaic Roman Religion, Op. cit.*, p.58

[21] *Ibid.*, p.50

[22] *Ibid.*, p.55

Roman foundation myth. But it is not true that they have no mythology; they have one fashioned out of legend and quasi-history. Roman mythology is concerned with the myth of the foundation of Rome. (a) That the Roman peoples are originally an amalgamation of migrants of Trojan origin intermingling with peoples of Latin origin, symbolised by the **marriage of Aeneas to Lavinia**, the daughter of king Latinus. (b) That there was a second foundation by a son of Mars, called **Romulus**. (c) That subsequently, there were a sequence of important events such as **the rape of the Sabines**, the reign of **Numa**, the story of the combat between **the Horatii and the Curatii** in the context of conflict with Alba Longa, the rise of the Etruscan monarchy culminating in the tyranny of **Tarquinius Superbus**, his overthrow by Lucius Junius Brutus, **the establishment of the Republic** and the successful defence of the Republic in its early stages. (d) Additional accretions to the legend/myth injected into the subsequent quasi-historical narrative, as found, for example, in Livy's history, to the effect that Rome time and time again beat off enemies and displayed the courage of her peoples and its leading members, mostly patricians.

The Roman anomaly must be accounted for, as does the appearance of the Roman foundation myth.

Two epochs. I postulate that Roman religion falls into two very broad stages. I would call these layers, subject to proviso that there are layers within layers. Let us call these layers of layers *epochs*. Granted this, then, the first broad original epoch (a layer of layers) would be one where we would have found the mythology of the Indo-European peoples that appears to have so remarkably disappeared. I shall argue that we would also have found many other mythologies. The second epoch concerns the development of a **reformed religion of Rome**, with a new mythology, whose focus is the myth of the foundation of Rome. Between the two epochs, there has taken place a **religious revolution**. Traces of the first epoch have been erased, and the mythology of the second epoch has been substituted. So effective does the revolution appear to have been, that the wholescale disappearance of the mythology of the first epoch presents the case of a "demythologized religion", otherwise almost unknown in cultural history.

The Roman "dark age". To the "dark age" between the traditional date of the foundation of the Republic (509), during which Romans could barely write, and war with Etruria (culminating in 283) and the war with Tarento (the Pyrrhic war of 280-275) I shall ascribe the revolution/reformation as such – that is, the erasing of the original religion and the foundation of the new one. The period of the struggle with Carthage from the First Punic War (264 – 241), is likely to have been decisive in the development of the foundation myth. The religious revolution also falls into stages or layers.

(a) The **underdog ideology** of Rome's constant struggle against a superior force, constellated the ideology of righteous war and moral superiority.

(b) Once Rome emerges victorious from this life and death struggle, which occurs only upon the defeat of the Carthaginians as the battle of Zama (202), Rome is confronted with its sudden rise to superpower status. This sets in motion the evolution of the **ideology of providence** – that Rome is destined to greatness. This corresponds in human psychology to ego-inflation; it is a **collective superiority complex**. But, as Jung assures us, there is no superiority complex without an inferiority complex, so that the more consciously Romans attempt to account for their greatness, the more subconsciously they are aware of their cultural inferiority. Hence, it sets in motion a desire to embed Roman destiny within an idealised picture of its place in universal history. This accounts for the importation of Greek mythology into Roman religion. The inflation invites myth formation, and the legend/myth of Rome's multiple foundation is developed. The pressure to do so continues into the fifth period of Roman history (see above), as Rome acquired a massive dominion over the Mediterranean, even dominating politically the culturally superior Greece initially acquired as a protectorate and then as a province.

(c) But the process of myth-formation is even further "contaminated" or formed by **the rise of the power of the *gens*** – the extended patriarchal family, usually, but not exclusively of patrician origin, and the conflict between those families ultimately for mastery of Rome and what will become its empire. Interwoven into this conflict of private interest groups there is the "class" or "economic" conflicts around the problem of agrarian reform, the social integration of the Italic peoples into the newly formed Roman state, and the extensive rise of slavery and the issue of the social management of these slaves. Backwards projection of contemporary politics gives further impetus to myth formation. Each Roman family (*gens*) sought to trace its origin to divinity. For example, the myth of Aeneas as son of Venus, was exploited by the Julian family, who could claim descent by blood from both Venus and Jupiter. This raised the status of the family in their own esteem, as well as others, and sanctioned their divine right to rule. But as poets and annalists are frequently the servants of the powerful, so too the foundation myth could take on the colouring of this or that family's esteem needs.

(d) Finally, once the Julio-Claudian dynasty (Augustus, Tiberius, Caligula, Claudius, Nero) was established the new foundation mythology and religion was fashioned in direct response to the demands for an **imperial cult**. Already Julius Caesar came to regard himself as semi-divine, god incarnate, and Augustus continued this trend.

The *Aeneid* of Virgil is the exemplary product of the imperial cult, sickening at times in its sycophancy. **Sycophancy** came to be the prevailing moral disease of the Roman peoples; in Livy with have that abstract sycophancy that sometimes masquerades under the guise of patriotism, in which the lionised object of sickening praise is Rome and its people, or Rome and its patricians. In Virgil the focus has become yet more restricted, as illustrated by **Aeneas's visit to the underworld**. In the *Odyssey*, Odysseus visits the underworld to find his way home (a profound symbol, capable of moral exploitation). In the *Aeneid* the purpose is so that Aeneas can learn of Rome's destiny to greatness. He is granted a vision of the future heroes of Rome. At the conclusion, Aeneas asks of his ghostly father Anchises, "Who is that, father, marching at the side of Marcellus? Is it one of his sons or one of the great line of his descendants?"

> Then his father Anchises began to speak through his tears: 'O my son, do not ask. This is the greatest grief that you and yours will ever suffer. Fate will just show him to the earth – no more. The gods in heaven have judged that the Roman race would become too powerful if this gift were theirs to keep. What a noise of the mourning of men will come from the Field of Mars to Mars' great city. What a cortège will Tiber see as he glides past the new Mausoleum on his shore! No son of Troy will ever so raise the hopes of his Latin ancestors, nor will the land of Romulus so pride itself on any of its young. Alas for his goodness! Alas for his old-fashioned truthfulness and that right hand undefeated in war! No enemies could ever have come against him in war and lived, whether he was armed to fight on foot or spurring the flanks of his foaming war-horse. Oh the pity of it! If only you could break the harsh laws of Fate! You will be Marcellus.'[23]

This is the climax of the visit to the Underworld. Virgil has already had father Anchises expound the Pythagorean-Orphic doctrine of the body/soul separation, of punishment in the afterlife, and of the necessity in certain cases for a reincarnation. (In accounting for the second epoch of Roman religion, we must not forget the possible influence of Pythagoras, though in general, and Virgil excepting, this did not appear to have been over-great.) At the reading, Virgil has already flattered his audience, which includes Augustus: both Augustus and Julius Caesar are illustrious descendants of Aeneas, and thereby of the goddess Venus. In the above passage the vision of Rome's future greatness concludes with two men called Marcellus walking side by side. The first is Marcus Claudius Marcellus, the general who captured Syracuse, and the hero who won the greatest honour a Roman can achieve, the *spoila optima* for killing an enemy general in personal combat, the Gallic king Viridomarus at the battle of Clastidium (222). The second is Marcus Claudius Marcellus, who died young, the nephew of Augustus, and son of his sister Octavia, reclining, we may imagine, by Augustus's side. Virgil flatters Augustus and Octavia firstly by making this Marcellus into the companion of the former, and secondly by making him into *the reincarnation of Aeneas*. Sycophancy at its best, and most heroic.

---

[23] Virgil, *Aeneid*, Book VI, 867-882.

Octavia is said to have swooned when she heard the line, *tu Marcellus eris*. An effective application of Platonic-Pythagorean-Orphic eschatology to the practical contemporary problem of *getting on in the world*.

Regarding Greek religion, the thesis which has been advanced here, is that Greek religion is a synthesis of matriarchal and patriarchal elements. The matriarchal elements form the original layer in which we see a religion of the Goddess and the ritual slaying of the god-king in the context of fertility.[24] The question, then, is whether this pattern is evinced in the evolution of Roman religion. If this pattern be true, and I have no doubt that some will dispute that, then we have every reason to expect the same pattern of evolution in Roman religion, and, moreover, it would be reasonable to anticipate that all these developments will be delayed by a number of centuries in comparison to processes taking place in Greece. In Greece human sacrifice as an institution had been predominantly superseded by 800, but we would not expect to see a parallel development in Italian religion at such a time. A delay of several centuries could be expected. But what may be expected is one thing, fact is stranger than fiction, and we need to see these things attested in the evidence, not merely to be the outcomes of speculations.

For those who wish to deny that human sacrifice occurred or that if it occurred then it is not Indo-European practice, it is not sufficient to merely demonstrate the presence of Indo-European structures within a religion, or to emphasise that such-and-such a peoples was an Indo-European race, as if Indo-Europeans could not possibly practice such horrors – these being left to other races – for the practice is manifest elsewhere and cannot be denied universally – it can only be plausibly be denied here or there, among these peoples and those. This is the strategy that Dumézil adopts, as he argues against a form of the thesis put forward here, in this case by André Piganiol.[25]

---

[24] **Summary**. I am taking over this interpretation from Frazer and Robert Graves. Over the course of the second millennium the matriarchal religion underwent some transformation in that the role of the god-king became more prominent in a role expressed by the archetype of Poseidon – the "capable husband of the Goddess Da". Since the Greeks themselves migrated into Greece during this period, it is possible to see this evolution as the outcome of a fusion of the patriarchal religion of the Greeks, who were Indo-Europeans, and the matriarchal religion of the Mediterranean peoples, the Pelasgoi and the Phoenicians. Subsequently, during the Greek Dark Ages, a further reformation of the religion took place, and the supremacy of the patriarchal principle came to the fore in the Olympian religion and the dominance of Zeus, the Father and embodiment of Justice. Socially, women were eclipsed and fell into the subordinate position, where their lives and property came under the domination of men. The Dionysiac religion of the Earth Mother, in which human sacrifice is so prominent, was also transformed into a chthonic religion in which the rites of fertility were preserved but in symbolic and ritual form only, and the burden of sacrificial victim was transferred to animals.

[25] André Piganoil, *Essai sur les origins de Rome*, 1916.

He [André Piganiol] admitted the authenticity of the "synoecism" which the annalistic tradition assigns to the beginnings. According to his solution, Rome was formed by the unions of Latins and Sabines, the former being Indo-Europeans and the latter Mediterraneans ... The Indo-Europeans brought into Italy the altar bearing the lighted fire, the cult of the male fire, that of the sun, that of the bird, and a repugnance toward human sacrifice; the Sabines used stones which they rubbed with blood as altars, ascribed the patronage of fire to a goddess, offered worship to the moon and to the serpent, and immolated human victims. This construction was and could be only arbitrary. Apart from the fact that the Sabines, who were themselves Indo-Europeans, could not play the role of "Mediterraneans" which was entrusted to them, there was then no means of taking an objective view either of Indo-European civilization or of Mediterranean civilization.

The rebuttal by Dumézil of the thesis of Piganiol fails. Both authors flounder on an agreed underlying assumption – namely, that indeed the Mediterranean peoples did practice human sacrifice to the Goddess and the Indo-Europeans did not. Thus, the question is transformed into the trivial one – were the Latins and Sabines Indo-European or not? Since their languages are both Indo-European, the hypothesis of a fusion of religious elements is abandoned. Piganiol's error is that in accepting this thesis he projects onto the Sabines the function of carrying into Roman religion the religion of the Goddess, and Dumézil's error is that in observing that the Sabines speak an Indo-European language, he concludes that they could not have any "Mediterranean" elements present in their religion and thereby could not act as vectors.

Frazer in *The Golden Bough* evidently does not make the distinction that Dumézil thinks is so important. Frazer assimilates without distinction the Aryans of Europe to the Aryans of India and to the ancient peoples of Europe.[26] He believes that he is elucidating Indo-European religion, not Mediterranean religion. However,

---

[26] For example: "In the ancient Vedic hymns of India, the fire-god Agni 'is spoken of as born in wood, as the embryo of plants, or as distributed in plants ...' A tree which has been struck by lightning is naturally regarded by the savage as charged with a double or triple portion of fire; for has he not seen the mighty flash enter into the trunk with his own eyes? ... It is a plausible theory that the reverence which the ancient peoples of Europe paid to the oak, and the connection which they traced between the tree and their sky-god, were derived from the much greater frequency with which the oak appears to be struck by lightning than any other tree of our European forests. ... This explanation of the Aryan reverence for the oak and of the association of the tree with the great god of thunder and the sky, was suggested or implied long ago by Jacob Grimm." Frazer, *The Golden Bough*, 927-28.

his approach is through comparative ethnology as much as through myth, and he does not sufficiently distinguish time and place – history and geography. In retrospect we see that the primary object of his study is the Mediterranean culture, which became the culture of the European Indo-Europeans – Latin, Sabine, Greek or any other – because they from the first adopted it. Whatever their Indo-European heritage, they too, became worshippers of the Goddess. But the core of Frazer's work, as a study of mythology, is concerned with the Mediterranean, Phrygian and Semitic deities – Adonis, Attis, Osiris, Dionysus.

A reconstruction. Suppose we postulate a pure form of Indo-European religion subsisting at the beginning before their migration, say, in the third millennium BCE. Let it be a religion of the three functions, patriarchal, subsumed under the authority of the great Sky-Father, involving no human sacrifice. Any such religion is a backward extrapolation from the religions that we do know about, for there are no documents to attest to it. But, let us grant this as a hypothesis. But what happens when these Indo-Europeans migrate into Europe, the Near East and India? Do they encounter a vacuum? Virgin lands, wholly unpopulated? Certainly not, the archaeological and historical record refutes that. Do they eradicate entirely the aboriginal populations? Certainly not, for the aboriginal populations are more advanced than they are in the record of civilisation and they assimilate them and their inventions. Do they impose their religion upon the aboriginal population? To some extent they may, as overlords, but the bulk of the population, even as the underclass, retain their ancient beliefs. The pattern is assimilation, not preservation of "ancient purity".

Once these Indo-European migrants settle down, they not only become the minority ethnically, they also share the same practical problems of the indigenous population. The Indo-Europeans were pastoralists – they herded animals; they did not grow cereal crops. Their god of the third function, Quirinus, had to do only with herding. But once they become farmers, then their third function must assimilate all the functions of farming; it becomes complex. As nature and the Goddess are one, so the god of the third function assimilates to itself the male gods of the Mother-goddess, and becomes at times Dionysus, the sacrificial god. The great pattern is assimilation and evolution. Hence, the Italic peoples, who gave birth to the Rome, were both Mediterranean and Indo-European – Latins and Sabines could not have been very different at any given stage of the evolutionary process. Frazer lays bare their common religion, the one that for the Latins had its cult centre at Aricia, where the god was Virbius and the Goddess, Diana Nemorensis.

As the Ionian-revolution of cognition occurred during the first millennium, we suppose that the Indo-Europeans at first shared the primitive materialism of the Mediterranean people. In this conception all things are simultaneously both material and living, as things imbued with vital spirit. The notion of personal rights is a long way off. The judgement "thou shalt not kill" has not yet emerged. People are things too, and as things they have their uses – sacrifice for example. We do not suppose that the Indo-Europeans theorised as such, but if they did theorize they could not find an objection in principle to human sacrifice – if the gods demanded it, it would be done. If we do not see human sacrifice as intrinsic to this religion, perhaps that is for another reason. For what was sacrificed must be a man, and these peoples are originally patriarchs. Perhaps they will sacrifice women instead, but there is no strong suggestion of such a rite developing as a cultural norm, despite the myth of Iphigenia whom Agamemnon is said to have sacrificed to appease Artemis in advance of a good wind to sail to Troy. The fertility cult requires male blood, for it is male seed that fertilises the land, and because it is male blood and seed we may suppose that the Indo-Europeans had an aversion to it. That is, so long as they did not assimilate and become Mediterranean people as well as Indo-European people.

Human sacrifice in the Celtic religion. Archaeology demonstrates that the Indo-Europeans did practice human sacrifice in the context of fertility worship and magic. The Celts are Indo-Europeans and their cult of human sacrifice is very well attested. **Bog bodies** in Ireland have been recovered.[27] They also ritually sacrificed children, which is attested at innumerable sites in Spain, for instance at La Escudilla near Castellón de la Plana in the Valencia region – where infant sacrifice was used in the C4 BCE for the sake of abundant crops and fecundity of livestock, accompanied by votive offerings, commemorated by slabs. The context is that of the Goddess.[28]

Celto-Ligurian cult of severed heads. The Celto-Ligurians are an example of a fusion of Indo-European people (Celts) with autochthonous people (Ligurian). At sites such as Roquepertuse, Entremont and La Cloche the severed heads were embalmed in oil or coated in fresh clay. They are associated with head hunting as opposed to ancestor worship.[29] This cult is not to my knowledge explicitly

---

[27] Bog bodies are men who have had their throats cut or have been stabbed in ways indicative of ritual sacrifice. The context is fertility and the usual interpretation is that the victim is a king married to the priestess as the personification of the Goddess. A bog body near Portaloise is dated to c.2000 BCE; it is of a male who has suffered violent death. Old Croghan Man was killed between 326 and 175 BCE; he died horrifically with holes cut in his upper arms through which a rope had been threaded. He was stabbed many times and his nipples were sliced; then he was cut in half. Clonycavan Man was disembowelled. These mutilations are interpreted to signify ritual dis-enthronement. Throughout Europe the Celts practiced human sacrifice.

[28] Polybius refers to a temple of Athena in the territory of the Insubrii. Posidonius refers to the Celtic priestesses of an island shrine at the mouth of the Loire. Hecateus quotes Diodorus as referring to a circular temple of Apollo. Libernice near Kolin in Bohemia dates from C3 BCE. The post hones may have contained adorned posts in carved human form, though now the remains are burnt. Remains of animal and human bones suggest sacrifices were conducted. A woman is also buried there, who may have been a priestess.

[29] At Saint-Blaise there are niches for skulls or severed heads. Roquepertuse (Bouches-du-Rhône) also has skull niches. At Glanum (St. Rémy-en-Provence) there are lintels, pillars and skull-niches. At Salurii (Entremont, Provence) there is a pillar with stylized human heads and fifteen adult human

connected to the Goddess, though perhaps that has not been investigated; it shows that contrary to the thesis of denial, Indo-Europeans can and do commit ritual murder, even if it is in battle. It is likely that head-hunting and the taking of trophies in battle is a product of the fusion of matriarchal and patriarchal elements. A cult of severed heads is attested in Homer; Achilles's tent was full of skulls.

A *nemeton* is a shrine or sanctuary that is based on a sacred grove or clearing in a wood.[30] The most famous Roman *nemus* is that of Diana at Aricia. Thus, we are brought back to **the continuity of the religion of the Latin peoples with that of the other Indo-Europeans.** There is no reason to postulate a distinct development for the Latin, Sabine and Roman peoples. If the Romans did not ever practice human sacrifice and never worshipped the Goddess, then they stand alone in the evolutionary record.

The vector of Mediterranean culture. We are discussing the thesis that Roman religion represents another form the synthesis of the Indo-European and Mediterranean religions – another fusion of patriarchy with matriarchy. For this, we require no vector for either side of the equation, for we can see the rise of patriarchy to be endogenous to the evolution of any European peoples. However, in the case of Rome we have a vector for the matriarchal religion, a people of Mediterranean origin, closely related by culture to the Carthaginians and Phoenicians – a people known to have exercised suzerainty and cultural dominance over the Latin peoples from an early time – the Etruscans.

---

skulls. It dates from before 123 BCE. There are indications that a head-cult was common throughout the Celtic world.

[30] Strabo records that the Galatian meeting-place in Asia Minor was Drunemeton, which would have been a sacred oak grove. The Galatians were Celtic peoples who migrated to Asia Minor. In Irish *nemed* stands for a sanctuary and *fidnemed* is a forest shrine.

18

The Etruscans

The origin of the Etruscans. For millennia the question as to the origin of the Etruscans has been debated. In Herodotus's account they emigrated from Lydia in Asia Minor, according to legend, during the reign of Atys son of Manes and under the leadership of his son, Tyrrhenus. Dionysius of Halicarnassus disputed that the Etruscans were either Pelasgians or Lydians, remarking on their very different language and customs.[1] Herodotus placed this migration C13, second millennium. DNA studies indicate the relation of Etruscan descendants to oriental peoples – Armenians, Hindus, Romanies. Skulls studied by Giuseppe Sergi are similar to skulls of the Mediterranean race of the Neolithic period.[2] According to Jacques Heurgon "a dualism which was no longer really horizontal – between Orient and Occident – but vertical would seem to be the true explanation of the ancient primitive world. One must imagine, at the outset, in Italy, as also in Minoan Crete, a civilization dominated by the importance of Chthonian cults and by the pre-eminence of women; then, after vast upheavals, the marriage of Heaven and Earth, Indo-European strength with Mediterranean grace, the conquest of an agricultural society by war-lords."[3] Perhaps what Heurgon means by "grandiose outlines of myth" is his own idealising and romantic backward projection contained in his words, "Indo-European strength with Mediterranean grace". The fundamental pattern is valid, though the many vortices and stagnant patches will exhibit details that may obscure it.

At the time Heurgon was writing, the origin of the Etruscans was still an open question; quite recently, it has been demonstrated at the European Human Genetic Conference in Nice in 2007 that the Etruscans are descendants of peoples of Turkey. The study was based on genetic investigations of Y chromosomes taken from Etruscan burial chambers of Voterra and Murlo. The Etruscans formed a racially and ethnically distinct people who became dominant in that part of Italy we name after them, Tuscany, from the C8 and for a time established a hegemony over much of the Italian peninsula. However, it is probably best to see them as a complex fusion of immigrants from Asia Minor (Lydia) and other migrants speaking Indo-European languages. At first, they formed a single culture, known as the **Villanovan culture**, whose most distinctive common feature was the use of biconical cinerary urns, which in Etruria were often covered with inverted pottery bowls or bronze helmets. The urns were buried in holes in the ground surrounded by stones and

[1] *The Roman Antiquities of Dionysius of Halicarnassus*, Loeb, 1937, I. 30.
[2] Jacques Heurgon, *Daily Life of the Etruscans, Trans*. James Kirkup, Phoenix Press – London – 2002, Original – 1961 – *La Vie quotidienne chez les Etrusques*, Original English version, 1964, Weidenfeld & Nicholson. p. 21.
[3] *Ibid.*, p.8.

accompanied by ornaments such as brooches, bracelets and razors, but not usually weapons.

The **Villanovan Iron Age** began c.750 around the time of Greek colonization in Italy at Ischia and Cumae. Subsequently, the Villanovan culture died out. It is likely the Villanovan peoples were absorbed into **Etruscan culture** in Tuscany and morphed into the Latin culture in Latium. By the C7 the Etruscan culture adopted inhumation, and the dead were laid in chamber-tombs cut into rock. Villages coalesced into small and wealthy cities. Greek pottery was imported. We tend to think of the Indo-Europeans as imposing themselves as overlords over a Mediterranean body of people, but in this case, it is likely that the Etruscans were a Mediterranean people who immigrated into Italy and imposed themselves as an aristocracy upon an Indo-European population. The Lydians are said by Homer to have been allies of the Trojans, and hence a migration from Asia Minor following the defeat at Troy, which I take to be historic, is not out of the question – there may be a kernel of historic truth in the **legend of Aeneas**. It was the Etruscans who first adopted this legend and made Aeneas into a cult hero of theirs.

The **Etruscan language** is not Indo-European and is hypothesised to have belonged to a now extinct language group known as Tyrsenian, which included the language of the Greek island of Lemnos. An inscription on a funerary stele has been found on Lemnos which is "the text most closely resembling Etruscan ever read outside Italy."[4] It is further evidence of the origin of the Etruscan people from Lydia. The Etruscans acquired the ability to write around the same time the Greeks relearned it, c.750, and in contrast to the Romans they have left around 13,000 inscriptions, dating from c.700. Their script is derived from the Euboean variant of the Greek alphabet, and was probably imported from Pithecusae and Cumae, which were Euboean settlements. The language is not completely decoded, but a lot is known about it, thanks to late inscriptions in both Etruscan and Latin. A significant more recent find is the Pyrgi Tablets which are in both Etruscan and Phoenician dated to c.500.

The Etruscans are also known through their many burial chambers and necropolises, so that in contrast to early Roman history, which is almost a complete blank as to certainly, we know a good deal about Etruscan history and culture.

Etruscan history. There was a rapid transformation of Villanovan culture after the Greek discovery of metal deposits of Etruria. Etruria rose to power by the acquisition of wealth arising from trade in these metals. In 770 the Chalcidians established a colony on the island of Ischia, which is near Naples. Gold from Etruria and iron from the island of Elba were exported. The Etruscans became wealthy and

[4] *Ibid.*, p.5

a coalition of twelve Etruscan cities united by religious solidarity was formed.[5] They had a common sanctuary in the territory of the Volsinii at the temple of Voltumna (Vertumnus).

There was an Etruscan expansion in C6. They moved into the Po valley, establishing new Etruria[6] and conquered Latium and Rome. The Roman tradition of an Etruscan dynasty, between 616 to 509 is confirmed by archaeology though the dates are disputed as later: 550 – 475. Etruscan power extended to Cumae and to territory in the Campania.

The Phocaeans from Asia Minor were the first Greeks to penetrate into the Western Mediterranean and they founded Massalia (Marseilles) in 600. This brought them into conflict with Etruria and with Carthage. The Carthaginian policy was to establish naval dominance in the Western Mediterranean and thereby control the trade with Iberia and North Africa. The Etruscans allied with the Carthaginians and defeated the Phocaeans at the Battle of Alalia c.535, driving them out of Corsica. But Etruria began to decline. The conflict with Greece was instrumental, as Syracuse in Sicily rose to be the most populous and powerful of the Greek states and became the champion of the Greek cause against Carthage and Etruria. The Carthaginians were defeated at Himera in 480, which ended for a time the Carthaginian bid to take control of Sicily. In 474 the Etruscan fleet was defeated by Syracuse at Cumae and the Etruscan cities of Tarquinii and Caere started to decline. During the C4 the Etruscans also came under pressure from Gallic migrations. But the Etruscans expanded into the north. Rome claimed to have liberated itself from Etruscan rule in 509, and subsequently destroyed the Etruscan city of Veii, which lay just beyond its territorial borders in 396. The Etruscan city of Volsinii was taken in 265. Etruria was conquered by Rome during the C3.

In Etruria, power was held by an exclusive aristocracy. There seems to have been no "middle class". Below the aristocracy was a mass of peoples in servile position.[7]

---

[5] One list gives these as: Veii, Caere, Tarquinii, Vulci, Rusellae, Vetulonia, Volsinii, Clusium, Perugia, Cortona, Arretium, Volterra.

[6] The cities founded included Marzabotto, Bologna (Felsina), Parma, Moderna, Ravenna, Spina, Adria, Melpum (Milan?), and Mantua.

[7] It is not known whether they were technically slaves or in principle free men. A special term, *penestes*, was used by Dionysius of Halicarnassus to describe them, and they are compared to Spartan helots. They made up the bulk of the population, comprising servants, entertainers, peasants, who were country slaves. These slaves or servants also served in the army. Dionysius suggested that they were "free men" – clientele – but were treated with contempt by their masters. They may have been serfs descended from Villanovans. Slave labour was used in the mining industry of Populonia and Campigliese. Junvenal describes Tuscan slave prisons – *in Tusca ergastula* – "in which there were prisoners or vincti whose manacles were never loosed." Martial (C1 CE) wrote "without rhetorical exaggeration, that the latifundia of Etruaria rang with the clanking of innumerable chains." Archaeological evidence of this cruelty has been uncovered. The Senate, a council of aristocrats, was

Etruria represents what I term a **developed matriarchy**. I suggest that it is the nearest approximation within the historical record of the first millennium to the Mycenaean-Minoan culture – the culture of the second millennium. There is a potential distinction between matriarchy, sometimes taken as indicative of descent through the female line, and **gynaecocracy** (gynarchy) as rule by women. This is what Heurgon indicates when he remarks, appropriately, that "It cannot be denied that Etruscan society in many respects has elements of both matriarchy and gynaecocracy," though he calls it "a very adulterated form".[8]

Terminology for matriarchy. A number of distinctions are appropriate. (1) Descent through the female line I indicate by the term *matrilineal*. (2) Female rule to the exclusion of male participation in government I shall denote by *gynarchy*. (3) Rule on behalf of a power that is conceived of as feminine, such as the Goddess, I shall denote by *matriarchy*. (4) We need a term also for a society which practices ritual male human sacrifice in worship of the Goddess. As there does not appear to be a term in the language for this, I shall coin one, *herarchy*. I name this practice thus after the Greek Queen of Heaven, Hera. This may be unfair to the Olympian goddess, but I feel that the name of the Goddess needs to be represented in the term used to denote this practice, and Hera as a goddess is far older than the tamed representation of her that we encounter in Homer. The ancient world, Virgil is a good exemplar, had no hesitation in identifying Hera with the great Goddess wherever she was met – with Tanit at Carthage for instance. Hence, *herarchy* for a system in which men, *heroes*, are sacrificed for the goddess, *Hera*. The association of Hera with her victim, her hero, renders this term most appropriate, for the victim should also be represented in the term employed. (5) The theology that claims that the world is a manifestation of female power, either the creation of it, or the embodiment of it, I shall call *Gaiaism*. (6) The term *matriarchy* is appropriate to describe the whole structure, as well as that part that concerns the notion of the origin of power.

Within these board categories there may be many variations. A pure system of gynarchy would exclude all men from power, but such a system is scarcely conceivable even in the ancient world, so we must allow it to encompass social systems where men have some power devolved to them by the dominant female power. As society is complex, or develops complexity, distinct functions of government split off from their common root, the *matriarch* or *patriarch*, and one may acquire functional or departmental power within the system. Thus, it may become traditional within a system that is broadly a gynarchy to devolve upon men responsibility for, say, war. That departmental power is devolved to men is not

---

the only political assembly of the Etruscan state. The Etruscan word *zilath* denoted a minister, a special magistrate, aedile, town councillor, praetor, or chief of State. There was a supreme zilath.

[8] Heurgon, *Etruscans*, *Op. cit.*, p.85.

indicative of an overall change in the ideology of a culture, for a man may exercise power for and on behalf of women, just as in the Middle Ages it occasionally happened that women held regnal power.[9] In the ancient societies, where men were co-opted into government, a form of equality between men and women begins to emerge. It may also develop that a king assumes the greatest responsibility for government, so that monarchy is a male preserve, and yet it is women who hold power in principle. The king rules on behalf of the queen, or derives his power theologically from the Goddess, as her representative, or consort.

In such a system, *herarchy* may still be practised. On whom does this onerous duty of sacrifice fall? In principle, upon the king, the Lord, Ba'al, who is the consort of the Goddess, but in the development of a matriarchal system, this duty may be transferred elsewhere – onto children, symbolic heroes, prisoners of war, slaves. Such a transference is likely to develop in a culture where the male aristocracy achieves near equality with the female; then ties of family and class divert the practice onto some other part of society.

Etruria was a developed matriarchy. (1) Descent was reckoned on both matrilineal and patrilineal lines. (2) Rule was exercised by men, but theoretically on behalf of the female power, which held the greater honour or dignity; in the terminology above, it remained a matriarchy, but was a diluted form of gynarchy. Both practically and symbolically power was conferred upon the king by the queen or priestess. (3) It practised *herarchy* (human sacrifice) but in ritualised forms in which the connection between kingship and the sacred duty of subjection to immolation was separated. (4) Its theology remained a form of *Gaiaism*.

The predominance of the Goddess in the worship of the Etruscans may be indicated as follows. Heurgon tells us that the "universe of Etruscan religion" was "dominated by the all-powerful female divinity, the Earth Mother whom Veii and Caere worshipped under the name of Hera or Juno, Mater Matuta or Leucothe." The appearance in this statement of Mater Mutata is a salutary adjustment to the claim by Dumézil that she is a purely Indo-European goddess, merely dawn, the emanation of male power. Just as Hera was equated with Uni or Juno, Turan was the Etruscan goddess of love, fertility and vitality, the patroness of the city of Velch, and identified with Venus or Aphrodite. Epithets of these goddesses included *ati* = "mother", *eel ati* = "mother earth", *turan ati* = "mother Turan". The gold Tablets from Pyrgi (c.500) in both Etruscan and Phoenician is the record a religious dedication of a gift, a statue, by the king of Caere, in gratitude for the protection of the Goddess. In it the goddess Astarte is identified with the goddess Uni.[10]

---

[9] For example, Emperor Charles V successively appointed his aunt Margaret of Austria and his sister Mary of Hungary to govern Burgundy on his behalf.

[10] An engraved bronze mirror from Volaterrae bearing a legal-religious inscription depicts Uni as an enthroned female deity, nursing a full-grown Hercle, witnessed by four standing gods, which include Apollo, identified by a laurel branch, an older god holding a trident or lightning bolt, identified as

There are frequent representations of dyads in Etruscan art.[11] These all relate to the fundamental mythologem of Dionysus – the Cybele and Attis pairing that is indicative of ritual sacrifice in the context of the worship of the mother.

The ongoing privileged status of women is shown in burial customs: women had more privileged burials – "… in these funerary chambers the sarcophagus was also destined for the mother of the family." An example is the Regolini-Galassi tomb at Caere (c 650). It is the tomb of a royal woman with two attendant male warriors, one cremated. Between 650 and 450 the Etruscans of Caere awarded women in death more status than men.[12]

---

either Nethuns or Tinia. The picture shows how Hercle becomes Uni's son by drinking milk – it is an adoption ritual. This is an example of a number of Etruscan representations of the mythological nursing scene. The recurring themes of Etruscan mirrors and wall paintings involve the importance of the mother, the prevalence of couples or "dyads", representations of the birth of gods mediated by midwives, and representations of souls or ghosts. A stone statue from Volaterrae (C3 BCE) is another example of the many mother-child representations in Etruscan art. It is a life-sized marble statue of a standing woman holding a baby, a cult statue, a *kourotrophos*. Hera, Uni appears as a *kourotrophos* in Etruria, suckling the child Herakles. A painted plaque from Caere, in the Louvre, depicts an Etruscan king, who is seated before the statue of a goddess and is holding a sceptre in his left hand. The axe symbol of Oriental and Mediterranean cultures, associated with the worship of Mother Earth or the Great Goddess, was adopted. The double-axe, designated by the word *labrys*, which derives from Minoan culture, is found in ancient Minoan depictions of the Mother Goddess. Labyrinth may mean the "house of the double axe". A labrys was used by female priestesses for bull sacrifices. The double-axe designates the authority of the king derived from the Goddess. A C7 stele from Vetulonia shows a bipennate axe. In Phrygia, the Mother of the Gods, Cybele is associated with mountains, town and city walls, fertile nature, and wild animals, especially lions. Likewise, in Etruria we have the Tomb of The Lionesses (c. 520) where on the main wall are depicted two lionesses with black spots amid multiple scenes of music, dancing and banqueting with male and female worshippers. Similar ideas are expressed on the murals of the Tomb of the Leopards, located within the Necropolis of Moterozzi (480 – 450).

[11] Dyads include Fufluns and Catha; Aita (Hades) and Phersipnei (Persephone or Proserpina); Atmite (Admetus) and Alsctei (Alkestis); Turan and Atunis. Turan is often represented as an older woman with Atunis as a boy or very young man. Some couples turn out to be mother-and-son groups like Semla and Fufluns. Other "dyads," as Pallottino calls them, are twins like the Dioskouroi, Castor and Pollux. See Massimo Pallottino, *The Religion of the Etruscans*.

[12] Men and women were buried in tombs representing beds or couches; masculine beds were generally eighty centimetres and the sarcophagi in which women were buried was one meter ten centimetres wide. The female bed was contained within a sarcophagus. The best-preserved tombs – The Regolini-Galassi (Cerveteri), and Bernardini and Barerini Tombs (Praeneste/Palestrina) – held gold and silver vessels and jewellery, wheeled vehicles, ivory-inlaid furniture, and rare imported goods such as Phoenician silver bowls as well as Nuragic-inspired beaked vases, Phoenician faience and ivory, and Baltic amber. Some tombs were erected for women, presumably the rulers or heiresses of kingdoms: at Caere, the Regolini Galassi tomb, now in the Vatican Museum, held a bronze bowl inscribed for "Larthia wife [or daughter] of Velthur" and at Latin Praeneste the Bernardini Tomb belonged to "Vetusia," presumably an Etruscan princess who had married into the ruling Latin family. See Gary D. Farney, Guy Bradley, *The Peoples of Ancient Italy*. Referring to the work of Raniero

Etruscan civil status of women is indicated in that "the women are provided with a first name," which contrasts significantly with Roman practice. The continuing status and independence of Etruscan women gave them a suspect, if not bad reputation, well into Roman times, and they are frequently criticised by Greek and Roman authors for their loose morals. Athenaeus represents the Etruscans as sybarites.[13] The same idea is found in the gossip of Theopompus also mentioned by Athenaeus.[14] Posidonius of Apamea remarks on "their indulgence in banquets and effeminate delights."

I have dealt so far with the evidence for the political and civil aspects of the developed matriarchy of the Etruscans, I must now turn my attention to the *herarchy,* which I remind the reader is my term for the practice of male human sacrifice in the context of Goddess worship.

The cruel core of "civilisation". The uncovering of this "custom" should be profoundly disturbing. No matter how civilised we like to think we are, we acknowledge that our civilisation is in direct descent by an evolutionary process from primitive peoples. That Neolithic peoples also practised human sacrifice is likely, and the earliest civilisations under investigation here were originally Neolithic cultures. However, the term "civilisation" is appropriate. While herarchy correlates in cognition to primitive materialism, the cultures under discussion are, within the confines of that primitive materialism, all highly advanced cultures that have learned the secrets of agriculture, of animal husbandry, of the wheel, of construction, of economic organisation, etc. Herarchy lies in the background of civilisation. While we may account for it in terms of a system of beliefs (primitive materialism), in terms of mitigated responsibility (borderline consciousness, divine possession), it must also be just cruelty.

Cruelty. Possibly, it is wise to postulate that at the earliest stages cruelty was a product of need, bound up with the experience of the numinous, the sacred. During the first millennium, when overcoming the practice of herarchy was the spiritual struggle of the age, then as culture evolved, so too did herarchy, and in a **developed herarchy** we see a decided expression of **cruelty for cruelty's sake**. The sincerity

---

Mengarelli. [Raniero Mengarelli (1865-1943), Etruscologist.] Heurgon remarks, "Mengarelli thus was lead to formulate a new law: in Etruscan tombs the body of the man, on the left, was disposed on a kline, that of the woman, always on the right, in a sarcophagus." [Heurgon, *Etruscans, Op. cit.,* p 93.] There are some exceptions. "But all things considered, we would consider that Mengarelli was right and so do the majority of etruscologists." Inscriptions from amphorae from the tomb of the Grecian Vases indicate ownership by women.

[13] Athenaeus in *The Deipnosophists XII* 519b makes the remark which is attributed to Timaeus. Sybaris was a city of Magna Graeca on the Gulf of Taranto founded 720 by Achaeans and Troezenians, which became very wealthy. Sybarites are people devoted to luxury and outrageous pleasure-seeking.

[14] See Heurgon, *Etruscans, Op. cit.,* p.34.

with which the Carthaginians during the Second Punic War exceeded the quota and sacrificed not two hundred but a further three hundred of their first-born offspring is a complex issue – the sacrifice was necessitated by an initial evasion on the part of the aristocratic families, thus bespeaking a crisis of faith, a collapse in the confidence in the ritual. Hence, in the twilight period between one system of cognition and another, when the efficacy and need for a cruel ritual conflict with a doubt as to that efficacy and a wish to evade its implications, then cruelty per se is born.

The **Etruscans were particularly cruel**. They delighted in cruelty and bequeathed it to their Roman descendants – for Rome's break from Etruscan monarchy may not have been as decisive as they later sought to make it seem.

The custom of human sacrifice takes several forms: (a) immolation, (b) live burial, (c) live burning, etc. The Greeks tended to practise less violent forms of herarchy by pushing heroes from cliff edges or allowing them to die in combat by being overpower by their successor. But in their mythological record the most violent form of all is attested for Greece – the rending limb-from-limb of the live victim in Bacchic frenzy.

It is against this outline of its history and its social institutions that we now examine the Etruscan record for cruelty. The story in Herodotus is that after the battle of Alalia (c. 535) the Etruscans of Caere (Agylla) stoned to death the Phocaean prisoners.

> The Carthaginians and Tyrrhenians drew lots for the possession of the prisoners from the ships which were sunk. Of the Tyrrhenians, the people of Agylla got by far the largest number, and they took them all ashore and stoned them to death. The result of this outrage was that when any living thing – sheep, ox, or man – subsequently passed the place where the Phocaeans had lain, its body became twisted and crippled by a paralytic stroke. Wishing to expiate the crime of the murder, the men of Argylla sent to Delphi, and were told by the Priestess to begin the custom, which they still observe today, of honouring the dead men with a grand funeral ceremony and holding of athletic and equestrian contests.[15]

This extract records the fact of the ritual sacrifice, which may be accepted as historic. It also expresses Greek outrage at the sacrifice and reflects the moral revolution that has by the time of Herodotus been in effect there. In line with this, Herodotus relates the wishful bringing down of a curse upon the land. Regarding the consultation with Delphi and the establishment of funeral games, it is not likely that the Etruscans felt any need to expiate a sin, but the evolution of funeral games, or we should say,

---

[15] Herodotus, *Histories*, Bk I, 167.

gladiatorial contest, was another aspect of their developed and developing *herarchy*. According to Nicolaus of Damascus, Rome borrowed the custom of gladiatorial contests from the Etruscans. "Once upon a time men believed that the souls of the dead were propitiated by human blood, and so at funerals they sacrificed prisoners of war or slaves of poor quality bought for the purpose."[16] The Etruscans celebrated games at the meeting of the federation at the Temple of Vertumnus every spring.

In the *Aeneid,* Vergil attributed to Mezentius, King of Caere a cruel form of torture: "… to bind living people to dead bodies, hands against hands, mouth against mouth, and these victims of a new form of torture, drenched in pus and poisoned blood, died slow deaths coupled in this wretched way."[17] There does not appear to be a tradition independent of Virgil for this story, and it may be his invention. It illustrates perceptions of the Etruscans, since the story was believable. Heurgon remarks: "We must assume that in the Etruscans there was an underlying cruelty which is revealed in the horror of certain of their tortures and in the persistence, right into historical times, of their human sacrifices."[18]

The Etruscans became avid connoisseurs of Greek art, but their most favourite representations were those connected to ritual sacrifice. They loved **the funeral scene of Patroclus** in which Achilles sacrifices Trojan prisoners of war in memory of his beloved companion. The ceremony is depicted everywhere. In the war of 358, Livy reports that consul "Fabius fought against the Tarquinians without caution or prudence; nor was the loss sustained in the field so much [a subject of regret] as that the Tarquinians put to death three hundred and seven Roman soldiers, their prisoners, by which barbarous mode of punishment the disgrace of the Roman people was rendered considerably more remarkable." He spares his Roman audience the details of the immolations.

The **Game of Phersu** is depicted in paintings inside four tombs in Tarquinia, for example in the Tomb of the Augurs (late C6). The rite involves blinding a man by placing a sack over his head and then forcing him to defend himself against a wild dog that has been angered by having a collar attached that has a nail embedded that digs into the animal's neck, provoking it to attack the man. These contests also have an official, a referee, who supervised it. His was the name Phersu, and as he wore a mask, the term has come into the Latin language and down to us as signifying persona, mask, dramatic role and person. He is an organiser of tortures, and his outfit evolved into the costume of the medieval Harlequin. In the Game of Phersu, we see in the dog the motif of the Hound of Hell, Cerberus. The man is armed with

---

[16] Quoted from Tertullian, *On the Public Shows*, by Keith Hopkins, *Death and Renewal*, Cambridge University Press, 1983. p. 3.

[17] Virgil, *Aeneid,* VIII, 489 – 94.

[18] Heurgon, *Etruscans, Op. cit.* p.39.

a club, which is a symbol of Hercules. It may be a dramatization of the struggle of the hero against fate and a perverse interpretation of the myth of Hercules capturing the hound of hell.

Immolation implies a definite degree of organisation, so it is hardly spontaneous. It must be planned, and the planning makes it into cruelty. The **history of crucifixion** is also revealing. Crucifixion is an elaborated ritual form of death by immolation involving at times the use of a tree or representation of a tree. It became the established mode of execution at Carthage, and generals who failed in battle were also crucified. The close **cultural ties between Etruria and Carthage** are evident. They are both forms and manifestations of developed matriarchy and herarchy.

The origin is religious ritual. The representation of a **high cross** with prolonged lower limb was in Phoenicia the symbol of Astarte and connected to sun-worship. Coins from Sidon show the Goddess standing on the prow of a ship with the high cross in her arms. Sacrificial crucifixion in the Baal cult is established among the Phoenicians and Carthaginians. That this was a common practice among Semitic peoples is illustrated by stories from Herodotus concerning the crucifixion c.519 by Darius I of 3,000 political opponents in Babylon.[19] One suggestion is that crucifixions were originally sacrifices to the sun-god. A votive stone from Numidia bears the inscription, "To Lord Baal, the Eternal Solar King, who has listened to the prayers of Hicembal." [20]

Since the practice of immolation has already been attested above in the rituals of the Celts and other Indo-European peoples from as far back as the second millennium BCE, it is not essential to look for a mechanism whereby this practice was transmitted from the Near East to Europe. However, as it was a Phoenician custom, the transmission to Carthage is automatic. After the long siege of Tyre, **Alexander the Great** crucified 2,000 survivors and so adopted it into the Macedonian culture and transmitted it independently to the West. I suggest the Romans, being in part at least an Etruscan people, may have adopted it early; they subsequently used crucifixion to punish slaves, pirates, and enemies of the state. There were mass crucifixions following the Third Servile War (73 – 71 BCE) and after the destruction of Jerusalem (70 CE).

Transmission to Rome. Hence, the cruelty inherent in Etruscan religious consciousness was transmitted to Roman culture, which is ironic since the Romans came to see themselves as the champions of the moral rejection of human sacrifice. That is also a case of split consciousness developing, since the line between the ritual sacrifice involved in a gladiatorial contest, the enjoyment of the spectacle of blood

---

[19] Herodotus, *Histories*, i. 128.2, iii 132.2, 159.1.
[20] Ghillany *Menschenopfer der Hebrder*, p. 531.

being shed in the Coliseum, could not to any intelligent observer be radically different in kind to the immolations practised by the Carthaginians and Celts. Seneca's observations are relevant here.

> The other day, I chanced to drop in at the midday games, expecting sport and wit and some relaxation to rest men's eyes from the sight of human blood. Just the opposite was the case. Any fighting before that was as nothing; all trifles were now put aside - it was plain butchery.
>
> The men had nothing with which to protect themselves, for their whole bodies were open to the thrust, and every thrust told. The common people prefer this to matches on level terms or request performances. Of course they do. The blade is not parried by helmet or shield, and what use is skill or defence? All these merely postpone death.
>
> In the morning men are thrown to bears or lions, at midday to those who were previously watching them. The crowd cries for the killers to be paired with those who will kill them, and reserves the victor for yet another death. This is the only release the gladiators have. The whole business needs fire and steel to urge men on to fight. There was no escape for them. The slayer was kept fighting until he could be slain.
>
> 'Kill him! Flog him! Burn him alive!' (the spectators roared) 'Why is he such a coward? Why won't he rush on the steel? Why does he fall so meekly? Why won't he die willingly?" [21]

Nonetheless, a kind of moral distinction can be made, for the Romans treated crucifixion as a punishment for crime, not as a religious observance, they rejected child sacrifice and defined human sacrifice as a form of murder. The gladiatorial contest was cruel, but the victims usually had some chance of survival, and were condemned criminals. Yet, cruelty was transmitted in this overt and latent form into the Western psyche.

Etruscan theology. Their belief in the afterlife is well-attested in their funeral decorations, and is consonant with their state of primitive materialism, as we have seen before. It seems that this conviction that the soul is a mere substance and hence survives, as substance, its separation from the body, goes together with a disregard for the consequences of death.

Fate. The Etruscans developed another theological concept to its limit – the idea of fate. I think that a belief in the overwhelming influence of fate goes hand in hand

---

[21] Seneca, *Epistle 7*.

with the spiritual disease of cruelty, probably as a **rationalisation of cruelty**. If it is fated that such-and-such a person is to die in such-and-such a cruel way, then the spectator is absolved. The burden of responsibility falls upon the gods, for it is their laws that make this spectacle immutable.

Evidence for an Etruscan theology of fate is at once thin and substantial; thin, because the cult itself is only partially attested, substantial because the concept of fate pervades every part of their Etruscan science – their *disciplina Etruria*. In Greek mythology, Atropos – fate, would seem to be a minor deity, and one introduced by the Orphic eschatology – she is one of the three Moirai and cuts the thread of life. In Etruria, Athrpa, Atropos was worshiped as Nortia at Volsinii, where her consort was probably the god Voltumna (Veltha), who was worshipped in Rome as **Vortumnus**. Given that Voltumna is the supreme god of the Etruscan pantheon, also the god of the underworld, it indicates that the Etruscan god Mantus, also said to rule the underworld, is another appellation or manifestation of his. Mantus is paired with the Etruscan goddess Mania (Manea), a goddess of the dead. This suggests that Voltumna-Atropos, Mantus-Mania are equivalent pairings of the Lord and Mistress of the dead, equivalent to Hades-Persephone. In Greek Persephone means "to destroy" or "murder".

With Nortia there is associated a **ritual of the nail**. In Book VII of his *Histories*, Livy remarks: "Cincius, a careful student of monuments of this kind, asserts that at Volsinii also nails were fastened in the temple of Nortia, an Etruscan goddess, to indicate the number of the year." The precise meaning of the nail ritual cannot be inferred from this comment alone; however, (a) the ritual relates to fate; (b) the use of the nail in the game of Phersu, and its association with Etruscan cruelty suggest that sacrifice is involved. I observe the similarity of the term Phersu to the Phersipnei, the Etruscan equivalent of the goddess of the Underworld, but I have not seen any learned discussion of the relation between the two: to whom or what was the game of Phersu dedicated? What was its religious meaning? The back of an Etruscan mirror depicts the story of Meleager and Atalanta. Athrpa (Nortia, fate) holds a hammer in her right hand and a nail in her left. We infer that this symbolises necessity, and the inevitability of death.

The core of Etruscan theology was the belief in fate. The mummy of Zagreb is a mummy of a young female that was brought to Croatia, and which turned out to have been wrapped in a linen volumen bearing the text of one of the Etruscan books of fate. This book has not been completely deciphered but appears to be an **Etruscan calendar**. As Heurgon remarks, "… there was nothing either in public or private life whose course had not been foreseen and fixed by the 'ritual books'." Everything – prodigies, celestial phenomena, the flight of birds – had a meaning. The works of a Byzantine antiquarian called Johannes Lydos (b.590 CE) include *De Mensibus*, a work on the Roman calendar, and *De Ostentis*, a work on omens, which incorporated the Brontoscopic Calendar of Publius Nigidius Figulus (c.98 – 45 BCE), a contemporary and friend of Varro. Thus, we have the entire Etruscan manual of divination by thunder (this is what **brontoscopy** means). The first month of the year is June. The calendar opens:

> Full Moon. 1. If in any way it should thunder, there will be an abundance of fruits, with the exception of barley; but dangerous diseases will be inflicted upon bodies.

And so, it goes on. It makes excellent bed-time reading; a catalogue of everything that concerned the Etruscans and their desire to know in advance what would happen. Not surprisingly, for a society founded upon cruelty and aggression towards the lower orders in the form of a species of slavery, worries about social disturbances figure significantly, as well as concern for crops and harvests.

These **books of fate**, and their **methods of divination**, were held to have been taught to the Etruscans by chthonic deities, that is beings that have emerged from the underworld. A version of the story is handed down to us by Cicero. In this extract he is speaking.

> "It seems useless to say more about soothsaying. However, let us examine its origin and thus we shall very readily determine its value. The tradition is that, once upon a time, in the district of Tarquinii, while a field was being ploughed, the ploughshare went deeper than usual and a certain Tages suddenly sprang forth and spoke to the ploughman. Now this Tages, according to the Etruscan annals, is said to have had the appearance of a boy, but the wisdom of a seer. Astounded and much frightened at the sight, the rustic raised a great cry; a crowd gathered and, indeed, in a short time, the whole of Etruria assembled at the spot. Tages then spoke at length to his numerous hearers, who received with eagerness all that he had to say, and committed it to writing. His whole address was devoted to an exposition of the science of soothsaying. Later, as new facts were learned and tested by reference to the principles imparted by Tages, they were added to the original fund of knowledge.
>
> "This is the story as we get it from the Etruscans themselves and as their records preserve it, and this, in their own opinion, is the origin of their art.
>
> "Now do we need a Carneades or an Epicurus to refute such nonsense? Who in the world is stupid enough to believe that anybody ever ploughed up —which shall I say—a god or a man? If a god, why did he, contrary to his nature, hide himself in the ground to be uncovered and brought to the light of day by a plough? Could not this

so-called god have delivered this art to mankind from a more exalted station? But if this fellow Tages was a man, pray, how could he have lived covered with earth? Finally, where had he himself learned the things he taught others? But really in spending so much time in refuting such stuff I am more absurd than the very people who believe it."[22]

The passage is interesting because it illustrates the breakdown of faith at the time of the late Roman republic, expressed in the scepticism of Cicero. The story itself communicates the Etruscan belief in a **chthonic origin of the revelations**; viewed from the late perspective in the wake of Ionian revolution in consciousness it has been transformed into a ridiculous, unbelievable story. But Cicero was himself appointed to the college of augurs in 30 BCE. The above passage was written in 44 BCE.

Etruscan science in principle is an articulation of the underlying worship of the Goddess. When cognition is at the stage of primitive materialism, there is nothing inconsistent in the notion of receiving prophecies from the dead, for they remain vital substances, and "alive"; prophecy issues from the underworld, that is, out of the ground. Likewise, in vision or trance, in the experience of *mania*, the goddess can appear and instruct. But we must add something to this metaphysics if we are to arrive at the Etruscan cognition – that everything that happens is rule by fate, and yet – and to us this may look like a formal contradiction – if one knows one's fate, one may yet be able to do something about it. But we are familiar with this. The trick of living is to live respecting the conditions and limitations of life. If the river is flowing that way, it is not exactly futile, but difficult to swim against the current. Thus, an Etruscan, if fighting a battle, naturally consults the will of the gods (or Goddess) by means of haruspicy, the interpretation of the entrails of a disembowelled sacrificial animal. If the prognostication turns out badly, then it is wisdom to avoid the battle, for that is running contrary to the will of the gods. In this way, we gain a measure of control over fate, though we are bound by it. Another device is to be sure to be in favour with the gods, that is, to make proper sacrifice and follow all the rituals precisely. If the gods demand a sacrifice, then the sacrifice must be given. The gods favour those who are pious. Yet, behind all of this, there lies the added ingredient of Etruscan cruelty, and whether it is true of the Etruscans, or merely true of ourselves, transferring the onus of our own guilt onto either nature or super-nature is a pretty way of evading moral responsibility.

The Etruscans believed that their religion was revealed to them through consultations with chthonic deities and revelations to prophets and seers by the Goddess. Thus, in this connection we not only find other Tages-like figures, such as

---

[22] Cicero, *Concerning Divination*, Book II, 50 – 51.

Cacus, but also nymphs and muses, such as the Sybil Vegoia to whom many of the books of fate are attributed – the *Libri Fulgurales*, part of the *Libri Rituales*, and the *Libri Fatales*.

There are many other things that may be said about the Etruscans, and among these is the subject of their fertility rites, which are associated with that sexual fecundity that we expect of a pure worship of the Goddess – their music, Bacchic and other dances – but it is time now to revert to the discussion of Roman history and religion.

19

Roman religion

Deliberately forgetting the past. Dumézil's interpretation of Roman religion in terms of the survival of an archaic Indo-European triad of deities represents only a fragment of the truth. In the case of Greek religion, we postulated a religious reformation of the religion of Dionysus taking place during the Dark Age, 1200 – 800. I suggest that we read Roman religion along the same lines, only that, given that the Romans are some centuries out of phase with the Greeks, their reformation takes the form a yet stronger amnesia. Forgetting the past features prominently in Greek religion, but as their transformation took place over four centuries of darkness, a rich tapestry of myth and legend could emerge alongside it. Not everything was forgotten. At Rome, the transformation occurred when they were literate, and a semi- if not fully-conscious revulsion against their own origins can be postulated. They deliberately lied about the past, they covered-up and destroyed the evidence, they eliminated from the record overt traces of the worship of the previous epoch. Hence, the Roman anomaly, the apparent oddity of a religion without myth. When Romans became interested in literature and history, they had only fragments to build upon; then they engaged in a corporate activity to construct out of these fragments a fabulous history, one that could only reflect their achieved common consensus over values, the chief of which is that *society ought to be governed by patriarchs* because *it always had been*, which is a lie. The central authority of the family and state is the *pater familias*; therefore, the authority *always has been the pater familias – pater Aeneas, pater Romulus* etc. The revolution had replaced a developed matriarchy by patriarchy.

On this account, Frazer's *Golden Bough* is a correct description of a state of religious consciousness that corresponds to the stages of matriarchy and what subsequently develops out of it; a correct description of Roman religion at its earliest stages, before Rome itself had been founded, whose ancestors existed as a community of Latin villages, of which Lavinium and Alba Longa were members. Then, indeed, the Latins were worshippers of the Goddess, and their tribal cultic centre was at Aricia, where they gathered together to worship *Diana Nemorensis* and sacrifice her consort, Virbius, the king of the wood. That these Latins were partly of Indo-European origin should not prevent us from coming to this conclusion. At some point, the presence of the Indo-European triad structure re-emerged.

The Etruscan culture was a developed matriarchy, and as such bears similarities with other developed matriarchies – those of Phoenicia and her colony Carthage, with whom she enjoyed excellent diplomatic relations. Dumézil tells us that in the foundation myth, Romulus "following a ritual which was said to be Etruscan, had thrown the 'first-fruits of all things the use of which was sanctified by custom as good and by nature as necessary.'"[1] The term for this ditch is *mundus*, used also for a trench that gave access to chthonic deities; the Latin word *mundus* probably has an Etruscan etymology. I conclude that Rome was founded by Etruscans, but if not, then it came under Etruscan dominance soon after, and for a period was governed by Etruscan kings. Rome inherited at is foundation a developed matriarchy from Etruria, which it subsequently overthrew in favour of patriarchy.

The relation between myth, legend and history in the construction of the Roman myth of its city's greatness, the work of the annalists, is complex. It is difficult to construct a genuine historical "narrative" out of it. I suggest is that we allow each motif in the annalist tradition to stand out separately, and then assign it to its possible layer.

(1) **The Capitoline triad of Jupiter, Juno and Minerva**. Dumézil tells us that this was a later institution than the original all-male triad of Jupiter, Mars and Quirinus, to which he attaches the three functions of the Indo-European common religion. It is said to have been an innovation of the Etruscan monarchy. Legend ascribes to the Etruscan monarch Tarquinius Priscus the vow to build the great temple of Jupiter Optimus, with *cellae* for Jupiter, Juno and Minerva, who together form the Capitoline Triad, which was later constructed by Tarquinius Superbus. The terracotta statue of Jupiter was made by Vulca, the master from Veii. The question of the meaning of this triad is raised. Dumézil admits that the presence of Minerva in it is a mystery, asking, "what did she represent in the Capitoline foundation, by the side of Jupiter and Juno?"[2] He finds the Triad itself an insoluble puzzle: "As for the meaning which the Tarquins gave to the triad, either of their own accord or by tradition, it escapes us so much the more because we know their work only through a distorting screen."[3] Dumézil does point us in the direction of the same triad in Greek religion, which is found in "the Phocian Building, where assemble the Phocian delegates from each city. The building is large, and within are pillars standing throughout its length. From the pillars rise steps to each wall, on which steps the Phocian delegates take their seats. At the end are neither pillars nor steps, but images of Zeus, Athena and Hera. That of Zeus is on a throne; on his right stands Hera, on his left Athena."[4] This marks out **the Phocian triad** as important, as it is at the centre of their confederacy. If one saw such a configuration in any other context, one would conclude that the deities were Dionysus, Demeter and Persephone or any equivalent: the dying god (ritually sacrificed) between the dual manifestation of the Goddess as mother and daughter. This interpretation is immediately supported by a doublet of the Capitoline Triad at Rome itself, **the Aventine Triad** of Ceres, Liber

[1] Georges Dumézil, *Archaic Roman Religion*, trans. Philip Krapp, John Hokins Press, London. 1966, p.351. He cites Plutarch *Roman Questions*, 11. 1-4 and Ovid's *Fasti* 4.281-24 as sources.

[2] *Ibid.*, 306.

[3] *Ibid.*, 308.

[4] Pausanias Book 10, 5, 2.

and Libera. Ceres is the ancient Roman Mother Goddess of agriculture, grain and fertility; Liber was a phallic deity, later identified with Bacchus and Dionysus; Libera, his consort was identified officially with Proserpina (Persephone) as the daughter of Ceres. This Aventine Triad is also known as the plebeian triad. The patricians had one triad, and the plebeians another, but both were essentially the same configuration.

Appeasing the gods in times of crisis. To interpret this configuration further, we have from Livy an intriguing account of events in Rome said to have taken place between 365 and 363. It begins in 365 with an outbreak of pestilence. The following year (364) "men's minds were completely overcome by superstitious terrors." To alleviate these concerns there was the introduction of the games of the Circus. Musicians were imported from Etruria. "However, the first introduction of plays, though intended as a means of religious expiation, did not relieve the mind from religious terrors nor the body from the inroads of disease. Owing to an inundation of the Tiber, the Circus was flooded in the middle of the Games, and this produced an unspeakable dread; it seemed as though the gods had turned their faces from men and despised all that was done to propitiate their wrath." The narrative continues.

> It is said to have been discovered that the older men remembered that a pestilence had once been assuaged by the Dictator driving in a nail. The senate believed this to be a religious obligation, and ordered a Dictator to be nominated for that purpose. L. Manlius Imperiosus was nominated, and he appointed L. Pinarius as his Master of the Horse. There is an ancient instruction written in archaic letters which runs: Let him who is the praetor maximus fasten a nail on the Ides of September. This notice was fastened up on the right side of the temple of Jupiter Optimus Maximus, next to the chapel of Minerva. This nail is said to have marked the number of the year – written records being scarce in those days – and was for that reason placed under the protection of Minerva because she was the inventor of numbers. Cincius, a careful student of monuments of this kind, asserts that at Volsinii also nails were fastened in the temple of Nortia, an Etruscan goddess, to indicate the number of the year.[5]

This equates Minerva with the Etruscan goddess Phersipnei, goddess of the underworld, also called Nortia, fate, and Mania, the goddess of death. The nail motif confirms this. (The explanation concerning the scarcity of written records is an attempt to explain away the meaning of the nail.) Then, we may ask, what was the

---

[5] Livy, *Histories*, Book VII, 1-4.

"religious obligation" that required the appointment of a dictator? In a state of primitive materialism, when things go wrong, it is because the gods are wrathful, and they need to be appeased by sacrifice. The institution of gladiatorial games where men are killed was a form of human sacrifice, but the flooding of the Campus Martius indicated that something more was required. Ritual human sacrifice was required, and a dictator having absolute power was appointed to see that the business was carried through. Some victim had to be selected, and where the choice falls, there is resentment. Thus, the story continues in Livy. L. Manlius once appointed as dictator. "caused a very angry feeling among the men liable to serve by the inconsiderate way in which he conducted the enrolment." This is attributed by Livy to Manlius being "eager to command in the war with the Hernici," and the issue of the nail and the "religious obligation" is forgotten. Manilius is forced to resign and almost impeached. "But what men most loathed was his brutal temperament, and the epithet "Imperiosus" (masterful) which had been fastened on him from his unblushing cruelty, an epithet utterly repugnant to a free State. The effects of his cruelty were felt quite as much by his nearest kindred, by his own blood, as by strangers. Amongst other charges which the tribune brought against him was his treatment of his young son." There then follows a spurious story about the "young son" and the vague hint that this young son might have been a sacrifice is ignored.

In case the reader thinks that I am putting too much meaning upon the text, consider that as a matter of historical record (so far as anything is) we know that in later times, the Romans did revert to human sacrifice. The festival of the *Argea* is described by Dumézil as "a macabre ceremony on 14 May. At that time, it designated effigies of men, bound hand and foot, which the pontiffs and the magistrates carried solemnly to the *pons Sublicus*, where the Vestals threw them into the Tiber." It is generally agreed that the effigies are substitutes for human victims, and that the ritual is a reformed one. Dumézil continues.

> We can only compare this ceremony with the unfortunately positive cases of ritual murder, if not human sacrifice, which are attested in historical times. The victims were generally paired couples, two men and two women, who were buried alive in the *Forum boarium*. Probably in 228 (Cichorius), the Insubres, allied with other Gallic peoples, threatened Italy. There was great consternation. Plutarch (*marc.* 3-4) thinks this was the first time that this barbarous procedure was resorted to. Following the recommendation of the Books, the Romans executed not only a Gallic man and woman but also a Greek man and woman.[6]

---

[6] Dumézil, *Roman Religion*, *Op. cit.*, 449. We note that in this account both men and women are sacrificed. That a sacrifice took place is surely historical; what form precisely it took may be

Plutarch had forgotten the real origin of the rite. The Gauls and the Greeks were the traditional enemies of the Romans. The same rite was reverted to after the battle of Cannae (216), and while Livy only refers explicitly to four people who were buried alive, the history of the Second Punic War and the terror it produced in Rome suggests that there were many more such sacrifices.

Reverting to the events of 363, there follows the story of **the self-sacrifice of M. Curtius**. An enormous cavern appeared in the Forum and "the seers declared, must be sacrificed on that spot if men wished the Roman republic to be eternal." On hearing this, M. Curtius "Then mounting his horse, which had been caparisoned as magnificently as possible, he leaped in full armour into the cavern. Gifts and offerings of fruits of the earth were flung in after him by crowds of men and women."[7] Stripped bare of the later gloss, the motif amounts to a sacrifice of a man and a horse in the forum to the chthonic deities. Livy remarks, "If any path would lead an inquirer to the truth, we should not shrink from the labour of investigation; as it is, on a matter where antiquity makes certainty impossible we must adhere to the legend which supplies the more famous derivation of the name." That is very Roman of him. But I agree with the sentiment, "we should not shrink from the labour of investigation."

(2) **The foundation of the Patres.** According to legend, **Romulus** founded Rome as a fortified settlement on the Palatine. He then summoned the people and gave them laws. He adopted rituals of the Etruscan type – the State Chair, purple-bordered toga and twelve attendants; he welcomed asylum seekers into the town which rapidly grew; and created a hundred senators, named "Fathers" (*patres*) or the heads of clans.

This legend summarises the religious, social and political revolution of Rome. The matriarchy has been overthrown. Matrilineal descent has been replaced by patrilineal descent; gynarchy (rule by women) has been replaced by patriarchy (rule by men).[8] But, when did this occur? And, who was responsible for it? The legendary foundation of Rome is 753, the legendary overthrow of the Etruscan monarchy is 509, yet in the period preceding that legendary overthrow it seems that Rome was a developed matriarchy; Tarquin was in the process of dedicating a Temple on the Capital of the Etruscan triad of Jupiter, Juno and Minerva – a dedication that was completed, according to legend, under the republic. The charges against Tarquin, in addition to despotism, are suggestive of Etruscan cruelty. It is said that he had his enemy Turnus "bound underneath a hurdle weighted with stones

---

questioned. In the primordial religion, it is a man that is sacrificed. But here we are in the state of a developed matriarchy, or even patriarchy, and the context is an act of sacrifice by way of bargain with the gods to secure victory in war, and not fertility of crops.

[7] Livy, *Histories*, Book VII, 5.

[8] There does not appear to be a direct antonym in the English language for gynarchy.

and flung into the water – a form of punishment which was a new invention of Tarquin's."[9] Patriarchy cannot perceive itself as an innovation, nor recognise that *really* in the past there was a time when the supreme force was the Goddess, so **history must be rewritten**. Rome had a founder, and that must be Romulus; therefore, Romulus instituted the patriarchy, which must also appear to be a natural institution. The patriarchal figure of Romulus, so far has his exploits go, is a fictional creation of backward projection. The revolution did not occur as early as 753. The institution of the Republic marks a more likely watershed for the decisive break, though 509 is also probably still far too early for this event.

(3) **Motifs of matriarchy and gynarchy**. (a) The legendary fifth king of Rome was Lucius Tarquinius Priscus, not native to Rome but an immigrant from Etruria. He was first hailed as king by his wife **Tanaquil**, a prophetess; then, he was "elected" king in preference to the sons of the previous king, Ancus Marcius. (b) Tarquinius Priscus was murdered; Tanaquil concealed the fact and appointed her "adopted" son **Servius Tullius** as king; Servius married Tarquinia, the daughter of Tanaquil. (c) Servius is said to have been a slave of Tanaquil. His younger daughter, **Tullia the younger**, murdered her elder sister, Tullia the elder. Tullia then married Tarquin (Lucius Tarquinius), who became seventh king of Rome, and took the title Tarquinius Superbus. (It is a double murder, for this younger Tullia had formerly married Tarquin's brother, Arruns, and this Arruns was also murdered by his brother.[10]) Servius was murdered by Tarquin; Tullia drove in a carriage over the dead body of her father, Servius; Servius was denied proper burial.

These three stories firmly indicate that power was conferred on men by women, who were priestesses and embodiments of the Goddess. Tanaquil was known as Gaia Caecila, the Roman Goddess of fire, the hearth, healing, and women – Vesta. We infer that the original Vestal Virgins were not "virgins" in the patriarchal sense, and they become such when patriarchy was instituted. The violent ends of Priscus and Servius point to ritual sacrifice of the king. Descent is not in the male line, and the "interrex" is a backwards fiction to conceal this fact by making the monarchy appear elective.[11]

Other motifs of matriarchy and **matrilineal descent** include: (a) Aeneas became Latin king by marriage to Lavinia, daughter of King Latinus. They founded a settlement called Lavinium. (b) Second legendary king, Numa Pompilius, was the consort of the divine nymph Egeria. (c) After the death of Aeneas, Lavina ruled as

---

[9] Livy, *Histories*, Book I, 52.

[10] The motif of this double murder, the similarity of the names of the two daughters, is suspect. This story contains within it the motif of child sacrifice.

[11] A device of a proclamation by the people serves the same purpose as the fictional notion of an interrex, diverting attention away from the mythologem itself – the old king is killed at the institution of his daughter, who appoints her son as the new king. If descent is patrilineal, why the need for election? If the monarchy was elective, then in these legends the election is by women.

regent. (d) Romulus and Remus were the sons of the Vestal Priestess *Rhea Silvia* by the god Mars. Romulus and Remus killed king Amulius and were jointly proclaimed king by the people.

(4) **Motifs of herarcy** (specifically, ritual sacrifice of the king). (a) Romulus Silvius, one of the kings of Alba Longa, said to have claimed to be a god, was struck by lightning and succeeded by Aventinus. (b) According to Servius,[12] Aventinus was killed and buried on the Aventine hill, which took its name after him. (c) Tullus Hostilius contracted plague and was burnt to death in a badly performed ritual to Jupiter Elicius which resulted in the temple being struck by lightning. (d) The Alban king, Mettius, planned to betray Rome when Veii and Fidenae started a war against her. Nonetheless, with Alban assistance Tullus defeated the men of Veii and Fidenae. Afterwards, Tullus transferred the entire population of Alba to Rome. He executed Mettius by having him torn apart by teams of horses yoked to chariots. (e) Romulus disappeared during a violent storm. He is said to have been murdered, and his body dismembered. A later story tells that he was directly subsumed into heaven, and later, he was identified with the Sabine god, Quirinus. (f) Amulius murdered his brother Numitor and usurped the kingship of Alba Longa. He ordered his daughter to become a Vestal Virgin and attempted to murder her children, Romulus and Remus. They murdered him instead. (g) Romulus murdered his brother Remus. (h) Tarquinius Priscus was murdered by the sons of Ancus. (i) Aeneas is said to have died in battle against the Rutili, but no tomb of his is known. Dionysius of Halicarnassus claimed that his body disappeared. Livy says that he was worshipped as a local god under the title of *Jupiter indiges*. (j) Conflict arose between Rome and Alba. However, the Alban king, Mettius, proposed that sovereignty should be settled by trial by combat between three champions on each side, to avoid bloodshed that would weaken the nation and expose them to Etruscan aggression. The Curiatii represented Alba and the Horatii Rome. In the fight the young Horatius was the only man left standing. However, his sister had been betrothed to one of the Curiatii and he killed her in rage when she was mourning her dead lover. Tullus arrested Horatius but contrived to have Horatius tried by the people, who acquitted him. This legend contains the motif of a gladiatorial contest, which is a form of ritual sacrifice. The image of the sister mourning the dead lover, is a variant of the Cybele-Attis motif. Ritual sacrifice is indicated, glossed over by a complex legend.

(5) **Romulus** is the son of Rhea Silvia, a priestess of Vesta by Mars. He was suckled by a she-wolf. His foster mother is Acca Larentia, a goddess, after whom the Larentalia festival is named. In another myth, Larentia is a temple prostitute who copulates with Hercules. Romulus's foster-father is Faustulus, a shepherd. He founds Rome. The foundation of Rome was celebrated on 21 April, at the festival of

---

[12] Maurus Servius Honoratus, late C4, early C5 CE, *Commentary on Virgil.*

Parilia, which was in honour of Pales, twin gods or goddesses of shepherds. The Romans called themselves Quirites in honour of the Sabine town Cures. Quirinus is also a Sabine deity that the Romans identified either with Mars or with the deified Romulus. All these motifs indicate that Romulus was originally a vegetation god, the son of the Goddess, and sacrificed as such. The foundation myth was projected onto this Romulus, because Rome was named after him. He was metamorphosed into the founder of patriarchy.

(6) The **Lupercalia** takes place on 15 February. Faunus was the god of the festival. Cicero said the rites were "instituted before human civilization and the laws." *Februum* was translated by Varro as "purgamentum", *februare* by "to purify". The Luperci are "dispellers of wolves". It was a ceremony of rites of purification and fertility. A dog may have been sacrificed, and goats certainly were. In the ceremony "youths of noble birth" touch their foreheads with a bloody knife, wipe the stain off with wool dipped in milk, and laugh. The Luperci gird themselves in the goat skins, and then race around the Palatine. Two teams, representing spirits of nature, the *Luperci Quinctiales* and *Luperci Fabiani*, naked but for the goatskins, run around the Palatine hill. They hit women with the thongs. An aetiological explanation is offered in a story related by Ovid: after the rape of Sabine women, it was discovered that they were sterile. There was a voice heard in a grove dedicated to Juno saying, "Let a sacred goat penetrate the women of Italy!" The mysterious meaning was unravelled by an Etruscan soothsayer – a goat is immolated, the skin is cut into thongs, the backs of young women are beaten, and nine months later, there were plenty of babies.[13]

A festival of purification, like that celebrated at Athens in the same month, surely formed a standard component of the religious festival calendar of any Romano-Greek city. The addition of the "wolf cult" is distinctive; it may be a remnant of a totem – the wolf being the totem of the original people of the Palatine hill. The ritual is clearly both a fertility rite and a rite of purgation. The symbolism points yet again to an original form in which human blood was shed, transferred in the "civilised" form onto goats. The rite is a dramatic representation of the idea of blood begetting fertility, though to describe it in such terms surely fails to express the breathless ecstasy that must have been involved in participation, as flagellator or flagellated, or even as mere onlooker. The presence of a dog in the sacrifice, hints at the symbol of the Hound of Hell.

Although we see the motif of rape in the story of the rape of Lucretia, the only episode of the Roman foundation myth in which rape figures as a mythologem is that of **the rape of the Sabine women**. The rape mythologem figures prominently in Greek mythology but hardly at all in Roman mythology. This points to differences in the way the reformation of the religion of Dionysus came about in Greece and in

---

[13] See Dumézil, *Roman Religion, Op. cit.* p. 347 – 350.

Rome. At Rome, notwithstanding the story of the deposition of Tarquin, overall less violence is recorded. The myth of the rape of the Sabine women is not historical. It extols literally naked masculine power and in the story of how the Sabine women bring about peace it represents a submission of women. It expresses a feeling among the Romans that they are racially a synthesis of Latin and Sabine peoples.

(7) The **Roman Calendar**. To discuss all the Roman festivals would be out of place here. There was hardly a day when something was not scheduled. The overall impression is that, just as with the Athenian calendar, the Roman year was dedicated to fertility and purification (expurgation of the dead). Roman religion is predominantly chthonic, and the upper Olympian layer of Greek religion is missing. What has taken its place is an idealisation of the maternal concept of fate, projected onto a masculine deity – Jupiter ultimately – the idea of the destiny of Rome. Among the myriad of festivals, in addition to the Lupercalia and Parila already mentioned, I draw attention to the following: (a) The **Compitalia** in honour of the *Lares Compitales* or household deities and related to crossroads and boundaries. The sacrifices comprised honey-cakes. During the festival, families put up statues of the goddess Mania at the door of their house, also hanging up figures of wool representing men and women; prayers were made to spare the house. According to Macrobius, Tarquinius Superbus restored the festival because of an oracle saying, "they should sacrifice heads for heads." It was interpreted to mean that children should be sacrificed to Mania, who is the mother of the Lares. Brutus substituted heads of garlic and poppies for the heads of children. In its original form the ritual points decidedly to sacrifice of children, probably the first-born as at Carthage. It was reformed into a less harmful variant, and the reformation is associated with the overthrown of the Etruscan monarchy. The Lares are twin gods and are sometimes indistinguishable from the *Penates*, whom Aeneas is said to have rescued from Troy.[14] Twins is a motif that occurs in the context of agriculture in both patriarchal and matriarchal religions, and hence both variants may easily fuse. (b) The

---

[14] "Penates – household god, deified ancestors generally of the Romans, whose images were placed and worshipped in the centre of the house, penetralia, where, in their honour, a perpetual fire burnt, and the first-fruits and salt-cellar were always on the table; the *Lares* were included in the Penates. The Roman state, considered as one family, had Penates whose images were believed to have been brought by Aeneas from Troy to Lavinium, thence to Alba, and, on its fall, to Rome." *Beeton's Classical Dictionary*. The sex and identity of these gods is unclear – however, Roman coins and images from the period contemporaneous with Cicero make the Penates into male twins and depict them on either side of the goddess Vesta, with the chthonic symbol of the snake below, emblem of the risen soul following violent death. That makes them into fertility gods in the service of the Goddess; hence in their most elementary layer, they are sacrificial twins symbolically close to that of Romulus and Remus, in which the mythologem of ritual murder may be detected in that Romulus kills his own twin brother. The Penates were adapted in the patriarchal epoch into titular gods of the family and adopted into Roman patrician religion as protective deities of the household – that is of the ancestral line.

Agonalia is not one but a whole series of repeated events. The festival occurred on January 9, May 21, and December 11, but there was also an Agonium Martiale held on March 17. On each of these days a ram was sacrificed. The Roman perplexity regarding the meaning of this festival is reflected in some words of Ovid's *Fasti*,[15] where he proposes various meanings. *Agonia* or *agonium* was the term for victim, but it derives from Greek and Sanscrit, *ago*, to lead, drive (cattle), or to drive and impel (men), from which *agones*, games, contests, *agon*, contest, *agonia*, agony, in ancient Greek, emulation, competition, struggle. Any festival in which a victim was sacrificed could be called an *Agonalia*. From the same root word, the idea of games or festivals arises, and these are linked to funeral rites. There is the implicit concept of a heroic struggle against fate. The ram stands in for the hero. It is related to the motif of the scapegoat. I conclude that the ram is standing in for the king, who would have been the original sacrifice. The context is fertility originally. That it was the king that was originally sacrificed is indicated by the site of the sacrifice, the Regia, the residence of the Roman king and later of the Pontifex Maximus, and the presiding priest was the *rex sacrificulus* (*rex sacorum*) who held the highest prestige, and officiated at sacrifices on behalf of the king, as his substitute in Republican times. In the earliest times the Regia was situated on the Quirinal and the Quirinal hill was originally called Agonus, and the Colline gate Agonensis.[16] Thus, each of these sacrifices is an occasion when a victim was selected to stand in for the king, who was the original sacrifice.[17]   (c) The **Carmentalia** held on 11 January and 15 January (the Ides of January) and the festival of Anna Perenna held on the 15 March (the Ides of March).[18] Very little is known about either of these festivals, which were observed primarily by women. The goddess worshipped, Carmenta (Revealer of Wisdom) in the first of these, and Anna Perenna (Everlasting Queen) in the second, appear to be the same, for they have the same attributes of being a dual goddess of prophecy: Postvorta, She-Who-Looks-Toward-the-Future, and Antevorta, She-Who-Looks-Toward-the-Past. Both goddesses may be identified with the Etruscan goddess Juturna, whose consort is Jupiter, a goddess of rivers and still waters, another manifestation of the Etruscan Great Goddess. Under the authority of

---

[15] Ovid, *Fasti*, 1. 318.

[16] William Smith, D.C.L., LL.D. *A Dictionary of Greek and Roman Antiquities*, John Murray, London, 1875.

[17] The presence of the Earth Mother is all but erased from the details of the rite, though there is a numinous trace of her in one of Ovid's lines, "Or because the victim fears the knife mirrored in the water" – which contains the motif of the pool of water dedicated to the Goddess, such as the Lake of Nemi at Aricia, where Diana of the Wood was worshipped, and where visionaries could commune with her in the mirror of the water. Water was used in this way by later Neo-Platonic magicians to evoke visionary experience.

[18] We derive the word carmen = song from Carmentia.

Carmenta came the Carmentae, the Sybils who were female priestesses that revealed wisdom.

Despite the war of liberation with Etruria, Rome continued to live after that great event on generally good terms with the Etruscans, and probably remained under its suzerainty for a time. The reverence felt for the old religion of the Earth Mother continued, and the older practices did not die out immediately. The respect for the Great Goddess was preserved in the festival calendar, where she appeared under different guises, sometimes as Carmenta, sometimes as Anna Perenna, sometimes as Ceres, sometimes as Fortuna, and so forth.

Romans did not disassociate themselves altogether from the power of the Goddess and her control of fate. They preserved not only her worship in the form of transformed rituals, but also her wisdom in the form of **the Etruscan books of fate**, the most important of which were the **Sibylline books**, said to have been sold to Tarquin by the Cumean Sybil. These books, being the works of the religion of the Great Mother, were kept under strict lock and key and guarded by a team of ten specialist priests known as the *decemviri sacris faciundis* until the time of Sulla, when their number was increased to fifteen. Whenever times were hard, and the Romans needed recourse to strong medicine, they consulted the Sibylline books. These extraordinary documents, said to have been destroyed by the general Flavius Stilicho (c.359 – 408 CE), were remarkably good at proposing solutions to problems and sanctifying atavisms to human sacrifice. Rome did not divest itself of its original matriarchal core, and in extreme cases it always remembered and reverted to it. Rome did not achieve a full reformation of its religion, and although all political and social power rested with the men, as *patres*, fathers of the family, yet their institutions still justified this in terms of a derivation from maternal authority.

(8) **Late historical details embedded in early legend**. (a) According to the legend, Numa Pomplius, (legendary dates 715 – 673) a Sabine, was elected king; his election was confirmed by augury. He is said to have founded the temple of Janus and established a religious calendar, dividing the year into twelve calendar months and establishing on which days it was lawful to transact business. He established priests of Mars and Quirinus and virgin priestesses for Vesta, which was a cult originating from Alba. He introduced the twelve Salli, or Leaping Priests, in the service of Mars Gradivus. He appointed Numa Marcius as pontifex. He established an altar on the Aventine to Jupiter Elicius. It is said he conversed directly with the goddess Egeria. (b) The legend ascribes to the Etruscan king Servius Tullus a series of reforms. We note that this is the king that the Emperor Claudius identified with the Etruscan Mastarna. The military reform organised the army upon a timocractic

basis – that is service in the army would be based on ownership of property. He constructed the Servian wall.[19]

In the hotchpotch of detail, some having historical content: (a) The religious reformation includes the reform of the calendar, the transformation of the cult of Vesta into one served by virgin priestesses, but these must belong to later dates, and are projected onto Numa. The establishment of a male pontifex maximus is likewise a backward projection. The cult of Janus and the altar on the Aventine belong to a much earlier layer; they are ancient. (b) The wall attributed to Servius was built in the early C4 and not in the early C6. Some part of the military reorganisation may be attributed to the C6; it may have laid the foundation for the religious transformation. Developing military and political power for men may bring about a transformation in which the head of the family passes even imperceptibly from the woman to the man. It may bring about a division within society between a religiously conservative monarchy led by Tarquin and a progressive aristocracy led by Brutus. The position of the lower orders, the plebeians, is ambiguous. In all the crises it seems that they are clamouring for a reversion to the older forms of matriarchal worship, and at times they are appeased, and sacrifice is restored. Potentially, a political alliance on religious grounds between the monarchy and the plebeians existed; after the reformation, the patrician order established a monopoly over religion, and all the priesthoods were exclusive to them. One can read the

---

[19] It is said that owing to the increase of the urban population a reorganization was required. The three original tribes were abolished, and twenty new ones created, with four city tribes named after the hills of Sucusana, Esquilina, Collina and Palatina. The country population was divided into sixteen tribes named after *gentes* – leading families. The census divided the people according to their property – those whose property was below the minimum level for military service were classed as lesser class citizens or *proletarii*. The classes were divided into centuries. There were 193 centuries in all. A new form of Assembly, the Comitia Centuriata, was instituted, which was summoned by trumpet and met on the Campus Martius. Whilst the Comitia Curiata continued to function for a while, the Comitia Centuriata gradually became the more important of the two Assemblies. The centuries voted in order of precedence, starting with the *equites*, and down through the classes. The centuries of cavalry, numbering 18, and those of the first class, numbering 98, gave them a majority in the Comitia Centuriata. The round shield and the sword were adopted as standard military equipment. Servius is believed to have established a cult of Diana on the Aventine hill, which was a plebeian quarter. Some of the neighbouring Latin towns accepted this as their federal sanctuary.

Comment on this "historical data" is appropriate. (1) The level of detail and the numbers involved all suggest a backward projection of later events onto an earlier time. (2) Such a reorganisation of the tribes, as with the Athenian case under Solon and Cleisthenes, in the context of the religious confrontation of matriarchy and patriarchy, is suggestive of a step towards patriarchy; it is indicative of religious revolution. (3) Hence, attributing the reorganisation to "population expansion" may be a much later aetiological explanation by way of concealing the real religious reasons for breaking up the original tribal configurations, which would have been constituted on different religious principles.

demise of the Republic as the overthrow of the aristocracy by a political alliance between the rising monarch (Julius Caesar) and the lower orders.

(9) **Ritual and insignia.** The ritual and insignia of the Roman state were all directly borrowed from Etruscan equivalents, which in turn were borrowings from other places.[20]

(10) **The Twelve Tables.** While the original document does not exist, the date of 450 – 449 is not disputed. It is customary to interpret this law as a victory of the plebeians, who had been agitating for some time for agrarian reform and a written code of law to gain "fuller security of person and property."[21] As a prelude the plebeians are said to have established an organisation based on the Aventine hill where they worshipped Ceres, Liber and Libera. They are said to have had connections with Greece and Magna Graeca. The aristocracy were said to be led by the gens *Fabii*. The plebeian leader, Spurius Cassius, elected as consul for the third time in 486, was condemned to death by the patricians a year later in 485. The plebeians threatened a general strike. While the Twelve Tables contain provision for legal protection of property and rights under the law on an equal footing, I do not see within it any provision for agrarian reform in the sense of redistribution of land, or of limitation on amount of tenure. The first such law is the *Lex Licinia Sextia* of 367.

I suggest that this conflict had a **religious dimension.** (a) The Plebeians had an alternative organisation based on the religious sanctuary of the Avertine Hill where they worshipped Ceres, Liber and Libera. This identifies them with the worship of the Corn Mother, Ceres. (b) The coda to the law made in 449 prohibits "Intermarriage (*conubium*) between plebeians and patricians" (Table XI.1). This statute was repealed in 445. It is a very strong statement of a religious division between the patricians and plebeians. (c) Punishment by sacrifice to the goddess Ceres is proposed for infringement of property rights.[22] This is effectively a

---

[20] The crown of gold, the throne of ivory, the sceptre bearing an eagle, the tunic of purple with gold, and the mantle of purple, were all derived through Etruria from the kings of Lydia and Persia. The lower garments, the *tunica palmata* and *toga picta* were similarly derived. Each Etruscan king had a lictor – that is an official carrying a ceremonial axe called a *faces*; the official walked in front of him; the axe symbolised his power to administer justice and capital punishment; in the event of war the chief king was attended by all twelve lictors. Italicus wrote, "Vetulonia, formerly the pride of the Lydian race, was the first city to place the twelve faces at the head of processions and to add to them the silent menace of the axes." Examples have been discovered there dating form C7. Under the Roman republic, each consul had twelve lictors.

[21] M. Cary and H. H. Scullard, *A History of Rome*, Macmillan, London, 1935, Third edition, p. 66.

[22] From the Twelve Tables: VIII. "10. For pasturing on or for cutting secretly by night [another's] crops acquired by tillage [shall be] in the case of an adult hanging and death [by sacrifice] to Ceres; a person under the age of puberty (under 15 years of age) [shall] either be scourged at the discretion [of the magistrate] or make composition by [paying] double [damages] for the harm [done]." The translator's note: "[Ceres is] properly the goddess of creation, occasionally (by extension) the goddess of marriage, usually the goddess of agriculture, especially the goddess of cultivation of grain and of

statement acknowledging the right of the plebeian Mother Goddess to exact punishment on behalf of the plebeians in the event of unlawful use of land. It constitutes an edict of toleration. (d) Table X, entitled "Sacred Law" prohibits excessive display of emotion at funerals or the creation of shrines to the dead.[23] These are religious laws designed at curbing the rites of Dionysus – the lamentations on behalf of the ritually sacrificed hero in the context of the worship of the Mother. The edict of toleration is accompanied by an edict of prohibition, which may be read as a coded prohibition against ritual human sacrifice.

The legendary history of Rome postulates that very soon after the Republic was established, Rome divided into two factions – the aristocracy or patricians and the common people or plebeians. We may surmise that the overthrow of the monarchy was not popular with the plebeians, or at least, brought into existence a plebeian opposition to the rule of the aristocracy. The provisions in the Twelve Tables are customarily read as a partial victory for women's rights: "In the matter of family law it sanctioned, under certain conditions, the emancipation of wives and children from the autocracy of the *paterfamilias*."[24] On the other hand, if the original norm had been greater equality if not dominance of women in matters of property and religion, as we have seen subsisted in Etruscan society, then **the provisions in the Twelve Table represent a victory for patriarchy**; the law might perhaps be interpreted as a concession to the plebeian community, though subject to the proviso against intermarriage, and in the framework of a shift in favour of patriarchy.[25] Another aspect of the laws are regulations against magical practices: death is prescribed as penalty for incantations, curses and enchantments. These practices, within terms of our schema, are reflections of primitive materialism in the belief structure of the plebeians, but their use is outlawed in a document that primarily serves the interests

---

growth of fruits in general. Ceres is represented commonly as a matronly woman, always clad in full attire of flowing draperies, crowned either with a simple ribband or with ears of grain holding in her hand sometimes a poppy, sometimes a sceptre, sometimes a sickle, sometimes a sheaf of grain, sometimes a torch, sometimes a basket full of fruits or of flowers, seated or standing in a chariot drawn by dragons or by horses." The translator and editor is P.R. Coleman-Norton of Princeton University.

[23] An interpretation of the following prohibition: "The bones of a dead person shall not be collected that one may make a funeral afterward."

[24] Cary and Scullard, *History, Op. Cit.*, p. 67.

[25] From the Twelve Tables: "Table V. Inheritance and guardianship: 1. Women shall remain under guardianship, even though they shall become of full age… 2. The conveyable or movable possessions of a woman who is under tutelage of her male relatives shall not be acquired rightfully by long usage or long possession, save if these [possessions] by herself shall have been delivered with the sanction of [her male] guardian." Translation slightly modified. The translator is P.R. Coleman-Norton of Princeton University. The term used for "male relatives" in the text is *agnates*, and we are told: *agnates* are relatives by blood or through adoption on male side only; *cognates* are blood-relatives on either male or female side. The family of the *ius civile* is the agnatic family; the family of the *ius gentiu* is the cognatic family.

of patriarchy. The law of the patricians is imposed upon the people. If we grant that Rome was originally a developed matriarchy, then the Twelve Tables represents a victory of patriarchy over matriarchy.

(11) **The story of the books of Numa**. A strange story recounted by Livy describes how some "books" appertaining to the legendary king Numa were discovered buried in the ground; these were examined by various magistrates, who decided to burn them. The details provided by Livy all point to the idea that the books are a forgery produced by a Pythagorean sect, and hence Livy invites us to agree with the dramatic act of censorship. The incident would not merit mention in this work were it not that we possess an alternative account of the story, which comes from Augustine's *The City of God*. Since Augustine is quoting from Varro, an earlier source than Livy, his account is closer to the original events.

> A man named Terentius had a farm near the Janiculum. His ploughman was driving his plough near the tomb of Numa Pompilius when he turned up the books of that author which dealt with the reasons for the established ceremonies of religion. He took them to the city and handed them to the praetor. The praetor took a look at the opening passages, and then reported the find to the senate, as a matter of great importance. When the leading senators had read some of the reasons given by Numa for various religious practices, the senate approved the action of the deceased king, and, as pious conscript fathers, decreed that the praetor should burn those books.[26]

There is no mention in this account of features in Livy's version: the freshness of the books, that the coffin in which they were buried was found to contain no body, that the books were in both Latin and Greek, and that it was a common belief that Numa was a pupil of Pythagoras. The events are historic and do point to a significant act of religious censorship. Numa is a legendary figure, but it does not follow that the books which were burned may not have contained disturbing revelations concerning the foundation of Roman religion, and its migration from matriarchy to patriarchy that the Roman authorities must deem as too disturbing to be preserved.

(12) The **Battle of Cannae** and the "introduction" of **Cybele** to Rome. In 216 the Roman army was massively defeated by the army of Hannibal at Cannae. The apprehensive and superstitious nature of the common people is captured by Livy's description of the portents seen before the battle.[27] The account of Polybius indicates

---

[26] Augustine, *City of God*, Book VII. 34.

[27] "... a couple of shields had sweated blood; some soldiers had been struck by lightning; an eclipse of the sun had been observed; at Praeneste there had been a shower of red-hot stones; at Arpi shields had been seen in the sky and the sun had appeared to be fighting with the moon; at Capena two moons

that the entire Roman army was engulfed and destroyed. Estimates of the casualties vary from between forty-five to seventy thousand slain. Ten thousand were said to have been taken prisoner; the Romans refused to ransom them, and Polybius does not state what their fate was. The consternation the defeat produced at Rome was extreme. "As soon as the news of this disaster reached Rome the people flocked into the Forum in a great state of panic and confusion."[28] Attempts to appease the gods were made with massive sacrifices of animals and other religious rites. Subsequently, "Two Vestal virgins, Opimia and Floronia, were found guilty of unchastity. One was buried alive, as is the custom, at the Colline Gate, the other committed suicide." Then, "in obedience to the Books of Destiny, some strange and unusual sacrifices were made, human sacrifices amongst them. A Gaulish man and a Gaulish woman and a Greek man and a Greek woman were buried alive under the Forum Boarium. They were lowered into a stone vault, which had on a previous occasion also been polluted by human victims, a practice most repulsive to Roman feelings."[29]

It was deemed necessary in 204 to respond to a further deterioration of public morale by the introduction of the Phrygian cult of the Mother of the Gods, Cybele, into Rome. There is some irony in this: the Mother of the Gods had always been worshipped in Rome, for Rome had formally been a matriarchy, and even in those days, the great Mother was worshipped as Ceres or Hera. But a developed polytheism of departmental gods, and the suppression of matriarchal deities meant that perhaps such things had been forgotten. The reintroduction of Mother worship into Rome is a symbolic statement of a partial reversion in Roman religion to the religion of its ancestors. In times of stress, the Sibylline Books were consulted, and it was the Great Mother in whom the common Roman people found comfort. The statue of the Phrygian Cybele was donated by King Atallus of Pergamum and conveyed in great ceremony to Rome – its final resting place, the Temple of Victory.

(13) **The end of the practice of human sacrifice** came very late in Rome's history. According to Pliny the Elder in 97 BCE "a decree forbidding human sacrifices was passed by the senate; from which period the celebration of these horrid rites ceased in public, and, for some time, altogether."[30] This passage has been much debated, for it seems to imply that the practice had been regular in Rome until that time. The whole effort of the Roman psyche aimed in some way to overcome this practice, as it was the challenge of the first millennium to do so everywhere; but the Roman psyche, conditioned by its past, never wholly overcame

---

were visible in the daytime; at Caere the waters ran mingled with blood, and even the spring of Hercules had bubbled up with drops of blood on the water..." Livy, *History*, Book 21, 1. 8.

[28] Livy, *History*, 22, 76.

[29] Livy, *History*, 22, 57.

[30] Pliny the Elder, *The Natural History*, trans. John Bostock and H.T. Riley, London. Taylor and Francis, Red Lion Court, Fleet Street. 1855, 30.3.

the tendency to ritual murder and cruelty, which it dressed up under the guises of gladiatorial combat and crucifixion of those guilty of crime. Pliny continues, and referring to the Druids of Gaul and Britain, he tells us:

> The Gallic provinces, too, were pervaded by the magic art, and that even down to a period within memory; for it was the Emperor Tiberius that put down their Druids, and all that tribe of wizards and physicians. But why make further mention of these prohibitions, with reference to an art which has now crossed the very Ocean even, and has penetrated to the void recesses of Nature? At the present day, struck with fascination, Britannia still cultivates this art, and that, with ceremonials so august, that she might almost seem to have been the first to communicate them to the people of Persia. To such a degree are nations throughout the whole world, totally different as they are and quite unknown to one another, in accord upon this one point!
>
> Such being the fact, then, we cannot too highly appreciate the obligation that is due to the Roman people, for having put an end to those monstrous rites, in accordance with which, to murder a man was to do an act of the greatest devoutness, and to eat his flesh was to secure the highest blessings of health.

Pliny expresses the high ideal of the Roman world, its aspiration to represent civilisation in its spiritual progress against barbarism.[31] But the habit of split consciousness has also been brought in alongside that, for Roman practice will not

---

[31] Two other expressions of a related idea are found in (1) Strabo. "The Romans put a stop both to these customs and to the ones connected with sacrifice and divination, as they were in conflict with our own ways: for example, they would strike a man who had been consecrated for sacrifice in the back with a sword, and make prophecies based on his death-spasms; and they would not sacrifice without the presence of the Druids. Other kinds of human sacrifices have been reported as well: some men they would shoot dead with arrows and impale in the temples; or they would construct a huge figure of straw and wood, and having thrown cattle and all manner of wild animals and humans into it, they would make a burnt offering of the whole thing." Strabo, *Geography*, 4.1.13. Trans. Benjamin Fortson, Koch and Carey, 1995. 18. (2) Julius Caesar. "All the people of Gaul are completely devoted to religion, and for this reason those who are greatly affected by diseases and in the dangers of battle either sacrifice human victims or vow to do so using the Druids as administrators to these sacrifices, since it is judged that unless for a man's life a man's life is given back, the will of the immortal gods cannot be placated. In public affairs they have instituted the same kind of sacrifice. Others have effigies of great size interwoven with twigs, the limbs of which are filled up with living people which are set on fire from below, and the people are deprived of life surrounded by flames. It is judged that the punishment of those who participated in theft or brigandage or other crimes are more pleasing to the immortal gods; but when the supplies of this kind fail, they even go so low as to inflict punishment on the innocent." Julius Caesar, *Gallic Wars*, 6.16 – trans. Anna Lea in Koch and Carey 1995. 22.

equal Roman ideals. Suspicions that both Julius Caesar and Augustus practised human sacrifice remain neither confirmed nor refuted. However, it is the damage done to the Western psyche by **the habit of lying about the past** that we need to attend to. Force was used to bring about the demise of the ancient religion, and the patriarchy that arose lost its connection with the vital forces that the primitive religion did represent, albeit criminally. In its long and intense struggle for survival, Rome was constantly under pressure to revert to an older form of consciousness and to the practices of its matriarchal core, which the Romans never had the courage to wholly destroy. A tendency on the part of the Roman government **to manipulate the religious superstitions of the people** arose, and in Cicero's *On the Gods*, Cotta is right, and when Cotta quotes Varro, then Varro is right to indict the Roman authorities of having instituted certain rites to control people for what they deem to be their own benefit, to permit the continuance of beliefs which they deem to be no more than "lying fables".

(14) The Roman habit of **making a deity out of an "abstraction"** exposed the Roman religion to the charge of the ludicrous.[32] "The Romans," writes Augustine, "assigned particular gods to particular spheres and to almost every single movement. They had a goddess called Agenoria, to arouse to action; a goddess Stimula, to stimulate to extraordinary action; a goddess Murcia to make a man extraordinarily inactive, … meaning slothful and inert, and a goddess Strenia, to make man strenuous."[33] When one looks back on this Roman tendency, the tendency is to explain these as personifications that have then been reified and deified into persons and divinities, which makes the habit appear ridiculous.

It is the explanation that makes this motif seen odd: firstly, the Romans have an abstraction, say action in the sense of stimulation to work, then they create a fiction, a personification of this abstract idea, as Strenia; then a narrative poem about Strenia; then, a real person out of her; then, a deity out of her, and then build a temple for Stenia and make prayers and sacrifices to her.

[32] The following is a list of deities that represent "abstractions": Copia, Porus, Volumnus, Agenor, Strenia, Fessonia, Terminus, Palatua, Portumnus, Consus, Tarpeia, Larenta, Libitina, Naenia, Genita-Mana, Ate, Discordia, Verminus, Febris, Mefitis, Scabies, Janus, Pavor, Volupia, Verplaca, Pallor, Stimula, Caca, Nerio, Flora, Edesia, Pomona, Fornax, Bivesia, Frutesca, Mellona, Molae, Fraus, Caia, Medtrina, Medica, Valentia, Angintia, Fruscinus, Citumnus, Furrina, Cluerca, Limentinus, Forculus, Lina, Epona, Agenoria, Adeona, Voltumna, Nemestrinus, Collatina, Sylvanus, Picus, Tellumn, Vallonia, Eventus, Jugatinus, Domitius, Juga, Subigus, Cinxia, Manturnae, Anteros, Soranus, Pecunia, Aesculanus, Cacus, Volta, Luna, Noctornus, Numeria, Fidius Dius, Sanctus Saber, Semipater, Semo Sancus, Panda, Saudela, Hora, Perfica, Mercia, Vaucna, Libentina, Comus, Voluptas, Lua, Pellonia, Fascinus, Poena, Fama, Cloacina, Muta, Tacita, Camoena, Libertas, Laverna, Antevorta, Postvorta, Angerona, Clementia, Fluonia, Juventas. This list is from a compilation made by Gregory Flood.
[33] Augustine, *City of God*, Book IV, Chapter 6.

This is probably not the way in which these developed. Indeed, from the list of "abstractions" taken to be deities, we may infer that the Roman psyche was quite different to ours, or our psyche may be quite like the Roman one, only we do not know it. We encountered this issue earlier when we examined the Greek concept of sin, and how in the first place, *they did not have one*. The terms we translate by the abstraction "sin" began as the goddess Ate, Hate. The Romans, like the Greeks at an earlier stage of cognition, experienced phenomena that we might denote by an abstract noun, as a vital force. The deity does not begin as a personification, for it had never been an abstraction either. When Romans talk of Strenia, they mean Strenia, the goddess, the vital force that flows through their psyche and enables them to get on with something strenuous; not strain in the abstract sense, but strain in the concrete sense of *that thing to be done, that battle to be won, that ditch to be dug, that fortification to be put up*. The Roman pantheon is real and concrete. They are not making gods out of abstractions, it only appears such to us.

It should not be too difficult for us to comprehend this as psychology. Jung tells us that certain complexes of our psyche can function as if they were autonomous in some sense; among these archetypes are the Shadow, the Anima (or Animus), the Father, the Mother and the Self. His list is not exhaustive, and he is open to the inclusion of other complexes. The Roman likewise experiences forces within his psyche as something "other", something that can be invoked. It's like what we do when we talk to ourselves and say, "Come on, you can do it!" We often experience ourselves as a "we" and not as an "I", and we allow one part of this "we" to talk to and appeal to another. What is distinctively Roman is that these "other parts" of the Self, were characteristically experienced as both personal and universal, and hence, as gods. The gods are archetypal forces of human nature, writ large upon the backdrop of the cosmos. As such, they can be invoked; theoretically, they can also be made to visualise, and can be talked to. We talk to them already, if the truth were known. So, the Romans are not exceptional in this respect, though something *very Roman* has got into it.

(15) **Roman piety** and **Roman bargaining religion**. The Roman religion became a religion whose central concept was devotion to Rome and belief in Rome's destiny. The Romans had as much metaphysics as was required to render this system of devotion serviceable. Their religion became a bargaining religion – a system of striking deals with the "gods" – **sacra and signa** – and its purpose was to promulgate their defence of their city when hard-pressed and expansion when they had the upper hand. The system was tremendously effective: in the late days of the Republic, not only did they survive the terrible war with Carthage, which saw humiliating defeats, enormous losses and terrible destruction of the land, but they went on to establish an empire.

20

Roman piety

Frazer's distinction between **magic-science and religion**. In magic-science, the universe is populated by forces that are capable of manipulation by man; by his magic he controls nature. The primitive has "a faith, implicit but real and firm, in the order and uniformity of nature." Like the modern determinist, he believes "the same causes will always produce the same effects."[1] Since he experiences nature as full of vital force, he also conceives of nature has populated by spirit beings, so he is a pantheist, only for him the distinction between man and god has not arisen, and he "hardly conceives the distinction commonly drawn by more advanced peoples between the natural and the super-nature. To him the world is to a great extent worked by supernatural agents, that is, by personal beings acting on impulses and motives like his own."[2] In the long twilight period before the emergence of Ionian consciousness, the distance between himself and the gods begins to increase – the gods become more powerful and he less powerful. He has not yet grasped the concept of infinity, but "large" and "larger" have come into his view. At the same time, because he belongs to a social structure, either as master or servant; the world is becoming more "objective" to him, separate and real; his ego-consciousness is evolving, and stabilising. He realises implicitly that nature is not subject to his spells. Then, he advances to religion – to the belief that nature is subject to the control "of powers superior to man." Likening those powers to himself, the focus of his conduct may take the form of the "propitiation or conciliation" of those powers.

> … no man is religious who does not govern his conduct in some measure by the fear or love of God. …But if religion involves, first, a belief in superhuman beings who rule the world, and, second, an attempt to win their favour, it clearly assumes that the course of nature is to some extent elastic or variable, and that we can persuade or induce the mighty beings who control it to deflect, for our benefit, the current of events from the channel in which they would otherwise flow.[3]

There is an implicit tension, if not contradiction, expressed between the two parts of Frazer's statement above.

---

[1] J. G. Frazer, *The Golden Bough*, Chapter IV – Magic and Religion.
[2] *Ibid.*, Chapter II – Priestly Kings.
[3] *Ibid.*, Chapter IV, Magic and Religion.

A.   Nature, governed by God, is "elastic" and "variable"; hence, the course of events cannot be predicted.

B.   By our actions, we can induce God to make Nature conform to our wishes.

The dichotomy within religion.   At one extreme, God is all-powerful and inscrutable, and we can merely submit to His will.[4] At the other extreme, we have what amounts to an extension of the ideas of primitive materialism into the domain of gods, onto whom we now project some kind of law-like behaviour. In magic, spell X produces effect Y by operating on the immutable laws of Nature; in magic-religion, *sacrificio X* produces an effect upon deity, who responds, *in law-like fashion*, by producing effect or *signa Y* in Nature. All we have done is to insert the supernatural being into the chain of causes; the freedom or free choice of the deity in the process is not considered. But this logic also creates a dichotomy, an Either/Or. At the one extreme, all that happens in the world, our fate, is subject to the now arbitrary will of God, his grace, or caprice, and at the other extreme, we have made God into nothing more than a part of the mechanism, capable of being manipulated.

In the second half of this dichotomy, a mediating concept is that of *moral law*. For we ask, why does *sacrificio X* produce an effect upon deity? The answer is that the *sacrificio* conforms to *moral law*, it is *moral*, that is *pious*, and God, who perceives this, rewards us with happiness, which takes the form of granting our wish. *He rewards the pious with happiness.* We stand in the right relation with God, because of our devotion to God. But then, in this case, moral law also takes the form of a deterministic system of causes and effects. In place of the physical determinism of Nature, we substitute moral determinism of God's Nature, or of Moral Reality.

Roman metaphysics of piety.   The Romans took it as "axiomatic" that "happiness is proportionate to morality" and that a power, God, or the gods, ensures that it is so. Hence, as soon as anything went wrong, demonstrating a dislocation between their happiness and God, they immediately sought to rectify their morality, that is, to piously place themselves in the right relation to God, by devotion. It is also "axiomatic" in their system that God reveals displeasure through signs, such as prodigies. After the defeat in first battle of Hannibal's campaign in Italy at Trebia in 218 as Livy tells us, "During this winter many portents occurred in Rome and the neighbourhood..."[5]

> With regard to the other portents, the decemvirs were ordered to consult the Sacred Books ... all the City was purified, and full-grown victims were sacrificed to the deities named in the Sacred Books; an

---

[4] This system may be found in the work of Spinoza.

[5] Livy, *History*, 21 62.

offering of forty pounds' weight of gold was conveyed to Juno at Lanuvium, and the matrons dedicated a bronze statue of that goddess on the Aventine. ... In Rome also a lectisternium [ceremony of propitiation] was ordered for Juventas and a special service of intercession at the temple of Hercules, and afterwards one in which the whole population were to take part at all the shrines. Five full-grown victims were sacrificed to the Genius of Rome, and C. Atilius Serranus, the praetor, received instructions to undertake certain vows which were to be discharged should the commonwealth remain in the same condition for ten years. These ceremonial observances and vows, ordered in obedience to the Sacred Books, did much to allay the religious fears of the people. [6]

These are the characteristic devices of Roman piety – sacrifice, dedications and vows. It affirms the Roman conviction that there is a power that produces the *signa* and responds to *sacra*.

The Sacred Books with this system. It is characteristic of Roman concrete thinking that they seek to mechanise the process. Such is the role played by "the Sacred Books," for therein are contained the mechanical rules for propitiating the gods – such-and-such sign followed by such-and-such a sacrament, and where the sacrament, as in human sacrifice, offends emergent moral conscience, then "the Sacred Books" can be called upon to sanction the crime, as required, by the gods. It is a mechanisation of the moral order, a form of "spiritual materialism" that reflects the backward pull of primitive materialism on the Roman psyche, the underlying core of Roman worship of the Mother-Goddess, or perhaps the inexorability of the Either/Or logic.

> Either – the universe is wholly at the whim of God, in which case no good work, or sacrament, can possibly avail, and, bereft of action, we are at the mercy of God's divine will, His Grace,

> Or – the Moral Law operates according to immutable laws, and is deterministic, not arbitrary, and it is given to us through revelation that such-and-such a sign is to be followed by such-and-such a sacrament, and there is justification through good works.

Either/Or. The first part affirms that it is not possible to "buy" one's way into Heaven, and the second affirms that it is. The Romans are devotees of the second path, and they do believe literally in the efficacy of money: "an offering of forty

[6] Livy, *History*, 21 62.

pounds' weight of gold was conveyed to Juno at Lanuvium." We note that the dedication is made to the Goddess – to Juno – to the Mother, not to the Father. A dedication was also made to the sacrificial son of Juno (Hera) – Hercules. The Either side of this dichotomy is represented by Augustine – the doctrine of predestination – interpreting Paul – justification by faith alone – leading to Luther and Calvin - or, in another respect by Spinoza.

At the back of Roman piety there is implicit the *moral argument for the existence of God*, or, rather, an inversion of it.

> Happiness should be proportionate to morality.
>
> There must exist a cause of the greatest good that is capable of bringing it to completion
>
> We must postulate the existence of God, as the necessary condition of the possibility of the greatest good.
>
> This is a moral law based on pure reason alone.[7]

The Roman inversion of the moral argument could proceed along these lines: accepting that God does exist, and that "happiness is proportionate to morality", then:

> Happiness is proportionate to morality (sacrament, piety). That is, God exists. Therefore:
>
> If any two sacraments are the same, then the happiness accruing must be the same.
>
> To he who demonstrates the greater morality (sacrament, piety), to him is allotted the greater happiness.

From this we derive **religion as a system of bargains**. Victory shall go to he who bids most. Bidding may take two forms: money, or sacra put down immediately, "on

---

[7] These phrases are adapted from Kant's presentation of the argument. "The same moral law now leads us also to affirm a second element in the summum bonum, which is that happiness should be proportionate to morality. This is affirmed by a line of reasoning that is as disinterested and unaffected by egocentric considerations as before; that is, it follows from impartial reason. This also leads us to conclude that there must exist a cause of the summum bonum that is capable of bringing it to completion; in other words, we must postulate the existence of God, as the necessary condition of the possibility of the summum bonum. God is an entity endowed with will who is capable of producing the summum bonum, which is a moral law based on pure reason alone. We proceed to exhibit this connection in a more detailed and convincing way." Kant, *Critique of Pure Practical Reason*, The Existence of God as a Postulate of Pure Practical Reason.

the table," and promissory notes, vows, made in advance, to be fulfilled on payment of victory.

The *devotio*. The law of proportionality expressed above argues that the greater the sacrament, the greater the reward. All these sacraments are sacrifices as well. Of course, when an animal is sacrificed, the burden falls upon the animal mainly, but that animal and the ceremony must be paid for, so it is no mere sham. In the scale of things, human life is more valuable, therefore, that is the greater sacrifice. But this is not the greatest: to he who wishes victory most, most should be offered. Therefore, the greater sacrifices involve – (i) a vow to die in battle, (ii) the sacrifice of one's son; (iii) the sacrifice in advance of battle of one's own life, for the sake of the victory. The most famous Roman example of the last is **the *devotio* of Publius Decius Mus**, Consul and general according to legend during the Samnite Wars.

> In the confusion of this movement Decius the consul called out to Marcus Valerius in a loud voice: "we have need of Heaven's help, Marcus Valerius, come therefore, state pontiff of the Roman People, dictate the words, that I may devote myself to save the legions." The pontiff bade him don the purple-bordered toga, and with veiled head and one hand thrust out from the toga and touching his chin, stand upon a spear that was laid under his feet, and say as follows: "Janus, Jupiter, Father Mars, Quirinus, Bellona, Lares, divine Novensiles, divine Indigites, ye gods in whose power are both we and our enemies, and you, divine Manes, — I invoke and worship you, I beseech and crave your favour, that you prosper the might and the victory of the Roman People of the Quirites, and visit the foes of the Roman People of the Quirites with fear, shuddering, and death. As I have pronounced the words, even so in behalf of the republic of the Roman People of the Quirites, and of the army, the legions, the auxiliaries of the Roman People of the Quirites, do I devote the legions and auxiliaries of the enemy, together with myself, to the divine Manes and to Earth." [8]

After that, he plunged fully armed on his horse into the battle and was so slain. The Romans win the battle. (a) There is a definite ritual involved, a formula that must be conducted in the right way etc. (b) The *devotio* is made to the chthonic powers of Earth. The Romans retain at the base level their Etruscan heritage – the belief that the ultimate power of the universe is a feminine power rooted in the Earth. (c) The divine Manes are the spirits of the ancestors. In Roman mythology the Manes are specifically the twin sons of Mania; the Goddess manifests primarily as the Terrible

[8] Livy, *History*, 8 9.5-6.

Mother, the Goddess of the Underworld. (d) The author, Livy, does not make explicit what "I devote the legions and auxiliaries of the enemy" means; but given that the general sacrifices himself, I presume that any prisoners taken in the battle were forthwith sacrificed by immolation, according to the Etruscan practice. This extract represents an idealised picture of Roman courage and piety; we cannot be assured that any part of it is historical.[9] The *devotio* was elaborated into a code of military-sacral conduct, and Livy goes on to expound details.

> It seems proper to add here that the consul, dictator, or praetor who devotes the legions of the enemy need not devote himself but may designate any citizen he likes from a regularly enlisted Roman legion. If the man who has been devoted dies, it is deemed that all is well; if he does not die, then an image of him is buried seven feet or more underground and a sin-offering is slain; where the image has been buried thither a Roman magistrate may not go up. But if he shall choose to devote himself, as Decius did, if he does not die, he cannot sacrifice either for himself or for the people without sin, whether with a victim or with any other offering he shall choose. He who devotes himself has the right to dedicate his arms to Vulcan, or to any other god he likes. The spear on which the consul has stood and prayed must not fall into the hands of an enemy; should this happen, expiation must be made to Mars with the sacrifice of a swine, a sheep, and an ox.[10]

The *evocatio* is another bargaining device for dealing with the gods of an enemy. Prior to an assault on an enemy city, it is a ritual formula to entice the gods of the enemy to desert that enemy by promising them better conditions and devotions at Rome. It is as if the power of the enemy city lay in the very earth beneath it, inhabited by chthonic powers, and if these powers will agree to be enticed out of their city dwelling and make their home in Rome, then that power of the earth will be transferred to Rome, and augment its power.

To address the **theological-philosophical issue** raised by Roman religion as a tool for bargaining: the implicit claim, since happiness is proportionate to morality, is that he who offers most, is most happy. It is this that inverts religion and turns it into a system of spiritual materialism, a system of bargains. It communicates itself

---

[9] It is customary at this stage to treat Livy's narrative as historical for the Samnite wars, but I think that the annalist tradition is so likely to be infected by backward projections and idealisations as to be very unreliable as to details. The history of Rome in its early stages, which includes periods down to the C3 BCE, is doubtful. The Roman annalists successfully created a fictitious and inflated history of Rome, and we remain constrained by it.

[10] Livy, *History*, 8 10

also into the religion of spiritual exercises – and it is in part the thinking behind the practices of asceticism. The idea is that the greater the personal sacrifice, or the greater the spiritual effort, the greater the reward. The tendency is to turn the cosmos into a system in which one can spiritually ascend by a bargain: to give up bodily desires in return for a higher seat in heaven; to exercise spiritually in this or that meditation or ascetic practice, in return for signs of spiritual elevation, visions and supernatural powers.

One solution to this is **the atheist-materialist solution**, and its ethical counterparts, ethical-egoism or utilitarianism, but my reader will appreciate that I am not inclined to go down that path, a path that is bankrupt and leads to despair if it is fully embraced without illusion. In principle I agree that happiness both should be and is proportionate to morality. The moral argument is valid – that is the true and only basis on which we can have confidence in the existence of God – though no god is singled out by it – not the Christian god, or a Roman god, but just this – it does behove us to consider what we do. Therefore, if I do not wish to embrace one of the horns of the dichotomy, I must reject the Either/Or logic that produces it.

(a) **No two ethical situations are ever the same**. Everyone confronts God – or the moral order of things – as an individual. I cannot compare my situation on some scale of spiritual weights and measures with another person's. No one knows exactly how either he or some other person stands with the gods. No one really knows what another person experiences and what that other person's inner state of being is – whether that person is or is not "happy".

(b) There is no such thing as good works without faith, and no such thing as faith without good works. The whole dichotomy – justification by faith alone, or justification by good works is false. The same applies to the moral argument. I may argue in a trick of spiritual materialism as follows: God exists, he makes happiness proportionate to morality, therefore, it is my duty to do X, and in return for X, I obtain reward, material or spiritual, Y. Hence, I only do the action commanded by my duty for the sake of the reward Y – which is spiritual materialism. But in the battle of life, when duty calls, so comes doubt, for there is no such thing as faith without doubt. Hence, if the duty is irksome, so I may slough off my so-called faith in the reward. Hence, even to do something for the sake of a reward is an article of faith. That applies to everything. If I make a deposit in a bank, I must have trust, that is faith, in the banking system.

(c) Justification by faith is already to do a good work, for it is to work on one's faith. But some error may be involved in this. If we wish to get into the realm of dirty psychology, and question the sincerity of this or that motive, then he or she who argues for justification by faith may well be finding a pretext, a rationalisation for shirking some other responsibility. But I will neither make a rod for my own back, nor for another's. I think it is high-time that we should drop the whole tendency of castigating our fellow men, of loading other backs with sins; time to be easy-going. Live and let live! Of course, I do not say that there is no such thing as morality and ethical living, but so often we exaggerate the injuries done to us, and the virtues that we have. How do I know that my faith is a virtue and pleasing to God?

(d) *Happiness ought to be, and is, proportionate to morality.* But what is happiness and what is morality? Romans interpret happiness as victory in battle, and honour thus accruing; we have other ideas. So often, it is possible to think one is unhappy, and be quite happy; or conversely, to form confused notions of happiness. All life is directed towards ends and the supreme end-of-ends we denote by happiness. But life is also a voyage of discovery, and what we sometimes think at one stage is happiness, turns out merely to be a fragment. Likewise, Romans interpret morality as *sacra*, ritual observance of certain rules of conduct in war and politics; we have progressed, so we think at least, and see this Roman system for what it is – a rather narrow-minded, egocentric vision of morality. A bargaining religion. The world will never be short of preachers to tell us what morality is, but in truth some of the formulas are exaggerated, and come down to meddling in other people's lives.

(e) We like to compare our own lives with our fellows, and at the back of that what is said is *my life is better than yours.* Even the most selfish people do this, because they make a virtue out of their selfishness and argue that they alone understand the world, how stupid it is to believe in God and morality, and they can by this virtue of cleverness make themselves happy. But, as against this principle of *my life is better than yours*, I am inclined to adopt another interpretation of human existence, which I shall call "the equivalence of life". I seem to have a kind of vision that suggests to me that one life is not so much better or worse, morally, than another, because all life represents progress, where progress is an advance of consciousness.

Is it religion? Is it reasonable to characterise Roman religion as a genuine faith and expression of piety? In accordance with the preceding discussion, I think the fears attaching to spiritual materialism are exaggerated. The moral law expresses itself as a kind of bargain, in legal terms, so much happiness in return for so much morality/devotion/religious observance but given that the whole equation is an expression of faith and the observance is no mere play-acting, then indeed I would classify the Roman religion, and any equivalent system, as a form of piety. It is no mere sham to fight a battle in the first place, and to make such vows as the Romans were wont to, is a powerful expression of faith.

Providence. Is there a Providence, or rather, was it providential that Rome came to power? The reader will undoubtedly by this stage have encountered in his own thoughts the issue of whether the history of Western consciousness evinces a kind of moral order – that kind that we call providence and think of as the action of God on earth. Among the many ways of reading this history, two may be singled out as being opposite in tendency.

(a) The materialistic explanation in terms of physical, biological and evolutionary forces acting impersonally – conscious life being the accidental product of these processes. On such a reading of history, the shock and horror of the reality of human nature – that grotesque theme of human sacrifice – confirms the conviction that man is no more than a primitive animal at core.

(b) Against that, the history of Western consciousness evinces the principle of increasing moral and spiritual order over time, and although we see many reversions, we sense progress to higher states of consciousness, both in the individual and collectively. We sense that history evinces a sequence of problems, each problem constellating a collective attempt at solution, but in the process constellating another problem. The difficulties of mankind in the Palaeolithic Period cannot be grasped with any clarity, though one would imagine that the sheer semi-consciousness and uniformity of experience are its spiritual problem. Man in such a condition is barely alive. Then, spirit postulates a way forward, and mankind begins, with the warming of the atmosphere, to congregate into social units, to practice agriculture and to make cities and settlements. Consciousness has gown, and now man begins to think and conceives of himself as offspring of the Great Mother, and his consciousness is bound by a form of cognition; he is a primitive materialist. Now the need is to transcend this bounded consciousness. His ethical thinking is rooted in a state of moral blindness – humans are things not persons. The struggle of the millennia preceding the first millennium BCE is for the growth of ideas; but as ideas grow and develop into a systematic magic-science or theological-science, Man advances to the concept of devotion, sacrament and piety, to genuine love of the Goddess, but this spiritual life is contaminated by his fears and material wants and takes the form of the increasing practice of ritual sacrifice, including human sacrifice. Spirit constellates its opposite – a religion of the Father emerges and comes into conflict with the religion of the Mother.

It would seem that the first peoples to overthrow the practices of the Great Mother, and reform the religion are the Greeks. They constellate a new Olympian religion, a fusion of matriarchal and patriarchal elements and reform their matriarchal-chthonic religion. This is the struggle into which Rome emerges. Greece, which we might imagine to be the ideal vector for the spiritual evolution, and in a manner is the ideal vector, being ahead of the times, is also the first to enter the newly constellated problem – the problem of split consciousness. For in overcoming the system of primitive cognition, Greece has invented the concept of an inert Nature, not a Mother at all, but an unconscious body subject merely to deterministic laws. Thus, psyche has split from matter, and we have the newly constellated problem concerning the relation between body and soul, implicitly conceived, not always explicitly, as the problem of interaction between material and spiritual substance. This creates a new dichotomy, and a terrible Either/Or, that has so far only been hinted at. This is Either materialism, Or dualism, and ethically, Either man is an empty shell, and has no identity, Or he is a Fallen Being, immersed in primordial sin, and must devote his life to returning to his original state.

This is the spiritual context we now live in. Medieval consciousness did not serve to bring an end to this terrible dichotomy; it served, rather, to bring to the foreground the increasingly horrible consequences of the first solution – dualism constellates the shadow problem. In the epoch of modern consciousness, the horror of that shadow caused Western consciousness to revert to the other solution – materialism – the turning point was the Renaissance, and now we are in the grip of the spiritual problem that materialism constellates, the problem of despair. But we have not overcome the shadow problem either, so we are strung between Shadow and Despair. Our situation could not be more painful.

However, spirit has already constellated the solution to the problem in the work and person of Immanuel Kant. But Kant was too bounded by the dregs of medieval consciousness and too persuaded by the needs of the Enlightenment to be able to bring that resolution to fruition. Furthermore, spirit was not yet ready for it. Spirit needed to constellate contemporary consciousness first, to bring to the foreground all the consequences of materialism as a system of Despair, and this is the epoch we find ourselves in now, on the brink of a new spiritual transformation.

From this providential reading of the spiritual history of Western consciousness, we do perceive rightly that Rome had its part to play. Given the paralysis of Greek consciousness owing to the internal strife occasioned by its inability to resolve the theological-philosophical problem of the age, spirit constellated another Western force, in many ways a simpler one, to take on the mantle of progressing consciousness and civilisation.

In the struggle between Rome and Carthage, would the world be a happier place, and more advanced spiritually, if Carthage had won? For all the faults of Roman piety, the narrowness of a religion that makes bargains with God and seeks to bully the spiritual world into keeping those bargains, that backslides into the very worst crimes that it seeks to overcome in its enemy, it was Roman bargaining religion that found the strength to overcome a defeat in which barely one man out of 80,000 came out alive.

The archetype of the Roman. In the *devotio* of Publius Decius Mus we have the epitome of the Roman ideal – a man prepared to die for his country, fearless of death. He represents the archetype of the Roman. Cicero remarked, "None ever encountered death for their country but under a firm persuasion of immortality!"[11] Given that the expression of Decius's vow is no mere ideal – Romans were prepared to be Roman and die for Rome – what were the Roman beliefs regarding the

---

[11] Cicero, *The Tusculan Disputations*, On the Contempt of Death, 15.

afterlife? Rome is not a uniform society, and the question must be related also to period. The "common-man", the soldier-farmer, what did he think? At the time of Cannae, at the time of the collapse of the Republic, during the reign of Augustus, and later? For the views of educated Romans, Cicero may be taken as exemplar.

The vow of Decius reported by Livy is a starting point – not a common man to be sure, but a Roman. Decius begins by invoking the major gods of the Rome, but the vow is directed primary to the Earth as a deity. Within the dedication we see "*Lares*, divine *Novensiles*, divine *Indigites*, divine *Manes*" and the dedication of the sacrifice of his life is specifically to the "to the divine *Manes* and to Earth." What the "*Novensilies*" and "*Indigites*" mean is a matter of scholarly debate. However, the *Lares* are accepted to be the spirits of deceased ancestors, heroes. The *Manes* are likewise chthonic deities, the souls of dead ancestors. Every deity originally began as a hero – a sacrificial human victim that was raised by devotion into a god. The idea that the gods were deified men was advanced by Euhemerus of Sicily c.300 BCE and brought into Roman culture through a redaction of the poet Ennius. While Euhemerism may appear as a form of atheism, that would be a reading out of context. The idea that men could become gods is nothing alien to primitive materialism, nor to Roman cognition. Decius is invoking the ancestors under many different titles, some local, some universal. He uses the terms "di", "divi" throughout – they are all spirits made divine though death. Roman belief in the afterlife surely followed Etruscan belief, where the lavish tombs attest to a belief in the survival of the person, as in Egypt. But the vow of Decius conjures a different or modified image – that in some sense all Romans merge in the afterlife with the corporate spiritual-body of the ancestors. Cognition is focused on the living, and from that vantage, it is possible to see the ancestors as a single "host", a kind of union of beings, and to conceive of one's death as a joining with this band. This, I suggest, was an aspect of the Roman belief in the afterlife, and although the source is literary and late, I suggest that this is consonant with what we know about the religion of the Roman common people.

Yet, the Roman archetype presents a puzzle, and particularly regarding the upper classes. Cicero and Seneca, for instance, both committed suicide – an act that is so-Roman, but neither of them believed with any security in the afterlife. Roman after Roman fell on his sword; yet if the ideas of Cicero and Seneca are indicative, as I surmise they are, by the late Roman Republic, and into the Roman empire, Roman aristocrats were all either materialists or sceptics. They had ceased to believe in God or the gods, but they still believed in Rome and being Roman.

This attests to the power of the Roman archetype. By living through an archetype, or by an archetype living through oneself, one becomes more than human – the archetype, which may be conceived of as a god – for it has been worshipped as such – elevates and transforms the psyche in extraordinary ways. It reconciles one to death.

Afterword

Throughout this volume the problems raised in Ionian and Cartesian consciousness have been analyzed from the vantage of Kantian, subjective consciousness, which is here posited as a higher, more evolved stage of human development. Terms such as "immortality", the "afterlife" and "eternity" have meaning relative to the stage of cognition which mankind works in; for Man in a state of primitive materialism, "eternity" cannot mean "everlasting and infinite duration" as it does in Ionian consciousness. Hence, the spiritual problems we face are in part generated by the bounds set upon ideation in the system of concepts that we unconsciously deploy.

The Either/Or predicament that we in modernity find ourselves in has been further characterized – the choice between on the one hand, a world-denying religion replete with threats of Hell, and, on the other, the materialist alternative and its view of human identity as a mere bundle of perceptions with its nihilistic consequence of anatta as utter impermanence. Already the path to freedom from this false dichotomy has been laid. There is the transformation of our ideas about human selfhood from the conception of a substance bounded in objective space and time to one of transcendent subjectivity, together with the realization that the world that is before us is a mirror of the Self. There is life-affirmation and a revitalized regard for human passions.

But there is still much to do: the enquiry into *what man is*, has not been completed. We need to learn more yet about the aetiology of our spiritual illness. The story of the emergence of medieval Christianity and the evolution of the archetype of Christ also needs to be told. This involves, too, a history of Hebrew religion.

While it is a contention that in the account of ideation the period of the Middle Ages can be "stepped over", if indeed it is the case that Kant's *Critique of Pure Reason* laid the foundation for a new collective happiness, then the question why this new consciousness has not been adopted by the West must be addressed. For, rather, our modern culture has witnessed a restoration of materialism, originally an Ionian Greek philosophy emerging within the confines of Ionian consciousness, and subsequently elaborated by the Stoics. If the solution to the Either/Or is just there for the taking, why are we still thus unhappy? And so, the history of the Either/Or does not end with the close of antiquity; we must investigate how it has come to persist into the late modern period. The transformation expected by Kantian consciousness may also be further examined. We anticipate yet a new stage in the evolution of the religion of Dionysus.